DEBUSSY'S MÉLISANDE

The Lives of Georgette Leblanc,
Mary Garden and Maggie Teyte

Debussy's Mélisande examines the colourful lives of
Georgette Leblanc, Mary Garden and Maggie Teyte, and
their involvement with Debussy's *Pelléas et Mélisande*,
illustrating the prejudices and difficulties faced by women
singers of their era. The three women presented here were
not only remarkable for the resilience and initiative they
had to develop, but also for their willingness to adapt
themselves to the opportunities offered by the emerging
technologies of recording, radio and film. It is also the story
of the background to the opera's creation, and the frequently
stormy relationships between the author of the original
play (Maeterlinck), the composer, director, conductor and
performers.

This book will be of great interest to scholars and students of
Debussy, opera, French music and theatre, Maeterlinck, and
those interested in women's studies and biography.

GILLIAN OPSTAD read Modern Languages at Somer-
ville College, Oxford, after which she taught for a number
of years in Buckinghamshire and Bristol. She has been
actively involved with music both at university and since.
This, her first book, is a result of her particular interest in
French music, especially that of Debussy.

DEBUSSY'S MÉLISANDE

The Lives of Georgette Leblanc, Mary Garden and Maggie Teyte

Gillian Opstad

THE BOYDELL PRESS

First published 2009
The Boydell Press, Woodbridge

ISBN 978-1-84383-459-5

The Boydell Press is an imprint of Boydell & Brewer Ltd
PO Box 9, Woodbridge, Suffolk IP12 3DF, UK
and of Boydell & Brewer Inc.
668 Mt Hope Avenue, Rochester, NY 14620, USA
website: www.boydellandbrewer.com

The publisher has no responsibility for the continued existence
or accuracy of URLs for external or third-party internet websites
referred to in this book, and does not guarantee that any content on
such websites is, or will remain, accurate or appropriate.

A CIP record for this book is available
from the British Library

This publication is printed on acid-free paper

Designed and typeset in Garamond Premier Pro and
Lucida Bright by David Roberts, Pershore, Worcestershire

Printed in Great Britain by
CPI Antony Rowe, Chippenham, Wiltshire

Contents

List of Illustrations

Acknowledgements

I have many people and institutions to thank for their help over the years whilst gathering information and resources for this book.

At the Royal College of Music in London: Paul Collen of the Centre for Performance History for his help with the Mary Garden Collection, a rich and fascinating resource originally obtained for the College by Dr Oliver Davies; also Dr Peter Horton, Deputy Librarian.

Fabrice van de Kerckhove, Saskia Bursens and Paul-Etienne Kisters at the Archives et Musée de la Littérature in Brussels for their help and permission to use material relating to Georgette Leblanc. I appreciated my access to the cupboard full of her memorabilia. Jan Van Goethem, Archivist at La Monnaie/De Munt, Brussels. Joris De Zutter at the Kabinet Maeterlinck in Ghent, and staff at the Stadsarchief, Ghent; the Theaterwissenschaftliche Sammlung, Cologne University.

The Bibliothèque Nationale de France and in particular Pierre Vidal and staff at the Bibliothèque-Musée de l'Opéra. Alexandra Laederich, Curator of the Centre de Documentation Claude Debussy in Paris. Denis Herlin for correspondence and for permission to cite from the invaluable tome, *Claude Debussy: Correspondance (1872–1918)*.

The staff at a number of other institutions and libraries assisted me in my research: the Archdiocesan Archives, Birmingham; the Lichfield Record Office in Staffordshire; the Oxfordshire Record Office; the Wolverhampton Archives and Local Studies; the Westminster City Archives; Notre Dame de France (RC) Church, London; the Archivists and Curators at the BBC; the Royal Opera House Collections, Covent Garden; the Department of Manuscripts, National Library of Scotland; the Edinburgh International Festival; John Pennino of the Archives of the Metropolitan Opera; Jennifer B. Lee of the Rare Book and Manuscript Library at Columbia University; Dr Fredric Woodbridge Wilson of the Harvard Theatre Collection, Houghton Library, Harvard University; staff at the New York Public Library; and Frances Barulich of the Pierpont Morgan Library, New York. I am also grateful to Dr Susan Rutherford of the University of Manchester for her communication about Mary Garden.

My visit to the Abbey of Saint-Wandrille in Normandy was most rewarding and I thank sincerely the Père Abbé for my introduction to the Frère Archivist who made the visit so interesting.

I am most grateful to Garry O'Connor, Michael Turnbull and Maxime Benoît-Jeannin for discussion and correspondence on the subjects of their biographies of Maggie Teyte, Mary Garden and Georgette Leblanc respectively and for allowing me to cite from their books.

I am greatly indebted to Richard Langham Smith for reading the manuscript, for sharing his expertise on Debussy and making most valuable suggestions. I also thank Bruce Phillips, Caroline Palmer and Michael Middeke of Boydell & Brewer for their advice.

My husband, Christopher's love of Debussy's opera is as great as my own. His collection of interpretations of *Pelléas et Mélisande* on CD must be unique! He has provided constant support and assistance, and has made many pertinent comments and most useful contributions to my research and the preparation of the typescript for which I can't thank him enough.

All translations in the text are by the author unless otherwise acknowledged. The original French has been included in many instances, but not of letters or footnotes contained in Debussy's *Correspondance (1872–1918)*, edited by François Lesure and Denis Herlin, published by Gallimard in 2005. This is an inspirational resource, the most up-to-date and complete volume of Debussy's correspondence. Careful reference has been made to the relevant pages on which the letters referred to can be found.

To Christopher

Introduction

WHAT MUST IT HAVE BEEN LIKE to witness the composition of one of the seminal musical works of the twentieth century, Debussy's opera *Pelléas et Mélisande*, to be in the same room as the composer as he played with sounds, changed harmonies as you sang, as you listened to chords you had never heard before and tried to make sense of a vocal line which was more like natural speech than song? What was it like to fall obsessively in love with the author of the inspirational play about a princess from a foreign land who brings light into a dark world, to dream of personifying her, then to play out the rest of your life constantly referring back to that ethereal character?

Mélisande was not Debussy's creation, but that of Maurice Maeterlinck, the Belgian author born in August 1862, not only in the same year but in the same week as Debussy. Debussy's music conveys the essence of Maeterlinck's imagination, capturing the spirit of the mesmerising character that is Mélisande and intensifying the atmosphere of Maeterlinck's shadowy symbolist play. It becomes a touching, infinitely memorable opera which insinuates itself into the mind.

By itself, the play resembles one of those childhood tales, redolent of medieval legend, which on the surface is a triangular love story of a handsome young prince wooing a fair princess away from an older man. Impenetrable dark forests surrounding a castle, glistening water with a golden crown in its depths, a ship mysteriously arriving and departing, a beautiful damsel gazing down at the prince from a tower, her long hair falling towards him – all elements of endlessly retold legends and tales. These familiar themes become laden with layer upon layer of significance as opposing elements are repeatedly woven into them, the more negative predominating: darkness over light, being lost over being found, lies over truth, age over youth, death over birth. Each word becomes pregnant with implication. Even the setting of the play with its different levels, from the high tower to the deepest vaults of the castle, or with its different shades of light, from the dark forest and dank cave to the sun glinting over the sea, makes us constantly question its perspective.

In truth, a whole universe is represented within the shores of Allemonde. Here the most basic of human emotions and experiences are played out, confined and concentrated, like a light shining through a lens – a pinprick,

yet concentrated enough to create fire. Here all ages of mankind are represented. Arkel, the old sage, nearly blind, at the end of his life, still wistful for his younger days, longing to experience Mélisande's youthful kiss.
Golaud, a widower, a father who loves his son Yniold, yet is frustrated at
his innocence, loath to grow old, envious of Pelléas's youth. Before meeting Mélisande he was resigned to a formulaic existence, destined to remarry
for political reasons. Now he has married impulsively for love. His violence
is an instinctive masculine response to his raw anger, his primeval jealousy.
Geneviève, mother of Golaud and Pelléas, who naturally wants the best for
both of them, like Mélisande brought to the castle as a bride forty years
earlier, who reassures her daughter-in-law that she too had difficulty getting used to the dark surroundings. She does not want to stand in the way
of Golaud's happiness, so pleads his case with Arkel. Nor does she prevent
Pelléas from keeping company with the young girl, leaving the couple alone
in the garden. Pelléas, passionate, impetuous youth, emotional, spontaneous,
who has not yet learned to stand back and take stock of a situation before
acting. Yniold, son of Golaud, boyhood personified, questioning, too young
to realise the implications of the relationship of Pelléas and Mélisande, too
young to realise the inevitability of death as the sheep pass by on the way to
slaughter. The immoveable rock is the inescapable fate which neither he nor
any of those around him will be able to change. Into this universe comes
Mélisande. Her presence is the sunlight piercing through that lens, lighting
the spark that spreads into a flame. Innocence, beauty, love, jealousy, protec-
tiveness, mendaciousness, anger, birth, motherhood, death. All are focused
around one woman. Finally, a newborn child. A baby, significantly a girl, will
now have to undergo this cycle once again. Motherless, possibly soon to be
fatherless, she will no doubt be all too anxious to escape her claustrophobic
environment, just as her mother escaped from somewhere far away to arrive
at Allemonde. Mélisande's last words encapsulate the realisation that conditions have been created for events to recur in perpetuum. 'Elle va pleurer
aussi ... J'ai pitié d'elle.'[1]

  Before Debussy's death in 1918, writer and critic Romain Rolland wrote
that Debussy had 'never sought to dominate Maeterlinck's poem, or to swal-
low it up in a torrent of music; he has made it so much a part of himself that
no Frenchman is able to think of a passage in the play without Debussy's
music singing at the same time within him'.[2] Others felt that Debussy's music
raised Maeterlinck's play to a higher imaginative level. 'To put it unkindly,

---

[1] Act V: 'She is going to cry as well ... I am sorry for her.' See David Grayson, 'Waiting
   for Golaud: The concept of time in Pelléas' in *Debussy Studies*. Edited by Richard
   Langham Smith (Cambridge, 1993) for a discussion of circularity in the play.

[2] Romain Rolland, *Musicians of Today* (London, 1917), p. 238.

Debussy saved Maeterlinck's play.'³ Yet in that play Debussy discovered a text that had so many layers of meaning that it will never be completely fathomable, a text that leaves so many possibilities for interpretation that it enables both the opera and the play to be open to many different types of production.

Despite Maeterlinck's eventual claim that the play had become a stranger to him, Debussy showed great respect for the original text, hardly surprising given the lyrical quality of the words. At the centre of this inspiration is Mélisande. Even her name evokes a lyrical response. Yet this is no showy operatic diva role destined to bring its intrepid interpreter instant glory. In fact there are virtually no good 'tunes', for the voice rises and falls as close to speech as possible lending the words their full significance, emotional, yet subtle and true to life. There is no opportunity for that sporadic applause which so often interrupts the flow of an operatic plot.

Debussy omitted four scenes of the play and shortened some speeches, certain modifications being in keeping with Maeterlinck's own revisions after seeing his play performed, even though the composer was working from the original text. The simplicity of the original words is sometimes simplified even further by the omission of repetitions. Conversely, Debussy occasionally adds a repetition, in both cases to heighten passion or tension.⁴ The spirit of the play remains intact, the intention of the words being underlined through the music.

The unique status of *Pelléas et Mélisande* was acknowledged by André Messager, its first conductor, when two years before the composer's death he called to mind the final scene and remarked, 'When asking for the window to be opened, Mélisande let in all modern music.'⁵ There is something so special about *Pelléas et Mélisande* that critics even today have difficulty in defining its uniqueness. The 'peculiar status of *Pelléas* in musical history', 'Debussy's strange, impossible, history-laden anti-opera' were words used in a recent review.⁶ 'It is the sphinx among operas' writes an enthusiast for the work.⁷ Going back in time, as one composer evaluating another, Lennox Berkeley commented, 'One cannot place *Pelléas* in any operatic category. It stands quite alone, owing very little to any previous opera ... and certainly not pointing in any direction that could be followed by the succeeding

³ Joseph Kerman, *Opera News,* 28 December 1953, p. 26.

⁴ See David Grayson, 'The Libretto of Debussy's Pelléas et Mélisande', *Music & Letters,* January 1985, pp.34–50 for analysis of Debussy's alterations.

⁵ 'En ouvrant la fenêtre, Mélisande a fait passer toute la musique moderne.' Yvonne Tiénot and O. d'Estrade-Guerra, *Debussy* (Paris, 1962), p.235.

⁶ Roger Parker, *Opera,* July 2007, p.856.

⁷ Rupert Christiansen, *The Daily Telegraph,* 2 May 2007.

generation.'[8] Sixty years after its first performance in Paris, Harold Rosenthal
found the 1962 Glyndebourne production 'a strange kind of work, not really
fitting into any known category of opera, and certainly a piece that must
be quite unlike anything in the experience of many of the Glyndebourne
audience.' However, the elusive Mélisande was not to his liking. 'She was
too knowing, and her art and effects seemed too contrived. Is there an ideal
Mélisande today?', he asked.[9]

An ideal Mélisande? Debussy certainly believed the first two singers
to perform the role fulfilled his ideal, yet neither of them was the woman
Maurice Maeterlinck had in mind. The part meant so much to these women
that Mélisande became a pivotal role referred to throughout their lives. They
were the interpreters of the role. Its creators were men, undoubtedly socially
and artistically more powerful and influential in this environment: author,
composer, director, conductor. Without them the women could never have
achieved such fame. This is the inescapable truth in the lives of Georgette
Leblanc, Mary Garden and Maggie Teyte. But what women! The toughness
of the life of a female opera singer, her inferior position in hierarchical society at the turn of the nineteenth century, meant that they had to be resilient
and to have unshakeable belief in themselves. And then there is a dichotomy.
Debussy's opera *Pelléas et Mélisande* is regarded as quintessentially French,
yet the two first great Mélisandes came from Britain. Both these women
were determined, characterful personalities, far removed from Maeterlinck's
child-like creation.

Larger than life roles in a larger than life art form must inevitably be won
by characters with a certain lack of compromise, and the willpower to succeed. To follow their story is to realise that women who were building their
careers over a hundred years ago were just as capable as those of today of taking charge of their own lives, demanding attention to get their way, and that
long before the age of television and mass communications, the press could
be manipulated by 'celebrities', in an age when such a term hardly existed.
The lives of the women who created Mélisande demonstrate the hardships
and sacrifices such dedicated professionals had to make to keep in the public
eye. Arguments and intrigues surrounding the casting of the role evoke the
atmosphere of the opera house of the era. The men needed the women to
bring to life the images filling their imaginations yet the praise of these men
is hard earned. How damning can be their comments. Georgette Leblanc in
particular suffered from their dismissive attitude. Not just contemporaries,
but even later writers who could not have heard her, insist on her lack of

[8] *Ballet and Opera*, September 1949, p.48.
[9] *Opera*, July 1962, p. 452.

talent. In *La Passion de Claude Debussy*, Dietschy claimed that Georgette was indirectly associated with the failure of Maeterlinck's play in 1893.[10] Yet she had not even met the author at the time of its first performance. He also finds it 'odd' that the *Chanson de Mélisande* set to music by Gabriel Fabre was dedicated to her, yet she sang this work with Fabre himself accompanying her many times. His assumption appears to be that Georgette claimed the role of Mélisande passionately as though she foresaw the dazzling success of the opera, implying that this was merely to further her own ends. Lockspeiser, in his two-volume biography of Debussy dismisses Georgette with the claim that she 'had a wretched reputation as a singer'[11] even though she received praise from both professionals and amateur music lovers on many occasions.

Recordings of Georgette Leblanc are very rare and, of course, the industry was in its infancy when both she and Mary Garden recorded songs so it is difficult to judge the true quality of their voices. A recent issue on CD brings us evidence of Georgette's voice as recorded by Gramophone and Typewriter Limited in Paris in 1903, just one year after the première of Debussy's opera, when she was thirty-four. Here she is accompanied at the piano by Jules Massenet in the aria *Pendant un an je fus ta femme* from his opera *Sapho*.[12] Massenet's playing is so discreet that he can barely be heard at all in the background, but despite the inevitable hiss, Georgette's voice is distinct. From descriptions of her manner, one might expect an overtly dramatic interpretation, yet whilst this aria is sung with feeling and a range of dynamics, the expression is not exaggerated. There is some vibrato, wider than Mary Garden's, but not excessive, some scooping up to the high notes, these – particularly the top A on the last syllable of 'ton coeur s'ouvrira' – being clear, if a little thin. The words are well projected but not over-enunciated. The same set of two CDs contains recordings of Mary Garden accompanied by Debussy (these will be discussed in a later chapter),[13] so a direct, although necessarily very limited comparison can be made of the two voices at about this time. On the basis of this brief extract, even if her rival has a purer, more lucid voice, Georgette Leblanc's performance here does not appear to merit the derogatory criticisms made of her vocally.

What follows is not a technical analysis of the opera *Pelléas et Mélisande*, but the story of the staging of the play which inspired the opera, its composition, and the relationships between author, composer, director, conductor

---

[10] Marcel Dietschy, *La Passion de Claude Debussy* (Neuchâtel, 1962), p.99.

[11] Edward Lockspeiser, *Debussy: His Life and Mind*, vol. 1 (London, 1962), p.201.

[12] *Legendary Piano Recordings*. Marston, 2008. 52054–2.

[13] See Chapter 9, p.118.

and performers. The lives of Georgette Leblanc, Mary Garden and Maggie
Teyte are interwoven, each not only remarkable for her resilience and initiative, but for her willingness to adapt to the opportunities offered by the
emerging technologies of recording, radio and film. Each wrote an autobio-
graphical account of her life, these books revealing intriguing styles and personalities, none of them reliably accurate, reflecting their desire to convey a
sympathetic artistic personality.[14]

What was it that drew them so irresistibly to the character of Mélisande?
Despite what may appear on first impressions to be a misty fairytale of love
and death, there is an uncomfortable psychological undercurrent which is
underlined by her fragmentary speech. Is Mélisande as innocent as she seems
at first sight? Neither Golaud nor Pelléas can resist her sexual attraction.
Even Arkel's ardently expressed desire to kiss her with his 'old lips' could be
interpreted as more than just grandfatherly affection. She is terrified of being
touched when Golaud finds her, and when questioned immediately admits
that she has been hurt, physically hurt, but will not say by whom or what
has been done to her, thus appealing at once to his protective nature. What
instinct leads her later to treat Golaud with such duplicity, to manipulate
him? Is she exploiting her femininity? Yet this power seems to be exerted
despite herself. Whilst the men express their feelings and desires, pour out
their emotions, Mélisande is inhibited, unable to utter more than a few
words at a time, often not completing a sentence. It is a paradox that she
seems so helpless and sweet, that she does not seem malicious, yet is innately
selfish. She insists on not being touched yet wants to be loved. She knows
she is beautiful, yet does not want to be seen by Pelléas when not at her best.[15]
Her huge eyes and long hair contribute to such striking beauty that they
make Pelléas feel intoxicated and drive Golaud mad. If a lie will allow her to
get her way, she will resort to it – many times over, both leading the men on
and misleading them. She misrepresents Golaud to Pelléas when describing
their first encounter, claiming that although Golaud had said nothing to her

---

[14] Georgette Leblanc, *Souvenirs (1895–1918)* (Paris, 1931). Version used here: *Souvenirs:
My Life with Maeterlinck*, translated by Janet Flanner (New York, 1932). Extracts
are included by permission of Methuen. Mary Garden and Louis J. Biancolli,
Mary Garden's Story. Reprinted with the permission of Simon and Schuster Adult
Publishing Group, copyright © 1951 by Simon & Schuster, Inc. Copyright © renewed
1978 by the Estate of Mary Garden and Louis J. Biancolli. All rights reserved. Maggie
Teyte, *Star on the Door* (London, 1958). Extracts are included by permission of Garry
O'Connor.

[15] The line 'Je suis affreuse ainsi' ('I look awful like this') (Act III scene 1) was replaced
by Maeterlinck in a later edition of the play, as he thought 'It really sounds like the
frightful flirtation of a milliner.' ('une affreuse coquetterie de modiste'). Letter to
Lugné-Poë, 22 February 1893, quoted in Lugné-Poë, *Le Sot du tremplin* (Paris, 1930),
p.238.

initially, he wanted to kiss her.[16] Likewise, she later tells Golaud that she can see from Pelléas's eyes that he does not like her.[17] To Golaud she fabricates events surrounding the loss of the ring, that ring that is more important to him than anything else, then asserts that Pelléas would not want to go alone with her to seek it, knowing full well that he will willingly collude in her lie.[18]

Why can Mélisande not tell Golaud more about herself? In her book, Maggie Teyte reminds us that Mélisande, before her meeting with Golaud and Pelléas, was one of the wives of Bluebeard. Having been brutally ill-treated by him, she has lost her memory and run away, to be found by Golaud by a pool in the forest. 'Because of what she has suffered', writes Maggie:

> she is afraid of any man she sees. But when Golaud, in a fit of jealousy, drags her about by the hair, she undergoes a kind of 'shock cure.' Her love for Pelléas, at first a shy uncertain thing, reaches the point where she can say, when he warns her that they may be discovered, 'I want them to see me!'[19]

In a later interview Maggie was at pains to stress Mélisande's innate sexuality. Because of Bluebeard, she hates men, and is terrified of Golaud, 'a real roughneck'. Maggie found her, 'an innocent, sexy thing – her hair is very sexy – and when Golaud drags her about by the hair, it is the shock treatment and brings back her memory.' But when she sees Pelléas murdered, 'she goes back again into the haze.'[20]

Maggie saw in both creators, Maeterlinck and Debussy, an underlying violence. She found Maeterlinck:

> a character with certain brutal aspects,[21] who was nevertheless capable of great refinement and delicacy of perception. Debussy himself was by no means free of violent feeling, which is no more than an undercurrent in his music – yet this undercurrent of violence and terror is, I think, in sympathy with Maeterlinck. It is a quality the two had much more deeply in common than the pastel colourings that shimmer on the surface of their work.[22]

Maggie even ascribed the quarrels between the two as another manifestation of this 'sympathy'. Certainly, in examining both personalities, it becomes evident that there are more than a few similarities between them, despite their eventual dislike of each other.

Mélisande has been abused by her first husband, only to be abused by her

---

[16] Act II scene 1.

[17] Act II scene 2.

[18] Act II scene 2.

[19] Teyte, *Star on the Door*, p.73.

[20] *Opera News*, 21 March 1970, p.16.

[21] Maeterlinck was able to vent his aggression by physical means as he was a keen boxer.

[22] Teyte, *Star on the Door*, p.73.

second. She seems passive in her acceptance of her fate, almost sleepwalking into her marriage, pregnancy and death, but at the same time colluding with Pelléas in the lie of their relationship. Perhaps the singers who first portrayed her identified with this ultimate feminine guile. The music contributes ineluctably to her mystery, fragility, and sensuality, making it possible for an interpreter to enter completely into the heart and soul of the princess. They certainly wanted to get under her skin and in their own lives to be as desired as Mélisande, whilst at the same time endeavouring to prevent the men who had the power to determine their futures from manipulating them.

Before analysing further the characters of Georgette Leblanc, Mary Garden and Maggie Teyte, it is essential to find out how the opera came to be created in the first place and to see why Debussy became obsessed with it for ten years and more.

1 *Pelléas et Mélisande: from Play to Opera*

*F*ROM THE MOMENT he finished reading a copy of Maeterlinck's play *Pelléas et Mélisande*, Debussy wanted to give up everything else he was doing and set it to music.[1] Thus wrote his friend René Peter, and whether it is exaggeration or not, it underlines the sense of excitement engendered in the composer and sets the scene for the composition and performances of a masterpiece which was to affect the lives and careers of so many musicians in the future. Of all operas, this must be the one where an ideal encapsulation of the charged atmosphere of doom and emotion is hardest to satisfy. Debussy certainly found it a challenge to fulfil his innermost desire for a perfect score. As Robert Godet wrote, reminiscing about the young Debussy, he never realised it would take ten years of his life, ten years of dreaming a thousand ways of looking at a fountain, a cave, moonlight or a human soul until he had discovered the most revealing, the one and only one that was right.[2]

Maeterlinck's characters cast an immediate spell on him. However, it was not just a matter of characterisation. This was a work that would enable Debussy to reach his artistic ideal as famously described to his teacher, Ernest Guiraud, in 1889: 'Music begins where words are no longer capable of expression; music is made for the inexpressible; it should seem to emerge from the shadows and return to them; it should always be discreet.'[3] When asked what poet could ever provide such a 'poem', he replied:

> One who by only half saying things enables me to graft my dream onto his; one who creates characters not associated with any specific place or time; someone who will not force his idea of performance on me like a tyrant and will leave me free to have more art than him, and to perfect his work.

He insisted on a balance between music and poetry, claiming that in opera there was too much singing. There should be singing only when necessary,

---

[1] René Peter, *Claude Debussy* (Paris, 1944), p. 163.

[2] 'En commençant son travail, Debussy était loin de se douter qu'il y consacrerait dix ans de sa vie ... à rêver mille aspects d'une fontaine, d'une grotte, d'un clair de lune ou d'une âme humaine, jusqu'à ce qu'il eût découvert le plus révélateur, car il n'en voulait fixer qu'un, mais décisif.' Robert Godet, 'En marge de la marge', *La Revue musicale*, vol. 7 (May 1926), p. 78.

[3] Maurice Emmanuel, *Pelléas et Mélisande de Debussy: étude et analyse* (Paris, 1929), p. 35.

and full-voiced singing should be saved only for moments when absolutely essential:

> There must be differences in the energy of expression. At some points it is necessary to paint only in monochrome and be satisfied with shades of grey … nothing should slow down the pace of the drama: any musical development not called for by the words is wrong; musical development, however brief, cannot fit the mobility of words.[4]

He dreamt of poems which did not condemn him to composing long, weighty acts. The scenes should move on, vary in place and character. The characters should not philosophise, but submit to life and their destiny.

How did Debussy find this play which met these demanding criteria? In Maeterlinck he discovered an author who did not believe in staging human drama with actors giving their all in full-blooded interpretations of their roles, who drew attention to themselves rather than the soul of the character they were conveying, thus destroying the very illusion they were supposed to be creating. In his early plays, Maeterlinck even envisaged employing wax figures or puppets in order to heighten the intensity of the words and avoid the interference of human personalities. A play without human actors – how close to Debussy's thoughts on an opera without arias.

Even though he had had little formal education as a child, Debussy read widely, eagerly devouring books and responding to the visual stimuli of paintings and illustrations. He frequently met artists and writers in cafés and through Edmond Bailly, musician, occultist and bookseller at the Librairie de l'Art Indépendant who published the early works of Gide, Claudel, and Pierre Louÿs. He was remarkably well informed about the latest trends in literature, and was to be seen at Stéphane Mallarmé's 'Tuesdays', amongst other salons. Little wonder that he was aware of the Symbolist movement and of writers such as Villiers de l'Isle-Adam and Edgar Allan Poe. He certainly did not want to ingratiate himself with well-known figures, but absorbed the essence of their ideas to reflect upon and develop in his own mind. He responded with affection only to those he recognised as like-mindedly genuine in their striving for artistic integrity. The external impression of an irascible, self-contained individual who did not seek popularity belied the searching going on inside the mind of the composer who desperately wanted to express a personal chemistry in his music that was pleasing to him, that gave him his own sense of fulfilment and satisfaction, that expressed innate beauty and the inner essence of an emotion, regardless of whether others would regard it as conventionally correct or melodic.

[4] Emmanuel, *Pelléas et Mélisande de Debussy*, p. 36.

Louis Laloy, the earliest French biographer of the composer, said that Debussy was strolling along the pavements of Paris one summer's evening in 1892 when he spotted a newly published book in the window of the bookshop Flammarion.[5] It is, however, more likely that he purchased the book the following year in order to prepare for attending the first performance of the play *Pelléas et Mélisande*. Indeed, he even wrote himself a little note to remind himself, 'Bought and read Pelléas 1893.'[6] Lugné-Poë, the play's director, claims that his friend and colleague, Camille Mauclair, had already suggested to Debussy that *Pelléas et Mélisande* should be set to music. The performances depended on subscriptions, so Debussy had to send his payment for a seat in the stalls directly to Lugné-Poë. With this he included a note saying he knew neither the play nor the author.[7] He can, therefore, never have met Maeterlinck before. Hardly anyone else knew the author either. The very day of this performance, *Le Figaro* published on its front page an interview with Maeterlinck carried out by Jules Huret including the statement, 'There are not twenty people in Paris who know the poet from Ghent.'[8]

On 17 May 1893 at the Théâtre des Bouffes-Parisiens there was a single performance of the play, a matinée directed by Aurélien-François-Marie Lugné-Poë. The autobiography of this remarkable actor and director reveals how closely related Debussy's opera is to the spirit and ethos of the young artists of his day. Lugné-Poë, like so much of the talent around him, was poor financially but rich in the company he kept. In 1891, aged twenty-two, he was sharing a studio with artists who were to become known as *Les Nabis* – Pierre Bonnard, Maurice Denis, Édouard Vuillard.[9] By now he already knew of the Belgian author Maeterlinck through fellow actor and founder of the Théâtre Libre, André Antoine. In Maeterlinck they saw the personification of all their hopes for a new type of theatre despite the scepticism of others, and struggled to mount his plays. The actors burnt their feet as they rehearsed Maeterlinck's early play *L'Intruse* on the hot metal roof of the Vaudeville Theatre, the stage having been commandeered for more highly regarded plays sharing the same programme! Lugné-Poë, like Debussy after

---

[5] Louis Laloy, *Debussy* (Paris, 1944), p. 21.

[6] 'Acheté et lu Pelléas en 1893.' Yvonne Tiénot and O. d'Estrade-Guerra, *Debussy: l'homme, son œuvre, son milieu* (Paris, 1962), p. 83.

[7] 'Claude Debussy … qui m'écrivit qu'il ne connaissait pas la pièce, ni l'auteur et à qui on avait suggéré par Mauclair, la possibilité d'une composition.' Aurélien-François-Marie Lugné-Poë, *Le Sot du tremplin* (Paris, 1930), p. 229.

[8] 'Il n'y a pas vingt personnes à Paris qui connaissent le poète gantois!' *Le Figaro*, 17 May 1893.

[9] Lugné-Poë, *Le Sot du tremplin*, p. 189.

him, was fascinated and inspired by the effect of silence in Maeterlinck's plays. He dreamt of creating a new type of theatre 'where poetry and silence would go together'.[10] Poetry and silence, a play without actors, an opera without arias – what creative stirrings in the minds of these young iconoclasts. Through Camille Mauclair, who knew Maeterlinck personally, Lugné-Poë was able to correspond and collaborate with the author, and persuade him to entrust his play *Pelléas et Mélisande* to them. Without the insight and inspiration of these young men, Debussy may never have created his masterpiece.

With Mauclair's support, Lugné-Poë persisted in finding a way to put on *Pelléas et Mélisande* as the sole work on a programme. Besides finances, the main problem was to find a venue. Ironically, one of the personalities later to be most closely and enthusiastically associated with Debussy's opera, Albert Carré, then Director of the Vaudeville Theatre, refused permission to mount the play there.[11] Eventually, after borrowing money left and right, including, to Maeterlinck's surprise, from Lugné-Poë's parents (his own would not have considered such folly), they managed to book the Bouffes-Parisiens for 17 May 1893. Maeterlinck came from Belgium to Paris only five days before the performance for just two rehearsals, and both Mauclair and another supporter of the author, Octave Mirbeau, tried to drum up enthusiasm by writing articles in newspapers.

Debussy may not have met Maeterlinck, but he was certainly familiar with at least one of his previous plays, *La Princesse Maleine*, written in 1889, the very year of those prophetic comments he made to Guiraud. Could it have been his immediate empathy with this style of writing that drew forth those statements on his ideal drama for setting to music? In a long article published on the front page of the newspaper *Le Figaro* in August 1890, writer and critic Octave Mirbeau had found this play 'an admirable and pure and eternal masterpiece ... comparable and – dare I say it? – superior in beauty to what is most beautiful in Shakespeare.'[12] This astonishingly generous opinion certainly brought it to the notice of composer Erik Satie, who expressed interest in setting it to music; it may have been he who drew Debussy's attention to it. Debussy must have asked the journalist Jules Huret, at that time working for *L'Echo de Paris*, to intercede with Maeterlinck, for on 23 June 1891 Huret received a letter from Maeterlinck refusing Debussy

[10] 'Je songeais à créer un théâtre où s'associeraient poésies et silences', Lugné-Poë, *Le Sot du tremplin*, p. 223.

[11] Lugné-Poë, *Le Sot du tremplin*, p. 225.

[12] 'Un admirable et pur et éternel chef-d'œuvre ... comparable – et oserai-je le dire – supérieur en beauté à ce qu'il y a de plus beau dans Shakespeare.' *Le Figaro,* 24 August 1890.

the rights and saying that he might give Vincent d'Indy precedence.[13] Thus, three composers had already been attracted to the musical qualities inherent in *La Princesse Maleine*.

Even before he arrived in Paris to assist with rehearsals for *Pelléas et Mélisande*, Maeterlinck had written to Lugné-Poë suggesting that the costumes for his characters should derive from the eleventh or twelfth centuries, or from Memling (fifteenth). With this in mind, after giving a talk on Maeterlinck on 30 April 1893, Camille Mauclair went to Bruges, taking with him a sketch-book. How to dress Mélisande? He was sure the panels of the Shrine of St Ursula in the Hospital of St John would provide inspiration.[14] Painted by Hans Memling in 1489, these panels show Ursula wearing a white tunic and long blue skirt as she lands at Cologne on the first stage of her pilgrimage to Rome.

In a later letter,[15] Maeterlinck was very specific about the appearance of Pelléas and Mélisande, demonstrating his commitment to the production of his play: 'Don't you think that for Mélisande, rather than green, the sort of mauve to be found at Liberty's would be more suitable? Pelléas could be in green which goes splendidly with mauve.' He drew a little hat with a red top and ermine rim to be worn with this, then suggested that Pelléas's tights should be a darker green than his tunic which could be green, brown or grey. He also reasoned that if Pelléas was in green then Mélisande should certainly not be, otherwise they would look as if they were emerging from a bowl of sorrel soup. Her dress should be simple, clinging, with a low neck, high waist, but long enough to hide her feet. She could wear a few precious stones at her neck and hips and have violet ribbons braided in her hair, or perhaps even just a few leaves. He enclosed with this letter a picture by Walter Crane, who provided inspiration for these ideas.

In Paris Maeterlinck was a reluctant presence, 'being there from time to time like a dog being whipped, at rehearsals of which he understood nothing',[16] grumbled Lugné-Poë. He was so nervous that 'he told us afterwards that his hair had grown measurably during the morning.' Apparently every time Maeterlinck came to Paris, nervous about a performance, his hair would grow so much in just a few hours that he had to go to the barber's.[17] Significantly, this reticence stayed with him throughout his life. How far

[13] Léon Vallas, *Claude Debussy et son temps* (Paris, 1958), p. 143.

[14] Camille Mauclair, *Le Charme de Bruges* (Paris, 1929).

[15] Stadsarchief Gent B LXXII.1 and 5.

[16] 'Assistant de temps en temps et comme un chien qu'on fouette à des répétitions auxquelles il ne comprenait rien.' Jacques Robichez, *Le Symbolisme au théâtre: Lugné-Poë et les débuts de l'œuvre* (Paris, 1957), p. 163.

[17] Lugné-Poë, *Le Sot du tremplin*, p. 229.

would he have progressed in the public eye without others – another in particular – to promote his works?

The idiosyncratic staging of Maeterlinck's play departed as far as possible from a realistic approach. Lugné-Poë himself acted the part of Golaud, as particularly requested by the author.[18] Eugénie Meuris played the first Mélisande. It was not a man but another woman, Marie Aubry, who acted the part of Pelléas. The scenery, also advised upon by Maeterlinck, was by Paul Vogler. It was painted on paper, but the stage hands were so unfamiliar with it that they mounted it back to front! Lugné-Poë had to rectify this himself.[19] Apart from the initial setting of each scene, there are few stage directions in the play. Few props were necessary, those required becoming evident from the comments of the characters. To enhance the haunting impression of distance in time and space and heighten the symbolism, a thin gauze curtain was hung between the stage and the audience, and behind this the lighting was very subdued.

The actors 'recited their roles in a uniform monotonous chant ... with voices of shadows as far as they were able' reported one reviewer.[20] Little music, then, even in the intonation of the words. There was just one song, 'Les trois sœurs aveugles' set to music by Gabriel Fabre, a song which Georgette Leblanc was later to sing passionately. This was *not* the one in the original 1892 printed version of the play, 'Mes longs cheveux', which Debussy had bought and was eventually to set in his opera. Maeterlinck had asked Lugné-Poë to replace the latter, saying he disliked it, and that Mademoiselle Meuris should choose any song out of thirty he had written. The song about three blind sisters must have been her choice.[21] This demonstrates that Debussy was initially setting the earliest printed version of Maeterlinck's play to music, not incorporating the changes Maeterlinck made for this performance.

The critics were faced with a unique occasion, one sole matinée performance of a play in a style and setting so removed from reality that it was as if written for puppets in limbo, little shadows emerging from semi-gloom.[22] One vivid impression of the extraordinary new drama begins: 'This afternoon at les Bouffes we saw strange things, so strange that they will never be seen again.' The writer emphasised that punctuality was essential, as no one was permitted entry to the theatre once the show had started. It was very dark and hot, and applause was forbidden as it would have disturbed

---

[18] Lugné-Poë, *Le Sot du tremplin*, p. 238.

[19] 'Les chassis se trouvèrent posés à l'envers.' Lugné-Poë, *Le Sot du tremplin*, p. 229.

[20] 'Ils ont récité leurs rôles sur le ton de la mélopée uniforme ... avec des voix d'ombre, autant qu'ils ont pu.' Jules Lemaitre, *L'Echo de Paris*, 21 May 1893.

[21] Lugné-Poë, *Le Sot du tremplin*, p. 238.

[22] Jules Lemaitre, *L'Echo de Paris*, 21 May 1893.

the flow of the performance. 'We watched the symbolic (and how!) drama by M. Maurice Maeterlinck unfold. Charming to read, delightful if acted by the marionettes at the Chat Noir[23]... but on the real stage and with real people it seemed to us rather childish and often banal.' There were certainly fierce supporters of Maeterlinck present, who would have shouted down any dissenting voices. The atmosphere, however, was depressing, for the play was 'set in a very primitive age, in a very unfamiliar country, but one which is very sad and surely very unhealthy: all the people seem to be ill and being in their company for a long time we cannot avoid catching the fever which has them in its grip.' The sardonic reviewer has to admit that Mlle Meuris acted the 'adorable' tower scene with Mélisande's hair 'adorably', together with the woman playing Pelléas, Mlle Marie Aubry. He adds that the play was dedicated by Maeterlinck to M. Octave Mirbeau, which was 'the least the poet from Ghent could do for the one who had proclaimed him to be "superior to Shakespeare". Oh! Oh!'[24]

In another colourful review of both the play and its reverential audience, an influential journalist found the atmosphere one of a religious service rather than an entertainment. He emerged dazed from the shadows, as if a lead weight were pressing on his head, gasping for fresh air, never wanting to see another play by Maeterlinck.[25] The artist Henry Lerolle was not quite so dismissive. The play had not been particularly well acted, was very fragmented with too many scene changes, and the obsession with repeating the same word three times was annoying. Nevertheless, he told his brother-in-law, the composer Ernest Chausson, that he considered it very artistic.[26]

Having described his ideal 'poem' as we have seen above, it is hardly surprising this production of *Pelléas et Mélisande* made such an impact on Debussy. 'Monochrome', 'shades of grey' were words he used in 1889. He had even said that the characters should not philosophise, 'but submit to life and to their destiny'. Nothing could be nearer to this conception. Author and composer,

---

[23] Chat Noir: cabaret founded by Rodolphe Salis.

[24] 'Nous avons vu cette après-midi, aux Bouffes, des choses étranges, si étranges qu'on ne les verra jamais plus ... Nous avons vu se dérouler le drame symbolique – Oh! Combien! – de M. Maurice Maeterlinck. Charmant à la lecture, délicieux peut-être encore s'il était joué au Chat Noir par des marionnettes ... à la représentation sur un vrai théâtre, et par des personnes naturelles, un peu bien puéril et souvent banal ... qui se passé à une époque très primitive, dans un pays, très inconnu, mais triste et sûrement très malsain: tous les gens là semblent malades, et à les longtemps fréquenter nous ne pourrions que gagner la fièvre qui les étreint ... C'était bien le moins que dût le poète gantois à celui qui l'avait proclamé «supérieur à Shakespeare». Oh! Oh!' Édouard Noël and Edmond Stoullig, *Les Annales du théâtre et de la musique* (1894), p. 367.

[25] Francisque Sarcey, *Le Temps*, 22 May 1893.

[26] Gordon Millan, *Pierre Louÿs ou le culte d'amitié* (Aix-en-Provence, 1979), p. 203.

born in the same week, shared the same creative philosophy. Recalling the
young Debussy, Robert Godet wrote that upon reading the play he immediately jotted down some ideas which remained in the final work nearly ten
years later,[27] although it has since been pointed out that the latter two of
these motifs do not appear in the earliest extant sketches.[28] Now he lived for
this strange work with its 'dreamy characters enveloped in a veil of mist'.[29] In
1902, reflecting on the process of composition, Debussy justified his choice
of drama, citing in particular the sensitivity of its evocative language which
could be extended in the music and in the orchestral setting. He insisted
that he was trying to obey an aesthetic law generally ignored when it came to
dramatic music: the characters of his opera try to sing like real people, not in
an arbitrary language built up over years of antiquated tradition. 'A character
cannot continually express his feelings melodically; dramatic melody has to
be quite different from what is generally called melody.'[30]

The puzzlement of the public at the incomprehensible manipulation of
the characters by an all-pervading sense of inescapable fate in Maeterlinck's
play was to be compounded in Debussy's opera with its musical extension
of this feeling. It is not surprising that some found the innovatory setting of
words to music following their natural stresses and intonation inappropriate
for the operatic stage.

Whilst Debussy kept quiet about his own impressions of the play following the critics' scathing remarks, this did not stop him from requesting a
friend, the poet Henri de Régnier, to write to Maeterlinck on his behalf to
request the rights to set it to music. In August 1893 Maeterlinck received a
letter telling him that Debussy had 'begun some charming music for *Pelléas
et Mélisande*, which deliciously garlands the text while scrupulously respecting it. Before going further with this work which is not inconsiderable, he
would like authorisation to continue.'[31] It was just as well that Debussy had
an intermediary, for Maeterlinck, knowing nothing of music and not being

---

[27] The outline of a theme accompanying Pelléas's words, Act IV scene 4, 'on dirait que ta
voix a passé sur la mer au printemps'; the rhythm for Golaud, the five-note arabesque
which is Mélisande's motif. Godet, 'En marge de la marge'.

[28] David Grayson, 'The Opera: Genesis and Sources', in R. Nichols and R. Langham
Smith, *Claude Debussy: Pelléas et Mélisande*, Cambridge Opera Handbooks
(Cambridge, 1989), p. 32.

[29] 'Les personnages de rêve, enveloppés d'une voile de brume légère'. Émile Vuillermoz,
Claude Debussy (Paris, 1957), p. 58.

[30] Claude Debussy, 'Pourquoi j'ai écrit Pelléas': note to George Ricou written in April
1902, *Comoedia*, 17 October 1920; translated in *Debussy on Music*, collected by
François Lesure, ed. and trans. Richard Langham Smith (London, 1977), pp. 74–5.

[31] Georgette Leblanc, *Souvenirs: My Life with Maeterlinck* (New York, 1932), p. 168,
translation by Janet Flanner of *Souvenirs (1895–1918)* (Paris, 1931).

familiar with the names of contemporary composers, would otherwise probably not have bothered to reply.

It was to his friend, Lugné-Poë's colleague, Camille Mauclair, that Maeterlinck wrote:

> I have received from a M. Debussy, of whom I know absolutely nothing ... a request for authorisation for my *Pelléas*. You know that as far as music is concerned I may as well be deaf. Do me the service of listening to the score and if you think it is good I will authorise it.[32]

So Mauclair, who had not until now met the composer, went to Debussy's flat with the writer Pierre Louÿs, the composer's close friend. Debussy insisted that Mauclair should give Maeterlinck a candid impression. He proceeded to sing all the parts, at the same time conveying the orchestral effects. By the end, Louÿs' and Mauclair's eyes were full of tears. When Mauclair asked him what he was thinking of doing with his score, Debussy modestly replied that he was writing it simply for his own satisfaction. Fearing no one would agree to put it on in a theatre, the most he could hope for was two or three private performances in the mansion of the aesthete Robert de Montesquiou, the Pavillon des Muses, in Neuilly. Mauclair thought otherwise. He wrote a telegram to Maeterlinck. 'I have just heard a masterpiece. Authorise it by telegram.'[33] On 8 August 1893 Maeterlinck answered: 'I wholeheartedly give him all necessary authorisation for *Pelléas et Mélisande*.'[34]

Already, therefore, there was enough music sketched out for judgements to be formed on its quality. Raymond Bonheur, reminiscing about his friendship with the young Debussy, loved to recall Saturday afternoons in the rue Gustave-Doré, when he and Satie would climb up to Debussy's lodgings on the fourth floor. There, Debussy would begin by making tea in his pernickety way, then after some small talk he would play them the latest pages of *Pelléas*, jumping from one act to another, just as the mood took him for 'he was totally possessed by *Pelléas*.'[35]

By 3 September Debussy had already finished a draft of a key scene, Act IV

---

[32] 'J'ai reçu d'un M. Debussy, dont j'ignore tout ... une demande d'autorisation pour mon *Pelléas*. Tu sais que la musique est pour moi aussi inintelligible que si j'étais sourd. Rends-moi le service d'aller écouter cette partition, et si tu la juges bonne, j'autoriserai.' Albert Carré, *Souvenirs de théâtre* (Paris, 1950), p. 274.

[33] 'Je viens d'entendre un chef-d'œuvre: accorde autorisation télégraphique.' Millan, *Pierre Louÿs ou le culte d'amitié*, p. 204.

[34] 'C'est de bien grand cœur que je lui donne toute autorisation nécessaire pour Pelléas et Mélisande.' Marcel Dietschy, *La Passion de Claude Debussy* (Neuchâtel, 1962), p. 101.

[35] 'sautant d'un acte à l'autre, suivant les caprices de sa fantaisie, pour ce *Pelléas* qui à ce moment le possédait tout entier.' Raymond Bonheur, 'Souvenirs et impressions d'un compagnon de jeunesse', *La Revue musicale*, vol. 7 (May 1926), p. 7.

scene 4, the climax of the work, which included the theme he had sketched out when his enthusiasm was first aroused.[36] In a letter to Ernest Chausson, after bitter complaints about the difficulty of writing music and the painful noises coming from the floor above him where a young girl was murdering a piece of piano music, he signs off, then adds his 'breaking news: C. A. Debussy finishes a scene from *Pelléas et Mélisande* "A Well in the Park" (Act IV scene 4) on which he would like the opinion of E. Chausson.'[37]

However, by 2 October he was, typically, dissatisfied with these early attempts. He had claimed victory for *Pelléas et Mélisande* far too early and was now having sleepless nights because it was all too Wagnerian, or as he put it, reminiscent of 'old Klingsor'. He had torn the whole lot up! What is intriguing, however, is his statement that he had turned to a new idea – unusual in music. Just as Lugné-Poë had wanted to combine poetry and silence in the theatre, Debussy was experimenting with the use of silence as a means of expression.[38] As we will see, the significance of this is that it entirely fitted the philosophy of Maeterlinck and his mistress Georgette Leblanc, therefore instinctively, before he had even met the author, Debussy had entered the soul of Maeterlinck's art. In the same letter he also said he had just met André Messager, composer and conductor, who had invited him to dinner. Messager was to prove indispensable in supporting and conducting Debussy's masterpiece.

On 27 October 1893 Debussy expected Bonheur to recognise his allusion to Act IV scene 4, when Pelléas and Mélisande realise they are locked out of the castle, for on that date he writes: 'I urge you to come next week to dine with your little friends, under penalty of having to see the gates close. Do you hear the great chains?'[39]

On 6 November 1893 Debussy travelled with Pierre Louÿs to meet the playwright. Writing to Chausson on 16 November he described how first the two of them visited the great violinist Eugène Ysaÿe in Brussels who yelled with joy at seeing Debussy and flung his arms around him, squeezing him to his vast chest. That evening Debussy played *Pelléas* to him, and Ysaÿe's reaction was a sheer frenzy of delight. Already, even in this embryonic form, the opera was moving the hearts of its listeners.[40] He and Louÿs then moved on to Ghent. As he related to his brother many years later (in 1914), Louÿs claimed that he did all the talking for Debussy, who was too shy to be able

[36] See n. 27 above.

[37] Claude Debussy, *Correspondance (1872–1918)*, collected and annotated by François Lesure, Denis Herlin and Georges Liébert (Paris, 2005), p. 156.

[38] Debussy, *Correspondance*, p. 160.

[39] Debussy, *Correspondance*, p. 173.

[40] Debussy, *Correspondance*, p. 175.

to ask for what he wanted.[41] Maeterlinck was even shyer, and as he could not put his answers into words, Louÿs replied for him too! Debussy described the author's reticence as being that of 'a young girl whose future husband is being presented to her, then he thawed out and became charming.'

The essential purpose of the trip was fulfilled, for Maeterlinck not only gave Debussy complete authorisation to do what he liked with the text, but agreed that Debussy could cut sections, some of which Maeterlinck suggested himself. However, Debussy realised that Maeterlinck had no understanding of music. The author himself confessed that for him to go to hear a Beethoven symphony was equivalent to a blind man visiting a museum. The essential thing as far as *Pelléas* was concerned was that when the composer thanked Maeterlinck for entrusting his play to him, the author did all he could to prove that it was he who should be grateful to Debussy for wanting to set it to music! Underlining his lack of any musicianship, the author was absolutely astonished that his play could provide material for a whole musical score. 'C'est curieux, c'est très curieux!', he muttered.[42]

From now on, Debussy lived with Pelléas and Mélisande as if they were his own children. By December 1893 there was enough music composed to play to a gathering at Henry Lerolle's house, even if he was initially reluctant to play it to his friends. Lerolle wrote a letter to Chausson,[43] giving a wonderfully evocative description of this musical evening, which had begun with Vincent d'Indy playing the last act of his opera *Fervaal*. Debussy, after at first insisting he had nothing to play, began tinkering at the piano. Lerolle discovered the current pages of *Pelléas* in Debussy's briefcase, and once started, Debussy got quite carried away. His little audience was amazed and appreciative. Only one, Benoît, was bored and wanted to go home.

In January 1894 Debussy wrote to another friend, the composer Paul Dukas, reluctantly refusing to play him any of *Pelléas* yet as the parts he had finished were too fragmentary, and would give the wrong impression.[44] He made excuses to Chausson for not contacting him earlier:

It's all Mélisande's fault – but please forgive us both. I have spent days pursuing that 'nothing' of which she is made ... I don't know if you have ever gone to bed like me with a strange desire to cry, feeling you had not been able

[41] Debussy, *Correspondance*, p. 176 (note).

[42] Peter, *Claude Debussy*, p. 164.

[43] In *Correspondance*, pp. 180–1 (note), the letter is dated 19 December 1893. Dietschy, *La Passion de Claude Debussy*, pp. 104–5, gives the same date, but refers to Tiénot and Estrade-Guerra, *Debussy*, p. 86, which gives December 1894. In Jean-Pierre Barricelli and Leo Weinstein, *Ernest Chausson: The Composer's Life and Works* (Norman, OK, 1955), the letter is dated two months earlier, 19 October 1893.

[44] Debussy, *Correspondance*, p. 186.

to see a beloved friend during the day. Now it is Arkel I am worrying about. He belongs to the world beyond the grave and has that disinterested and far-seeing love of those who will soon be here no more. And all this has to be said with doh ray me fah soh la te doh. What a job![45]

Yet this 'job' was far enough advanced by May 1894 for others to hear several excerpts. Pierre Louÿs had a piano taken to his flat especially so that friends could listen to Debussy playing and singing *Pelléas*. He was to remember to bring with him the first act, the scene by the well, and 'the scene with the hair, even if incomplete'.[46]

However, Debussy's 'children' did not always behave. 'Pelléas and Mélisande are sulking and won't descend from their tapestry', he told Henry Lerolle:

> so I was forced to play around with some other ideas. Then they got a bit jeal-ous and returned to lean over me and Mélisande, in her sweet little wheedling voice which you know so well, said to me: 'leave those mad ideas alone, flirting with the cosmopolitan audience, and save your dreams for my hair. You know very well that no love matches ours.'[47]

Hair! How important this was to be for future Mélisandes! He had finished the scene in the vaults, 'full of impending terror, mysterious enough to give vertigo to the most hardened souls, and also the scene when they come out of the vaults, in a blaze of sunlight, but sunlight bathed by our good mother, the sea.' The scenes with Yniold were now occupying him, particu-larly Golaud's problematical interrogations of his son. The words 'petit père', which recurred so often, were giving him nightmares.

In January 1895 Debussy's obsession with his characters was made clear to Louÿs when he described Pelléas and Mélisande as his 'only friends at the moment ... Perhaps we are even getting to know each other too well and we are only telling each other stories whose ending we already know perfectly well; but then when you finish a work, isn't it a bit like the death of some-one you love?'[48] It was something deeper than simply coming to the end of his composition that was troubling him. He was in mourning. One day in April, he was hoping to see Louÿs, but 'I have been detained by the death of Mélisande. It upsets me and I am trembling as I work on it.'[49] Indeed, those words of Mélisande he had imagined, 'No love matches ours', were ringing true.

---

[45] Debussy, *Correspondance*, p. 189.

[46] Debussy, *Correspondance*, p. 208.

[47] Debussy, *Correspondance*, pp. 219–20.

[48] Debussy, *Correspondance*, pp. 237–8.

[49] Debussy, *Correspondance*, p. 254.

So the end was in sight. Debussy reminded his publisher and sponsor Georges Hartmann at the beginning of August 1895 that 'I am expecting you tomorrow afternoon for the agony of poor little Mélisande.'[50] Yet he must still have been revising his work as only a few days later he told Bonheur, 'I thought the second act of *Pelléas* would be child's play, but it's absolute hell!'[51]

Just eight days later, Debussy told Henry Lerolle that he had at last finished *Pelléas*. He was not going to find it easy to let go of his beloved characters, though, for he was anxious to express his empathy not just with Pelléas and Mélisande, but with Golaud. The scene between Golaud and Mélisande (Act IV scene 1), he explained, was 'where you begin to sense catastrophe, at the point where Mélisande begins to lie to Golaud and to understand herself, helped along by Golaud, who is a good man despite everything.' He was pleased with his setting of the scene by the cave, where he had tried:

> to convey all the mystery of night where everything is so silent that one blade of grass disturbed in its sleep makes a frightening noise. Then there is the sea nearby telling the moon of its sorrows. And there are Pelléas and Mélisande, a bit afraid to speak amongst so much mystery ... Now my worries are just beginning. How will the world react to these two poor little creatures?[52]

It is clear from these remarks that Debussy was apprehensive about how his audience would respond to the death of his dearly beloved couple being expressed in such quiet, understated, one might say unoperatic, musical terms. He saw disaster looming, for here there was to be no elaborate, long-drawn-out farewell. 'People can't accept that you just slip away from this life discretely like someone who has had enough of planet Earth and you go to where flowers of tranquillity bloom.' Despite what must have been an emotionally significant moment for Debussy, he was just as insistent on understatement when he told Pierre Louÿs: 'Pelléas was finished on 17 August. Nothing was disturbed in the order of things because of this, the earth did not move.'[53]

In September Debussy told Lerolle that only two people (Bonheur and Dupin) had heard the ending of *Pelléas*, thus confirming that he had once again reached some sort of conclusion to his score.[54] Most significantly, however, on 17 October 1895 Maeterlinck again confirmed to Debussy that, 'As for *Pelléas*, it goes without saying that it belongs entirely to you and you

---

[50] Debussy, *Correspondance*, p. 267.

[51] Debussy, *Correspondance*, p. 267.

[52] Debussy, *Correspondance*, p. 266.

[53] Debussy, *Correspondance*, p. 270.

[54] Debussy, *Correspondance*, p. 272.

can have it performed where and when you want.'[55] Twice, therefore, the composer had received unequivocal permission from the author to have free reign with the play – three times if you count the very first written response to Henry Lerolle.

What was happening meanwhile to Maeterlinck's play? That same year Lugné-Poë's theatre company, the Théâtre de l'Œuvre, was invited by J. T. Grein of the Independent Theatre Society to give a week of performances, in French, of Maeterlinck's plays in the Strand in London. What a disaster the London venture could have proved! When they came to unpack the wardrobe, it was discovered that the costumes for Pelléas had been left behind. It was a Saturday and the shops were shutting. In the street Lugné-Poë came across a Scottish boy wearing kilt, sporran and Glengarry. Allegedly the boy was persuaded to lend his outfit and this provided the costume for Pelléas – or so Lugné-Poë's story goes![56] Suzanne Després (later to become Lugné-Poë's wife) played Mélisande. As in Paris, a gauze veil was stretched across the stage through which the audience viewed the actors, helping to convey an impression 'of fascinating mystery and spiritual penetration', enhanced by the 'dim lights and lengthy silences, and slow rhythmical movements'.[57] This production was therefore very similar to that seen in Paris two years earlier.

In October 1896 Debussy was once again in touch with the violinist Ysaÿe, who had been trying in vain to organise a performance of the opera at the Théâtre de la Monnaie in Brussels, and now had the idea of giving excerpts in a concert performance. But Debussy was convinced that this would destroy the essential link between movement on stage and the movement of the music. The 'special eloquence' of the silences so essential to the work would fail to be understood. The simplicity of the means used to tell the story could only be achieved in a fully staged performance. 'At a concert performance people would throw back at me the American wealth of Wagner and I would look like a poor man who couldn't even afford to pay for ... contra bass tubas!' Typically, he stood up for his characters: 'In my opinion, Pelléas and Mélisande must introduce themselves as they are and people can take them or leave them.'[58]

Debussy knew that Lugné-Poë's productions involved some musical accompaniment, but consistently refused to have anything to do with them. Just like the singers who were later to be so determined to create Mélisande, Mrs Patrick Campbell, the great English actress, was mesmerised by the

55 Debussy, *Correspondance*, p. 284.
56 W. D. Halls, *Maurice Maeterlinck: A Study of his Life and Thought* (Oxford, 1960), p. 52.
57 Virginia Crawford, *Studies in Foreign Literature* (Boston, 1899), p. 167.
58 Debussy, *Correspondance*, p. 325.

character, having read an English translation of Maeterlinck's play by J. W. Mackail, son-in-law of Burne-Jones. 'I *knew* Mélisande as though she had been part of me before my eyes were open. I *knew* I could put the beauty of the written word into colour, shape and sound', she wrote.[59] She approached Debussy to provide incidental music for forthcoming productions in London, but typically he remained steadfast in his resolve not to compromise his conception of the opera. Pierre Louÿs, knowing Debussy's perpetually impoverished circumstances, found it difficult to sympathise with this high-mindedness.[60] This did not disturb Maeterlinck, who was only interested in the success of the play and not at all in its relation to the music.

Thus it came about that in June 1898 Maeterlinck's play was again performed in London at the Prince of Wales Theatre in Mackail's translation with incidental music, but not by Debussy. This was the occasion for which, at Mrs Patrick Campbell's request, Fauré composed his suite *Pelléas et Mélisande*. Maeterlinck might well have wondered why Debussy was taking so long to finish his operatic version, for Fauré's incidental music was completed in just over a month, the orchestration having been entrusted to Charles Koechlin. On 9 August Debussy told Georges Hartmann that three years earlier, Mauclair, on Maeterlinck's behalf, had already broached with him the subject of incidental music for this London performance, but there was simply no way he was prepared to separate words and music. Knowing Debussy's deep instinctive feeling that the music should underline the intention of the words, convey their intangible essence and extend their meaning, it is not in the least surprising that he remained intransigent. On hearing that Fauré had fulfilled this commission, Debussy expressed his real feelings about the author: 'Surely, Maeterlinck should have informed me about it since it has been done in spite of everything. But he is Belgian! Therefore rather uncouth and definitely badly brought up.' Neither was he flattering about Fauré, who had not had the grace to let him know about this commission. He found it impossible to believe that his music would last or that there could be any confusion between the two versions.[61]

On reading the review in *The Times* of this London performance,[62] Debussy's opinions seem to be supported, for here Fauré's music is deemed to have taken the place of the intervening gauze veil which separated the audience from the happenings on stage in the original performance of the play. The music was 'decidedly less transparent than the curtain it has

[59] Mrs Patrick Campbell, *My Life and some Letters* (London, 1922), p. 126.

[60] Debussy, *Correspondance*, p. 290 and n. 4.

[61] Debussy, *Correspondance*, p. 414.

[62] *The Times*, 22 June 1898, p. 12

supplanted, and if its purpose is to supply the angularity of effect which was formerly given by the gestures of the actors it must be held to have succeeded perfectly.' It lacked both charm and dramatic power, and was even described as 'ugly' at various points. Had he read it, this negative reaction would surely have strengthened Maeterlinck's dislike of any musical interference with his masterpiece.

Mrs Patrick Campbell as Mélisande wore a gold dress designed by Sir Edward Burne-Jones; Pelléas was played by Martin Harvey, who designed his own clothes, paying great attention to his wig, which was made of the hair of a Tibetan yak. On top of this he had wings on his head. Johnston Forbes-Robertson played Golaud. Apart from the music, the *Times* reviewer had words of the highest praise for all. However, Virginia Crawford, the writer on European literature who had so appreciated Lugné-Poë's London production in 1895, found this staging too material. It was produced with such grand scenery and elaborate detail in order to conform to what she described as 'the orthodox traditions of the English stage', that it became 'little more than a drama of domestic intrigue', some episodes being of almost childish triviality. The only actor to receive praise was Harvey as Pelléas, and even his interpretation of the love scene in the fourth act was questionable. In Crawford's opinion it should have been played 'on a level of tender soul-communion rather than of passionate human emotion'. Thus the play lost its 'weird elusive beauty' and at the same time any semblance of symbolism seemed to have vanished. Mackail's translation, which she found 'prosaic and here and there painfully colloquial', contributed to this effect.[63]

Maeterlinck, however, was simply delighted with the performance. He wrote to Mrs Campbell telling her that she had been 'in reality more lovely and more lifelike than in [his] most vivid and beautiful imaginings' and he poured lyrical praise on 'the delightful, the ideal Pelléas' of Harvey.[64] In a letter to Lugné-Poë he said he hoped he too had seen the performance. 'Not bad, was it!' Significantly, he then expressed his concern that if they put it on again in Paris, it might clash with the version Carré was organising at the Opéra-Comique, one which was supposed to be even more brilliant than the one in London. They were going to have to meet to discuss this.[65] Clearly, already talk was spreading of Carré's plans for performing Debussy's opera. How had this come about?

The music publisher Georges Hartmann, who published under the name of Eugène Fromont, liked to encourage young French composers, and

[63] Crawford, *Studies in Foreign Literature*, pp. 165–7.

[64] Campbell, *My Life and some Letters*, p. 131.

[65] Stadsarchief Gent B LXXII.6.

provided considerable support to Debussy. From 1895 he granted him an income of 500 francs a month. Indeed, it was Hartmann who had originally decided that the conductor at the Opéra-Comique, André Messager, must hear the opera.[66] Although at first taken aback, Messager was moved by the music as Debussy sang him scene by scene, and was gradually persuaded that *Pelléas* was a masterpiece, something completely new, expressed in unique, subtle language. Convinced that the work should be staged, he approached Albert Carré, now Director of the Opéra-Comique, suggesting that he should give the opera a hearing and meet Debussy. 'I would be delighted to listen to it', replied Carré. 'Bring him to me.'[67]

This was not as straightforward as would have been the case with most aspiring composers. Debussy was not the sort of musician who would vaunt his wares. Any interview with him would have to be conducted in the privacy of his own home. In the second fortnight in May 1898, Carré climbed up the stairs to Debussy's flat with Hartmann.[68] 'Do I need to tell you that I did not regret it?', he asks.[69] Carré, in common with many who met Debussy, found him a puzzling character. He recalled his 'revolutionary' qualities: he remembered Debussy applauding and protesting so vociferously at the 1882 première of Lalo's ballet *Namouna* when others had booed, that he had had to be removed from the hall and be reprimanded by Ambroise Thomas, Director of the Conservatoire. Then as now, he found him distant, coarse and brutal in his directness, indeed 'a bear'. He was extremely reticent, sensitive and generally indifferent to others, apart from his very closest friends. Carré insisted that Debussy's belief in his own music was always subordinate to his pure love of Music with a capital M, which meant that he always suffered doubts as to its true worth, and often destroyed the rough sketches he composed. Having climbed those stairs to Debussy's room, Carré had no doubts as to the special qualities of what he heard: 'I was struck by the novelty, the originality of this music, following exactly the inflections of speech and arousing such strong emotions, and I told Debussy his work was accepted by the Opéra-Comique.'[70] Even so, Carré took three years to finalise a contract.

This delay caused Debussy considerable anxiety. In July 1898 he asked Hartmann if there was any possibility of getting some sort of contract from

[66] Peter, *Claude Debussy*, p. 168.

[67] Carré, *Souvenirs de théâtre*, p. 275.

[68] Debussy, *Correspondance*, p. 400.

[69] Carré, *Souvenirs de théâtre*, p. 275.

[70] 'Je fus frappé par la nouveauté, l'originalité de cette musique, calquée sur les inflexions de la parole et dont se dégageait une si grande émotion ...' Carré, *Souvenirs de théâtre*, p. 275.

Carré, for talk was already spreading about the opera and he did not want to lose the impetus from this interest. Unfortunately, Debussy continued, he had been suffering from acute neuralgia for a week and maybe because of this he had been having awful nightmares: at a rehearsal of *Pelléas*, Golaud had suddenly changed into a bailiff and adapted the terms of his summons to be sung in character![71]

In his memoirs Carré wanted to scotch all rumours that he might have been reluctant to stage the work and that Messager had had to 'impose' *Pelléas* on the Opéra-Comique. Moved and fascinated, he was by no means reluctant to put it on, but how? In his position he obviously had to weigh up the risks of negative reaction and resistance to a work which broke with the familiar principles at his opera house and one which could potentially be a particularly heavy financial burden. As Messager later wrote, 'he worried greatly about how he could present this exceptional work to the public.'[72] 'Cette œuvre exceptionnelle' here implies not just an extraordinary work, but one not of the sort usually mounted at the Opéra-Comique. Audiences there were used to works with a lighter touch, often containing spoken dialogue. The plots were certainly dramatic, often tragic, but the music was immediately appealing, comprehensible, not too demanding intellectually. Bizet's *Carmen*, Charpentier's *Louise*, Massenet's *Manon* as all his other operas, presented a style with which the audience was comfortable and familiar. Messager and Carré had frequent discussions, Carré wondering whether to keep *Pelléas* off the main agenda and give it special matinée productions, whilst Messager tried to persuade him to present it without emphasising its unusual qualities.

What an enormous relief it was for Debussy at last to receive a promise from Albert Carré that *Pelléas* would indeed be performed at the Opéra-Comique in the 1901–2 season. On 5 May 1901 he wrote joyfully to Louÿs on the latter's return from Egypt wanting to be the first to tell him the good news that he had Carré's promise in writing.[73] At long last, nine years after Maeterlinck published his play, after adopting its characters as his own, moulding them in the day time and dreaming of them at night, he was assured that he would see them come to life on stage – not without continued modifications to the orchestral parts, though, for as late as December 1901 he wrote to Louÿs to tell him: 'I have set my mind on re-orchestrating *Pelléas* (not a word to anyone).'[74]

[71] Debussy, *Correspondance*, p. 412.

[72] André Messager, 'Les premières représentations de Pelléas', *La Revue musicale*, vol. 7 (May 1926), p. 110.

[73] Debussy, *Correspondance*, p. 596.

[74] Debussy, *Correspondance*, p. 631.

Now the anxious time had arrived when he would have to entrust his dear children to others, to allow someone else to breathe life into his 'poor little creatures.' Who was going to breathe that life into Mélisande?

2 *Georgette Leblanc*
(1869–94)

O F THE THREE WOMEN first associated with the role of Mélisande in Debussy's opera, Georgette Leblanc was perhaps the most extraordinary. She had a great propensity to dramatise every aspect of her life, an enduring belief in her own ability, and the instinct to take every opportunity and make the best of it as her life progressed, which often led her down unbeaten and somewhat wayward paths. The story of Georgette's life is inextricably linked with that of Maurice Maeterlinck. The translation of her first published autobiography, entitled *Souvenirs (1895–1918)*, is subtitled *My Life with Maeterlinck*.[1] It is, indeed, a strange tale initially of worship and adoration of the author of *Pelléas et Mélisande*, which in itself led to the eclipse of her own abilities as a writer and was even a handicap to her as a singer.

Significantly, each of our three Mélisandes elaborated tales of their ancestry to give themselves a veneer of romanticism and show themselves as somehow destined for a career in the public eye. Georgette's claim was that her father's real name was Emilio Bianconi. In her wishful thinking, he was a dashing Italian *condottiere* who left his native Venice at the age of fifteen to become an itinerant violinist. On reaching Rouen, despite only carrying out menial work, he met and married Blanche de Brohys, the aristocratic daughter of wealthy ship-owner, upon which he changed his name to Leblanc, and changed his nationality.[2] The truth was more prosaic. Émile Leblanc was a native of Rouen, born on 12 July 1830. He was a merchant and importer of coal before joining the firm of a ship-owner. Both he and his wife, Blanche, born near Rouen in 1843, were members of the prosperous bourgeoisie, whatever Georgette might have pretended.[3]

Marie Blanche Georgette was born in Rouen, unplanned, unwanted, on 8 February 1869. She regarded this situation as being germane to her whole personality: 'A child is usually born as a triumph. For my parents, I was a defeat … I have spent all my life winning the battle I innocently lost by being born.'[4]

---

[1] Georgette Leblanc, *Souvenirs: My Life with Maeterlinck*, trans. Janet Flanner (New York, 1932).

[2] Georgette Leblanc, unpublished manuscript, 'Histoire de ma vie', Archives et Musée de la Littérature [AML], Brussels. Also e.g. Georgette Leblanc and René Chambrillac, 'Confessions d'une amoureuse', *Voilà*, 21 October 1938.

[3] Information kindly provided to the author by Maxime Benoît-Jeannin.

[4] Leblanc, *Souvenirs: My Life with Maeterlinck*, p. 283.

Georgette's bitterness at this situation led to her elaborating further tales of having been carried up to the garret to be fed by her wet-nurse, a humble actress with an illegitimate baby son, thus suckling the milk of a thespian. She had a sister, Jehanne, five years older, and a brother, Maurice, four years older, whom she would watch as they played together. Her enforced loneliness was the clue to her desire for drama and pathos. She was convinced that she was virtually ignored: 'I therefore had to create situations in which I could applaud myself. I played heroic roles for myself alone.'[5] Maurice entered the Lycée Corneille at the age of eleven and Jehanne married at the tender age of seventeen whilst Georgette was educated and received piano and singing lessons at home.

Georgette's loneliness was compounded by the fact that she had few friends. At the age of twelve she had been allowed to sing to the accompaniment of a younger girl, Nelly-Rose, who was said to be a prodigy at the piano. However, the little pianist could never meet Georgette's extreme emotional and melodramatic demands in her interpretation and this led to Nelly-Rose's parents informing Georgette's parents that she was no longer welcome at their house as she was 'too artistic' and was leading their daughter astray.[6] Her friendship with another young girl proved to be even more heart-breaking. Isabelle was able to sing and play the piano exquisitely by ear, yet could not read a note of music. Her beauty and talent inevitably wrought their spell on Georgette, but she committed suicide, a decidedly operatic death: 'Her letter of farewell reached me in the morning. It had snowed the evening before and all the night. The city covered with white shone in the sun. Isabelle was found lying on her balcony in an immaculate shroud.'[7]

In 1885 when Georgette was nearly sixteen, although she refers to her age as only thirteen, an even greater drama occurred. The death of her mother, Blanche, was to have a huge impact on the impressionable girl. She describes the moment as if it were a scene from an opera. 'Dressed for a ball, lighted by her jewels beneath the great chandelier, she fell dead in my arms.'[8] Perhaps unsurprisingly, Georgette was always to feel the need for a mother figure. She was left in the care of her bereft elderly father, legally unable to receive the inheritance due to her from her mother until she was twenty-one.

Now, feeling lost and lonely yet brim full of emotion and with a vivid imagination, she managed to escape every day to the establishment in the rue de la Ganterie in Rouen run by the elderly organist and composer

---

[5] Leblanc, *Souvenirs: My Life with Maeterlinck*, p. 284.

[6] Georgette Leblanc, *La Machine à courage: Souvenirs* (Paris, 1947), p. 167.

[7] Leblanc, *Souvenirs: My Life with Maeterlinck*, p. 45.

[8] Leblanc, *Souvenirs: My Life with Maeterlinck*, p. 45.

Aloys Klein, a venue which attracted musicians from far and wide. There she received organ lessons which her father only permitted because Klein managed to convince him that the organ produced mystic vibrations which would excite religious sentiment in the young girl.[9] It was probably not too difficult to hide from her father the amount of time she spent on music, for Émile became morose and taciturn after the death of his wife. He rarely left his office in town. However, there was a public garden in front of their house, and from her balcony Georgette took to singing to the outside world. 'The passers-by collected. I sang madly, anything at all, provided it dealt with a broken heart.'[10] The drama, the pathos, the passion, and the need to express these emotions publicly are portents of the extrovert life to come.

The lonely girl had to keep her depressed father company when he returned from work. Whilst she pitied him, she also had grounds to fear the lonely widower. The evenings were passed alone with him in his austere bedroom. 'The lamplight brutally outlined his profile and clung to the knees of a silver Christ hanging above the bed. Suddenly he would throw aside his newspaper and pace the floor cursing God. Overcoming my own grief, I would sit silent, and my apparent apathy excited him to a greater fury.'[11]

Yet more tragedy was to follow. Georgette fell in love with a young man who wanted to marry her, but when her father refused to allow the match, her suitor poisoned himself.[12] No wonder Maeterlinck said to her long after they had met: 'I saw in your eyes, that first night, something sorrowful which was more salient than your smile or the triumph of your walk.'[13]

How to escape this incarceration?

Georgette was doing her best to develop her gifts as a singer. One day (according to her, 13 April – how these singers loved to attribute the number thirteen to significant occasions!) at Aloys Klein's music establishment, he asked her to start singing as soon as she saw someone entering the room. To her delight, she recognised the visitor as the composer Jules Massenet, who immediately seated himself at the piano and proceeded to accompany her in the prayer scene from his opera *Manon*. When he leapt up exclaiming over her talent, Aloys Klein cried back in delight, 'I told you so! I told you so!'[14] 'Where did she find all that passion?', asked Massenet – a question many were to pose during her career![15] The composer invited her to the opera that night

---

9 Leblanc, *La Machine à courage*, p. 169.

10 Leblanc, *Souvenirs: My Life with Maeterlinck*, p. 34.

11 Leblanc, *Souvenirs: My Life with Maeterlinck*, p. 41.

12 Leblanc, *Souvenirs: My Life with Maeterlinck*, p. 45.

13 Leblanc, *Souvenirs: My Life with Maeterlinck*, p. 45.

14 Leblanc, *La Machine à courage*, p. 170.

15 Leblanc, 'Histoire de ma vie'.

and fortunately her father agreed to accompany them. Although Georgette put every effort into dressing up to make herself look as old as possible, she was frustrated when Massenet told her father what a 'delicious little girl' he had![16] From then on she benefited from his encouragement.

One evening Georgette managed to persuade her father to take her to a performance by Sarah Bernhardt at the Grand Théâtre in Rouen, which made an immediate and indelible impression on her. Afterwards the young fan sewed a portrait of the actress into the lining of her dress. For the rest of her life Bernhardt was to remain an inspiration. Desperate to realise her ambition to appear on stage, a few months later Georgette impulsively caught the train to Paris. There, she bought a bunch of flowers and took a cab, simply giving as her direction the name of Sarah Bernhardt. Somehow granted entry to the great star's dressing room, she was delighted to hear Bernhardt exclaim that she looked just like her when she was a child. Georgette was made to sing and recite in front of the twenty or so people in the room. 'Astonishing, she's an astonishing child' was the verdict. 'You can either be a tragedienne or a singer, exactly as you choose.'[17]

The extraordinary Sarah Bernhardt will recur in these chapters, for she inspired both Georgette and Mary Garden. One reason for this may be that many of the roles in which she achieved huge success could almost be termed 'operatic'. For example, Arthur Symons wrote that Edmond Rostand's play *L'Aiglon* 'was composed like a piece of music, to be played by one performer, Sarah Bernhardt ... one seemed to see the expression marks; *piano, pianissimo, allargando,* and just when the *tempo rubato* comes in.'[18] She achieved two of her greatest successes in works that were later to be turned into operas: *La Dame aux Camélias* and *La Tosca.* The same would happen with *Pelléas et Mélisande.*

On her return to Rouen, Georgette had to face the anger and incomprehension of her father. The year was 1890; she was twenty-one years old; there was no sign of a suitor in contrast to her older sister who had married so young. Even her brother Maurice was disapproving of her flight to Paris. He, meanwhile, had become a writer, much to his father's annoyance and lack of understanding.[19] A woman singer, though – that was something different, not the sort of career to be followed by a young lady from a 'good' background. Lady singers had a certain reputation. Georgette remembers: 'My family did everything to discourage my interest in a career considered

[16] 'Sa fillette était délicieuse': Leblanc, 'Histoire de ma vie'.

[17] Leblanc, *Souvenirs: My Life with Maeterlinck,* p. 35.

[18] Ruth Brandon, *Being Divine: A Biography of Sarah Bernhardt* (London, 1991), p. 369.

[19] Author of the Arsène Lupin books about a gentleman confidence trickster.

dangerous. In Rouen prejudices are broad and points of view narrow.'[20]
What could she do to follow her dream?

Georgette had an invincible belief in her ability as an opera singer. She
knew that it was imperative to begin her singing career in Paris. Her father
was aware of her lessons and she was, after all, being encouraged by Massenet.
But singing as a vocation? Completely out of the question. This was no career
for the daughter of a wealthy ship-owner. She must marry and conform to
expectations. So Georgette evolved a bold, dangerous, and totally naïve plan
– something she would have to keep completely secret. She decided to marry
the first young man who presented himself, whatever her feelings for him,
and to force him never to consummate the marriage. The reward for him
would be her dowry: her inheritance from the death of her mother.

Georgette does not explain how she met thirty-one-year-old Buenaventura
Minuesa. He was a Spaniard from Zaragoza living in Paris. She had no problem in persuading her father to agree to the marriage – indeed, it may have
been he who introduced them to each other – as he assumed with relief that
this would put an end to her scandalous desire to sing on stage. Meanwhile
Georgette managed to arrange to stay with her father's commercial representative in Paris and organised an audition with a singing teacher at the
Conservatoire. Her father succeeded in dashing her hopes, however, for after
the successful audition, the wife of his representative, as instructed, told the
teacher about the girl's forthcoming marriage. Suddenly the teacher's enthusiasm melted. Singing lessons and family life were incompatible.[21]

On 19 April 1891 the marriage contract was signed, the dowry handed
over, and on 22 April the religious ceremony was celebrated, the bride wearing a typically dramatic and eccentric brocade dress decorated with silver. So
now to the next stage of Georgette's plan. What about the vow never to consummate the marriage? Her husband made her life a misery – not just out
of frustration. Georgette claims not to have known that he had lost all his
money gambling. 'For him this marriage replaced a revolver shot.' Truth or
exaggeration? Whatever the case, he wanted not just her money but his con-
jugal rights. If he had implied before their marriage that he would support
her quest to become a singer, this certainly was not the case afterwards. She
had little idea how to run a household of those days, when it was normal for
a cook and a maid to be employed and supervised. Her life of fantasy had not
given her any preparation for mundane housekeeping. In his fury Minuesa
physically abused his young wife, but Georgette could hardly go running to
her father for sympathy. It was not until a new maid, Eugénie, offered her

---

[20] Leblanc, *Souvenirs: My Life with Maeterlinck*, p. 38.

[21] Leblanc, 'Histoire de ma vie'.

help and took her to a lawyer that she escaped her husband. Bruised and exhausted, Georgette fell ill, but was legally separated from her husband and sent to a sanatorium in the rue du Ranelagh.[22] In 1892, the very year in which she was being abused by her Spanish gambler, Maurice Maeterlinck saw the publication of his play *Pelléas et Mélisande*. Of this, as far as we know, she was unaware.

There was never to be a divorce. Minuesa was a Spanish Catholic to whom divorce was not permitted. With no divorce, there could be no second marriage, even if she had desired it. Maeterlinck would propose marriage at a later date, but she would never agree to it.

Whilst Georgette recuperated in a nursing home in Paris run by nuns, her brother Maurice came to her aid and interceded with their father. He managed to persuade him to let her have the remainder of the dowry that Minuesa had not appropriated and to allow Georgette to remain in Paris out of the eyes and ears of Rouen. Eugénie, her maid, was to become her constant companion; together they moved into a flat which Maurice helped her find in the avenue Victor Hugo.

Georgette never doubted that she would become a singer and to this end returned to the teacher who had originally been ordered to reject her, Saint-Yves Bax. He was well known in Paris, numbering amongst his pupils the famous Californian, Sibyl Sanderson, of whom more later. Massenet also continued to keep an eye on her and in January 1893 she went to the Paris première of his opera *Werther*. It was with his encouragement she attended an audition held by the Director of the Opéra-Comique, Léon Carvalho, for a part in *L'Attaque du moulin*, by Massenet's pupil, Alfred Bruneau, which was based on a novel by Zola. Despite her inexperience, she captivated her listeners, amongst whom were both Bruneau and Zola, and as a result she was granted the role of Françoise. On 22 November 1893 Zola himself was present at the dress rehearsal.[23] How qualified he was to judge her performance is debatable, for, rather like Maeterlinck, he disliked the intrusion of music into drama. This interfered with the representation of reality. 'I cannot pass the Opéra without feeling silent anger', he once said.[24] On 23 November *L'Attaque du moulin* opened to critical acclaim. Georgette had entered the world she had been dreaming of, never having been to a music conservatoire, never having had to pass through the novitiate of a series of minor roles, having no rich sponsor, equipped with nothing but determination, ambition and the single-minded desire for self-fulfilment.

[22] Leblanc, *Souvenirs: My Life with Maeterlinck*, p. 41.

[23] Maxime Benoît-Jeannin, *Georgette Leblanc (1869–1941)* (Brussels, 1998), p. 38.

[24] Robichez, *Le Symbolisme au théâtre*, p. 29.

Her beauty, strength of mind and independence quickly made her a sought-after personality. How she revelled in her new-found freedom! This was an age in which the salon was a meeting-ground for artists, writers and musicians to converse and exchange ideas. Georgette encouraged all and sundry to converge in her studio apartment. At first it must have been a strange mixture of poverty-stricken seekers after the artistic ideal: 'My studio was like a railway station. I opened my doors to all the artistic-minded ... all the homeless rushed in; a pianist without a piano, a painter without canvases, a singer without engagements, a writer without a publisher. With me they found what they lacked – fires, food and enthusiasm.' Eventually, to her delight, the apartment became a magnet for artists, sculptors, poets and novelists, composers and anyone else who wanted to mix with like-minded contemporaries, discuss the arts and revel in the eccentricities of their hostess and the extraordinary décor with which she surrounded herself. She described the scene with pride:

> The Sâr Peladan surrounded by Rosicrucians took possession of the studio ... One smelled incense and the candles' waxen tears; a lectern held an old Bible. On the dark grey walls I had written Arab proverbs in chalk and quotations from Shakespeare, profundities from Plato ... Ladies with their hair in precise braids and their waists thin as stalks sighed and palpitated. Men smoked enormous pipes ... Their velveteen suits, stained with ink, paint or clay, carried the signature of their profession ... I was happy.[25]

Regular visitors included the painter and sculptor Henry de Groux, who was later to make a bust of Debussy; the poet Georges Rodenbach; Louis Fabulet, who translated Kipling, Thoreau and Whitman into French; the pianist Rollinat, and the composer Gabriel Fabre. Fabre set many poems to music which Georgette was to sing, often to his accompaniment. He was in fact the first composer to set Maeterlinck's poems to music.

Georgette was not exaggerating. Fifteen years later the journalist and writer Georges Maurevert still recalled the extraordinary scenes at the atelier in the avenue Victor Hugo which he had visited in his twenties, presided over by the woman who 'all her life despised anything banal, silly or vulgar', whose desire was to surround herself with beauty. She would jump up from her great leather, iron-studded armchair to the sofa which was 'deep as a grave' then leap towards the Pleyel piano to sing Fabre's music in her magnificent, captivating, voice. He remembered how she loved to cause a sensation with her outrageous clothes, her magnificent hair topped with a damask-rose velvet bonnet, a gold chain around her forehead bearing a diamond.[26]

---

[25] Leblanc, *Souvenirs: My Life with Maeterlinck*, p. 43.
[26] See illus. 4.

He saw Debussy's close friend, the young Pierre Louÿs there, a first link between Georgette and the composer. 1893 was, after all, the very year that Mauclair visited Louÿs' flat to listen to *Pelléas* in order that Maeterlinck (as yet unknown to Georgette) should give Debussy permission to set it to music. One would love to know what tales Louÿs told Debussy about her. Maurevert relates the extraordinary anecdote of the scandal caused by Georgette in medieval attire, partnered by the artist Joseph Granié, wearing an eye-catching velvet suit and strange little green hat entering a *pâtissier* near her apartment. The clientèle, already laughing and joking at the apparition, were stunned to see Georgette order a whole selection of delicious cakes, not to eat herself, but to feed to two splendid white hounds![27]

It was through Gabriel Fabre that the writer and poet Camille Mauclair was introduced to Georgette's studio. Mauclair was to be the vital link between Georgette and the author Maurice Maeterlinck, and thus her first step on the path to the sombre land of Mélisande. Mauclair himself fell in love with Georgette at first sight. The name of this young man (born in Paris in 1872) was originally Camille Laurent Séverin Faust, but he discarded the teutonic surname for the gentler, more French-sounding Mauclair.[28] By the time he entered Georgette's life he had only published a collection of poems and a few articles yet he was already earning respect in literary circles. Besides having good looks, his obvious intelligence and passion for the arts immediately appealed to Georgette who was always attracted to an intellectual. He was twenty-one; she was twenty-four.

Even before he fell in love with Georgette, Camille Mauclair had regarded Maeterlinck as the greatest writer of his generation. He was not the first to praise him to the skies, however. As we have already seen, in 1890 Maeterlinck's play *La Princess Maleine* had been given an astonishingly generous review in *Le Figaro* by the highly respected critic Octave Mirbeau. Mauclair's friendship with Maeterlinck was the result of correspondence following his own glowing praise of the author's work published in *La Plume* in October of the same year. In 1892, when Mauclair was only twenty years old, he gave the first of several lectures on Maeterlinck.

1892 was also the year in which Maeterlinck's name was to become known internationally. Following its publication, *Pelléas et Mélisande* was translated into English by Laurence Alma-Tadema, daughter of the rich London artist Sir Lawrence Alma-Tadema. She too was a writer and poet, and as we shall see, was later to play a role in the drama of the relationship between

---

[27] Georges Maurevert, *L'Art, le boulevard et la vie* (Paris, 1911), p. 84.
[28] See illus. 3. There was a trend for adopting different names, e.g. Lugné added Poë to his surname, Maurevert was born Georges Leménager.

Georgette and Maeterlinck. Although Maeterlinck's name soon spread to Germany and Austria, it was not easy for new young writers to make their voices heard in Paris and it was fortunate that he had such fervent support from Mirbeau and Mauclair, the latter collaborating with Lugné-Poë in that production of *Pelléas et Mélisande* which Debussy attended on 17 May 1893.

It should be emphasised that Georgette Leblanc, meanwhile, knew virtually nothing of Maeterlinck before meeting Camille Mauclair. It was Mauclair who introduced her in 1894 to the poems, *Serres chaudes*, then the plays, *La Princesse Maleine*, *Les Aveugles*, *L'Intruse*, and eventually *Pelléas et Mélisande*. She was certainly not present at the performance at the Bouffes-Parisiens in 1893. But what was it that made her so determined to meet the Belgian writer? It was not so much his plays that had struck a chord, but his introduction to a French translation of Emerson's essays, a book lent to her by Mauclair. She was ecstatic. Having read and reread Maeterlinck's preface all night long, by morning she was sure that 'in all the universe he was the one man I could love.'[29] What was the attraction? In her words, 'because in his preface I had discerned a tendency of mind, a vision, ideas and even a being whose secret inner existence corresponded to my own.'[30] How was she going to engineer an introduction to a man who had been described to her as 'a bear who never left his native town of Ghent'?[31]

Inspired by the Wagnerian influences in Bruneau's *L'Attaque du moulin*, Georgette, in common with her generation of musicians in France, experienced a huge awakening of enthusiasm for the operas of Wagner and travelled to Munich to hear a performance of *Tristan und Isolde*. This swept her away emotionally, as can be seen from letters quoted by Maurevert in which she describes her reactions with typical hyperbole: 'I am worn out, overwhelmed, dead, and despite my tiredness, too on edge to be able to sleep ... Immense joy and at the same time bitter suffering are making little cold tears run continually down my cheeks.'[32] Swearing that she was suffering from 'Isolde-sickness' ('le mal d'Yseult'), she was so desperate for the opportunity to sing Wagner which would not be available to her at the Opéra-Comique, that she managed to arrange a formal audition with Édouard-Fortuné Calabresi, Co-Director of the Théâtre de la Monnaie in Brussels. She claimed that if she failed she would move to the country outside Paris and spend the rest of her life working on the role of Isolde![33] There was, however another, even

---

[29] Leblanc, *Souvenirs: My Life with Maeterlinck*, p. 18.

[30] Leblanc, *Souvenirs: My Life with Maeterlinck*, p. 12.

[31] Leblanc, *Souvenirs: My Life with Maeterlinck*, p. 19.

[32] Maurevert, *L'Art, le boulevard et la vie*, p. 89.

[33] Maurevert, *L'Art, le boulevard et la vie*, p. 89.

more urgent reason for wanting to go to Brussels. This would narrow the distance between her and Maeterlinck, whom she had not yet met, but who was now the object of her fervent admiration and who lived in Ghent, only sixty kilometres from that city.

Whatever later critics and biographers may have written to denigrate Georgette's voice and singing ability, she must have impressed both the Opéra-Comique and the La Monnaie panels, for now she successfully passed her audition for the latter just as she had the former. Calabresi suggested she should be employed at La Monnaie, not yet to sing Wagner, but to take on any parts available for one year, followed by a year's full contract. Always one to follow her heart, she decided to leave the Opéra-Comique despite the security it offered. Once in Brussels it was not Isolde on which she was asked to begin work, but the role of Anita in *La Navarraise* by Massenet, to be performed on 26 November 1894.

Meanwhile, at the end of 1893, Mauclair had received the letter from Maurice Maeterlinck telling him of Debussy's desire to set his play, *Pelléas et Mélisande*, to music and had advised him to authorise it. What could be more natural than that Mauclair should tell his mistress, Georgette, about this project? And whatever could be more likely to awaken in her an intense desire to sing the role of Mélisande? Her ever-increasing fervour for the writing of Maeterlinck combined with her ambition to express herself in great operatic roles converged to point her in one direction. This was encouraged by Mauclair, who tried to help her fulfil this desire by writing to Maeterlinck in the autumn of 1894:

> She has been my mistress for six months. I love her very much. She has the nature of a true artist. I am teaching her to recite verses and I think this winter she will come to play Isolde at La Monnaie ... I think that if she did anything of yours it would be the Mélisande which Debussy has composed to your play; that would suit her perfectly.[34]

So, almost eight years before the première of the opera and before he had even met Georgette, the seeds of the idea were sown in Maeterlinck's mind that here was a singer waiting to portray his princess in music. It is also significant that both Mauclair and Georgette realised the potential of this work.

Unfortunately, Georgette soon found out that Maeterlinck was a very solitary figure who hardly ever went to the theatre or to social gatherings. Not only this, but his growing reputation was pulling him regularly to Paris, so, ironically, she could have remained there to meet him. As in Paris, Georgette soon became a magnet in Brussels, her beauty and eccentricity as well as her intellectual powers drawing attention to her, besides her dramatic

---

34 Letter from Mauclair to Maeterlinck, quoted in Debussy, *Correspondance* p. 633 n. 1.

way of dressing. But Maeterlinck did not yet have the opportunity to witness her extrovert way of life. He, in contrast, at the age of thirty-two, still lived quietly at home with his parents in Ghent. Whilst he was actually practising as a lawyer specialising in cases in the Flemish language, a profession chosen to please his parents, he was far more interested in writing, even though his compatriots did not appear to appreciate his work as much as the French.

One has to wonder at the blindness of Mauclair's love for Georgette. He was so sure of her reciprocal affection, perhaps also because Maeterlinck was ten years his senior, that it clearly did not occur to him that he might lose her to the writer he so admired and desired her to meet. Those words to Maeterlinck, 'I think if she performed anything of yours it would be the *Mélisande* that Debussy has written to your play', are proof that even before their meeting, Maeterlinck had received the suggestion that she should be the first singer of the role and also show that at this point, by the beginning of 1895, Mauclair was under the impression Debussy had completed his composition. Little did he know the passions he would unleash and the consequences of his suggestions for the career of his mistress and for the history of Debussy's opera.

3 *Georgette Leblanc meets Maurice Maeterlinck (1895–8)*

*T*HROUGH ACQUAINTANCES they had in common, Madeleine and Octave Maus,[1] Maeterlinck heard of the desire of the young singer, Georgette Leblanc, to meet him. In Brussels Edmond Picard, a lawyer, held a dinner party for the cast of Strindberg's *The Father*, which was being performed by Lugné-Poë's company at the Théâtre du Parc, to which both Georgette and Maeterlinck were invited. Teasingly, Picard led Georgette to believe she was going to meet a 'vieillard' (old man).[2] Knowing Georgette would be there, his inquisitiveness aroused and, no doubt, desiring to see this proposed Mélisande, so eagerly suggested by Camille Mauclair, Maeterlinck accepted his invitation.

The very beginning of Georgette's autobiography, *Souvenirs*, is an ecstatic account of that evening of 11 January 1895. On reading Georgette's description of her carefully prepared appearance, one can't help feeling a certain sympathy with Maeterlinck's reaction to the vision confronting him. Mélisande was already her point of reference:

> I had arrayed myself in a costume highly Mélisandesque and absurd. On my forehead blazed brighter than ever the diamond which had already scandalized Brussels. Like wood-shavings my hair quivered in curls about my head and my trailing gown of gold-flowered velvet prolonged my person indefinitely ... There before the fireplace stood a man in a long macfarlane. He was smoking a pipe ... In spite of myself I cried, 'How wonderful. He is young.' And the poet, abashed, took refuge in the smoking room.[3]

When their host, Picard, proposed a toast to Georgette's success, she felt curiously panic-stricken. She had uprooted her career scarcely begun at the Opéra-Comique in Paris and abandoned everything upon reading Maeterlinck's preface to Emerson's essays. On looking back at this first meeting she likened it to a religious experience, 'the highest level that our human nature can attain.'[4]

When Georgette was prevailed upon to sing after the meal, for the first

---

[1] In 1883 Octave Maus formed Les Vingt, also known as Les XX, a group of 20 Belgian artists. In 1893 this was dissolved and La Libre Esthéthique, an annual salon, was formed, in which many different types of art, including music, were presented.

[2] Leblanc, 'Histoire de ma vie'.

[3] Leblanc, *Souvenirs: My Life with Maeterlinck*, pp. 7–8.

[4] Leblanc, *Souvenirs: My Life with Maeterlinck*, p. 13.

time she learned that the author understood nothing about music. She would
not allow this to put her off. Nothing daunted, accompanied by Octave
Maus, she put everything she could into the dramatic presentation of the
song about three blind sisters, which had been composed by Fabre for the
performance of *Pelléas et Mélisande* at the Bouffes-Parisiens, published in
March 1893 as the *Chanson de Mélisande*. Georgette claimed there was much
more to see than to hear in her particular way of singing the chants of Fabre.
'All those little tales in three lines concerned exclusively with golden crowns,
golden keys, golden doors and rings, seemed to me to conceal Aeschylean
tragedies.' The author seemed delighted, but assured her prosaically, despite
her dramatic interpretation, that there were no hidden meanings in the
poems.

Georgette was completely and utterly blinded by her emotions. She
described her love in telling terms: 'I carried it within me as a mother carries
her child, ready to accept and adore it whatever it would be.' How prophetic
was this instinct, for it was virtually as a child that Georgette was later to nurture and protect Maeterlinck, to the extent of writing to him and addressing him as 'Bébé'. Now, as always, she would hungrily accept every aspect
of the man, eagerly rationalising those aspects which were less than attractive: 'Maeterlinck's rustic air, his long greatcoat, his nails eaten by acids, had
slightly disconcerted me but he seemed more picturesque that way, more
simple.'[5] As the time came to go home she had the presence of mind to say
to him that she would love to visit Ghent one day. He, without this prompt,
would probably have said nothing.

At La Monnaie Georgette was still performing *La Navarraise* by Massenet,
for which she had received glowing reviews, referring in particular to the
intensity and extraordinary power of her portrayal, and at the same time she
was rehearsing *Carmen*. She was longing, however, to portray a more ethereal eponymous heroine: 'Day and night Carmen and Mélisande tore at each
other's hair in my brain. Caught between the Belgian angel and the Spanish
demon I could no longer sleep.'[6]

When Georgette eventually visited Maeterlinck in his own home, her
impression of his rustic air was compounded. What a contrast to her metropolitan life style. His elderly parents had no understanding of his writing,
appreciating only the interest he took in the bees and roses they were so
fond of. The importance to him of three copious meals a day, the regularity
of his daily routine: work in the morning, meals, and twice a day a trip to
the café to drink beer, physical exercise, in particular boxing, skating and

5 Leblanc, *Souvenirs: My Life with Maeterlinck*, p. 21.
6 Leblanc, *Souvenirs: My Life with Maeterlinck*, p. 21.

cycling, all were essential aspects of the taciturn writer. For the twenty years of their relationship, she claims, she was never to change his desire for placid routine. She discovered he loved dogs and hated cats. This was not irrelevant: some years later he shot dead Georgette's own cat when it was prowling the garden and yowling.[7] Another fact might have disturbed her, but she took it philosophically: Maeterlinck always had several mistresses at once. To him this was a pastime like any other, for happiness did not exist outside pleasure and good health. To Georgette it just magnified the challenge to offer him both love and happiness.

In view of this simple life, Maeterlinck's first visit to Georgette's apartment must have been in complete contrast to anything he had ever experienced. She transformed the room in which she planned to receive him with 'black tulle walls and silver ornaments. I fancied this lugubrious effect was mystical – made for him.' She did not have time to remove a puce-coloured armchair in the room next to this before he rang the bell. Whilst he untied a present of some books he had brought her she lifted the curtain of the little room from which waves of incense were escaping and invited him in. He approached, sniffing the air. 'And what's that catafalque? I wouldn't go in there for anything on earth.' Lighting his pipe he settled in the puce chair. Apparently he had a horror of antique furniture and liked only white walls, bright rooms, everything precise and shining. How could Georgette ignore this complete dismissal of her painstaking preparations? Later, when her faithful maid Eugénie brought tea into the room, the poet looked distressed and explained that in his house one only drank tea when one was ill. Georgette dutifully sent Eugénie to fetch a bottle of port.

She could have been completely disillusioned. Here was a man so unlike the smooth, elegant intellectual she might have imagined. Reality was the exact opposite.[8] Yet this contradiction intrigued her. She regarded it as territory to explore. Her instinct drove her to want to communicate her strong convictions, share her knowledge, to provide inspiration, and will Maeterlinck to produce works of beauty.

Significantly, after their next meeting, a visit to a church at Malines (Mechelen), Georgette received a letter from Mauclair with which he enclosed a letter his friend Maeterlinck had written to him. Proudly Mauclair passed on the author's impressions of Georgette, which culminated in the words: 'What other woman could seem beautiful and interesting after seeing her?' Still no alarm bells rang for the younger man. He simply revelled in the fact that his friend admired his mistress so much.

---

7 Leblanc, *Souvenirs: My Life with Maeterlinck*, p. 26.
8 Leblanc, *Souvenirs: My Life with Maeterlinck*, p. 29.

Now Georgette's letters to Maeterlinck began. Letter after letter, pouring out her emotions, her philosophy of love and life, letters which were to continue throughout their relationship. She wrote every night after her performances. Since she had fallen in love with him through his books, she thought he would grow to know her through her letters. The subject of mutual silence preoccupied her. 'We do not yet know each other because we have not dared to be silent together.'[9] The ability to be silent together was to bare one's soul. He answered her on the same subject and from this exchange was born his essay 'Le Silence' which appears at the beginning of his collection *Le Trésor des humbles*.[10] This is only the first of many examples of the inspiration Maeterlinck received, if not direct appropriation of ideas, from Georgette's letters and conversations.

The pair could not meet regularly due to Georgette's rehearsal schedule, but when they did she dressed in fantastic costumes whilst he wore a big travelling coat, huge hunting boots and an old hat. 'I always dressed as a painting', she remembers. 'I went about as a Van Eyck, as an allegory of Memling or a Rubens Virgin.' She caused quite a stir at a performance at La Monnaie when, as a member of the audience, she appeared dressed as an exact reproduction of a figure by Da Vinci. The opera had begun and, just as the singer was making her entry, the entire house turned towards Georgette in her box instead. Inevitably she denies that she had tried to ruin the soprano's entrance.[11] No wonder people were astonished at the odd couple, this 'rough, almost peasant-like man and this woman whose appearance indicated the most frenzied research'. Yet she insists that beneath this show they were two people 'of authentic simplicity'.[12]

Georgette's interpretation of the role of Carmen was as eccentric as her own clothes, anything but typically Spanish. This Carmen had blond hair bound in gold – 'a gypsy who had taken hashish', as she describes her.[13] After the première on 23 March 1895, the reception of this novel blond Carmen was positive, the critics, as always, emphasising Georgette's intensity of expression. This was to be Maeterlinck's introduction to the opera house, for she finally persuaded him to overcome his aversion to 'something he held in horror'. Between the acts, her friends eagerly reported back to her: 'He's still there, he's been applauding you, his opera glasses are trained on you.' He was

[9] Leblanc, *Souvenirs: My Life with Maeterlinck*, p. 36.

[10] Maurice Maeterlinck, *Le Trésor des humbles* (Paris, 1896). Several essays were originally published in journals, 'Le Silence' appearing in *La Revue franco-américaine*, July 1895.

[11] Leblanc, *Souvenirs: My Life with Maeterlinck*, p. 48.

[12] Leblanc, *Souvenirs: My Life with Maeterlinck*, p. 50.

[13] Leblanc, *Souvenirs: My Life with Maeterlinck*, p. 52.

completely smitten. He wrote to her the next day of the almost terrifying effect of seeing her in direct contact with others:

> You seem to be the only living being. It has exactly the same effect as if a being from a superior world should suddenly appear in the midst of a crowd. Those who surround you become frightful. Really they seem like spectres and I never more clearly felt the absence of life, the absence of existence, which there actually is in most men ... besides you the others have the air of not even knowing how to walk or stand.[14]

Her portrayal in this role so inflamed the tenor singing opposite her one evening that only at the last moment did Georgette see he had a real dagger in his hand when he was to stab her on the steps of the arena. She put up her hand to defend herself and claims that for ever more she bore the scar. She explained this near tragic event by supposing he could not bear to be outshone by this blond Carmen. She, needless to say, was thrilled by the drama of real blood running down her gold satin skirt.[15]

Having been compared to the actress Eleonora Duse in the excellence of her portrayal,[16] Georgette was able to take the opportunity of meeting the great tragedienne who at the time was acting in *La Femme de Claude* by Alexandre Dumas.[17] She learnt of Duse's worry about the sad state of her love affair with d'Annunzio, a figure who was to feature later in both Georgette's and Debussy's lives, and whom Mary Garden was also to meet.

A few days after *Carmen*, on 28 March 1895, Georgette was seen by Ernest Chausson in a performance of his *Légende de Sainte Cécile* which took place at La Libre Esthéthique, the salon in Brussels formed by Octave Maus. The Ysaÿe Quartet also took part.[18] Chausson was so impressed by Georgette's performance that he approached her with the proposition that she should sing the role of Genièvre in his own opera, *Le Roi Arthus*. He believed the part was made for her and was pleased that the music appealed to her when he showed it to her.[19] The opera did not actually receive its première at La Monnaie until eight years later, on 30 November 1903, nearly three years after the composer's death, and then the role of Genièvre was sung by Jane

---

[14] Leblanc, *Souvenirs: My Life with Maeterlinck*, p. 52.

[15] Leblanc, *La Machine à courage*, p. 182.

[16] *L'Art moderne*, 15 April 1895.

[17] Her conversations with Duse were published in Georgette Leblanc, 'Mes conversations avec Eleonora Duse', *Les Œuvres libres*, no. 66 (1926).

[18] Barricelli and Weinstein, *Ernest Chausson*, p. 81.

[19] Jean Gallois, 'Le Roi Arthus d'Ernest Chausson à La Monnaie', *La Monnaie symboliste*, ed. Manuel Couvreur and Roland van der Hoeven (Brussels, 2003), p. 148.

Paquot d'Assy, but the very fact that Chausson would have liked Georgette to sing it demonstrates that she could make her own way successfully in the world of opera in works not associated with Maeterlinck.

Georgette also performed one of another composer's most celebrated compositions in Brussels in 1895: Henri Duparc's *L'Invitation au voyage*, the words of which are by Baudelaire.[20] Evidence of Duparc's appreciation of her interpretation can be found in the dedication of this song which reads: 'A Madame Georgette Leblanc en témoinage de reconnaissance et d'admiration. H. Duparc.'[21]

For his part, even at the age of thirty-three, Maeterlinck was too anxious about the reaction of his parents to his relationship with a mere *singer* to declare it openly. She, Georgette, a freer spirit, felt swept away by ecstasy. She was, as she puts it, 'dazzled' by meeting the author of *Pelléas*.[22] Any question of marriage was brushed aside. She says that he once spoke of it while they were walking in woodland and on seeing the bewilderment of her expression did not continue. They swore an oath not to fall into the trap of jealousy, domination, the curtailing of liberty, but, whatever words they exchanged on the subject, for Georgette there was no question of marriage for she was still married to her Spaniard in the eyes of the Vatican. She further justified her stance by claiming that she had never found one man in history who had been made greater by marriage. It would have compromised the divinity of her poet and their mutual happiness.

Elegiac letters flowed between them. On Easter Sunday 1895 Maeterlinck echoed a phrase Georgette had used when writing to him: 'It is impossible to leave each other spiritually at the precise moment we separate physically.' He philosophised about the necessity for separation, the anxiety about returning to the one one loves – a test they had passed. He was thrilled that she had used the familiar 'tu' to him when they parted, something he declares he would have never dared to do. Right from the start it becomes clear that Georgette was feeding him inspirational ideas. By her mere presence, he wrote, she gave life to thoughts he would not otherwise have had, thoughts that she had sown in him without realising it.[23]

Neither Maeterlinck nor Georgette revealed the true nature of their relationship to Camille Mauclair. Georgette met the latter in Paris whilst visiting her brother Maurice Leblanc, who had recently divorced, and behaved

[20] Elaine Brody, *Paris: The Musical Kaleidoscope, 1870–1925* (London, 1988), pp. 254–5.

[21] 'To Madame Georgette Leblanc. As a mark of my gratitude and admiration.' Pierpont Morgan Library, New York, Dept. of Music Manuscripts and Books, Record ID 114451.

[22] Leblanc, *Souvenirs: My Life with Maeterlinck*, p. 53.

[23] 14 April 1895, Stadsarchief Gent B LXIII.1.

as if nothing had changed.[24] On her return to Brussels at the end of May 1895, Georgette had some days free, and she and Maeterlinck took the opportunity to travel together to Middelburg on the Isle of Walcheren in the Netherlands. Typically she arrived at the station weighed down with flowing medieval garments, but only a tiny bag containing a powder box. A sense of unreality enveloped the couple. With heightened emotions, from the church tower of Veere, Georgette and Maeterlinck watched the sun set as little fishing boats came towards the shore. Determined to watch until the last boat appeared on the horizon, Georgette realised too late that the last sail was black, which both regarded as a fateful omen. She saw a shadow pass over Maeterlinck's face. Writing to him later, she wanted to erase the memory of his distress. 'The accident that made the last sail black could have given us excuse for melancholy, but like all lovers who have accepted life we accepted it again and once again understood each other.' Just as with her thoughts about silence, Georgette claimed later that the author made good use of her ideas on achieving happiness in *La Sagesse et la Destinée*, a collection of 117 short essays, to be published in 1898. For now, though, it was time to return to their hotel where, for the sake of convention, they had separate rooms. Georgette, ever eager to converse, even all night through, rushed to her room and pushed the sofa towards the window. He, however, hesitated and remained by the door. Georgette gabbled on, uttering words at random, but suddenly was overcome with unhappiness, feeling foolish and embarrassed. Maeterlinck, as on their first meeting, preferred to withdraw. 'For the first time we were a man and a woman who hid themselves behind words', reminisced Georgette. Maeterlinck departed, 'leaving the elegiac lady alone with the night and lost in contemplation of a moonlight that did not exist.'[25]

Soon after this break Georgette returned to Paris, where she kept company not only with her brother and sister, but again with Camille Mauclair. Had Mauclair seen the passionate fervour the taciturn author was expressing in his letters to Georgette, he would have been in no doubt that he had lost her to the older man.

In view of later events and recriminations when blame was heaped on Georgette from all quarters for exploiting her relationship with 'the Belgian Shakespeare', Maeterlinck's letters provide evidence that he was enraptured by her beauty, her intellect, her passion. He did not *have* to submit to her desire to nurture him and provide him with a sympathetic environment, yet he willingly responded to her outpourings with expressions of astonishment at the intensity of his own reactions. Telling her, 'I'm almost ashamed to

[24] Benoît-Jeannin, *Georgette Leblanc*, p. 85.
[25] Leblanc, *Souvenirs: My Life with Maeterlinck*, p. 68.

repeat yet again how much you amaze me, Georgette', he tried to express the
sensations of a heart beating deep inside his very soul, his ardent admiration
of her philosophy of the closeness of their spiritual life. 'It is astonishing how
I am moving into you – soon I will have no need of any other land, any other
abode.' Whilst working, he was having difficulty finding the right words to
express his thoughts, but 'I was thinking all the time of your *lucidity*. You
would have seen straight away what I wanted to say.'[26] A few days later he
again quoted her words back to her, which he acknowledged came to her so
simply and spontaneously. She was unique, at the very heart of things. He
had never seen in any of her letters one phrase which was not living and had
not lived inside her. She was 'a being of life and light.' They would meet death
with a smile, for they would have lived something admirable and unique.[27]

Georgette believed their letters were of essential significance. 'Here
our true nuptials took place.'[28] Yet their love, however ardently expressed,
did not prevent Maeterlinck from continuing his relationships with other
women. In June 1895 Georgette travelled to Switzerland with her brother,
whilst Maeterlinck went to London, where Lugné-Poë's company was to
perform his plays in French. From Switzerland as usual Georgette wrote
constantly to Maeterlinck, but worryingly received no reply. The mysterious
silence eventually came to an end when with no explanation he joined her
for a few days in the Vosges. When she asked him for a reason for that 'horrible silence' his reply was 'To make you suffer ... Love wants that. One never
has pity for the being one loves.'[29]

Jokingly, Maeterlinck had spoken to Georgette of a 'fiancée', none other
than the first English translator of two of his plays, *Pelleas et Melisanda* [sic]
and *The Sightless* (*Les Aveugles*), Laurence Alma-Tadema.[30] When this book
appeared, *The Times* was none too flattering about either the play *Pelleas
and Melisanda* or its translator, describing Miss Alma-Tadema's preface as
'ecstatic and rather mystical', finding that 'either the translation is sadly at fault
or the original must be a tissue of pointless inanities'. The review continued
that the play was 'not without dramatic intensity of a kind, but its motives,
situations, and characters belong to a world of which we at least have no
experience.'[31] In her introduction Laurence did indeed try to explain in her
own words that Maeterlinck was seeking 'to draw near the unapproached, to

---

[26] July 1895, Stadsarchief Gent B LXIII.2.

[27] 9 July 1895, Stadsarchief Gent B LXIII.3.

[28] Leblanc, *Souvenirs: My Life with Maeterlinck*, p. 70.

[29] Leblanc, *Souvenirs: My Life with Maeterlinck*, p. 90.

[30] *Pelleas and Melisanda and The Sightless: Two Plays by Maurice Maeterlinck*, trans.
Laurence Alma Tadema [sic] (London and Felling-on-Tyne, [1895]).

[31] *The Times*, 27 September 1895.

see the unseen, to hear the unheard, to express the inexpressible.' She clearly empathised with his awareness of the limitations of humans to penetrate beyond the forces of fate, her assertion that 'we live within the shadow of a veil that no man's hand can lift' showing how near she had come to the philosophy of the man she loved, unbeknown to Georgette.

In September 1895 Georgette was travelling between Paris and Brussels, still writing letters to her lover, delving deeper and deeper into her psyche, analysing the capacity for love, beauty, our 'human and spiritual machine', always relating her emotions to her union with Maeterlinck. *Pelléas et Mélisande* provided a constant point of reference for her:

> You remember Golaud lifting up the child in his arms so that his simple eyes would tell him what he had seen through the window of the tower ... in the same way you who are so much bigger will lift me in your arms and my ignorance will see clearly into what is happening on a higher level than life.[32]

The opera *Fidelio* was her next challenge, not a great personal success, followed in March 1896 by *Thaïs* by Massenet. The composer had originally written this opera with Sibyl Sanderson in mind for the eponymous role and it had received its première in Paris in March 1894. When it was to be performed in Brussels his thoughts naturally turned to Georgette, whose friend he had remained since her childhood in Rouen and who had made a success of his opera *La Navarraise* at La Monnaie. Georgette took the opportunity to dress scantily and shock the Brussels public with her bare shoulders and arms as she wore an almost transparent Greek-style tunic. She certainly impressed a young woman teacher, Mathilde Serrure, who began to correspond with her, and would play a major role in her life many years later.

In the middle of this run of performances she received an unannounced visitor – Laurence Alma-Tadema, Maeterlinck's English translator. Having learnt of Georgette's relationship with her 'fiancé' she wanted to ensure for herself that this obstacle to her happiness was removed. Georgette learnt that Laurence had met Maeterlinck at a dinner party given in honour of her famous father, the eminent artist Lawrence Alma-Tadema, and after reading some of his works had determined to translate them in order to maintain contact with him. In this extraordinary circumstance, Georgette kept cool, insisting that she was not intending to marry Maeterlinck and would not stand between them if Laurence would bring him true happiness. She invited her to dine with both of them.

What an evening for the poet! Georgette magnanimously helped to transform Laurence's frumpy appearance before the poet arrived, then both women wooed their lover with intelligent conversation. He simply smoked

---

[32] Benoît-Jeannin, *Georgette Leblanc*, p. 95.

his pipe, gazing into the middle distance.[33] The three of them spent several days together, but Laurence was eventually persuaded to take the train back to London from Paris. According to Georgette, Maeterlinck's play *Aglavaine et Sélysette* mirrors this triangle, she being Aglavaine and Laurence, Sélysette. She points out that the author borrowed dialogue for the love scene between Aglavaine and Meléandre from letters which had passed between himself and Georgette, thus making use of her own words.[34] In fact by now Georgette's influence on Maeterlinck's writing was becoming evident, for his women characters were becoming stronger, less ethereal. As she wrote herself, 'With childlike intransigence I made fun of the little princesses he liked to shroud in such a lavish cloak of mystery.'[35] Maeterlinck's own admission was 'I feel that I am through with marionette plays, with the Maleines and the Pelléas.'[36]

In 1896 Georgette had to face the disappointment of her contract at La Monnaie not being renewed. She left Brussels for Paris in order to earn money, but Maeterlinck did not follow her. He still wished to remain with his parents in Ghent. He preferred the quiet life, slept better, avoided the expenditure of a big city. She, back at her brother's apartment received daily visits from Mauclair, anxious and as much in love as ever. Maeterlinck still did not want her to tell her younger admirer the truth. Could this be because he still needed his approbation and useful literary contacts? When Georgette again had to travel to Bordeaux, letters again passed backwards and forwards between them, expressing and developing ideas and philosophies. 'The poet often told me that by a curious coincidence my letters were perfect answers to what he was thinking about.'[37] How convenient!

Performing Massenet's *La Navarraise* in Bordeaux, Georgette took out her frustration at not being near her lover on this role, acting her final convulsions so dramatically that, according to her, the orchestra forgot to play the last bars of the score![38] When at last he did travel to see her, reality did not meet the expectations of the couple, although Georgette would be the last to admit it. Maeterlinck did not hide from her that he had been seeing another mistress. She prevented herself from revealing her natural reactions, listening with a false calm and simulated indulgence. Their farewell at the

[33] Leblanc, 'Histoire de ma vie'. Georgette here gives Laurence the pseudonym Hilda de S. Maxime Benoît-Jeannin has identified her as Laurence Alma-Tadema.
[34] Leblanc, *Souvenirs: My Life with Maeterlinck*, p. 93.
[35] 'Avec l'intransigeance des enfants je me moquais des petites princesses qu'il se plaisait à envelopper d'un si somptueux vêtement de mystère.' Leblanc, 'Histoire de ma vie'.
[36] Leblanc, *Souvenirs: My Life with Maeterlinck*, p. 96.
[37] Leblanc, *Souvenirs: My Life with Maeterlinck*, p. 105.
[38] Leblanc, *Souvenirs: My Life with Maeterlinck*, p. 104.

station had a strange sense of fatality about it as she saw his pale face and his eyes clinging to hers. A strange little memento of this period is preserved in a notebook which Georgette must have picked up and used much later, for other scribblings in it date from around 1926. Her inimitable handwriting on the front reads 'Bordeaux en Décembre 1896. Cette semaine j'ai passé à prier.' ('I spent this week praying.')[39]

Letters continued to flow between Bordeaux then Nice and Ghent until February 1897, when Georgette decided to settle in Paris. She moved to a rented flat, 5 Villa Dupont off the rue Pergolèse, but Maeterlinck did not join her there. She did, however, manage at last to make her break with Camille Mauclair, even asking him to return to her the many letters she had written to him.[40] He took out his frustration at his treatment in an extraordinary permanent 'souvenir' of his relationship with Georgette. He wrote a novel called *Le Soleil des morts*.[41] This was first published in serial form in *La Nouvelle Revue* between 15 February and 1 May 1898 and is a work which contains portraits of many famous contemporary writers and artists under invented names. The book is dedicated to Ernest Chausson. The characters in this *roman à clef* meet at the home of Mallarmé in the rue de Rome where the poet held his legendary Tuesday salons. Mallarmé appears as Calixte Armel, and Mauclair as André de Neuze. Almost against his will, de Neuze falls in love with a woman called Lucienne Lestrange, in whose appearance we immediately recognise Georgette. Lucienne's overpowering intelligence and intense emotions are irresistible, despite de Neuze's attraction to Sylvaine, Calixte Armel's much quieter and more submissive daughter. There can be no doubt that this is a vivid manifestation of Mauclair's initial strong passion for Georgette. Debussy is given the extravagant name Claude-Eric de Harmor and is depicted as trying to complete his lyric drama, complaining about the lack of understanding of the public for the plight of the true artist and the torment of creation. Regretting his attachment to Lucienne, de Neuze (Mauclair) insists that he could not but submit to the desires of this strong-willed woman. De Neuze's assertion that Lucienne's intelligence ruled her emotions as she analysed closely every feeling she experienced is typical of Georgette.[42]

Meanwhile, Maeterlinck also managed to terminate his so-called 'engagement' to Laurence Alma-Tadema. One might have imagined that he would then move to join Georgette in the city where she was once again hostess

39 Notebook in AML, Brussels, Georgette Leblanc Collection.

40 Benoît-Jeannin, *Georgette Leblanc*, p. 137.

41 Camille Mauclair, *Le Soleil des morts* (Paris, 1898).

42 Mauclair, *Le Soleil des morts*, p. 117.

to a number of famous literary figures. The names of those invited to a private recital on 14 April at Georgette's flat are impressive, including Stéphane Mallarmé, Henry Gauthier-Villars, otherwise known as Willy, and his wife Colette. It was not until the end of May 1897, however, that Maeterlinck conquered his aversion to moving to Paris and even then it was only possible after Georgette made special arrangements to enable him to work in peace. She had purposely chosen her apartment in a very quiet little avenue. His working environment had to be just right, for although the move was 'the natural work of love', she also makes it quite clear that she wanted to further his career, helping his fame to spread world-wide.[43] To make Maeterlinck feel at home as well as to indulge her own taste she had decorated the rooms in rustic 'Isle of Walcheren' style with 'white-washed walls, trimmings in violent colours, ruddy copper vessels.' But this did not solve the problem of the battle between two enemies: music and silence. So that he would not be disturbed by the noise of the piano and her singing practice, Georgette rented a completely separate room on the fifth floor of 4 rue de Lalo. There she put a table, two chairs and a coat-rack. Now the author was able to work in solitude on *La Sagesse et la Destinée*. Also, by using this address for correspondence, he was able to keep concealed the fact that he was actually living with his mistress. Despite organising her life to the rhythm of his work, it was only for a few months that this arrangement lasted, however, for her indefatigable energy, her fraternising with the literary and artistic figures of the day, his dislike of living in a big city soon drove him back to Ghent.

Almost at once she was writing letters again, telling him of meetings with Paul Adam, Mirbeau, Rodin. On 25 May 1898, when Emma Calvé had to go to London to fulfil previous engagements, Georgette took over the role of Fanny Legrand in Massenet's *Sapho* at the Théâtre du Château d'Eau. There she met 'a queer little man who rushed at me in the wings. He had a head like a witch, an umbrella under his arm and an excitable lisp.' This was Saint-Saëns believing he had found the ideal interpreter for his *Proserpine*.[44] This situation was to repeat itself twenty years later. 'He was then a very old witch.' Never did she sing this role, which had been created in 1887 by Caroline Salla. Georgette's performance as Fanny Legrand, however, was also admired by Massenet, who wrote her a note of appreciation.[45] Since it is an aria from this opera that has survived in the rare recording made in 1903, referred to in the Introduction,[46] it is worth noting the praise given by critic Edmond

---

[43] Leblanc, *Souvenirs: My Life with Maeterlinck*, p. 111.

[44] Leblanc, *Souvenirs: My Life with Maeterlinck*, p. 124.

[45] Benoît-Jeannin, *Georgette Leblanc*, p. 169.

[46] See Introduction, p. 5.

Stoullig. Her interpretation was quite different from that of her predecessor, he wrote, but it brought her personal success as an actress, singer and woman.[47]

To entice Maeterlinck to her side once more Georgette rented a house for a peaceful holiday near Bagnoles-de-l'Orne in Normandy. Here once again she gave him the best of the rooms, bright and sunny. For herself she had to make do with a room at the opposite end of the house where she too tried to write. 'The window framed a dead pine, its posture set and sad. I pretended I liked it better.'[48] He wrote assiduously whilst she found herself suffering from lack of inspiration. Each day he would ask her how her work was going and could not fail to notice her eyes, red from tears of frustration.

One evening, when reading his day's efforts to her, he laughingly said, 'I steal from you, don't I?' She realised then that the only way out of her impasse would be to leave him, but immediately dismissed this thought. However, on a hot day when they were both watching an ant-hill, Maeterlinck teasing the insects with a stick, she suddenly asked him in spite of herself why he never acknowledged the true source of his ideas when he quoted her, but always referred to 'an old philosopher' or 'an old friend' or simply put quotation marks around the words. How his reply must have cut her to the quick: 'But don't you see it would be ridiculous to mention you. You're on the stage, a singer, nobody would believe me, it would be ridiculous.' As she ruefully thought: 'Obviously I was an actress, I sang *Thaïs* with a diamond on my brow, my face painted, my arms bare, my hands gloveless, my body uncorseted ... Obviously all this excludes the capacity for thought.'[49] This attitude had already been conveyed to her by Maeterlinck after he had received a visit from Jules Huret, editor of *Le Figaro*. He had not hidden from her his hurtful words: 'I'll never meet your wife. I can't imagine Maeterlinck living with an actress.'[50]

At the end of the holiday Maeterlinck returned to Ghent, but Georgette needed isolation to review her position. She stayed on for a while in Normandy, searching her mind for a solution, but finding none apart from deciding to return to Paris and throw herself into performing, carrying out further operatic engagements and recitals. In her *Souvenirs* Georgette proudly quotes Mallarmé's opinion of this 'extraordinary and exciting

---

47 'Une interpretation toute différente de celle de sa devancière lui valait un succès très personnel de comédienne, de chanteuse et de femme.' *Les Annales du théâtre et de la musique* (1899), p. 123.

48 Leblanc, *Souvenirs: My Life with Maeterlinck*, p. 133.

49 Leblanc, *Souvenirs: My Life with Maeterlinck*, p. 136.

50 Leblanc, *Souvenirs: My Life with Maeterlinck*, p. 125. Georgette made a point of meeting Huret and disabusing him of his negative opinion!

woman' he saw in a *matinée musicale*.[51] The poet visited her in her house and she often went to see him in the rue de Rome, feeling quite at ease in his presence.

Another famous visitor, whom both she and Maeterlinck entertained in Paris in May 1898, was Oscar Wilde. After Georgette had received a letter of appreciation from Wilde of a performance he had seen, she was eager to invite him to dinner, despite Maeterlinck's lack of enthusiasm, for he regarded him as a superficial character. Georgette wanted to show her sympathy with Wilde, whose *Ballad of Reading Gaol* had been published earlier that year. Having told them that he was in mourning for his life,[52] Georgette was gratified to hear Wilde say to her, 'You have comforted me', when he left.[53]

Georgette's brother, Maurice, meanwhile supported her efforts to make Maeterlinck acknowledge his debt to her by allowing her name to appear next to his own at the front of *La Sagesse et la Destinée*, but the author's response, once again, was that he could not let the public know the secrets of his private life – that he lived with a mere singer and actress. However, he suggested that perhaps a dedication might be in order. This duly appeared at the front of the book when it was published in September 1898, but Georgette was horrified years later to find that in the 1926 edition Maeterlinck had suppressed this dedication. It was a petty revenge, and she felt he had no right to touch this 'smallest act of justice'.[54]

Contrast Maeterlinck's attitude with Debussy's. Debussy did not forget his former mistress when he inscribed a score of *Pelléas et Mélisande*: 'To Gaby, princess of the mysterious kingdom of Allemonde. Her old devoted friend Claude Debussy. June 1902.'[55] Even though he had left Gaby four years earlier, Debussy still recognised the significance of her role in their partnership and expressed his gratitude for facing trials and tribulations with him. The difference between this and the support given by Georgette is that Gaby was self-effacing, working as a seamstress or doing other menial work for the eight years of their relationship, staying by the composer's side despite hardship, not seeking her own glory. No doubt Maeterlinck would have had little difficulty acknowledging the tacit support of a similarly intellectually modest woman. But he was dealing instead with a strong-minded, aspiring singer and writer, so astute that he could steal her ideas.

51 Leblanc, *Souvenirs: My Life with Maeterlinck*, p. 123.
52 Richard Ellmann, *Oscar Wilde* (London, 1987), p. 531.
53 Leblanc, *Souvenirs: My Life with Maeterlinck*, p. 130.
54 Leblanc, *Souvenirs: My Life with Maeterlinck*, p. 142.
55 'A Gaby, princesse du mystérieux royaume d'Allemonde. Son vieux dévoué Claude Debussy. Juin 1902.' Dietschy, *La Passion de Claude Debussy*, p. 88.

Debussy by this time was certainly not unaware of Georgette Leblanc, for her name occurs in a letter from Pierre Louÿs on 14 October 1898 questioning which singer is going to perform at a talk on the *Chansons de Bilitis*. Achille Segard, who was presenting it, wanted a singer from the Opéra-Comique, where Debussy's powerful influence would give him the pick of the bunch. Georgette Leblanc had been suggested, but Louÿs did not think she would do at all. He naughtily suggested that Debussy should go and seduce some pretty little song bird with his winged words and in a postscript added the address, 12 rue Chabanais. This happened to be the address not of some song school but of a famous brothel![56]

Meanwhile, in the hope that Maeterlinck would feel more at ease in the country than in Paris, Georgette took out a lease on an old presbytery which they had discovered in 1897 in Normandy at Gruchet-Saint-Siméon. This was to be their base when together for nearly ten years. Here he would write *Ariane et Barbe-Bleue*. Yet here again she subordinated her needs to his. Once more, she confirms Maeterlinck's dislike not just of noise, but of music. 'At Gruchet, behind the salon and in a corner shut off by two doors, I had placed the piano, always relegated to shameful exclusion', she stated.[57] Not only was her career relegated to second place, but to her frustration, Maeterlinck sulked, although she was never able to discover why, 'considering that our life was as invariable as that of a convent'. No wonder she called him 'mon bébé'. Even though he was behaving like a spoilt child, Georgette consistently put his needs before hers and did all in her powers to make life comfortable for him. One benefit that did accrue to her locally was her meeting with a young girl, Mathilde Deschamps, who was to be her constant help and loving companion for many years. Clearly though, she needed to earn money and keep her own career as buoyant as possible, so had to go where her opportunities lay.

[56] Debussy, *Correspondance*, p. 424.
[57] Leblanc, *Souvenirs: My Life with Maeterlinck*, p. 153.

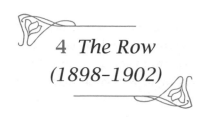

4 *The Row*
(1898–1902)

GEORGETTE'S CAREER now took her back to Paris, where on 14 January 1898 Albert Carré had become Director of the Opéra-Comique. She was to play the role of Carmen in a new production being prepared to inaugurate the new Salle Favart, housing the Opéra-Comique, on 8 December 1898 and therefore she moved into a rented apartment at 69 rue Raynouard.

Prior to this, however, a significant visit to London took place in June when she and Maeterlinck went to the Prince of Wales Theatre for a matinée performance of the play *Pelléas et Mélisande* in English, the one for which Debussy had refused to compose incidental music.[1] The next day Georgette wrote to her brother and commented enthusiastically, but not without criticism, on the production, one incidentally, in which Maeterlinck's cuts had not been observed. Her views are similar in some respects to those of Virginia Crawford,[2] who found that the drama had become a mere domestic intrigue. Georgette thought that Mrs Patrick Campbell had misinterpreted the character of Mélisande, making her little more than charming and weepy.[3] Whilst Pelléas was excellent, Golaud became too ordinary, too normal.[4] Georgette also knew that the following afternoon Albert Carré would be attending a performance with Messager to ensure that Fauré's music was not going to compromise Debussy's version.[5]

Meanwhile Georgette had to prepare for her performances in *Carmen*. In Brussels, when Maeterlinck first saw her sing her blond Carmen, she had born no resemblance to a southern gypsy. Now her quest was to seek authenticity. To this end she persuaded Carré to accompany her to Spain to do some research in Madrid, Seville and Granada. At least, this is her version of events. Albert Carré, in his *Souvenirs du théâtre* makes no mention of her role in *his* decision to visit the country to collect authentic material and ideas for updating the scenery. Georgette did manage to persuade Maeterlinck to go with them, despite his reluctance to travel and dislike of foreign food.

[1] See Chapter 1, p. 23.

[2] See Chapter 1, p. 24.

[3] 'charmant et pleurnicheur': Benoît-Jeannin, *Georgette Leblanc*, p. 194.

[4] 'plus proche du connu, de l'habituel': Benoît-Jeannin, *Georgette Leblanc*, p. 194.

[5] Benoît-Jeannin, *Georgette Leblanc*, p. 194.

She describes her efforts to minister to his grumbles and his relief at being able to settle quietly in a corner of a train carriage with his pipe. Carré must have found the contrast between Maeterlinck's lack of enthusiasm and Georgette's ebullience striking. Certainly she waxes enthusiastic about the director, especially after they had discovered 'Carmen herself, the real gypsy' in Granada. This was a woman called Trinidad la Chatta, whose posture and gestures Georgette was to transpose to the stage in Paris. Indeed, Carré tells us that they brought back not only Trinidad, but also her ten-year-old daughter to provide an example for the corps de ballet. This little girl turned out to be such a good little dancer that he had the bright idea that she should perform on a table on stage to provide even more local colour. On the first night the child received tremendous applause. However, next morning Carré was summoned in front of the Directeur des Beaux-Arts who said this was to be stopped forthwith as several spectators had found it 'shocking and immoral' for such a young girl to be in such a 'place of ill repute'.[6]

On 7 December 1898 the grand inauguration of the new Opéra-Comique took place. It was certainly an occasion 'fertile in incidents' to translate literally the words of Carré.[7] When the President, Félix Faure and his wife entered the foyer, *La Marseillaise* was struck up by two bands simultaneously: the Opéra-Comique orchestra and the Band of the Republican Guard. Unfortunately it had been quite overlooked that the national anthem when played by military bands was always in the key of B flat and when played by a symphony orchestra it was in A. 'So the new director is a fan of modern music!', was one sarcastic comment. Just as the band struck up, Madame Faure fell down some steps, landing in a mass of crumpled dress, fur and feathers, and could only join her husband at the end of the anthem. The programme commenced with a selection of operatic scenes, and all was going smoothly until *Carmen*. The toreador was singing, when to his horror Carré saw one of the lamps on the set tip over, spilling oil over the stage floor. A quick-thinking member of the chorus snatched off his cloak and snuffed out the snake of flame that was winding towards him. This incident appears to have gone unnoticed by the audience. The same cannot be said for Georgette's performance. It may not have been one of the disasters at the inauguration, but Carré certainly has much to complain about when describing the revival of the full opera which began the next day. Georgette, as ever larger than life, claims, 'my costumes, my gestures, my walk … disconcerted the lovers of routine and enchanted everyone else.'[8] Carré, however,

---

[6] Carré, *Souvenirs de théâtre*, pp. 239–40.

[7] Carré, *Souvenirs de théâtre*, p. 232.

[8] Leblanc, *Souvenirs: My Life with Maeterlinck*, p. 164.

had to remonstrate with her. She 'revealed herself to be inadequate vocally and, as for her acting, extreme in her interpretation of the role.' Despite her authentic costume and jewellery, her hair and makeup, the way she swayed her hips turned her Carmen into an exaggerated caricature. Worse still, she took the artificial oranges from the baskets held by the chorus on stage and threw them in all directions 'without sparing the scenery, her fellow actors, and not even the audience'. She only stopped when one of the oranges was returned, 'hitting her in her most mobile parts in the swaying movements of the *meneo*'.[9]

The next she knew, she was suspended from the Opéra-Comique. Carré claimed she had made a complete travesty of her role. However, Arsène Alexandre wrote a long and complimentary review in the journal *Le Théâtre*,[10] the cover of which was adorned with a colourful picture of Georgette as Carmen. In the very first sentence appears that word which always seems to come to mind whenever people talk or write about Georgette: *l'intelligence*. Alexandre appreciated her determination to break with tradition and create something new out of the role, and commented fulsomely on her propensity to analyse her thoughts and dash them down on paper. Most significantly, he refers to her ability to create a modern work. 'She will be sure to prove this in *Proserpine* by Saint-Saëns, in *Pelléas et Mélisande* by Claude Debussy.'[11] Clearly, this critic had heard somewhere that Georgette was going to be creating the role of her dreams, and this at the beginning of 1899.

Georgette's explanation of her dismissal is only incidentally linked to *Carmen*. Her version of events is that there could only be one person responsible for her downfall and that was not for reasons of poor performance. 'Free in my manner, spontaneous and naïve, when *Carmen* was being given I found myself in situations which I only knew how to meet with contempt or the most insulting laughter.' To Georgette's mind, it was entirely her intransigence in refusing to grant Carré his desires by submitting to the indignity of what others called the 'casting couch' which was to blame for her dismissal from the Opéra-Comique and ultimately for 'the Maeterlinck-Debussy quarrel.' As we will see with regard to Mary Garden and Maggie Teyte, this is not entirely implausible.

---

9 'Prenant de fausses oranges ... elle se mit à les jeter en tous sens, sans épargner ni décor, ni ses partenaires, ni même le public qui en reçut quelques-unes aussi. Mme Leblanc mit fin à ce jeu de scène lorsque l'une d'elles lui revint on ne sait d'où, l'atteignant dans la partie d'elle-même qui s'activait le plus au roulement du *meneo*.' Albert Carré, *Souvenirs de théâtre*, p. 240. *Meneo* is an Andalusian dance.

10 *Le Théâtre*, February 1899, pp. 16–18. See illus. 5.

11 'Elle est une de ces rares qui soient vraiment aptes à créer une œuvre moderne. Elle doit en donner la preuve un de ces jours dans la *Proserpine* de Saint-Saëns, dans *Pelléas et Mélisande* de Claude Debussy.' *Le Théâtre*, February 1899, p. 17.

At the beginning of 1901 Georgette was described in a review as 'one of the most admirable *tragédiennes lyriques* we know' when she appeared at the Opéra-Populaire in the musical drama *Charlotte Corday* by Alexandre Georges. Besides photographs, over half a page of Georgette's handwritten notes are reproduced which she had actually done when sitting on stage during her act, not simply to look authentic, but to record her immediate impressions of what was going on around her. Georgette, ever the writer, thinker, emotional and intellectual, did not want to let one moment of life pass her by without comment, even when acting. Incidentally, the reviewer's warmest compliments are paid to the 'young and distinguished conductor', Henri Büsser [*sic*], soon to be chorus master for *Pelléas et Mélisande* at the Opéra-Comique.[12]

Maeterlinck was adamant that Georgette should create the operatic role of Mélisande. Back in 1894 he had given Debussy permission to do what he liked with the play when setting it to music, and Mauclair had suggested Georgette for the role of Mélisande even then. As René Peter points out, at the time of her suspension Albert Carré could not already have had Mary Garden in mind for the role, for she had not by then entered the Opéra-Comique, did not know Carré and probably had never even been to France.[13] He had also heard that Maeterlinck had told Debussy of his definite desire for the role of Mélisande to be sung by Georgette Leblanc, to which the composer's reaction had been prevarication: 'We'll see ...'[14] In view of what one of Debussy's piano pupils later wrote, this reaction is hardly surprising. Of the mordant criticisms she heard Debussy make regarding certain singers, she remembered in particular his reference to 'the wife of a man of letters' who dreamed of singing the role of Mélisande. 'Not only did she sing out of tune, he said, but she spoke out of tune.'[15] However, this recollection was not noted until 1933, and therefore has the benefit of hindsight. Debussy's views on many of his interpreters, even of those he admired, were often contradictory.

On 3 May 1901 Carré wrote to Debussy at last confirming formally that he would mount *Pelléas et Mélisande* the following year.[16] Not long after, on 30 May, from Georgette's address at 69 rue Raynouard, Maeterlinck wrote to the composer arranging to meet him there between then and 6 June any day from five o'clock onwards. 'I shall be pleased to see you again, to shake hands

[12] *Revue Æolienne*, vol. 3, no. 25.

[13] Peter, *Claude Debussy*, p. 174.

[14] Peter, *Claude Debussy*, p. 173.

[15] 'Non seulement, disait-il, elle chante faux, mais elle parle faux.' Mme Gérard de Romilly, 'Debussy professeur par une de ses élèves', *Cahiers Debussy*, no. 2 (1978), p. 7.

[16] Debussy, *Correspondance*, p. 596.

and talk about our *Pelléas*.'[17] Obviously he must also have been determined
to ensure that, despite any ruptures at the Opéra-Comique, Georgette
would be given the role she had coveted for so many years.

Indeed, Georgette was present throughout the interview when Debussy
came to discuss matters with Maeterlinck and more than ready to grasp the
opportunity to claim the part for herself. Her account is typically vivid:

> I watched him enter the room. His extraordinary head was already known
> from photographs. But his presence revealed a special quality. By small details
> of colour, manner, gesture, one guessed much of his hidden personality. His
> toneless skin was as white as wax, his fine crinkly hair misted the massive out-
> line of his formidable skull. Beneath the bulging brow his sheltered glance
> shone dimly. His gestures were rare and he seldom smiled.[18]

As had happened at the first meeting of the two men in Ghent in 1893,
there was a certain reticence and an atmosphere of wariness between them.
Georgette observed them as both equally on the defensive. In the intervening eight years the author had heard not a note of the composer's setting of
his words. Why had it taken so long to compose?, he must have wondered.

Georgette saw her lover, the writer, as being the more balanced of the two
personalities: 'Debussy's reserve was physical. In him one felt a painful sensitivity and even something morbid which was biding its time. In Maeterlinck
the physical and moral balance made itself felt at once.'[19] One can't help
remembering at this point Maeterlinck's insistence on peace and quiet and
regular meals. His was the more mundane, down-to-earth personality. He
was certainly blessed with greater financial and emotional security than the
composer. Georgette realised that: 'The musician suffered from the little
things of life. The poet refused to endure them. With him the "Do not enter"
sign meant "Do not disturb me." With Debussy it seemed to mean "Do not
make me suffer."' A physical comparison of the two men led Georgette to
believe Debussy's body was 'built for strength and yet apparently uninhabited by it. His strength had been drained by his genius.' Her lover's body
was never neglected. Instead, he cultivated strength through regular boxing
practice and physical exercise.

It is paradoxical that the text that inspired Debussy's greatest work
should have been written by one 'not understanding music in the least'.[20]
When Debussy played through his score at Georgette's piano his back was
to his little audience. This enabled Maeterlinck to make desperate signs to

[17] Debussy, *Correspondance*, p. 599.
[18] Leblanc, *Souvenirs: My Life with Maeterlinck*, p. 168.
[19] Leblanc, *Souvenirs: My Life with Maeterlinck*, pp. 168–70.
[20] Leblanc, *Souvenirs: My Life with Maeterlinck*, p. 169.

Georgette. 'Several times he wanted to escape but I held him back. Resigned, he lit his pipe.' Even Georgette admits that 'At this first hearing of *Pelléas* many of its beauties escaped me.' The afternoon must indeed have seemed long, for it was not until the prelude for the death of Mélisande that she felt 'that special, that unique emotion that we undergo in the presence of a masterpiece'. By then it was late. 'Two candles on the piano outlined Debussy's silhouette. Maeterlinck was half asleep in his armchair.' Just before Debussy's departure the longed-for topic was broached. Georgette expressed her desire to sing the role, and Maeterlinck urged Debussy to allow her to do so. According to Georgette, Debussy said he would be delighted. Are we to believe this? Even if he did express delight, could this not have been out of politeness? He did not have Carré's authority to distribute the casting and he must surely have been aware that Georgette was *persona non grata* at the Opéra-Comique. Georgette has to admit, 'He told me that after having seen me so violent in *Carmen* he had at first doubted me, and that he had not known to what an extent I could adapt myself.'[21]

Debussy went so far in his pretence that Georgette could sing Mélisande that they had five rehearsals: two at Debussy's flat and two or three in Georgette's.[22] Was he doing this just to pander to Maeterlinck? Or could he not be the one to face the singer's disappointment? Whatever the situation, the two found it difficult to communicate in the pauses between making music. 'We were like two savages, each one drawing back from the other's presence. I thought Debussy walled in by his pride.' She has no problem in describing dramatically every emotion she experienced faced with the composer. But what can have been going on in his mind? Shame at not being able to tell her the truth? Frustration at wasting time rehearsing with someone he knew was not going to sing the role? Such a fulsome, extrovert, overpowering personality as Georgette's must have been completely at odds with his introvert, self-contained nature.

She may not have been able to speak to Debussy about her passion for the role of Mélisande, but as ever Georgette had no difficulty in expressing her innermost emotions in a letter. Had he been chiding her for overacting? At the end of 1901 she wrote to the composer emphasising her passion for the work, but claiming that she did not think an interpreter played only a minor part in creating a role:[23]

> Obviously you draw a wonderfully precise circle for her and that around
> Mélisande is necessarily the tightest (given her fearful, unknowing little soul),

[21] Leblanc, *Souvenirs: My Life with Maeterlinck*, p. 170.

[22] Debussy, *Correspondance*, p. 634 n. 1.

[23] Debussy, *Correspondance*, p. 633.

but your work is so humane that it seems to me to have more elements of interest, more colours and more life in the little space you have reserved for the
interpreter than in works with vaguer outlines or other musical forms which
do allow for development.

She begged him not to think she would perhaps not be 'flexible', assuring him
she was happy 'to bow to what is right and beautiful.' She admitted that she
had a tendency to 'seek beyond what is' and sometimes to go astray more easily than others, then told him, 'I sang some of Mélisande's music to Maurice
– and he understood perfectly – the words, he said, were "prettier like that". It
is the triumph of your logic.' In view of later events, Maeterlinck's admission
that his words were *'prettier like that'* must be emphasised.

Strange though it may seem, there is no reason nor any complaint given
by Georgette for the cessation of these rehearsals. There is a letter in which
she postpones a rehearsal giving as an excuse that having just arrived back
from the country she had found letters waiting for her which upset her
plans,[24] but that is all. Perhaps her mind was preoccupied with other personal matters, for in 1901 the question of marriage to Maeterlinck arose once
more. Apparently such an announcement must have been made prematurely
by a newspaper and the marriage may have been planned for the following spring.[25] Legally by now Georgette could have divorced Minuesa, but
Maeterlinck would never have been satisfied with only a civil wedding. He
wanted a religious ceremony, and the complications this would bring about,
as well as Georgette's continued reluctance, meant that eventually they
abandoned the idea. From then on, however, she called herself Georgette
Leblanc-Maeterlinck. Many believed they were, in fact, married.

Albert Carré stated adamantly that it had been solely Debussy's decision to 'promise' the role of Mélisande to Georgette. As soon as he heard
of it he categorically vetoed it. Having made one error in giving her the
part of Carmen, he did not want to commit another. Physically she did not
fulfil his image of Mélisande. 'I thought that this singer whose beauty was
in full bloom did not possess the physical qualities of the childlike woman
Melisande, her voice, her gestures, her natural grace, her melancholy smile,
her featherlight walk', all of which were attributes of Mary Garden.[26] He
himself extricated Debussy from his promise. Carré insists that it was not
for personal reasons that he exerted influence on Debussy. He underlines

[24] Debussy, *Correspondance*, p. 634.

[25] Benoît-Jeannin, *Georgette Leblanc*, p. 201.

[26] 'J'estimais que cette cantatrice, à la beauté épanouie, ne possédait pas les qualités
physiques du personnage de femme-enfant qu'était Mélisande, la voix, le geste, la
grâce naturelle, le sourire mélancolique, la démarche ailée ... tout ce qui, enfin, se
trouva si merveilleusement réuni en Mary Garden.' Carré, *Souvenirs de théâtre*, p. 277.

the point that 'Not then, not before nor after was this type of pressure in my nature.'[27] In taking full responsibility upon himself for the casting of the role, Carré made the author, whom he insists he admired so much, into an irreconcilable enemy.

Carré's emphasis on the maturity of Georgette's figure lends support to the belief of René Peter that both Albert Carré and Debussy were more concerned about the appearance of their Pelléas and their Mélisande than their vocal performance. Someone young – above all they had to be young. Their characters would be incomprehensible otherwise. Even someone who was not a professional singer but who looked youthful and could sing might be more suitable than one with experience. René Peter was amazed when Debussy asked him point-blank: 'Have *you* got a voice?' 'A voice?', replied René. 'Yes, you have the right voice and it is *young* ... but do you know how to sing?' 'Why?' 'Because you wouldn't have displeased me ... as Pelléas!' René Peter realised to his astonishment that Debussy was not joking. 'Poor Pelléas!', he thought.[28]

Carré's aesthetic preoccupations meant that he had to cast as Mélisande someone who might have been a vision in a dream, with child-like, innocent features, someone who might have stepped out of a medieval stained glass window (just as Debussy saw his beloved creatures stepping out of a tapestry). Discussions took place between Carré, Debussy and Messager at the Café Weber, where they picked to pieces the whole Opéra-Comique company.[29] They even suggested names from elsewhere, but no one fitted the physical image they had imprinted on their imaginations. Meanwhile, even at this stage Debussy was still working on the opera. Whilst at the café they were urging him to finish writing the last tableaux.[30]

Georgette was to hear of the decision to appoint Mary Garden to the role when it was announced in *Le Ménéstral* of 29 December 1901. Her shocked reaction to the news was immediately to blame Carré and not Debussy. She linked it inevitably to her 'disagreeable adventure connected with *Carmen*'.[31] Later on, looking back on the fracas, Carré was to comment wryly that Georgette sent everyone angry notes which achieved record sums of money when sold at auction![32]

When Maeterlinck read in the paper that another artist was to sing Mélisande he was incandescent. He referred his case to the Société des

---

[27] Carré, *Souvenirs de théâtre*, p. 279.

[28] Peter, *Claude Debussy*, p. 169.

[29] Peter, *Claude Debussy*, p. 170.

[30] Carré, *Souvenirs de théâtre*, p. 276.

[31] Leblanc, *Souvenirs: My Life with Maeterlinck*, p. 174.

[32] Carré, *Souvenirs de théâtre*, p. 278.

auteurs et compositeurs dramatiques (SACD), but found that where a writer
and a composer collaborated it was the composer's rights which took precedence. Also it must be remembered that even though Maeterlinck's work
pre-dated that of Debussy, he had granted the composer complete freedom
to do what he liked with the play so many years ago. His fury could not be
contained. The scene that followed became legendary. In front of Georgette,
Maeterlinck grabbed his cane and leapt out of the ground-floor window.
He rushed round to Debussy's flat and with his stick threatened the composer, who dropped into a chair. Lilly Debussy ran towards her husband
with a bottle of smelling salts, begging Maeterlinck to go away. What more
could he do? He left, grumbling, 'They're all crazy, all off their heads, these
musicians!'[33]

Maeterlinck's own recollection of events is to be found in a letter he wrote
to Henry Russell in 1925.[34] He asserts that if he did have a big stick, it was just
his normal walking stick.[35] 'I did not have to threaten to make use of it, for
Debussy, seeing I was in quite a bad mood, in order to get rid of me, quickly
promised anything I wanted. Today I realise that all the fault was on my side
and he was a thousand times right.'

However, at the time, Maeterlinck's anger did not subside, and there was
even talk of a duel. He is said to have used a black cat as target practice and
shot it dead! Debussy's 'seconders' were to be Robert de Flers and Albert
Carré, but fortunately, despite talk of others preparing to stand in for the
composer, no duel materialised.

Carré and others[36] report that Maeterlinck, in his efforts to make the
director give in, even consulted a medium, and later went so far as to make
use of the experience in an essay entitled *L'Avenir* (*The Future*),[37] in which
the character of 'the enemy' and 'the man who wishes me evil' is said in fact
to be Carré. The medium prophesies the illness and imminent death of
this enemy. Carré, in his *Souvenirs*, apologises to her via his readers for his
untimely longevity![38]

On 7 February both Debussy and Maeterlinck had to present their case
to the SACD. Maeterlinck tried to show that Debussy had not registered
his opera until 30 December 1901, but had pre-dated his application, which
was recorded as 3 May 1901. He also tried to prove that his letter to Debussy

---

33 Leblanc, *Souvenirs: My Life with Maeterlinck*, p. 174.

34 26 November 1925, Stadsarchief Gent BC62.

35 This stick is preserved in the Cabinet Maeterlinck in Ghent, to which the contents of
    Maeterlinck's study have been transferred.

36 Germaine and D.-E. Inghelbrecht, *Claude Debussy* (Paris, 1953), p. 149.

37 Maurice Maeterlinck, *Le Temple enseveli* (Paris, 1902).

38 Carré, *Souvenirs de théâtre*, p. 278.

of 19 October 1895 had not been intended to give the composer *carte blanche* with his play. The minutes of the hearing state that 'In spring 1901 M. Maeterlinck ... demanded that the role of Mélisande be interpreted by Mlle Georgette Leblanc. M. Debussy did not reject this demand, but was of the opinion that one should not rush M. Carré and should wait.'[39] Arbitration was the next stage considered in the row, but it was refused by Maeterlinck. His lawyers also dissuaded him from taking his case to court. Then on 27 February 1902 René Peter received a handwritten note from Debussy saying, 'Dear friend, Maeterlinck is in the bag and Carré, like me, thinks his is a pathological case. But there are still mental homes in France.'[40]

Maeterlinck still did not give up his battle, but resorted to the means he was most familiar with: words. Mysteriously, on Wednesday 19 March he attended a rehearsal, but then disappeared silently. On 13 April 1902 it was announced that the première of *Pelléas et Mélisande* would take place on 23 April.[41] The next day a letter from Maeterlinck, dated 13 April, was published in the newspaper, *Le Figaro*. This stated categorically that *Pelléas et Mélisande* would be performed 'in spite of me'. Spitefulness, indeed, is the all-pervading sentiment conveyed by the letter, in which he summarised the arguments he had presented to the SACD. Maeterlinck insisted he had been excluded from his own work, and that arbitrary and absurd cuts had been made which made it incomprehensible. 'In a word, the *Pelléas* at issue is a piece that has become a stranger to me, almost an enemy. And, deprived of all control over my work, I am reduced to hoping that its failure will be prompt and resounding.'[42]

Obviously Maeterlinck deeply regretted that he himself had agreed to cuts to the text and had even initially suggested some himself. In fact the composer, in an eternal quest for perfection, went on making revisions to the text[43] and the music even well after the initial performances, but it is difficult to see how Maeterlinck could find the finished result alien to his conception. His complete lack of musical sensibility must have contributed to a prejudice against any interpreter of the role of Mélisande apart from his mistress, to the extent that his comprehension of the extra dimension

[39] Debussy, *Correspondance*, p. 633 n. 2.

[40] Peter, *Claude Debussy*, p. 175.

[41] It was postponed first to 29, then to 30 April.

[42] 'Cette représentation aura lieu malgré moi ... En un mot, le *Pelléas* en question est une pièce qui m'est devenue étrangère, presque ennemi; et dépouillé de tout contrôle sur mon œuvre, j'en suis réduit à souhaiter que sa chute sera prompte et retentissante.' *Le Figaro*, 14 April 1902.

[43] Detailed in David Grayson, 'The Libretto of Debussy's *Pelléas et Mélisande*', *Music & Letters*, vol. 66 (1985), pp. 34–50.

the music added to his words was utterly clouded. This was anything but a rational reaction of an adult intellectual and, if anything, tends to lend support to Georgette's treatment of him as her 'Bébé'. Maeterlinck also made it quite clear on several occasions during his life that it was not simply the interpretation, but also the stage sets of this Opéra-Comique production that he disliked. The period was too specifically gothic for a story which was supposed to be taking place in some unspecified time.[44]

Octave Mirbeau, who had been such a support to Maeterlinck since praising his work twelve years earlier, tried to bring about some sort of reconciliation between the two opponents, but had to admit of the poet that he simply could not get him to reason any more. The anger of this 'mild-mannered and very sensible man' had become 'a veritable raving madness'. He had never seen a man 'possessed to this degree by the evil genius of a woman'.[45] Evil genius? Why was all the blame to be laid at the feet of Georgette?

Even stranger and distinctly hostile was the spoof programme entitled 'Select Programme' sold for six sous on the pavement outside the Opéra-Comique before the public dress rehearsal on Monday 28 April. The management had no knowledge of it. The summary of the plot of the opera was a ridiculous parody, rude and full of infantile innuendos. For example: 'Scene III. – Pelléas, brother of Golaud, walks in the shadowy gardens with his little sister-in-law. Ha ha!' 'Scene VI. – Mélisande spinning her distaff[46] ... and perfect love with Pelléas. Little Yniold, a terrible child, sees ... and will tell.' It ended: 'And there we are! This little play is a masterpiece and Maeterlinck is a genius. At least, that's what they say.' Authorship was attributed by many to Maeterlinck himself, who hoped that it would contribute to the failure of the opera. This is quite likely, although as others say, it was not in Maeterlinck's nature to ridicule himself and his work. Its authorship remains a mystery.

Maeterlinck was not present at the dress rehearsal, the first, or any other performance until two years after Debussy died. Not until 1920 did he write to Mary Garden, whom he had just seen perform in New York: 'I had sworn to myself never to see the lyric drama *Pelléas et Mélisande*. Yesterday I violated my vow and I am a happy man. For the first time I have entirely understood my own play, and because of you.'

Who was Mary Garden?

44 Reported in *L'Eventail*, 30 September 1906 and 6 January 1907.

45 'une véritable folie furieuse ... Je n'ai jamais vu un homme possédé, à ce point, par le mauvais génie d'une femme.' Inghelbrecht, *Claude Debussy*, p. 149.

46 This scene is not in the opera, so presumably whoever wrote this summary had not been to rehearsals nor seen the score.

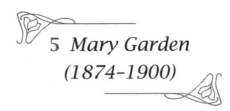

5 *Mary Garden*
(1874-1900)

*M*ARY GARDEN should have been born in the late twentieth century. She would have been an ideal subject for *Hello* magazine, *OK*, or any of today's tabloids. The paparazzi would have had a field day, with no problem making up quotations or acquiring a good photograph, for she would have thrived on the publicity from feeding the press juicy titbits about her latest lover, her views on the position of women in society, hints on her sexuality, her scanty costumes for her latest production, romances with royalty, and denial after denial of liaisons with an endless succession of men – or women. She would have been completely suited to today's fads for the latest diet, the urgent need for exercise, the quest for the perfect hair colour. She had a gift for manipulating the press that would be an example to many an aspiring star of today – in an age where there was no television, when films were only just becoming a viable proposition, and long distance travel was measured in days rather than hours from one side of the Atlantic to the other. Endorsing a product was not beneath this star singer. Newspapers and magazines were vehicles of advertising, and to turn one's nose up at such publicity would have been folly for a personality who thrived on any exposure – even over a hundred years ago.

A character further from the elusive, fragile Mélisande is difficult to imagine. Yet if it were not for this little creature, would Mary have achieved the level of fame and celebrity that she did? It speaks volumes for her acting ability and stage presence that she could subdue the extrovert excesses of her nature and enter into the heart of the 'poor little being'.

Mary's autobiography, *Mary Garden's Story*[1] was published in 1951. The original typescript of the first draft is to be found at The Royal College of Music in London, but Mary's first attempts to write her life story were not to any publisher's satisfaction. Her book is therefore the result of interviews with Louis Biancolli, who is acknowledged as the co-author, yet it is virtually impossible to unravel truth from fiction. Interestingly, in this context, in 1951 Mary showed her publisher, Simon & Schuster, a biography of Bizet written by Douglas Charles Parker,[2] who had previously corresponded with her about her interpretation of the role of Carmen. A letter dated 22 December

[1] Mary Garden and Louis J. Biancolli, *Mary Garden's Story* (New York, 1951).
[2] D. C. Parker, *Bizet* (London, 1951).

of that year which Mary wrote to Mr Parker tells him that unfortunately Simon & Schuster were not interested in publishing his book as it did not reveal enough of Bizet's private life.[3] This could surely be a clue as to the number of personal 'revelations' she included in her own book, which has often been criticised in this respect.

Writing her preface in December 1949, she tells her readers that she has found public speaking fun. Now her friend, Biancolli, has been urging her 'to tell all' – to include, as he puts it, the men as well as the music. And 'tell all' is what she proceeds to do – and more besides! The order of events, meetings, performances, is confused. Fabrications abound. Hints at relationships, dramatic exaggerations all help to create a portrait which is true in as much as it is an expression of her personality, but not one that is a reliable life story. Others must have regretted this lack of reliability. When Mary Garden's death was announced in the magazine *Opera* in February 1967 a full obituary was promised in an issue to come. But where is it? One searches in vain. Was this, perhaps, because of the near impossibility of quickly tying together so many loose ends? When *Opera* reviewed *Mary Garden's Story* in July 1952, the reviewer found it so entertaining that it only remained to make a movie out of her story. Maggie Teyte felt 'a little bewildered' by the book. She declared she could not reconcile 'the wonderful illusions she gave us before the scenery with what, Miss Garden would have us believe, happened behind it.'[4] This public review was more tempered than her reaction in private. She told her friend and companion, Grace Vernon that it was 60 per cent drivel.[5] There is another version of Mary's story in French entitled *L'Envers du décor* (Behind the scenes) which has the subtitle *Souvenirs d'une Grande Cantatrice*.[6] This book is shorter than the English version, some events occurring in a different order, and others omitted.

None of this detracts from the extraordinary, vital, larger-than-life personality of Mary Garden, the first Mélisande. In fact, it provides a convenient smoke-screen for someone who remained extremely close to her family throughout her career, thus maintaining some sort of private home life wherever she was living or performing. How did a young singer from Aberdeen come to meet Debussy and create the girl of whom the composer wrote: 'I have spent days in pursuit of that "nothing" of which she is made'?[7]

---

[3] Letter from Mary Garden to Douglas Charles Parker: National Library of Scotland, MS 21555, fol. 216.

[4] *Sunday Times*, 2 March 1952.

[5] Copy of correspondence in Royal Opera House Collections, JC 7/06/05.

[6] Mary Garden, *L'Envers du décor: souvenirs d'une grande cantatrice* (Paris, 1952).

[7] Debussy, *Correspondance*, p. 189.

Records show that Mary was born at 35 Charlotte Street in Aberdeen on 20 February 1874, only one month after the marriage of her parents which had taken place on 8 January. Her father, Robert Davidson Garden, the son of a farmer, had married well at the age of twenty-three. He was a clerk at the Blaikie iron works. Her seventeen-year-old mother, Mary Joss, was the daughter of Patrick Joss, who had risen from being agent to manager of the stone merchants at Bucksburn, north-west of the city. His father in turn had been a merchant in Aberdeen. Mary had three younger sisters: Amy, born in 1875, and Agnes, born in 1877, both in Scotland. Helen was born in America, in December 1886.

Mary liked to be thought of as something of a prodigy in her early childhood, although she had no music lessons. She fondly remembered standing on a table and rendering *Three little redcaps growing in the corn* to assembled family members.[8] Two other memories are recalled from those early Aberdeen days. The first was being taken to hear Marie Roze, the French soprano, at the Music Hall, which left an indelible impression, opening up a whole new world for her.[9] The second was a ghastly encounter with one of her grandfather's dogs who jumped at her when she greeted him and sunk his teeth into her just above the throat. Mary's dramatic depiction of her descent down the stairs from the bedroom into the drawing room of the large house where this occurred, her white silk dress a mass of blood, the effect of her entry on the assembled company, and her insistence that she still carried the marks of the dog's teeth, demonstrate her love of the dramatic effect and her realisation of its power. It is also remarkably similar in style to Georgette Leblanc's romanticised portrayals of memorable incidents which coloured her early life.

It is unlikely that the image Mary paints of her grandfather is truthful. She describes him as one of the biggest landowners in Aberdeenshire, having enormous granite quarries in Aberdeen, and remembers fine horses, dog-carts and a beautiful country place where the family spent a good part of the summer.[10] If there were such wealth and grandeur in the family, she would surely not have needed the valuable sponsorship she was to receive. The similarity in this evocation of grandeur, the wistful memories of a 'lost childhood' in wild haunts, to the early pages of Maggie Teyte's recollections, lead one to suspect that both women wanted to obliterate the truth of their much more prosaic origins. Later in life, Mary's sister Amy lived at Pitmurchie House, Torphins, of which there are many photographs in the family albums.

[8] See illus.7.

[9] *Mary Garden's Story*, p. 2.

[10] *Mary Garden's Story*, pp. 271, 274.

Perhaps in her old age, Mary believed this property had always been in the family.

There can have been no financial security, for in 1880 Robert Garden set sail for America to seek work to support his family.[11] Not until April 1882 did Mrs Garden and her three daughters, Mary (then eight years old), Amy and Agnes, cross the Atlantic on the SS *Anchoria* and join him in President Street, Brooklyn. Mary loved their new home, but her mother pined for her beloved Scotland. Quite naturally, the children were shy, and must have found it embarrassing to be surrounded by their intrigued classmates and asked to talk in their Scottish accents.[12] From Brooklyn the family moved to Chicopee, Massachusetts, where Mary's third sister, Helen, was born in 1886.

Mary paints an idyllic picture of a childhood spent cycling through beautiful countryside, skating and tobogganing, but she disliked what she described as 'girlish pursuits'. She attributed her delight in cutting off the heads of her sisters' paper dolls to her belief that they were wasting their time.[13] Her father is portrayed as a figure full of energy, endeavouring to make his daughters into athletes, encouraging literary knowledge by prizes for poetry recitation, which Mary always won, and certainly not discouraging his daughter's singing. When their neighbour, the wife of the church minister, heard her, she not only asked her to sing at the church festival, she taught her the little song, *The birds were singing in every tree at five o'clock in the morning*. 'That was the beginning of my public career', claims Mary. A violin teacher was found for her in Springfield and the following year it was this instrument that she played at the church festival. 'I was always musical. Only the media changed – one time it was violin, then piano, then voice', she later told an interviewer. She loved the expressive, one might say operatic qualities of the violin, for she could make it speak just by drawing a bow over it. Although her father encouraged her, believing she could become a great violinist, her interest in the instrument soon waned as she realised progress was not instantaneous. When told it would probably take twenty years to become a good amateur violinist, she immediately sickened of the instrument and dropped it for ever.

At this point, in 1889, Mary's mother decided to move back to Aberdeen for a year, taking the girls with her. They were sent to St Margaret's School for Girls, where it was not the school, but her private piano lessons that were

[11]   Michael T. R. B. Turnbull, *Mary Garden* (Portland, OR, and Aldershot, UK, 1997), p. 3. Mary says her father was an 'engineer' and left because he wanted to see America: *Mary Garden's Story*, p. 271.

[12]   Unpublished typescript in Royal College of Music [RCM], London, Mary Garden Collection.

[13]   Mary Garden, 'The "Know How" in the Art of Singing', *The Etude*, July 1920, p. 439.

to make their mark on fifteen-year-old Mary, for she developed a crush on her piano teacher. This had the beneficial effect that she worked and worked at the instrument in order to impress him, but she claims he never noticed the state of excitement in which she arrived at her lessons. Later she did acknowledge that the piano was an invaluable aid throughout her career, for 'long, supple fingers, combined with my musical experience gained in violin playing, made that certain.'[14]

On returning to America in May 1890, it was Chicago that was to become Mary's home, for her father was employed by the firm of George Pope, which made bicycles. There Mary attended Hyde Park High School. A visit to the theatre to see Clara Morris in *Article 47* brought a similar reaction to Georgette Leblanc's when she saw Sarah Bernhardt in Rouen. Overcome by the dramatic portrayal, ill from excitement, Mary ate no dinner and was unable to sleep for the intensity of her feelings.[15]

Now aged sixteen, Mary sang in various amateur operatic productions, revelling in her costumes and the reactions of her audiences. One evening her father's employer came to dinner. Mary no doubt took little persuasion to sing to him after the meal and impressed him so much that he suggested she should meet Mrs Sarah Robinson Duff. This singer had just returned to Chicago after studying in Paris and was eager to find pupils in her home town. Mary found her 'handsome, tremendously charming and oh! so French in manner ... She was *so* everything that I had dreamed of, and never seen in my life.' She became her pupil and is quick to acknowledge her debt: 'I owe much of my vocal success to Mrs Duff. I was very young and very emotional, and I had a long pigtail down my back.'[16]

Despite being bored by her exercises, Mary worked very hard, concentrating on technique. Her efforts at local concerts were rewarded with praise and appreciation in the papers. Mrs Duff realised that she had an exceptional pupil, but that the family was not rich. It was, therefore, a hugely important moment in Mary's life when, in 1894, Mrs Duff engineered the introduction of Mary to another of her pupils, Mrs Florence Mayer. Mrs Mayer's husband was a wealthy partner of the dry goods firm Schlesinger & Mayer, which was to become the largest department store in Chicago. This couple agreed to sponsor Mary. To support his family, Mary's father had to take a job in Hartford, Connecticut, but since Mrs Duff was insistent that Mary should return to Chicago, it was arranged that she should live with the Mayers and in return help to look after their children. This golden opportunity has its

---

[14] Garden, 'The "Know How" in the Art of Singing', p. 439.

[15] William Armstrong, 'The Girlhood of Mary Garden', *Women's Home Companion*, August 1911.

[16] Garden, 'The "Know How" in the Art of Singing', p. 439.

parallel in the story of Maggie Teyte, who was also to move in with the family who sponsored her. On visiting her own family in their new surroundings, Mary found that one of their neighbours was Hayden Eames, brother of the soprano Emma Eames. She listened eagerly to his wonderful stories about his sister, and was made very aware of the sacrifices she had had to make to achieve a successful career.

At this point, Mary's penchant for dramatic tales once again resembles Georgette's highly charged accounts of her early years. A young naval officer, who lived next door in Hartford, fell in love with Mary whilst she was visiting her parents. During a romantic sleigh ride, he proposed. Mary rejected her suitor with the explanation that she would never marry. She knew music and marriage could not be combined. 'I've made up my mind. I've decided I want music. I'm perfectly reconciled to what I'm going to miss, and I know there will never be room in my life for marriage.'[17] Are we to believe the melodramatic timing of what followed? Just then, the horse took fright at an oncoming vehicle, swerved and the sleigh overturned. Her suitor's dog took fright, dashed in front of the vehicle and was run over and killed. Mary's statement of intent never to marry was to be repeated many times in her life, and she remained true to her vow.

In 1895 the family moved to Philadelphia, where Mary's enterprising father opened his own bicycle shop and repair business. She continued to live with the Mayers in Chicago. This was a vital stage in her development, for she was given every opportunity to practise and to attend the opera at the Chicago Auditorium. She has fond memories of hearing Nellie Melba and Jean de Reszke. The latter, a great tenor who was virtually the equivalent of a matinée idol to the Chicago audience, was not only eventually to become a neighbour of Mary's in later life, but to play a significant part in the life of Maggie Teyte. In 1896 Mary witnessed an extraordinary performance of Gounod's *Romeo and Juliet* which became one of the legends of the history of opera in Chicago. As Romeo, de Reszke was facing towards the balcony where Melba, as Juliet, was about to appear. Suddenly a man rushed down the aisle, forced his way onto the stage and aimed a revolver at de Reszke. De Reszke remained calm, but called for the curtain to be rung down. The drama over, terrified Melba took some persuasion to come out from behind the shutters on the balcony. She kept shouting backstage, 'My voice is gone!', until de Reszke called up to her, 'For God's sake, keep quiet Melba, open the window, and come out!' Much to his surprise Melba obeyed him, 'meek as a lamb'![18]

[17] *Mary Garden's Story*, p. 11.
[18] Ronald L. Davis, *Opera in Chicago* (New York, 1966), p. 61.

On following Mary's progress in recitals and concerts, Mrs Mayer was impressed, and had no hesitation in offering to pay for her to go to Paris with her teacher Mrs Duff and to study there for three years. Mary's parents supported this plan, and in May 1896 the two women left for France.

Paris was a magnet for young aspiring opera singers from America. In the latter decades of the nineteenth century Americans loved to acquire a veneer of French sophistication, Paris being regarded as a cosmopolitan and romantic environment where they could live cheaply and free of home restraints. On reading Mary's autobiography, one might reasonably assume that she and her teacher travelled alone, but in fact Mrs Duff was also bringing several other students to seek suitable teachers in the capital.[19] Many retired opera singers, eccentric and bombastic personalities from various countries in Europe, must have made a considerable income from teaching these ambitious and lucrative young hopefuls. The young ladies and their families were proud to aim for a career on the operatic stage. This was in stark contrast to the attitude of their European counterparts, whose bourgeois families viewed this world as demeaning. As we have seen, Georgette Leblanc was strongly discouraged by her family and despised by her lover for desperately seeking to become a singer.

Having become used to being showered with praise, Mary was full of confidence in her eventual success. She was now twenty-two, full of vital energy and enthusiasm. She was pleased to relate, 'I never saw America again until I came back as an established artist.'[20] For the second time she crossed the Atlantic back to Europe, this time not to chilly Aberdeen but to Cherbourg. From there she and Mrs Duff took a train to Paris, then a taxi to their hotel. When they passed the great Opéra, Mrs Duff clasped Mary's arm exclaiming, 'Look, Mary, that's where you're going to sing someday!'

First Mary had to find a suitable teacher. It took four attempts. Her account of their exploratory visits is highly entertaining. Jacques Bouhy, a Belgian baritone, the first to sing the role of Escamillo in Bizet's *Carmen* at the Opéra-Comique in 1875, was struck by Mary's prettiness. She hardly understood a word he said. 'All I could get from the torrent of French that poured from him was the one word, *"jolie!"* repeated again and again.' He claimed he could put Mary on the stage of the Opéra in twenty-six weeks. 'But who wants to go on the stage of the Opéra in twenty-six weeks?', cried Mary. 'I certainly don't – and won't.'

Then she tried Giovanni Sbriglia, an Italian tenor who had taught the

---

[19] Jack Winsor Hansen, *The Sybil Sanderson Story: Requiem for a Diva* (Pompton Plains, NJ, Cambridge, UK, 2005), p. 278.

[20] *Mary Garden's Story*, p. 13.

two de Reszke brothers, Edouard and Jean, and the 'Californian nightingale', Sibyl Sanderson. 'He began by making me hum scales through my nose. And of course all he succeeded in doing was to tie my voice into knots. Then he told me to unbutton the front of my dress. What he was looking for I can't possibly imagine, possibly my method of breathing.' This was an exploratory investigation that Sbriglia apparently carried out on all the young ladies who turned up for auditions with him. When Sibyl Sanderson had sung for him for the first time he had likewise excitedly rushed forward to unbutton her dress and, to her mother's horror, begun to behave with embarrassing familiarity toward her daughter. However, the volatile professor was merely explaining his breathing methods to both of them as he pressed and probed Sibyl's rib cage.[21] Mary managed to undergo ten lessons with Sbriglia, but could take no more.

Mathilde Marchesi was the next experiment. This seventy-five-year-old German contralto was a formidable lady with an international reputation as a teacher. She numbered many top divas amongst her pupils, including Sibyl Sanderson and the Australian Mrs Nellie Armstrong, later to become Nellie Melba. Mary and Mrs Duff were admitted into magnificent surroundings where Mary found Mme Marchesi 'an old, curt, haughty woman who came forward like an empress and just deigned to bow to you – almost didn't bow'. Marchesi's goal was to make a coloratura singer out of Mary, declaring, 'That is the only beautiful singing there is, young lady.' Having stayed with her new teacher for three weeks, Mary had had enough, and went on holiday with Mrs Duff, but six weeks later was persuaded to return to Marchesi for one more try. When she entered Marchesi's drawing room, she was greeted with the words, 'I've never seen you in my life, young lady. Who are you?' They arranged a date for a lesson the following week, but Mary wrote at once to cancel it. A few days later she received the cryptic reply: 'A rolling stone gathers no moss. Don't cry till you come out of the woods. Mathilde Marchesi.'[22]

Despite this inauspicious introduction, whatever Marchesi's attitude to the ambitious young lady, she was not sparing in her praise of Mary once she was established at the Opéra-Comique, for she was later to say, 'Of the Americans singing at the Comique she is the greatest.'[23]

Fortunately for Mary and Mrs Duff (and no doubt to the relief of Mary's sponsor, Mrs Mayer, who must have been wondering how her money was being spent), the next teacher they tried was a success. This was the Marquis

[21] Hansen, *The Sybil Sanderson Story*, p. 54.

[22] *Mary Garden's Story*, p. 16.

[23] William Armstrong, *The Romantic World of Music* (London, 1923), p. 128.

Ange-Pierre de Trabadelo,[24] an eccentric Spaniard, only five feet tall, who wore rouge to hide smallpox scars and a black wig to cover his bald head.[25] He too had become a teacher of Sibyl Sanderson in 1895, only a year before Mary's quest to find her ideal mentor. 'Sing for me in a normal, natural way, as if you were singing by yourself at home', he requested. With relief Mary turned to Mrs Duff saying, 'This is my teacher.' Mary felt reassured by Trabadelo's method of teaching as she practised many scales and also many roles in Italian. In an interview in which she described the exercises he gave her, she expressed appreciation of his demand that she should sing 'in a normal, natural way, not as a freak'.[26]

It was obvious that Mary needed to gain fluency in French, and fortunately she was able to move in with the family of Jean-Ferdinand Chaigneau, an artist of the Barbizon school, who lived in Clichy. There she lived for almost a year, dining with the parents and four children, speaking nothing but French.[27]

Towards the end of 1896 Mary at last met Sibyl Sanderson herself. This was not mere coincidence, for in fact, one of Sibyl's sisters, Marion, had met Mary's grandmother whilst visiting a friend in Aberdeen, and Mary was therefore armed with a useful letter of introduction.[28] Everybody raved about 'the incomparable Sibyl', as Albert Carré described her. He believed that Massenet (although married) was madly in love with her.[29] Not only his *Thaïs*, but previously *Esclarmonde*, had been composed especially for her to sing. The composer's possessive jealousy was said to be so great that whenever Sibyl disappeared behind the curtain of foliage covering the heroine and her operatic lover he would hide in the wings to spy on the couple to ensure they were not taking advantage of the situation! Carré claimed he would never forget her 'almost superhuman beauty' or her 'pure and limpid voice'. Mary also heard that at the sight of her 'there was a gasp of admiration from one end of the house to the other.'[30]

Mary later expressed strong views about Massenet, the composer who, it will be remembered, had also given Georgette Leblanc so much encouragement. 'I'm afraid I never cared for Massenet', she wrote. 'Massenet was the yes-man par excellence.' For Massenet, everything was 'All right, fine, perfect.'

---

[24] Also spelt Trabadello.

[25] Hansen, *The Sibyl Sanderson Story*, p. 258.

[26] Garden, 'The "Know How" in the Art of Singing', p. 439.

[27] *Mary Garden's Story*, p. 18.

[28] Jack Winsor Hansen: 'Mary Garden: Queen of Chutzpah', *Massenet Society Newsletter*, July 1990.

[29] Carré, *Souvenirs de théâtre*, p. 243.

[30] *Mary Garden's Story*, p. 24.

She found him gushing and hypocritical, paying people compliments to their face, but saying the opposite once their back was turned. His letters were 'dripping with the most sickening kind of sentiment ... He hadn't the genius of Debussy. Not by a long shot.'[31]

Sibyl's mother, Margaret, used to hold Sunday evening soirées. Mary was invited to one of these occasions when Saint-Saëns was also present. Both he and Massenet were charmed by her ebullient personality. A strong friendship grew between Sibyl and Mary, and as a result Mary was able to glean useful information about teachers and other contacts.

In Spring 1897 Sibyl invited Mary to see some of the gowns she had worn in Massenet's *Manon*, the operatic role which Carré regarded as her greatest triumph. From then on Mary was invited to Sibyl's house every Sunday, and often taken by Sibyl and her fiancé to the opera. By this time, however, Sibyl Sanderson was already passing the climax of her operatic career. The reason for this can partly be found in Carré's explanation: 'Unfortunately, in 1898, Sibyl Sanderson had just retired from the theatre at the height of her glory in order to marry one of her fellow countrymen, Mr. Terry.'[32] This is only half the story, for Antonio Terry was in fact from Cuba, and although legally separated, was having great difficulty in procuring a divorce from his strictly Catholic first wife. Massenet was so horrified that the Cuban sugar magnate should insist on his fiancée retiring from the stage, not only depriving him of his beloved protégée but also of the income that she brought him, that he is alleged to have concocted an evil plan. He introduced her to a certain lady whom he knew was a lesbian in the hopes that this would prevent her continuing her relationship with Antonio. Perhaps he already had some inkling that Sibyl might not be averse to sexual advances from Madame X, for, indeed, it is claimed that she did succumb whilst the worse for drink, but was horrified by her error and quickly ended this brief liaison.[33] Stories of her lesbianism, even of her soliciting women, never disappeared, and bear a certain relevance in the ensuing tale of Mary Garden. Sibyl's decline from glory was hastened by alcoholism, a vice shared by her fiancé, and frequent ill-health, not helped by a miscarriage shortly after her wedding in 1897. Whatever her own role in her own deterioration, it is a fact that, once again, the combination of the career of opera singer and marriage was discouraged by the men around her. This great opera singer was to die in 1903 at the age of only thirty-eight.

Finding the home of the Chaigneaus too far from her work, Mary moved

[31] *Mary Garden's Story*, p. 138.
[32] Carré, *Souvenirs de théâtre*, p. 243.
[33] Hansen, *The Sybil Sanderson Story*, p. 252.

into a *pension de famille* on the avenue Marceau, near the Arc de Triomphe. She retained fond memories of evenings spent with American students who also lodged there: Clarence Whitehill, the American bass-baritone, three years older than Mary, studying with Sbriglia, and Herbert Witherspoon, only one year older. To perfect her French, Mary entered the Yersin School. Her singing lessons continued. There is an undated and unidentified newspaper cutting in one of her scrapbooks entitled *A future star in Paris* which describes an occasion when Mr. Trabadelo presented some of his most promising singers to the Italian publisher, Mr Ricordi. This gentleman was particularly impressed by the timbre and richness of voice of one in particular, who was already being described as 'the future Patti', Miss Marie [*sic*] Garden. Mary declined Ricordi's tempting offer to sing a role at La Scala in Milan, saying she wished to complete her vocal education first.³⁴ Thus, in August 1898, following an introduction from Sibyl Sanderson, Mary also commenced studies with Lucien Fugère, a bass-baritone at the Opéra-Comique.

Mary always remained devoted to her family. Throughout her career her mother or one of her sisters was often by her side. In spring 1899 she and her mother were joined by a young man, Ed Mayer, a relative of her American sponsors. He took them out to restaurants, the theatre and the races, and clearly the enjoyment was mutual. However, the pleasure did not last for long. Someone must have reported these activities to the Mayers with a malicious twist, for back in Chicago rumours were received of scandal and impropriety. Once a month Mary used to go to the office of her sponsor's financial representative in Paris to collect her allowance, until one day the man looked at her coldly and said 'Miss Garden, there is no more money for you. Those are my orders.' She had no idea who or what had brought about this crisis. Could it have been someone in her group of male American friends at her lodgings, jealous of her talent and perhaps even a rejected suitor, who had told tales? After all, the informer must have been familiar with America and known how to contact her sponsor. Or was it that the Mayers suspected that Ed was becoming too close to Mary, not a desirable match, and wanted to distance her from him?

In a daze, Mary went to her teachers to inform them that she could no longer receive lessons from them unless she received credit, to which they instantly agreed, but she had problems raising money for her accommodation. It was not long before she had to pay up or move out, so leaving some possessions behind as security, she found a tiny room to lodge in. In her original typescript at this point, Mary has handwritten, 'Why I didn't

³⁴ RCM, London, Mary Garden Collection, album XI.

write home'. Frustratingly, the answer is not forthcoming.[35] Was it a matter of pride? In contradiction to this, she states in her *Story* that her father
did send her a little money, implying that he did know of her predicament.
Eventually, however, her lessons had to stop. Desperate letters to her sponsors bore no fruit. Despite trying to convince them of the sorry plight of an
attractive woman alone in Paris at the mercy of predatory males, no more
money was forthcoming.[36] That is not to say that Mary stopped seeing any
men, for she claims that a 'very rich count', whom she knew at this time of
crisis, wanted her to go with him to his château in the north of France. She
felt strongly tempted to go.[37]

Mary then persuaded the general manager of the Opéra-Comique, Émile
Bertin, to write to the Mayers, explaining how carefully her début had to be
timed and that her prospects were excellent. Eventually there was a knock
at her door. It was a woman sent by her sponsors in Chicago. At last she
could receive an explanation as to why her allowance had been stopped.
She was told they had been hearing stories about her private life, receiving
anonymous letters about her activities in Paris, where she had been doing
'Just about everything – except work ... They said you had lovers ... Also that
you had a child.' Mary always vehemently denied allegations that she bore a
child, but the rumour reaching the other side of the Atlantic in 1899 was still
to haunt her some ten years later, when the American press were greedy for
scandal concerning the newsworthy soprano.

Now, more desperate than ever, Mary left her room to walk through
the autumn leaves in the Bois de Boulogne. Penniless and distressed, she
recognised a lady walking her dogs but wearing deep mourning. It was Sibyl
Sanderson. Though Mary did not greet her, Sibyl turned, lifted her veil and
said: 'Why, Mary Garden! What are you doing out at this time of day?' On
seeing Mary's misery, Sibyl invited her into her waiting carriage where, overcome by this show of sympathy, Mary burst into tears and related the whole
story. 'You call that trouble?' was the response, for since Sibyl had last seen
Mary over a year previously she had experienced a series of tragedies culmi-
nating in the death of her new husband, Antonio, and besides calming her
nerves with alcohol, was suffering increasingly from an illness which would
prove to be fatal.

Sibyl provided a lifeline for the young bereft singer. Mary was immediately taken back to her flat at 104 Champs-Elysées, and the butler was sent
to her lodgings to pay off her rent and retrieve Mary's belongings. She was

---

[35] Typescript in RCM, London, Mary Garden Collection.
[36] Letters to F. Mayer at Chicago Historical Society.
[37] *Mary Garden's Story*, p. 20.

given the room belonging to Sibyl's stepdaughter, Natividad, known as Natica, who, when describing Mary later, said she was 'skinny as a reed'.[38]

What a blessing Mary's friendship with Sibyl was to prove. 'When I think of her it is as a sister who never failed me till the day she died. I have never known anyone with such a divine sense of loyalty.'[39] Not just friendship, but the vital link that was to lead Mary to the Opéra-Comique. Sibyl had not heard her sing for a while and on doing so now, suggested, 'Mary, how would you like to sing for Monsieur Carré?' She offered to invite the Director of the Opéra-Comique for dinner and let him discover Mary for himself.

In fact Carré dined at least three times at Sibyl's house that winter. Mary met more important people in Sibyl's home in five months, November 1899 to May 1900, than she had during the three previous years she lived in Paris. It seems inexplicable therefore that when the time came for Mary to perform a kindness to Sibyl it was not forthcoming. Perhaps one should be aware that Mary was now living with an alcoholic who suffered from severe bouts of depression and who was also gaining a reputation as a lesbian. How willing was she going to be at a later date, when her own name needed protection from unwanted scandal (as opposed to that which brought welcome publicity), to be linked in people's minds with such behaviour?

[38] Hansen, *The Sybil Sanderson Story*, p. 324.
[39] *Mary Garden's Story*, p. 24.

6 *Mary Garden's Breakthrough (1900–1902)*

*I*T IS AT THIS POINT that, unbeknown to either of them, the lives of
Mary Garden and Georgette Leblanc began to converge. In 1900 Mary
was inspired by the same actress Georgette had been so desperate to see that
she had escaped from Rouen to Paris to meet her. Mary went to see Sarah
Bernhardt acting in *L'Aiglon* by Edmond Rostand, a role in which trium-
phantly, at the age of fifty-six, Bernhardt played a boy barely past adolescence.
Many years later she was to stick a picture of Bernhardt in just this role into
one of her many scrapbooks.[1] Just as Georgette had experienced, she was able
to go backstage after the performance and found her surrounded by flowers
and people. Not surprisingly, Bernhardt, whose capacity to convey seductive sexuality in her roles was renowned, had a great influence over Mary's
style of acting, just as she did over Georgette's. Besides being received in
Bernhardt's own theatre, Le Théâtre Sarah Bernhardt, she was also invited to
Bernhardt's house. There she saw the immense drawing room which looked
down on to a court where Bernhardt kept her lion cubs, and the coffin in
which she famously used to take her repose.[2]

The inevitable link between Mary Garden and Georgette Leblanc, however, was the Opéra-Comique and the person there with the most influence, Albert Carré, who had been appointed its Director in January 1898.
As planned by Sibyl Sanderson, early in 1900 he was invited to dinner and
introduced to Mary. 'At table M. Carré looked at me through and through
till I was thoroughly embarrassed', writes Mary. 'You know that's a very
special kind of girl', was his judgement. 'I have a feeling she will make an
interesting Louise.'[3] Mary is usually accused of exaggeration in her memoirs
and interviews, but her account of this meeting does not stray far from the
truth, for Sibyl's sister Marion, who was also at the dinner, confirmed that
Carré kept his eyes on Mary for the rest of the evening. He told Mary he did
not have time to audition her at the moment, but that after the première of
Gustave Charpentier's *Louise* he wanted to hear her sing.[4]

Louise was of very personal significance for Carré, for it was the opera

---

[1] RCM, London, Mary Garden Collection, album XI.

[2] Typescript in RCM, London, Mary Garden Collection.

[3] *Mary Garden's Story*, p. 25.

[4] Hansen, *The Sybil Sanderson Story*, p. 324.

which he regarded as his own first contribution to his new régime at the Opéra-Comique.[5] Messager had brought Charpentier, a pupil of Massenet, to Carré's house where, on listening to the composer playing through his score at the piano, the music had made a direct emotional appeal, not just through the social drama of a young working girl, a seamstress, seduced by a young poet, but in its realistic depiction of everyday Parisian life. Carré was further delighted with his discovery of the young singer, Marthe Rioton, with whom he was preparing the role of Louise, having had to wait for her to finish her studies at the Conservatoire.

Sibyl arranged with Carré for Mary to visit the Opéra-Comique and watch a rehearsal of Charpentier's opera before Carré auditioned her formally. The effect on her was electric. 'We sat there, and I was just drunk, as if I had taken wine. As I listened to this magnificent music, I was in a dream.' From the moment she got hold of a score she studied it intensely every waking hour until she had every note and word in her 'mind and body.' At the weekend Natica, Sibyl's stepdaughter, would accompany her at the piano, and Sibyl herself gained some comfort from hearing the opera brought to life in her apartment.

At last Albert Carré sent a message to Mary, asking her to come and sing to him. She sang first 'Ah, fors è lui' from *La Traviata*, in French, then the Saint-Sulpice scene from Massenet's *Manon*. No sooner had she begun than Carré stopped her to ask what language she was singing in! 'He made me promise to correct my pronunciation', Mary remembered, but nevertheless he was impressed. Carré relates that the 'petite Écossaise' introduced to him by Sibyl Sanderson was a very young, very beautiful girl with 'a very charming voice' whom he engaged despite her strong British accent.[6]

There was no role vacant at that time, but he wanted Mary to accept a contract dated the following October, beginning with a salary of 250 francs. She was overjoyed to have achieved this accolade and, since this opened the door for her to attend all rehearsals and performances, she studied *Louise* even more assiduously. The première of the opera took place on 2 February 1900. On Tuesday 10 April one of those golden opportunities occurred that all young hopefuls in the music world dream of: the leading singer fell ill. Rioton warned Carré before the evening performance that she might not be able to sing the whole work. Her official understudy was also indisposed. Immediately Carré's thoughts turned to the young Scottish girl whom he knew had spent so many hours observing and learning the part. Mary was instructed to attend the performance that night dressed in costume and

[5] Carré, *Souvenirs de théâtre*, p. 252.
[6] Carré, *Souvenirs de théâtre*, p. 256.

made up ready to take over at a moment's notice. Rioton managed to get through two acts, but during the next interval panicked when she felt her throat constrict and ran out of the theatre, not to return. Mary received the sign from the stage manager.

'I was taken behind the curtain on the stage of the Opéra-Comique. Never in my life have I seen such absolute confusion.' Out of the chaos stepped Albert Carré. 'Eh bien, ma petite Garden, can you finish *Louise* for me tonight?' 'Certainly, M. Carré', was her calm reply.

Mary claims in her *Story* that the conductor, Messager, was so horrified at the whole idea of an unknown taking over that he exclaimed 'Give them back their money!' It was her teacher, Fugère, who was given the task of announcing the substitution to the audience. He, incidentally, was singing the part of le Père in the opera.

'I wasn't a bit nervous. I have never been nervous in all my life and I have no patience with people who are', wrote Mary. 'If you know what you are going to do, you have no reason to be nervous. And I knew what I was going to do.'[7]

Carré was entranced. As the curtain rose, everyone in the wings strained forward anxiously to watch the 'little Scottish girl' walk forward and sing Louise's great aria with great self-assurance, in such a pure voice and with such depth of feeling that loud cheering broke out for several minutes from the whole auditorium and even from the orchestral pit.[8] Mary wrote:

> After the third act, I remember Messager made the whole orchestra stand up in recognition of what I had done ... and by then everybody in the audience was asking: 'Who is she? Where does she come from?' ... There were curtain calls and curtain calls, and they all shouted and threw their programs and little roses, and handkerchiefs on the stage.[9]

Sibyl Sanderson's sister Marion described it as 'an unheard of thing to do and she did it magnificently!' She also commented on Mary's dreadful Scottish accent![10]

The newspaper reviews were full of praise for the newcomer for her performance on that auspicious night. How typical of Mary that she should insist in her *Story* that these fateful events took place on Friday 13 April and that the seat she was allocated in the auditorium during her wait to be called was number 113! How typical, too, that she should want to impress on her readers her sang-froid. When 'everybody began writing and talking about

[7] *Mary Garden's Story*, p. 32.
[8] Carré, *Souvenirs de théâtre*, p. 256.
[9] *Mary Garden's Story*, p. 33.
[10] Hansen, *The Sybil Sanderson Story*, p. 328.

me, and I found myself *the* person of Paris', she claims it had no effect on her. It did not change her one bit. 'I didn't become pompous or arrogant. My way of living was that way at the beginning, and it is that way now – simple.'[11]

Whilst this can hardly be an honest description of Mary's lifestyle a few years after *Louise*, it has to be said that her living conditions not long after her début were sparse. Her friend and mentor Sibyl Sanderson was advised to move to Nice for the sake of her health, for, apart from her advancing illness, manic depression and alcoholism, she was probably taking drugs to cope with her symptoms. Before she closed up her flat and left for the south, she was considerate and generous enough to pay six months rent in advance on Mary's room back in the rue Chalgrin where she could keep her piano as well as her bed, wash-stand, writing table and clothes.

How Mary rewrote history in her *Story*! 'Mlle Rioton never sang Louise again at the Opéra-Comique. The role became exclusively mine', she claimed.[12] In fact Mary did not perform the complete role from beginning to end until the end of April, for Rioton recovered sufficiently to sing it again as soon as the following week. Albert Carré blames himself for Marthe Rioton's eventual departure from the Opéra-Comique. One day when she wanted to view a performance from the auditorium he found her a seat which by chance was next to that of a young man who had adoringly watched her every time she had appeared on stage. The inevitable happened, and she eventually asked for the two remaining years of her contract to be cancelled, for the family into which she was to marry insisted that she renounce the theatre.[13]

Amongst Mary's mementos is a card of the seaside on which Gustave Charpentier, composer of *Louise*, told Mary of his appreciation of her performances: 'Gracieuse interprète, actrice merveilleuse, divine chanteuse – la mer me donne de l'éloquence! Je travaille et je pense souvent à vous!'[14]

In June 1900 Mary began rehearsals for *La Marseillaise*, an opera by Lucien Lambert about Rouget de Lisle who wrote the French national anthem. This only survived for three performances, perhaps justifiably, for it must have been rather ridiculous to hear Mary, as de Lisle's fiancée, suddenly stand up from the piano where she was accompanying the song and declaim with aplomb in her foreign accent: 'Je suis française!' No wonder everybody laughed.

[11] *Mary Garden's Story*, p. 33.

[12] *Mary Garden's Story*, p. 35.

[13] Carré, *Souvenirs de théâtre*, p. 234.

[14] 'Gracious interpreter, marvellous actress, divine singer – the sea is lending me eloquence! I am working and I often think of you!' Undated card in RCM, London, Mary Garden Collection, album x.

Mary's notebooks emphasise her determination never to marry and have
to give up the stage. As she wrote, 'I could not have two careers, as I hear marriage is *quite* a career. Taking care of your husband – sometimes that must be
quite a task.'[15] However, she is proud to demonstrate time and again that this
was not through any lack of opportunity. Neither was there any shortage of
drama. There was the tale of a young doctor who wanted to marry her and
duly informed his father of this. The match was regarded as totally unaccept-
able for a professional male, as the doctor's father explained to Mary in no
uncertain terms. She declared she had no intention of marrying his son, and
relates that in his despair her thwarted lover shot himself (not fatally). She
never saw him again, but when one of her sisters once visited his house she
found it adorned with pictures of Mary.[16]

Mary's first real close relationship was much nearer to her musical home
and with a man far older than she was. André Messager, who had conducted
her through that first appearance as Louise and all her performances since,
had fallen in love with her. Not only was there an age difference,[17] he had
been married to his second wife, the Irish composer, Hope Temple, since
1896 and had an eighteen-year-old son by his previous wife. Mary's tone was
honest when she later wrote: 'Our great love for Charpentier's opera had
brought us close together, and I suppose I was dazzled by the fact that a man
of his position in the world should be taking a fancy to me.'[18]

During the summer months of 1901, when the Opéra-Comique was
closed, Mary went to Aix-les-Bains to sing at the Casino. Here she sang *Thaïs*
for the first time, a role for which she was coached by Sibyl Sanderson, who
had created it for Massenet in 1894. Mary was able to stay with Sibyl who
was renting a chateau at Aix. When she saw her in rehearsal, with typical
generosity, the older women exclaimed: '*Thaïs* must have pearls.' And she
threw around Mary's neck her own precious, priceless pearls.

Whilst in Aix Mary received a note from Messager saying he was going to
drop in on her. In the French version of her memoirs, Mary relates that his
note implied he would stay for a couple of hours. Their relationship, however, was to last for two years. 'He was completely carried away. Me too', she
wrote.[19] In both versions she describes him as 'charming' and insists there
was no thought of *grande passion* or marriage. 'I liked him and he liked me,
that's all.' In the French version there is an extra sentence: 'Incidentally, I was

[15] Notebook in RCM, London, Mary Garden Collection.
[16] *Mary Garden's Story*, p. 39.
[17] Messager, 1853–1929.
[18] *Mary Garden's Story*, p. 43.
[19] 'Il était très emballé. Moi aussi.' Garden, *L'Envers du décor*, p. 63.

very friendly with his wife. It is normal to become the mistress of a friend's husband. It is shocking to marry him.'[20] She absolutely insists, however, that she never loved him: 'I was enchanted perhaps, but never really in love.' She is adamant that she always knew what she was doing, with Messager and with those who came later. Never did she succumb to 'that mad passion, where you say mad things and sometimes do them.'[21]

Mary dwelt with particular affection on one afternoon when Messager and she went to the top of nearby Mont Revard. There, in a lovely house perched high on the hillside, they discovered a copy of the magazine *L'Illustration*. It contained a copy of Debussy's song *Extase*,[22] which excited both of them. Surely she is elaborating upon the truth when she describes a subsequent conversation with Lilly Debussy in which Debussy's first wife claimed that it was on seeing this particular song in the magazine that she had felt she had to meet Debussy. Mary assured her that in her own case she had fallen in love with the music, but not with Debussy, the man.

Mary made another conquest in Aix. In the audience was King George I of Greece, who assured her that *Thaïs* would become one of the greatest operatic successes in the world. He invited her to sing the role in Athens, an event never to materialise. She was even on the same train as the king travelling back to Paris at the end of August.[23] Their paths were to cross several times from 1901 onwards.

'And so it went', wrote Mary.[24] 'There was nothing in my life but work, work, work – and André Messager. I was at the theatre almost every day.' The dichotomy that dictated the path of Mary's life and which had to be dealt with by each of the women desperate to fulfil her ambition to sing a major role in opera was ever present in their formative days: they worked and worked, practised their hearts out, looked after their appearance, their figures, their hair. They were necessarily extremely attractive women who were enormously talented. The music they sang was emotionally charged, the roles they were singing and seeking to perform concerned women at the mercy of powerful men. And who was it who allocated the desired prizes? None other than the director, the conductor, men who had it in their power to grant their dearest wish. The influence they exerted professionally could be used as blackmail to achieve their sexual desires. If the woman did not agree to meet the manager's demands he might not agree to cast her in a role

[20] 'Au demeurant, j'étais très liée avec sa femme. Il est normal de devenir la maîtresse du mari d'une amie, il est choquant de l'épouser.' Garden, *L'Envers du décor*, p. 64.

[21] *Mary Garden's Story*, p. 43.

[22] 'C'est l'extase langoureuse': the first of the *Ariettes oubliées* published 1885–7.

[23] Turnbull, *Mary Garden*, p. 29.

[24] *Mary Garden's Story*, p. 46.

for which she had been striving for years. Then, once she had succumbed (or even if she had not), she would be denounced as a mere singer, not worthy of marriage to any man with professional aspirations and certainly with no brain worth respecting.

Mary Garden often asserted that no relationships with the men who were in control of the roles she sang were meaningful to her, indeed that men were unimportant to her emotional fulfilment and she required no more than their friendship. It is, however, impossible to believe that Messager's desires were not reciprocated when they travelled and spent time together. But what about the Director of the Opéra-Comique, Albert Carré? One day he called her to his office and stated: 'Mary, you know that I am a free man again.'[25]

'Yes, M. Carré.'

'Will you be my wife?'

True to her resolution, Mary assured Carré that she was fond of him but never intended to get married. To reinforce her stance she had to inform him that: 'There is someone else in my life ... André Messager.' Carré was not to be put off, and wrote to Mary, asking her to change her mind and marry him. Mary wrote back boldly underlining the statement that she was in love with Messager. On commenting on her action in her *Story*, she is amazed at her audacity: 'When I think of it, the nerve I had at the beginning of my career, defying the man who could break it so easily!' How quickly all that young promise and hope could have been dashed. She was summoned to Carré's office. He waved her letter furiously, pulled open a drawer of his desk, took out her contract and tore it up violently, flinging the pieces into the wastepaper basket. He was finished with her. 'Now you can do what you like and go where you like and with whom you like!', he shouted.

Recalling her situation later, Mary expressed her great regret at so upsetting the man who had provided her with her first big break, but in the circumstances she had no other option than to leave the Opéra-Comique. Fortunately she had recently received an offer to create *Louise* in Italian at La Scala in Milan, a request which had come originally from Guilio Gatti-Casazza, later to become Director of the Metropolitan Opera House in New York. This she now accepted, but when she informed Carré of this turn of events, he soon sent for her. Now he was calm and smiling. He even put his arm around her as he said, 'Sign that!' – a new contract. 'M. Carré became one of my greatest artistic friends', she writes. But one wonders how true this statement was. Did he ever really forgive her relationship with Messager?

---

[25] Carré was divorcing his third wife, Madeleine Verneuil. Carré, *Souvenirs de théâtre*, p. 180.

In view of her position later at the Opéra-Comique it is a legitimate question.

What sort of relationship did Mary have with Messager? After a while it was certainly anything but smooth. Her account of his character is in distinct contrast to that described by his biographer, Henry Février, and the convivial portrait drawn by Albert Carré. According to Mary, the conductor had a violent temper. 'For no reason at all he would say the most savage things to me.' Besides being vindictive and rude to Mary, he was 'jealous, frightfully jealous'. There was a nineteen-year age gap between them. Mary was young and beautiful. He always tried to dominate her. 'All the men in my life were jealous, but perhaps Messager was the meanest of them all in his jealousy', Mary wrote. After two years of this turbulent liaison he came to her apartment one day and took out of his pocket a huge roll of money. He flung it at her and shouted, 'This is for you!' Mary took the money and threw it right back in his face, crying 'You get out of my house!'[26]

It is all very well to dismiss Mary's *Story* as wishful thinking and fanciful embroidery of the facts, but there is something sincere about her self-pity when she says: 'That man just broke me, trying to dominate me all the time, saying wretched things to me.' One day she saw him coming towards her door, and was literally nauseated at the thought of his being there in her apartment with her again. She ordered her maid to tell him she was out, feeling she had been humiliated more than any woman had a right to be. Physically and mentally he was destroying her. Messager knew that she was really at home and had to accept that the affair was over. But what must it have been like from then on to see each other and work together as artistic colleagues? They certainly coped, for later, looking back, Mary was to write, 'We quarrelled and quarrelled, but our friendship was too strongly rooted to be ever really broken.'[27]

In 1901 Mary sang *La Fille de Tabarin* by Gabriel Pierné. As Albert Carré points out, this was the first meeting of the future Pelléas, Jean Périer, with the future Mélisande.[28] She also continued to give performances of *Louise*, sang in *Manon* and was still on very good terms with André Messager when she performed in his opera *Madame Chrysanthème* in Monte Carlo in December 1901, with the composer conducting,[29] receiving excellent reviews.

In May of that very year Messager persuaded Albert Carré to listen to

[26] *Mary Garden's Story*, p. 52.

[27] Typescript in RCM, London, Mary Garden Collection.

[28] Carré, *Souvenirs de théâtre*, p. 261.

[29] See illus.9.

Debussy playing his *Pelléas et Mélisande*. Mary and the other selected singers were invited to Messager's home on the boulevard Malesherbes, where she was assigned to read the role of Mélisande, knowing nothing about it. She did not know what was about to overwhelm her:

> We were only there a short while when the door opened and in came Debussy. We were all presented to him, and he spoke the usual words of greeting. Without another word, he sat at the piano and played and sang the whole thing from beginning to end.
>
> There we sat in the drawing room – M. Carré, and M. and Mme Messager and the whole cast – each of us with a score, heads bowed as if we were all at prayer. While Debussy played I had the most extraordinary emotions I have ever experienced in my life. Listening to that music I seemed to become someone else, someone inside of me whose language and soul were akin to mine. When Debussy got to the fourth act I could no longer look at my score for the tears. It was all very strange and unbearable. I closed my book and just listened to him, and as he played the death of Mélisande, I burst into the most awful sobbing, and Mme Messager began to sob along with me, and both of us fled into the next room. I shall never forget it. There we were crying as if we had just lost our best friend, crying as if nothing would console us again.
>
> Mme Messager and I returned to the drawing room just as Debussy stopped. Before anyone could say or do anything, he faced us all and said: 'Mesdames et messieurs, that is my *Pelléas et Mélisande*. Everyone must forget that he is a singer before he can sing the music of Debussy. Oubliez, je vous prie, que vous êtes chanteurs!' Then he murmured a quick 'Au revoir' and, without another word, was gone.[30]

Carré relates how Mary first had to rehearse with the repetiteur Louis Landry before her work with Messager.[31] As she began studying her role intensely she found she had to work her way into Debussy's idiom, but it became easier as she progressed through the acts. By the time she came to practise the death of Mélisande, 'I discovered I had absolutely nothing to study. I just knew it. How, I haven't the slightest idea.'[32]

She explains this ability to enter the heart of a role by describing it as a psychic experience:

> There was nothing for me to study at Mélisande's death. Why? Because, I suppose I just died ... I never saw where Salomé lived. I never was with that great dancer of Egypt, Thaïs, but I knew her. I knew them all. That sort of thing was always happening to me – the feeling of being someone else and having been somewhere else. I never knew anything about the lives of these women of

[30] *Mary Garden's Story*, pp. 61–2.
[31] Carré, *Souvenirs de théâtre*, p. 279.
[32] *Mary Garden's Story*, p. 63.

opera. I had them all in me, in my very flesh and blood ... Was it a sixth sense? Maybe. I just don't know.[33]

Then came the day when Carré invited Debussy to hear the cast individually. He led the composer to a small rehearsal room and left each singer alone with him. Mary never forgot the experience:

> Without any preliminary chatter, except a quick exchange of 'How do you do's' we began. I opened my score, and Debussy sat down at the piano. We did the first act, Debussy singing the role of Golaud. His voice was very small and husky ... Debussy was a magnificent pianist. So there he sat, singing the part of Golaud, playing the piano and never saying a single word. When we came to Pelléas, he sang that too, and all the other roles as well, except mine. Then we came to the scene of the Tower. I was singing my lines when, without a word, he got up abruptly and left the room. I stayed there a while and waited, quite bewildered. I had a feeling I had offended him in some mysterious way and I began to prepare myself for the shock of not singing Mélisande.[34]

Mary was about to leave the rehearsal room when a boy came in to summon her to Carré's office. Albert Carré takes up the tale from that moment onwards.

Debussy had rushed into his office, quite overcome. 'Where does that woman come from?', he asked. Carré replied, 'I think she was born in the north of Scotland.' 'That's her! ... *C'est ma Mélisande!*' exclaimed Debussy.

Carré called in Mary who was fretting outside, thinking she had displeased him. When she entered the room, covered in confusion, Debussy walked towards her, took her hands in his and said, his voice choking: 'You have come from the mists of the north to create my music. I feel now that you alone can be my Mélisande.'[35]

These were the first words Debussy spoke to her, for 'the bear', as Carré described him, had been listening to her for an hour, his head in his hands, without uttering a word and had dashed out like lightning after the last note.

Now Debussy had made up his mind that Mary Garden and not Georgette Leblanc should create the role. According to Mary, he turned to Carré and said: 'Je n'ai rien à lui dire.'[36] He paused, as if embarrassed, and still looking at M. Carré added, 'What a strange person, this child!' 'With that', continues Mary,

> he fell silent, in that curious detached way of his, took his hat, and mumbling

---

[33] *Mary Garden's Story*, pp. 63–4.

[34] *Mary Garden's Story*, pp. 66–7.

[35] 'Vous êtes venue de ces brumes du nord pour créer ma musique. Je sens maintenant que vous seule pouviez être ma Mélisande.' Carré, *Souvenirs de théâtre*, p. 279.

[36] 'I have nothing to tell her'.

a 'good-bye' walked out of M. Carré's office. Debussy was always doing that –
suddenly walking out. He walked out of Lily [*sic*] Debussy's life that way, he
walked out of mine, and he even walked out of Mélisande's. When he was
finished, he was finished.[37]

Rehearsals went on for four months, every afternoon except Sunday,
beginning on 13 January 1902. On 21 January Debussy heard Mary again,
and, despite the physical threat he had received from Maeterlinck, was resolute that she should have the role. According to Mary, when Maeterlinck,
still determined to have his way, made the announcement: 'I don't wish Miss
Garden to sing Mélisande!' Debussy himself faced him to say, quite firmly:
'You are mistaken, Monsieur. It is Miss Garden who will create Mélisande,
my Mélisande.'[38] To settle the matter, Debussy called together a jury of musicians and they heard Georgette sing an act of the opera. They decided quickly
that Mary should continue with the role and from that day on, Maeterlinck
only ever attended one rehearsal, that on 19 March.[39] Why he was there we
shall never know.

Fortunately, Mary became good friends, 'inseparable friends', she wrote,
not just with Debussy, but also with his wife, Lilly. They often dined together,
at least twice a week, on Tuesdays and Fridays,[40] at Mary's apartment on the
rue Washington which she had recently moved into – tiny, but quite charming, as she described it.

> I was getting sixteen hundred francs a month, and that was a good deal of
> money for me – and it would have been even more for Debussy, who never
> had any. Debussy loved good eating, and he adored everything that was rich
> and flavoursome. He also secretly loved sumptuous and luxurious things. In
> his craving for things, he had the most extravagant brain I had ever known.
> But he could never do what he wanted and he never could buy what he wanted
> because he hadn't the money.[41]

These recollections of Debussy's taste for the finer things and luxury
foods are corroborated by many others. She also remembered his dislike
of walking, for at least once he arrived at her flat before Lilly, having taken
a carriage, leaving his wife to make her way on foot. Indeed, he never followed doctor's orders to take more exercise, a fact which may have exacerbated the illness which eventually led to his death.[42] Whatever else Mary

---

37 *Mary Garden's Story*, p. 67.

38 *Mary Garden's Story*, p. 69.

39 See Chapter 4, p. 63.

40 Notebook in RCM, London, Mary Garden Collection.

41 *Mary Garden's Story*, p. 74.

42 Inghelbrecht, *Claude Debussy*, p. 240.

may have exaggerated, her feelings for Debussy seem to be told as they were, and her early memories of him are reported fondly and without too much elaboration.

After dinner Mary and Lilly would sit and chat whilst Debussy sat at the piano and improvised. Mary treasured those hours:

> I have never heard such music in my life, such music as came from the piano at those moments. My God, how beautiful it was, and haunting, and nobody but Lily [*sic*] and I ever heard it! Debussy never put those improvisations down on paper; they went back to the strange place they had come from, never to return. That precious music, lost forever, was unlike anything Debussy ever published. There was a quality of its own about it, remote, other-worldly, always saying something on the verge of words.[43]

When she had to miss a couple of rehearsals on 24 and 25 January because of illness, already the composer was concerned for her well-being, writing to her from the Café Riche, near the Opéra-Comique:

> My dear little Mélisande, I have learnt that you are ill and that pains me (as I hope you believe). I wanted very much to ask you if you would work on Friday, but I don't dare to now and so we will have to agree to meet for *Pelléas* on Saturday.

Signing off, he included Lilly: 'With tender affection from your two little friends, Claude Debussy.'[44]

There was no understudy, but Mary quickly recovered from her slight illness and maintained her rigorous régime of rehearsals. At last Mélisande was ready to be brought to life.

[43] *Mary Garden's Story*, p. 75.
[44] Original letter in RCM, London, Mary Garden Collection. See illus.10.

7 Preparations for Performance of Pelléas et Mélisande (1902)

$\mathcal{M}$ARY GARDEN was to embody Mélisande's fragile mystique, her foreign accent lending a certain authenticity to the stranger of unknown origin landing in the kingdom of Allemonde. Pelléas was to be sung by Jean Périer. Just as he had been more concerned about Mélisande's looks than her voice, Albert Carré wrote: 'I thought that it wasn't so much the voice which mattered for this role as much as acting ability and physical appearance. With his tall, slim build, his beautiful sad gaze, Jean Périer seemed to me to be the personification of Pelléas.'[1] Hector Dufranne[2] was Golaud, and Félix Vieuille (with whom Mary had also performed in *Louise*) was Arkel. Jeanne Gerville-Réache sang Geneviève. Carré had first employed her in the eponymous role of Orphée in 1899 and he commented on this niece of a member of Parliament (*député*) that he wished all those singers whom he had had to take on at the request of politicians were so worth while.[3] A boy called Blondin was little Yniold.

When rehearsals began on Monday 13 January 1902, Carré had to put up with grumblings from all the cast except the two main characters: 'My other interpreters had hardly any confidence in the new work, which they found very disconcerting, with its long recitatives and absence of any great arias. 'They will make us rehearse for three months but it will only run for three days', muttered the singers.'[4] Yet Messager wrote: 'As the weeks went by, rehearsals progressed with growing zeal and enthusiasm; each scene was repeated twenty times without any of the interpreters becoming impatient with the demands of the composer, which were very difficult to satisfy.'[5] To cap it all, as Robert Godet remarked, Debussy had all the orchestration in his head, but it was getting it down in black and white that was the problem,[6] for there was as yet no full printed orchestral score in existence. Messager had to harass him continually and threaten to down his baton altogether if he did not get the manuscript to him in time. It arrived page

---

[1] Carré, *Souvenirs de théâtre*, p. 280.

[2] Spelt 'Dufrane' in the programme of the opera.

[3] Carré, *Souvenirs de théâtre*, p. 249.

[4] Carré, *Souvenirs de théâtre*, p. 280.

[5] Messager, 'Les premières représentations de Pelléas', p. 111.

[6] 'Il portait l'orchestre dans sa tête; mais encore lui restait-il à en établir, noir sur blanc, le texte complet et définitif.' Godet, 'En marge de la marge'.

by page. The handwritten orchestral manuscript bears many corrections, in particular Debussy's own and Messager's annotations.[7] 'No one will ever know how much work Messager put into bringing the masterpiece to life, spending night after night with Debussy correcting orchestral parts', commented Henry Février, Messager's biographer.[8] When the musicians started to play, not only did they find the music different from anything they had performed previously, sometimes even incomprehensible. The situation was exacerbated by the numerous mistakes in their parts. Poor Debussy had had 'the generous and unfortunate idea'[9] of giving the task of copying them to a young neighbour in the rue Cardinet, who was 'more devoted than competent', wrote Maurice Emmanuel.[10] According to Godet, he was a piano pupil who used to reel off his scales on the floor above, whilst a young girl practised her trills on the floor below.[11] This incompetent copyist forgot to insert time changes when writing in the silent bars for each instrument. Not only that, when questions were raining down on the composer: 'Is this a sharp here, is that a flat there?', he sometimes replied, 'I don't really know!' Debussy had to ask Godet to take over the corrections. One wonders what the leader of the viola section had to say, for this was Pierre Monteux, later to become a world famous conductor. Messager expressed his admiration of the orchestral musicians for their patience and good will and was impressed that they showed due deference to the composer.[12] Louis Laloy, however, was passing a pavement café one day with a friend who noticed one of the orchestral musicians, hunched over his glass of beer. When asked why he was looking so depressed, the answer was, 'The *Pelléas* rehearsals are a scandal. The orchestra is refusing to play.' When this was passed on to Debussy, he did not appear surprised. 'Hateful brute!', was his response. He threw away his cigarette and changed the subject.[13] As Laloy points out, however, the notoriously conservative musicians were having to come to terms with an extremely innovative score, which contained no big instrumental solos such as the *Méditation* in *Thaïs*. Far from giving them an opportunity for their own moment of glory, there was even a whole scene (Act III scene 2, in the vaults) where the violins did not play at all.

[7] For details, see O. d'Estrade-Guerra, 'Les Manuscrits de *Pelléas et Mélisande* de Claude Debussy', *La Revue musicale*, Carnet critique no. 235 (1957).

[8] Henry Février, *André Messager: mon maître, mon ami* (Paris, 1948), p. 104.

[9] 'la généreuse et malencontreuse idée': Messager, 'Les premières représentations de Pelléas', p. 111.

[10] Emmanuel, *Pelléas et Mélisande de Debussy*, p. 45.

[11] Godet, 'En marge de la marge', p. 82.

[12] Messager, 'Les premières représentations de Pelléas', p. 111.

[13] 'Une brute haineuse': Louis Laloy, *La Musique retrouvée, 1902–1927* (Paris, 1928), p. 95.

It was not long before the majority of the musicians fell under the spell of the colours and harmonies of the new language. Those who still resisted had no option other than to submit to the hard work of familiarising themselves with it, and gradually the score became comprehensible to all. Hostility, lack of understanding, turned into enthusiasm, and one day a trombonist, Potier, said to Messager: 'The brass doesn't have much to do in this score. But what we do play is amazing! When Arkel sings: "If I were God I would have pity on the hearts of men", I don't know what it sounds like from your podium, but where we are it's simply beautiful.' There is an echo of this statement in the appreciative review of the opera by Louis Schneider. As he says, Debussy hardly uses the trombone, but when he does, 'in this ashen atmosphere, the trombone sounds like thunder'.[14]

There were over sixty rehearsals which took place almost daily from January to April with various combinations of singers and players. By the middle of March the scenery for the forest and the room in the castle had been tried on stage and at the end of the month the vaults and the grotto were tested. A full costume rehearsal took place on 11 April, and on 14 April all scenery, lighting, props, curtains, were run through. Mary must have been exhilarated – or exhausted, for despite rehearsing Mélisande daily, at night she still had to appear as Louise and Manon several times between January and March, until on 2 April Sibyl Sanderson took over as Manon. On the one and only occasion Maeterlinck turned up to watch a rehearsal, on 19 March, Mary was singing Manon that very night! Maeterlinck saw Act I, most of Act II and Act III of *Pelléas*, first with orchestra alone then with orchestra and singers.[15]

The scenery was painted by Jusseaume and Ronsin. Mary would have been very familiar with the style of the former, who had already been employed at the Opéra-Comique for four years, for he had painted the sets for *Louise*, *Grisélidis* and *Manon*. He was well known for his landscapes, and painted the forest in the first act, the park with the well and Golaud's room, whilst Ronsin painted the gallery, the terrace, the tower and the cave.[16] Albert Carré claims to have been very influential in determining the design. In his *Souvenirs* he recalls his family's holidays in Lichtental, a village near Baden-Baden, where his father had opened a branch of his business. Here the medieval fountain near the chapel of Saint Lendolin remained forever imprinted on young Albert's mind, and he claimed it was this scene, hardly

14 'Dans cette atmosphère cendrée le trombone fait l'effet d'un tonnerre.' *La Revue musicale,* May 1902, p. 199.

15 Register (livre de bord) of rehearsals at Opéra Comique held at Bibliothèque de l'Opéra, Paris.

16 Emmanuel, *Pelléas et Mélisande de Debussy*, p. 49.

altered at all, which became one of the most beautiful pieces of scenery in *Pelléas et Mélisande*.[17] Carré insists that Debussy himself was not just a musician, but also a poet who was just as sensitive to lines and colours as to sounds and words. Nothing concerning the décor was done without his wishes being regarded or his agreement.[18] In fact Debussy was delighted, and even sketched his favourite scene for René Peter, the old castle surrounded by woodland, on which he wrote the words 'tour' (tower) and 'tilleul' (lime tree).[19]

The sets were romantic paintings of shimmering water reflecting tall fir trees reaching high into the sky, castle towers appearing to right or left. Ronsin's tower had medieval casement windows, their lattices covered in creeper and roses. A gnarled lime tree shaded the low stone well in Act II. The reviewer in *Les Annales du théâtre et de la musique* adored the 'veritable masterpieces of Jusseaume and Ronsin representing forests with dense foliage, old gothic castles with crenelated towers, the horizon over the sea with its changing tonalities. It will be a long time before we forget the lake with its sleeping, deep water and reflections of the shadows of great poplars.'[20] Émile Henriot wrote: 'For the first time, shades, outlines, the play of light were intentionally placed at the service of the new work. For the first time not just the musician and poet but the designer created a work of art himself.' He believed that one of the most influential factors helping to win over the initially hostile audience was the 'close attention to the production, this series of perfect mistily poetic tableaux by a designer who dared both to be an artist and to take the work itself into account whilst painting the backdrops.'[21] Victor Debay was enchanted with the russet and golden colours of the forest, the tree trunks dotted with green moss, the ivy covered tower, the reflections of stars in the pools in the park,[22] whilst another critic, Auguste Mangeot, found the scenery even more beautiful and truer than nature.[23]

However, during rehearsals it was found that more time was needed for scene changes. Messager described the problem: 'The stage of the Opéra-Comique looks quite large, but the headroom is so inadequate and the wings are so narrow that it's impossible to manœuvre even a flat through

[17] Carré, *Souvenirs de théâtre*, p. 10.

[18] Carré, *Souvenirs de théâtre*, p. 277. However, Debussy later disliked it, finding it too sugary, wrote Charles Koechlin, '*Pelléas et Mélisande*, étude de Charles Koechlin', ed. Aude Caillet, *Cahiers Debussy*, nos. 27–8 (2003–4), p. 36.

[19] André Gauthier, *Debussy: Documents iconographiques* (Geneva, 1952), plate 82.

[20] *Les Annales du théâtre et de la musique* (1903), p. 103.

[21] Gauthier, *Debussy: Documents iconographiques*, plate 74.

[22] *Le Courier musical*, 15 May 1902, pp. 145–7.

[23] *Le Monde musical*, 15 May 1902.

them and we were having to make on average three quick scene changes per act!' Debussy's music linking the tableaux was far too short, so he had to set to work again. Messager had to face the composer's grumbling and cursing when he fetched the pages from him that he had written between one rehearsal and the next.[24]

These interludes composed at such short notice certainly give the lie to those who claim that Debussy was a slow composer. Albert Carré's opinion was that they were 'veritable symphonic jewels and it must be acknowledged that someone who could dream them up and orchestrate them in such a short time was certainly not a musician lacking in imagination or short of ideas.'[25] Mary Garden recalled how 'Debussy was always making changes in those interludes, and I remember that while they were being rehearsed none of us was permitted to talk or move.'[26] To the listener, the only sign that they were composed at such speed is that they contain the most Wagnerian elements of the opera. The symphonic orchestration and rich imposing harmony of the first interlude at the end of Act I scene 1 could almost come from *Parsifal*, despite Debussy's diatribes against its composer, showing the extent to which he had, after all, assimilated the sounds and idiom of music he had so admired in his youth.

The costumes were designed by Bianchini, another regular employee of the Opéra-Comique and familiar to Mary from *Louise*. Their descriptions and cost are listed in a volume preserved at the Bibliothèque de l'Opéra in Paris. All were new, except for the dress which Mélisande wore in Act I when Golaud discovered her, which had previously been used in *Esclarmonde*, perhaps because this blue brocade silk was to be dirty and ragged. To go with it was a crêpe de chine top printed with dark grey squares sprinkled with sequins. The sleeves were grey muslin. Her belt and neckline were silver with red stones. The shoes were blue satin. Her second costume was sea-green ('vert d'eau') crêpe de chine embroidered with mauve silk, the jersey silk sleeves decorated with coloured stones, and covered with a layer of muslin. In her hair she wore a twist of mauve velvet decorated with coloured studs. At her neck was a brooch and around her waist a belt of many flowers. The third dress was lavender crêpe de chine with a pleated skirt and embossed velvet top, worn with lavender satin shoes. With this went a brooch and belt of old silver set with amethysts. For the death scene she wore a white chemise with lace inserts.

[24] Messager, 'Les premières représentations de Pelléas', p. 111.

[25] 'Ce sont tous de véritables bijoux symphoniques et l'on conviendra que celui qui, en si peu de temps, les imagina et les instrumenta, n'était pas un musicien dépourvu d'imagination et à court d'idées.' Peter, *Claude Debussy*, p. 194.

[26] *Mary Garden's Story*, p. 68.

Mary paid particular attention to her hair, for:

> I was shown the wigs that the Opéra-Comique had ready for me and I knew at once they weren't the hair of Mélisande. So I sent my coiffeur to Brittany to buy up real hair ... and he got it from the girls of Brittany, the lovely daughters of the *paysans*. The whole thing cost me six thousand francs. I've not worn such beautiful hair since.[27]

When not let down, this hair was gracefully looped and intertwined with a beaded coil or held back with a simple jewelled band. She must have been wildly exaggerating the cost. 6,000 francs would have been about ten times the cost of all the rest of her costumes put together! She may well have had to pay for it herself, as her wig is certainly not amongst the costumes originally listed.

Letters from Debussy to his friends written in extreme haste in March show a sense of panic at the amount of work he had to fit in. Constant rehearsals took their toll. Arranging an appointment with René Peter, he added, 'I'm not a pretty sight.'[28] To another friend: 'Please don't begrudge me for not replying earlier to your charming – and useful – letter. In this hectic life I am leading, manners vanish, but friendship remains.'[29] To Peter again, 'I've got a rehearsal at 1.30 – you have no idea how much there is to do. It's frightening.'[30] And whatever had happened to make him write, 'Something most embarrassing has happened, so much so that I have just withdrawn *Pelléas* from the Opéra Comique! (Don't tell anyone yet ...) I therefore can't go out, at least today.'[31] Was he just looking for an excuse to get out of his meeting with his friend, or was he simply suffering an overwhelming lack of confidence after the initial orchestral rehearsals? Was he even perhaps disappointed with the standard of production at the Opéra-Comique whose members had never had to cope with such a ground-breaking creation for which Debussy would expect accurate playing, so different from crowd-pulling successes such as Charpentier's *Louise* and Massenet's *Manon*? He told Henri de Régnier he was 'in the hands of singers, orchestral musicians and other theatre people which is enough to drive one mad ...'[32] When composing the interludes, Debussy grumbled to another friend that

---

[27] Although she wore it again in 1908 and 1918. E.g. *New York Times*, 1 February 1918 described the wonderful wig of real hair, reaching to her feet, said to have been obtained from a peasant girl at a fair in Normandy.

[28] Debussy, *Correspondance*, p. 640.

[29] Debussy, *Correspondance*, p. 641.

[30] Debussy, *Correspondance*, p. 642.

[31] Debussy, *Correspondance*, p. 643.

[32] Debussy, *Correspondance*, p. 643.

Messager had come to him at ten o'clock at night to ask him to compose a link of seventy-five bars for the second act of *Pelléas*.[33]

Lighting was also proving a problem. On April 18 Debussy wrote to Albert Carré to say the theatre was too dark, for the musicians and the singers could not even see the conductor. He gave very specific advice for improvements to the positions and movements of Golaud and Mélisande in the fifth tableau and requested an extra orchestral rehearsal the next day.[34]

More letters and notes from Debussy to his friends issued reminders and invitations to attend the open dress rehearsal and it is encouraging to find Pierre Louÿs rallying acquaintances round to form a claque which would applaud loudly. 'Count on me, Claude, I am inviting five friends to fill the box with applause. We've hardly seen you since the XIXth century, but that won't change my opinions on *Pelléas*.'[35]

The letter Maeterlinck sent to *Le Figaro* publicly disowning the opera appeared on 14 April, only a couple of weeks before the première, but the main proponents of the enterprise refused to let this get them down. Carré told Debussy of his delight at receiving a letter of support from Octave Mirbeau, the very writer who almost ten years earlier had heaped praise on Maeterlinck. Mirbeau was unable to comprehend Maeterlinck's obtuseness and was unable to appeal to his reason, this man normally so gentle and full of good sense now mad with rage.[36]

At the same time as all this was going on, Debussy was, as usual, suffering financial worries. Two years earlier a devastating event had occurred with far-reaching consequences. We read in a letter to Pierre Louÿs on 25 April 1900 that the composer's publisher, Georges Hartmann, who had been providing him with 500 francs per month for some years, and often additional odd sums when Debussy was really broke, had died unexpectedly. Debussy, always short of money, naturally worried about what would happen to his opera now, but felt sure that Hartmann would have left his affairs well organised. He expressed his appreciation of his benefactor by eventually dedicating *Pelléas* to his memory. Unfortunately, however, Hartmann's nephew and heir, General Bourgeat (or Bourjat), now pursued Debussy for the repayment of the money which had been so generously advanced to him,[37] and sent the bailiffs round to Debussy's apartment. Mary Garden must have been aware of Debussy's precarious financial situation, for many

33 Debussy, *Correspondance*, p. 644.
34 Debussy, *Correspondance*, p. 646.
35 Debussy, *Correspondance*, p. 650.
36 See Chapter 4, p. 64.
37 Godet, 'En marge de la marge', p. 82.

years later her sister Helen recalled that Debussy was so afraid to leave the house for fear of his creditors that Lilly used to let down a basket which their friends would fill with food![38] The situation was eventually resolved with the help of Eugène Fromont, the publisher under whose name Hartmann had worked.[39]

Financial stress, the row with Maeterlinck, the rush to copy out orchestral parts by hand – not a calm run up to the public dress rehearsal on 28 April 1902 at 1.15 p.m. to which the press were invited. Such dress rehearsals had an atmosphere of their own, for the audience was not that of a typical night at the opera. Koechlin describes them as comprising businessmen, protégés of politicians, shady bankers, old rogues.[40] Mary lists 'musicians, writers, society people, government officials – everybody who is anybody.'[41]

The first intimation that things might not go smoothly was the spoof programme sold at the door which has already been described in Chapter 4. Mary was disgusted by it:

> What language, and what illustrations! I have never in my life seen such obscenity – clever perhaps, but in a foul disgusting way. One of the drawings showed the scene in which Golaud puts his child up to Mélisande's bedroom window to see if Pelléas and Mélisande are together and report to him what they are doing. In France, when you try to find out anything that way, they call it 'tirer les vers du nez'.[42] It's an ugly expression, and it went with the illustration in the programme book. And of course, it explained why the people in the house were in paroxysms of laughter. They had been stealing glimpses at these booklets during the performance and showing them to one another.[43]

According to Henri Busser, who was initially the chorus master, the first two acts were accepted quietly. The trouble began in the scene between Golaud and the child Yniold in Act III. At the point where Yniold spies on the couple through the window and refers to Golaud as 'petit père' repeatedly, there was much mirth. The boy was nervous and he had a pronounced Parisian accent. Carré bitterly remembers the laughter that broke out when, having had her hair pulled by Golaud, Mélisande sang the words: 'Je ne suis pas heureuse' in her Scottish accent. A man stood up and shouted: 'What do you expect?' The person sitting next to René Peter was glad he had come to watch, for the opera was almost as funny as a Feydeau farce. 'See, she's not

[38] Madeau Stewart notebook for BBC talk *c.* 1963, Oxfordshire Record Office, P143/04/ MS/001.

[39] Debussy, *Correspondance*, p. 557n.

[40] '*Pelléas et Mélisande*, étude de Charles Koechlin', ed. Caillet, p. 36.

[41] *Mary Garden's Story*, p. 70.

[42] Literally 'to pull the worms out of your nose'!

[43] *Mary Garden's Story*, p. 70.

happy, that little woman. Her young brother-in-law is going to make it his duty to give her a bit of fun when he's finished doing her hair!'

André Messager wrote a vivid description of the occasion:

> It was in the second Tableau of the second act when Mélisande replied 'Je ne suis pas heureuse!' that the storm broke. All those who were there simply to demonstrate their hostility used the text as an excuse to beat time to the music. Phrases like: 'simplement parce que c'est l'usage'[44] or the 'petit père' in the scene between Golaud and little Yniold provoked gales of laughter and indignant cries of 'Oh! Oh!' To my right, in the first row, a fat woman indirectly associated with the world of theatre, who always used to come to dress rehearsals where she was famous for her ugliness and ill will, drew attention to herself through her indignant protestations and squawking like a frightened guinea-fowl. I can still see her rolling about in her seat like a rowing boat in a storm, raising her short fat arms and shouting: 'Oh! ... petit père ... petit père ... it's a scream! ... enough! enough!'[45]

Backstage, wrote Messager, there was just as much stress. During the intervals the musicians were wandering around moaning 'It's the end!' Apart from a few, most agreed it was impossible that such a work would succeed. On stage, however, everyone kept cool. Eventually, the performance and the emotions aroused by the final part of the work made an impression on even the most hostile and the rehearsal at least came to an end in silence.[46]

Debussy's friend Robert Godet has one overriding memory of that afternoon: the scandal caused by the word 'bed' when uttered by the child Yniold. When Golaud asked, 'Are they near the bed?'

> without any embarrassment, his brow glowing with a halo of innocence from a ray of light emanating from the orchestra, the child replied, in such a fresh and natural way that it might have been an angel speaking and you thought you were listening to Childhood itself: 'I can't see the bed.' It seems that this was beyond all limits, for all at once the entire hall, united in the defence of morals, burst out in such a roar of 'Oohh' it might have brought down the curtain.[47]

Debussy, still trying to look calm, then received from the under-secretary of the Beaux-Arts an official message ordering him to cut the bed scene. 'And this is how the maeterlinckian bed prevented him from being able to go to his own, which he needed so badly', writes Godet, ruefully.[48] It was also decided to cut Act IV scene 3, the scene with Yniold watching the sheep being taken to slaughter, which had aroused yet more sarcastic comments.

---

[44] Act IV scene 2.

[45] Messager, 'Les premières représentations de Pelléas', p. 112.

[46] Messager, 'Les premières représentations de Pelléas', pp. 112–13.

[47] Godet, 'En marge de la marge', p. 83.

[48] Godet, 'En marge de la marge', p. 83.

He had two days to make the cuts before the première. Émile Vuillermoz is at pains to point out that it was not Debussy's music which antagonised the audience, but Maeterlinck's text.[49] The music simply underlined the naïveté of some of the dialogue, particularly the examples mentioned above, and never provided any excuse for the protestors to disrupt the performance. Perhaps it should be noted that the enunciation of the singers must have been excellent, for obviously the audience did not miss a word!

Messager's stress leading up to the dress rehearsal was exacerbated when, that very morning, he had to leave Paris to attend the funeral of a much loved brother. During the interval Carré found him in a quiet corner in tears. What admiration and satisfaction he aroused in the director when he assured Carré that these were not for the death of his dear brother, but because he was so moved by *Pelléas*. Vuillermoz calls Messager Debussy's 'guardian angel'.[50] In his opinion it was Messager who produced the definitive version, the perfect materialisation of Debussy's musical vision and made it so persuasive. Only he held the secret to the enchantment, the nuances and delicate inflexions of the voices.

According to some, Debussy remained calm and inscrutable. Busser, however, reported that Debussy 'was hiding in Messager's office and nervously smoking one cigarette after another.'[51] Henry Février remembers finding him in Messager's office in an interval (again, not as calm as others report), and when he expressed his whole-hearted admiration for the work and the new horizons it was opening up for music, all Debussy replied was: 'I wanted to prove that Wagner's system was wrong!'[52]

At the end of this stressful experience, Robert Godet and Erik Satie waited for Debussy whilst Debussy made the required cuts to the score. When he came out they went to his publisher, Fromont, where Debussy picked up the piano reduction (the nearest to a full score in existence at that time), wrote a dedication to Godet in it and marked the cuts 'with a tired hand, but steady penstroke.'[53] In the rue Cardinet Debussy insisted they came in for a cup of tea, but there made no mention of his hectic day. Instead the topic of conversation was Weber's *Oberon*.

Two days later, the première took place.

---

[49] Vuillermoz, *Claude Debussy* (1957), p. 96.

[50] 'un ange gardien', Vuillermoz, *Claude Debussy* (1957), p. 89.

[51] Debussy, *Correspondance*, p. 651n.

[52] Février, *André Messager*, p. 108.

[53] Godet, 'En marge de la marge', p. 85.

8 First Performance and Reactions

T HE FIRST PERFORMANCE of *Pelléas et Mélisande* on 30 April 1902 went more smoothly than might have been expected from the dress rehearsal. Lilly Debussy watched from a box, very pale, trying to hide her emotions, but there were three or four curtain calls for each act. Although there were still some mutterings about Golaud's interrogation of little Yniold, they soon died down and there was positive enthusiasm for the last two acts. Debussy's name was warmly applauded at the end whilst that of Maeterlinck raised some protests. Carré and Messager had calmed down and were convinced the work would have a lasting success.[1] When René Peter rode through the Bois de Boulogne with Debussy and Lilly after the performance, what did they talk about? The beautiful sky, the glorious evening – not one word about *Pelléas*![2]

When press reviews started to appear, the audience seemed to be of as much interest to the critics as the opera itself. Eugène d'Harcourt in *Le Figaro* divided the musicians present into two schools – its 'arriviste' young supporters and their friends, determined to defend the work noisily, and the reactionaries, loath to accept any infringement of the holy trinity of melody, harmony and rhythm.[3] On the same page, 'Un Monsieur de l'Orchestre' gave his own reactions, noting that 'Some said it was a musical event of the greatest importance; others said disrespectfully that it was just a practical joke'. Amongst the audience he heard on the one hand the phrase, 'The power of orchestral sonorities' and on the other, 'monotonous psalm singing'.[4] But only a few days later Henry Bauer was writing in the same paper: 'Today or tomorrow Debussy's score will be recognised for what it is. It's a matter of time, just a little time.'[5]

---

[1] Debussy, *Correspondance*, p. 652 n. 2.

[2] Peter, *Claude Debussy*, p. 186.

[3] 'un groupe d'arrivistes qui ont des amis bruyants décidés à les défendre ... les fervents de l'art, qui trouvent que la musique est une trinité sainte, dont les trois éléments, la mélodie, l'harmonie et le rythme ont des lois qu'on ne peut continuellement enfreindre au détriment de la raison et de l'oreille.' *Le Figaro*, 1 May 1902.

[4] 'Les uns disaient que c'était un événement musical de la plus haute importance ... d'autres disaient irrespectueusement que c'était de la blague ... puissance des sonorités orchestrales ... psalmodies monotones.' *Le Figaro*, 1 May 1902.

[5] 'Aujourd'hui ou demain la partition de Claude Debussy s'imposera. C'est l'affaire de temps, de peu de temps.' *Le Figaro*, 5 May 1902.

The correspondent of the London *Times* seems never to have heard of the composer, for he referred to a M. Gaston Debussy![6] He was 'a daring innovator', his music 'so exceedingly modern as to belong to no hitherto known species, it being the most unexpected and enigmatic ever offered to the public.' He had to ask his fellow critics what to make of the music, but each gave a different opinion. His only comment about Mary Garden was that she had been much applauded as Mélisande.

Mary herself kept a cutting from as far afield as the *Chicago Tribune* of July 1902, a review including the sentence, 'All the artists were excellent, but it is Mélisande who takes hold of you.' No wonder she has handwritten around the margins, 'This seems to me to be all one could desire.'[7]

Henry Février met Gabriel Fauré the day after the first performance, who confided in him his amazement at 'such a successful curiosity'. In his opinion Mary Garden's foreign accent had contributed to its success.[8] 'You must go to see this work', wrote Auguste Mangeot, 'for it represents a type that will probably be unique.'[9] How perspicacious! 'Monsieur Maeterlinck would be hard-pressed to meet a musician more respectful of the spirit and letter of his work than Monsieur Debussy', was Victor Debay's opinion. He found Mary's Mélisande charming, sweet, plaintive, naïve and mysterious.[10] The review in *Les Annales du théâtre et de la musique* of 1903 described Mary Garden as 'the ideal Mélisande with golden hair, a little princess of legend, in love, mystical, wonderfully conveying to us with her whole being the atmosphere of the unreal.'[11]

Writing in *La Revue musicale*, Louis Schneider was entranced by the words, the music, the scenery. One wonders how Maeterlinck could have been so precipitate in separating himself from the opera he had inspired, for here was a critic so touched by the beauty of the text that he reproduced whole passages. Rather than interpreting Maeterlincks's repetitions as puerile, he regarded them as a quest for naïvety. The music, he wrote, 'clothed' the text, and 'was impregnated' by it. There were many pages of the score

---

6 *The Times*, 3 May 1902.

7 RCM, London, Mary Garden Collection.

8 'un tel succès de curiosité, auquel ... tout contribuait grandement, jusqu'à l'accent étranger de Miss Mary Garden.' Février, *André Messager*, p. 109.

9 'Il faut aller voir cette œuvre, car elle représente un type qui sera peut-être unique, d'un art tout special.' *Le Monde musical*, 15 May 1902.

10 'charmante, douce, plaintive, naïve et mystérieuse': *Le Courier musical*, 15 May 1902.

11 'L'idéale Mélisande aux cheveux d'or, petite princesse de légende, amoureuse et mystique, nous donnant merveilleusement en toute sa personne la sensation de l'irréel.' *Les Annales du théâtre et de la musique* (1903), p. 110.

which deserved repeated hearings. The humanity in the music allowed the audience to identify themselves with the characters.[12]

Whilst reactions to *Pelléas et Mélisande* veered between derision and disparagement on the one hand, and on the other enthusiasm and fierce commitment to campaigning for its acceptance, some influential people went further than deriding the work verbally. Théodore Dubois, Director of the Conservatoire, forbade his composition pupils to attend performances in case they were sullied by its influence![13] No doubt, all the more incentive for them to go. Catulle Mendès showed his complete misunderstanding of the work by expressing two desires: 'to hear M. Claude Debussy's score in orchestral concerts without the soloists and to see M. Maurice Maeterlinck's charming lyrical tale acted without singers or instruments in some theatre.'[14] It should perhaps be noted that his opinion might have been coloured by the fact that Debussy had never completed work on his libretto for *Rodrigue et Chimène*, begun in 1890.[15]

Amongst the members of Debussy's audience in the expensive seats were society ladies who were familiar with his music from performances in their salons, such as Madame de Saint-Marceaux. However, the *debussystes*, the most fanatical supporters of the opera, were certainly not to be found in the front rows with high society and official critics. No, they were right up in the 'gods', the top gallery of the auditorium, just as descriptively named *paradis* in French, where impoverished music lovers gathered. There students, office workers, artists, poets, listened, many of whom came to every performance of the work. One of their number, Émile Vuillermoz, enthused about the delicate and bewitching music, discrete yet so rich in timbres, the total correspondence of words and music, the clarity of Messager's conducting so that not one syllable of the text was lost, the palette full of colours in the orchestration.[16] Paul Dukas, in a long, sympathetic and sincerely appreciative review, wrote cuttingly, 'It's an old story which will end like all the others: in a few years the whole world will want to have been the first to proclaim the beauty of the work.'[17] He was deeply moved by the

[12] 'une partition qui «habille» le texte et qui en meme temps s'en imprègne ... des lambeaux d'humanité s'attachent à toutes ces situations, et voilà pourquoi nous vivons avec tous les personnages du drame.' *La Revue musicale*, May 1902, p. 196.

[13] Peter, *Claude Debussy*, p. 191.

[14] *Le Journal,* 1 May 1902.

[15] See Chapter 9, p. 117.

[16] Vuillermoz, *Claude Debussy* (1957), p. 106.

[17] 'C'est une vieille histoire qui finira comme les précédentes: dans quelques années tout le monde voudra avoir été des premiers à proclamer la beauté de l'ouvrage.' Paul Dukas, *Chroniques musicales sur deux siècles, 1892–1932* (Paris, 1980), p. 148.

unique way in which Debussy had caught the essence of the human tragedy in musical terms, illuminating Maeterlinck's poem, keeping the natural
inflexions of the words to the extent that music and language were fused
inseparably. The composer was not violating rules of melody, rhythm and
harmony as critics were complaining, but building on basic principles in his
own inimitable way. On the other hand, Vincent d'Indy said, 'This music
will never survive because it has no form.'[18] Carré was exasperated to find
the majority of critics talking about 'nihilist art', 'shadows and incoher-
ence', 'dissonances which drive you mad', 'defying common sense', 'a huge
flop'.[19] He felt sympathy for Debussy who he knew was not quite as impas-
sive as some had suggested. After all, Debussy had simply let the characters
sing inside him. 'I tried to listen to them and to interpret them faithfully.
That's all.'[20]

Carré claims that if Messager and he had not restrained him, Debussy
would have cut some of the most beautiful pages of his score. Debussy recognised the support of both men by dedicating his score to them. The first
dedication is to Georges Hartmann, who had died before the completion of
the opera, then follows that to André Messager, 'as an expression of my deep
affection'.[21] In the copy he gave to Albert Carré he wrote: 'To Monsieur A.
Carré, and even more, to the artist who knew how to create the unforgettable dreamlike atmosphere without which *Pelléas et Mélisande* would not
have been able to live.'[22] In an article published on 16 May 1902 he expressed
his relief in the face of all the criticism at having their support: 'What a joy
for me to have colleagues such as MM Albert Carré and André Messager,
interpreters such as those in *Pelléas et Mélisande*, and to remain, after the fray,
their grateful and devoted friend.'[23]

Mary Garden was exaggerating when she wrote that 'every critic in Paris
denounced *Pelléas* in the most dreadful language'. She was right, however,
when she said:

[18] 'Cette musique ne vivra pas, car elle n'a pas de forme.' Vuillermoz, *Claude Debussy*
(1957), p. 98.
[19] 'd'art nihiliste ... ténèbres et d'incohérence ... dissonances qui agacent jusqu'à
l'exaspération ... défi de bon sens ... four magistral.' Carré, *Souvenirs de théâtre*, p. 281.
[20] 'J'ai tâché de les entendre et de les interpreter fidèlement. Voilà tout.' *Le Figaro*, 16
May 1902.
[21] 'en témoinage de profonde affection'.
[22] 'et plus encore à l'artiste qui sut créer l'atmosphère de rêve, inoubliable, sans laquelle
Pelléas et Mélisande n'auraient pu vivre.' Emmanuel, *Pelléas et Mélisande de Debussy*,
p. 52.
[23] 'Mais quelle joie pour moi, d'avoir eu des collaborateurs tels que MM. Albert Carré
et André Messager, des interprètes comme ceux de Pelléas et Mélisande, et de rester,
après la bataille, leur ami reconnaissant et dévoué.' *Le Figaro*, 16 May 1902.

But the public – ah, there was another story! What I had myself predicted to M. Carré came true. They soon saw what confronted them. For by the time we reached the fifth performance, the Opéra-Comique had become a cathedral. No one dared to speak, even in the faintest whispers; no one came late; no-one moved in his seat or made any kind of noise.[24]

She too recognised that it was the people in the *paradis* who had the power to influence the rest of the audience. She witnessed their arguments, even scuffles as they fought to win people over. Her own complete empathy with the soul of the work is evident in her words:

> Think only of the silences in that opera – they are what make Mélisande – the silences that Debussy put there. In her silences, Mélisande has the orchestra to tell her what to do. On most operatic stages nobody is silent. They all sing, so they can never realise what a silence means. I've had more power over an audience with a silence than I ever had with a note. That's where I would look if I went into an opera house hunting for a genius – I would look into their silences.[25]

Mary's ability to maintain a statuesque stillness contributed to this power which became legendary: 'During moments when the orchestra was playing and the singers silent on stage, she would be frozen in whatever position she had assumed during the last note, never moving a muscle until the orchestral interlude was finished – she was like a carved figure which had stepped out of a medieval frieze.'[26]

Another witness to the spell Mary cast was the conductor Désiré-Émile Inghelbrecht, who in 1933 referred to her method in a talk entitled *Comment on ne doit pas interpréter Pelléas* (How not to interpret *Pelléas*). Discussing the closeness of the rhythm of the music to the words of the libretto, he advised performers to practise speaking the text, then to add the melody afterwards. To demonstrate this he pronounced the words to his audience, then asked them to remember how Mary Garden sang them, implying they sounded as if they were spoken. 'Right from the start, and quite brilliantly, she solved the mysterious problem of interpretation in a work in which the question of "neither too much, nor too little" is urgently posed on every page.'[27]

Sure enough, the success of the opera grew and grew. By the seventh performance over 6,000 francs were taken in the box office. Annual takings up

[24] *Mary Garden's Story*, p. 71.

[25] *Mary Garden's Story*, p. 72.

[26] Jack Winsor Hansen, 'Mary Garden, Queen of Chutzpah', *Massenet Society Newsletter*, January 1991.

[27] D.-E. Inghelbrecht, 'How not to interpret Pelléas', in booklet to CD *Inghelbrecht conducts Debussy: Pelléas et Mélisande*, Montaigne Archives, V4854.

to 1922–3 are listed by Maurice Emmanuel to demonstrate the rapid change of mind of the public and the ever-growing popularity of the masterpiece.[28]

Mary knew all too well that Debussy was upset by the initial reaction and realised that his behaviour was typical of the man, for after the last rehearsal, 'Debussy did the very characteristic thing of walking out of the life of Mélisande. He never came to a single performance of *Pelléas*.' Although she beseeched him to come and watch the complete fulfilment of his dream, his response was, '*Pelléas* is my child. I had it in my hands for ten years. I gave it to the public, and now it does not interest me any longer.' She could only remember him being present once again, and that, too, was at a rehearsal when she was creating Mélisande in Brussels several years later. For now, 'Debussy lived in a world of his own, where no one, not even his first wife, Lily [*sic*], with all her care and adoration, could reach him.'[29]

As if he knew that his dream would be lost when he gave his work to the public, in April 1902, before the first performance, Debussy had already expressed his worries in a note written in response to a request from Georges Ricou, the manager of the Opéra-Comique.[30] Whilst theatre audiences demanded 'something new', he complained, as soon as they heard someone trying to create just this, they jeered in their bewilderment. A work of art, an attempt at beauty, seemed to be taken as a personal insult by some people.[31] Inghelbrecht, in the talk referred to above, realising Debussy's total identification with the music he was composing or playing, recalled the composer telling a friend, 'You see, you should not love music too much!'[32]

Debussy's anxieties surrounding the 'birth' of his dear, beloved 'children' were expressed again in 1908 in such vivid language that it is evident that the anxiety and raw emotion experienced upon first seeing them personified on stage remained with him for years after. In an article published in *Musica* it is clear that he had feared that the practical realisation of his work would never match the pictures in his mind. Movingly, he wrote of 'the dream inside him', 'the beautiful lie' in which he and his characters had lived for so long, who were always about to emerge live from the pages of his manuscript, whom he almost felt he could touch. He dreaded them being ruined by the intervention of stage designer and performers. Most of all, he feared his dreams of Mélisande could have been shattered:

---

[28] Emmanuel, *Pelléas et Mélisande de Debussy*, pp. 64–8.

[29] *Mary Garden's Story*, p. 73.

[30] See also Chapter 1, p. 16.

[31] Debussy, 'Pourquoi j'ai écrit Pelléas', translated in *Debussy on Music*, pp. 74–5.

[32] 'Vous voyez bien qu'il ne faut pas trop aimer la musique!' Inghelbrecht, 'How not to interpret Pelléas'.

In my music I had tried to convey her fragility, her distant charm. But there was still her bearing, her long silences which one false movement could have ruined or even made her incomprehensible. And above all, Mélisande's voice, which inwardly I had heard as so tender, what would it sound like? – even the most beautiful voice in the world could be completely wrong for the special sound unique to her character.[33]

To Debussy's immense relief he had the perfect interpreter. He was deeply impressed and moved by Mary's interpretation. From amongst the great artists working with infinite dedication:

one in particular stood out. I hardly ever had to tell her anything; little by little the character of Mélisande took shape; I waited, remarkably confident, yet curious.

Eventually we came to the last act, – the death of Mélisande, – and I was so amazed I can't describe the feeling. This was the gentle voice I had secretly heard, with that faltering tenderness, that appealing artistry I had not dared to believe possible until then, that artistry which has caused the public to bow in ever-increasing admiration before the name of Mlle Mary Garden.[34]

This article also reveals why Debussy so hated attending actual performances of his opera, as opposed to assisting at rehearsals. It was as if some exterior force came between him and his work:

Applause, disgruntled grumblings sound like noise from a distant fair, a fair where you are scarcely more than a parasite feeding off glory which you do not particularly want to receive in this way, for success in the theatre is most often achieved through responding to public taste and arousing easy emotion.[35]

Rehearsals were more pleasurable to him, for working with dedicated artists were 'some of the best times I have spent in the theatre'.

[33] 'J'avais bien essayé d'en noter musicalement la fragilité, le charme distant; il restait son attitude, ses longs silences qu'un geste faux pouvait trahir, ou même rendre incompréhensible. Et surtout la voix de Mélisande, secrètement entendue si tendre, qu'allait-elle être? – tant la plus belle voix du monde peut devenir l'ennemie inconsciente de l'expression propre à tel personnage.' Claude Debussy, 'Mary Garden', *Musica*, January 1908, p. 5.

[34] 'Parmi ces derniers se dégageait une artiste curieusement personnelle. Je n'avais presque rien à lui dire; en elle se dessinait peu à peu le personnage de Mélisande; j'attendais avec une confiance singulière, mélangée de curiosité. Vint enfin le cinquième acte, – la mort de Mélisande, – et ce fut un étonnement dont je ne puis rendre l'émotion. C'était la douce voix secrètement entendue, avec cette tendresse défaillante, cet art si prenant auquel je ne voulais pas croire jusque-là, et qui depuis a fait s'incliner l'admiration du public avec une ferveur toujours grandissante devant le nom de Mlle Mary Garden.' Debussy, 'Mary Garden'.

[35] 'Des applaudissements, des rumeurs agressives semblent les bruits d'une fête lointaine, fête où vous n'êtes guère que le parasite d'une gloire pas toujours désirée telle qu'on vous la décerne, car réussir au théâtre c'est, le plus souvent, répondre à des vœux anonyms et de l'émotion assimilable.' Debussy, 'Mary Garden'.

Following the première Debussy sent Mary a copy of the score dedicated 'To Mademoiselle M. Garden. In the future others will sing Mélisande. You alone will remain forever the woman and the artist that I hardly dared hope for. Your grateful Claude Debussy. May 1902.'[36] Years later, he was still publicly praising Mary. No other person sang the role at the Opéra-Comique from 1902 to 1907. There was no understudy.

Mary often hinted at more than a professional relationship with Debussy. No doubt as she got older, wishful thinking may have become confused with fact, for what could be more calculated to excite curiosity and envy in her audiences than a love affair with the composer? It is to her benefit to remember, however, that Debussy, usually so taciturn and clumsy in his external manner, certainly expressed unstinting admiration for her on more than one occasion, and it is perhaps unjust to reject completely Mary's account of events three years after they met. One day she and Debussy were walking in the park at Versailles when he suddenly stopped to tell her of his obsession: 'Ten years I lived with this Mélisande, and I never thought I would ever find anybody who could make her come to life as the woman I lived with. And you did that, Mary.' She claims he then avowed his love for her, to which she replied, 'I love and adore your genius, I like you as a friend, but Debussy the man means nothing to me.' Finally she realised the truth of the matter. 'It isn't *me* you love, much as you believe it ... It is Mélisande you love. You've loved her for ten years, and you still do, and it is Mélisande that you love in me, not myself.'[37]

Debussy used to address letters to Mary as 'Ma chère Mélisande',[38] and this encouraged Mary to believe she had interpreted the situation correctly. Their farewell at the end of this visit to Versailles was to be the last time she and Debussy met socially in person. She was later to make the claim that she was to have been the inspiration for a new dramatic project: in both her autobiography and her private notebooks she asserts that Debussy was considering writing a *Romeo and Juliet* for her. When he used to visit her with Lilly, he would sit beside her and talk about the best way of arranging the libretto from Shakespeare's play, but with the end of their friendship the project never materialised. 'Think of it, *Romeo and Juliet* by the composer of *Pelléas et Mélisande*! It is the most heartbreaking might-have-been of my whole career.'[39]

We have no further evidence of this closeness of the composer and the

[36] Debussy, *Correspondance*, p. 2221.

[37] *Mary Garden's Story*, p. 77.

[38] See illus. 10.

[39] *Mary Garden's Story*, pp. 88–9, and notebooks in RCM, London, Mary Garden Collection.

singer, and most remain sceptical. Carl Van Vechten even sneers at Debussy's dedication of Mary's score, saying, 'It must be remembered that composers are notoriously fickle; that they prefer having their operas given in any form rather than not at all; that ink is cheap and musicians prolific in sentiments.'[40] However, the number of references to Mary in letters certainly shows his thoughts often turned towards her. Nor was this the only dedication she received. In 1902 Debussy wrote in the front of a copy of *La Damoiselle élue*, '*La damoiselle élue* pays respectful homage to Mélisande. Permit me to add my affectionate devotion, Claude Debussy, Oct. 1902.'[41] The following year there was yet another tribute to Mary when the *Ariettes oubliées* were reprinted by Fromont. 'To Miss Mary Garden, unforgettable Mélisande, this music (already rather old) in affectionate and respectful homage.'[42]

Mary's success was appreciated and rewarded by Albert Carré. She received a new three-year contract beginning at 2,000 francs a month, rising to 5,000 francs. There is no doubt that the director was immensely proud of having been instrumental in bringing about the success of *Pelléas et Mélisande*. His comments on this opera take up more pages in his book than any other single work. He said: 'This will remain one of the best memories of my life, my collaboration with this man who appeared so impenetrable to everybody and whose sparkling genius I had the great joy of discovering during our friendship.'[43]

Others who knew about the Maeterlinck and Georgette Leblanc fiasco were just as impressed by Mary's performance. It is ironic that Camille Mauclair, who had been so in love with Georgette Leblanc, wrote in praise of Mary in June 1902: 'To interpret Mélisande one needs a slender young woman, without the domineering demeanour of an actress, an excellent musician, but having nothing of the hateful manner of a "chanteuse". Mlle Garden seems to me to embody these qualities.'[44] The 'chanteuse' that he had in mind may well have been Georgette. Mauclair was not the only man to sound embittered after an affair with Georgette had ended, as we will see.

---

[40] Carl Van Vechten, *Interpreters and Interpretations* (New York, 1917), p. 74.

[41] 'La damoiselle élue présente son respectueux homage à Mélisande, permettez-moi d'y joindre l'affectueux dévouement de Claude Debussy, Oct. 1902'. Debussy, *Correspondance*, p. 2221.

[42] 'A Miss Mary Garden, inoubliable Mélisande, cette musique (déjà un peu vieille) en affectueux et reconnaissant hommage.' François Lesure, *Claude Debussy: biographie critique* (Paris, 1994) p. 235.

[43] 'Cela restera un des plus beaux souvenirs de ma vie, cette collaboration avec cet homme qui paraissait hermétique à tous et dont j'avais la joie, dans l'intimité qui fut nôtre, de découvrir l'étincelant genie.' Carré, *Souvenirs de théâtre*, p. 276.

[44] Dietschy, *La Passion de Claude Debussy*, p. 156 (note), quoting *Revue universelle* of June 1902.

We know Georgette came to a performance, for André Gide wrote a letter of fulsome praise to Debussy, adding:

> Has anyone told you Georgette was at the matinée of 1 June? She applauded heartily and said she only regretted that Pelléas was not a bit more feminine and a bit younger, and that the costumes were of a less precise age. I'm only telling you this out of simple curiosity! I don't share her point of view at all.[45]

Frustratingly, Georgette's opinion of Mary as Mélisande is not recorded. Gide's letter also demonstrates the way in which word of the extraordinary spell cast by the opera and in particular the role of Mary Garden as Mélisande was spreading. He asked Debussy if he had heard about an association of a dozen young enthusiasts who had to save up to pay for their tickets, not one of whom had missed a single performance.[46] Maurice Dumesnil, who was later to write many articles and a book on Debussy, was a member of this early fan-club, but as he explains, their number was far in excess of one dozen. There was a long queue of young fans waiting on the pavement of the rue Favart on *Pelléas et Mélisande* nights![47]

Looking back nostalgically, the conductor Inghelbrecht wrote:

> The young generation approaching the age of twenty around 1902 had the rare experience of being spiritually moved by the first performances of *Pelléas et Mélisande*. It was like a moment of enchanting light for those young people who twelve years later would fall into the atrocious blazing furnace of war.[48]

Two such young writers overcome with emotion at the beauty of the opera and in particular of its Mélisande were Henri Alain-Fournier, author of the evocative and atmospheric novel *Le Grand Meaulnes*, and his friend Jacques Rivière. In an article entitled *La Chanson du Grand Meaulnes*, José Bruyr specifically commented on this passion. He too was conscious of the transience of the lives of these young men. Echoing Maeterlinck's concept of 'les avertis', the idea that certain people were aware that they would only live short lives, he believed that Alain-Fournier, who was indeed to be killed in action in 1914, aged twenty-eight, possessed 'that air which Pelléas has of those who are not going to live long.'[49] When working alone in London in 1905, *Pelléas* had come to represent for Alain-Fournier everything which was 'far away, French and a friend'. Rivière believed that people simply did not

[45] Debussy, *Correspondance*, p. 669.

[46] Debussy, *Correspondance*, p. 669.

[47] Maurice Dumesnil, *The Etude*, January 1935.

[48] Inghelbrecht, *Claude Debussy*, p. 161.

[49] 'N'a-t-il pas naturellement cet air qu'a aussi Pelléas, de ceux qui ne doivent pas vivre longtemps?' José Bruyr, 'La chanson du Grand Meaulnes', *La Revue musicale*, vol. 15 (November 1934), p. 284.

realise what *Pelléas* meant to the young people who were present at its birth: 'a beloved paradise to which we escaped from all our troubles. All week at school we waited for it, we talked about it, and with what love and respect! It was the consolation for our imprisonment ... We escaped there knowing the way in through the secret door, and the world outside meant nothing to us any more.'[50] When appointed critic for the *Mercure Musical* in 1905, he wrote to Alain-Fournier telling him his first review had included two phrases sung by Golaud, for he wanted his first words in print to be a hymn to Debussy.[51] Whilst in Bordeaux, he wrote of the agony he was suffering missing Paris life and in particular Mary Garden. He had tears in his eyes whenever he thought of her. Whilst doing military service, Rivière was told by Alain-Fournier about a performance of *Pelléas*, but to attend it would have led to punishment by imprisonment.[52] As he admitted, both family and friends regarded him as unbalanced, he had seen the opera so often.

Inghelbrecht also had to put up with teasing from his family. A friend, the poet Léon-Paul Fargue, was amongst those who endeavoured to go to every performance with Ravel, Florent Schmitt, Ricardo Viñes, but not only was he often late, he would sometimes have to wait for them at the exit having spent the whole time searching unsuccessfully for the money to make up the full price of the ticket. When they emerged from the performance his first question would be 'Mary Garden? As fantastic as ever?'[53] Pasteur Vallery-Radot tells of one of his friends who always carried around with him a thread from the dress that Mary Garden wore at the première.[54]

In 1906, when Alain-Fournier was queuing up for *Pelléas*, he heard an impoverished-looking young man chatting to a friend and giving a perfect rendering of Yniold's role, including the cut scene with the sheep. On questioning him he discovered it was in fact Blondin, the original Yniold.[55] The adult Blondin keeps turning up in various people's reminiscences. Felix Aprahamian remembers the conductor Désormière telling him 'of an elderly taxi-driver who seemed amused to be asked to take him to the Opéra-Comique on one of the evenings he was conducting *Pelléas* there in the 1940s. Depositing him at the stage door, he revealed his identity – the boy Blondin, who had sung *le petit Yniold* at the first

[50] Bruyr, 'La chanson du Grand Meaulnes', pp. 285–6.
[51] 'J'ai voulu que mes premiers mots imprimés fussent un hymne vers Debussy.' Letter of 5 April 1906: Jacques Rivière and Henri Alain-Fournier, *Correspondance, 1905–1914*, 4 vols. (Paris, 1926–7), vol. 1, p. 220.
[52] Letter of 22 October 1906: Rivière and Alain-Fournier, *Correspondance*, vol. 2, p. 372.
[53] Inghelbrecht, *Claude Debussy*, pp. 171–7.
[54] Pasteur Vallery-Radot, *Tel était Claude Debussy* (Paris, 1958), p. 49.
[55] Letter of 9 November 1906: Rivière and Alain-Fournier, *Correspondance*, vol. 1, p. 383.

performance!⁵⁶ Maurice Dumesnil recounts that a lady friend of Madame Debussy wanted to visit the new memorial to Debussy on the outskirts of the Bois de Boulogne and hailed a taxi. The driver said immediately he knew where the memorial was and when the lady alighted, followed her. By the monument tears ran down his cheeks. When she gently inquired what was the matter, he explained that during the day he was a taxi driver and at night he directed a little music hall. 'But many years ago, I had other ambitions. It was I who created the part of Yniold in *Pelléas* at the Opéra-Comique, in 1902, in my boyhood days.'⁵⁷

Even in the earliest days of the opera changes had to take place. Messager only conducted the first three performances for he had been appointed Director of Covent Garden in 1901 and now had to relinquish the baton at the Opéra-Comique to the chorus master, Henri Busser. Audience numbers still rose, but Debussy was disappointed. He wrote to Messager on 9 May 1902, expressing his desperate desire to see him again. 'I'm about as sad as a footpath that no one passes along any more.' Busser, he complained, was nervous and looked as if he didn't know what end to open the score. Périer was singing in a voice sounding as if it was coming from under his umbrella! Mary Garden was refusing to look at Busser's face, on the pretext of being used to contemplating an infinitely more agreeable one. On Friday, they played to a full house, including Jean de Reszke. Debussy continued his impression of Busser as looking like 'someone about to take a cold bath and who does not relish the idea ... He does not bother at all about the singers and only throws some chords in their direction without worrying in the slightest about their harmonic virtue.' However, the composer was clearly satisfied with the end result, saying it had settled down after a fashion, and after the fourth act there were three curtain calls.⁵⁸ Eight performances took place in May, five in June. The opera had completed its first season.

⁵⁶ Felix Aprahamian, *Opera on Record*, ed. Alan Blyth (London, 1979), p. 635.
⁵⁷ Maurice Dumesnil, *The Etude*, March 1933, pp. 156, 204.
⁵⁸ Debussy, *Correspondance*, pp. 655–6.

9 *Mary Garden Reaps Success (1902-7)*

As DEBUSSY INDICATED, the change of conductor had a disappointing effect on the cast of Pelléas et Mélisande. Although he never attended an actual performance, he told Robert Godet that he could not wait for this season to end. His opera was beginning to be treated like any old work in the repertoire. The singers were improvising and the orchestra was sounding ponderous.[1]

This baptism of fire over, it was not just Messager who went to Covent Garden. He must have been influential in the casting of Mary Garden in two operas, after she had finished her season at the Opéra-Comique. This was, after all, the second year of their love affair. However, during the 1902 season Messager conducted at Covent Garden only twice. For her *Manon* on 3 July the conductor was Philippe Flon. Mary's star qualities were immediately recognised. Besides her 'very pure, rather light soprano' voice, her charming stage presence and the delightful freshness of her acting were praised.[2] She followed this on 14 July with an appearance in the now forgotten *Princess Osra* by Herbert Bunning, conducted this time by Messager. It is ironic, however, that in the land of her native language she was singing a British opera in its French version, *La Princesse Osra*!

Messager then asked Debussy to visit London, an invitation accepted with enthusiasm. Messager had told him of Mary's warm reception to which Debussy replied that he was not at all surprised. 'You would have to be wearing ear plugs to resist the charm of her voice. I simply can't imagine a more sweetly insinuating timbre. It is like a tyrannical power, it is so impossible to forget.' He even quotes Pelléas's words in Act IV scene 4, saying that when he thinks of seeing Messager on Sunday 'Mon cœur bat comme un fou jusqu'au fond de ma gorge.'[3] Confirming what Mary was later to tell her readers, he provides further proof that he thought of her and Mélisande as one and the same, for after signing off he added: 'Kiss Mélisande for both of us, and thank her for the charming letter I received this morning.'[4]

---

[1] Debussy, *Correspondance*, p. 670.

[2] *The Times*, 5 July 1902.

[3] 'My heart beats madly right up into my throat.' Debussy, *Correspondance*, p. 674.

[4] Proof that there was further correspondence between them. Only one letter survives (that quoted in Chapter 6, p. 89).

Leaving Lilly in Paris, on 12 July Debussy arrived at the Hotel Cecil in the Strand where Mary was also staying. He did not restrict his activities to the opera whilst there. On 15 July both he and Mary went to see Forbes-Robertson as Hamlet at the Lyric Theatre. Knowing Debussy was 'mad about Shakespeare' she enjoyed seeing him 'like a child in a trance. So profoundly was he affected that it was some time before he could speak. I have never known anyone to lose himself so completely in the spectacle of great art.'[5] Debussy had little knowledge of the English language, so must have been following the words from memory of the French translation.

One wonders how he felt about his Mélisande's behaviour towards Messager once he was with them both in London. He was certainly aware of the state of affairs between them, for on the evening of his theatre visit he wrote a letter to his wife, delighted with the room Messager had booked for him which overlooked the Thames, 'like the Seine, but twice as big and three times as dirty'. He then commented that Mary Garden was behaving 'like a mad little girl[6] and kicking up an enormous dust with Messager, her Director, her Maestro.'[7] He had been out shopping with them both that morning to buy a present for Lilly. 'Messager and Garden' sent their love when he wrote again to her that very day, expressing the view that absence makes the heart grow fonder and in which he not only commented on the difficulty in finding a good cup of tea in England but also on the unattractiveness of English women![8]

Pelléas et Mélisande continued to take up Debussy's time and energy on his return from London. Rehearsals for the new season began on 18 September 1902 and only a month later he was complaining to his friend, the novelist and poet Paul-Jean Toulet, that these had caused his delay in writing to him.[9] There were new members of the cast. Jean Périer had had to be replaced as he was singing elsewhere, which was a problem, for as Messager told Carré, the role was too high for a baritone and too low for a tenor.[10] Carré suggested a woman, Jeanne Raunay, might sing the role – not implausible as it was, of course, acted by a woman in the very first performance of Maeterlinck's play. Debussy was not mincing in his opinions to Messager: 'She sang me excerpts

[5] *Mary Garden's Story*, p. 76.
[6] 'une petite folle'.
[7] Debussy, *Correspondance*, p. 675.
[8] Debussy, *Correspondance*, p. 676.
[9] Debussy, *Correspondance*, p. 694.
[10] Letter of 26 May 1902, quoted in 'Lettres d'André Messager à Albert Carré (Extraits relatifs à *Pelléas et Mélisande* et présentés par Henri Borgeaud)', *Revue de musicologie* (July–December 1962), p. 102. The high baritone is often referred to as a *baryton martin*.

of *Pelléas* in a voice sounding like an excited, rather breathless old man.'[11] In the end it was a baritone, Lucien Rigaux who was chosen. Little Yniold was no longer sung by Blondin, but by a woman, Suzanne Dumesnil, and Jeanne Passama was Geneviève. These changes meant that on 30 October Carré and Messager found it feasible to reinsert the scene with the sheep, which had been omitted since the first performance.[12]

By June 1903 Debussy was still getting the proofs of the full score corrected for his publisher, Fromont. Meanwhile, he was also exercising his pen and somewhat barbed tongue as an idiosyncratic music critic on the review *Gil Blas*. In view of the fact that he was not one to mince his words about a work or a performer, his praise of Mary Garden's performance as Violetta in *La Traviata* at the Opéra-Comique on 12 February 1903 is all the more striking. She was:

> the star of the evening ... Her delicate and fragile crystal voice sometimes seemed at breaking point, before being reborn almost supernaturally. All the human suffering of a heart full of sacrifice was contained in this voice, and an understanding of art that went far beyond the written music.[13]

Debussy's criticisms were often trenchant and could be contradictory, but he remained consistent in his views about Mary's voice and interpretations, and never hid his admiration for her unique qualities.

In April 1903 Debussy travelled to London once more in his role as music critic, sending three articles to *Gil Blas* on the subject of Wagner's *Ring*, which he heard complete at Covent Garden, conducted by Hans Richter. He was complimentary about the opera house and praised his friend, André Messager, who 'looks after the artistic side of things in the best possible taste, and nobody seems to be in the least surprised. How strange all this is: they actually think a musician can run an opera house! Such positions are usually reserved for fools, or at least sticks-in-the-mud.'[14] It has to be said, though, that this opinion may not have been shared by all, for as in his first season at Covent Garden, Messager in fact spent most of the time in Paris, and did not conduct a single performance in London in his second season there.[15] On this occasion Debussy's room in the Hotel Cecil was not overlooking the Thames, but merely a dirty little yard. His mind was clearly still preoccupied with memories of his own opera, for on 1 May he wrote to Lilly commenting that there had been no joyful celebration on the first anniversary of *Pelléas*

[11] Debussy, *Correspondance*, p. 673.

[12] Debussy, *Correspondance*, p. 683. See Chapter 6, p. 98.

[13] *Gil Blas*, 16 February 1903: translated in *Debussy on Music*, p. 121.

[14] *Gil Blas*, translated in *Debussy on Music*, p. 189.

[15] Harold Rosenthal, *Two Centuries of Opera at Covent Garden* (London 1958), p. 298.

the day before. Instead he had heard *Siegfried*, which bore no relation to it. 'I have never been so bored. Afterwards Messager had a headache and we went to bed without any further distraction.'[16] He was to return with huge relief to the familiarity of his native land.

Back home again, he wrote a letter to Messager with an interesting post-script, for he obviously knew that Messager's relationship with Mary was at an end. He reports: 'Saw Garden ... seems very ill-disposed towards you.'[17] This might well have been her reaction after the encounter she describes in her autobiography which took place when she was staying in London. She unexpectedly met Messager on the stairs of the hotel, upon which he declared, 'I've got to see you again.' The stirrings of the old familiar emotion overwhelmed her. 'As he spoke there was all that desire, or sex, call it what you will, all over again, and I had thought myself completely cured.'[18] This was the man who had made her feel ill from the storminess of their relationship, whose temper and possessiveness had worn her down. But now something gave way in her and she agreed to lunch with him the next day. However, she was persuaded by friends to return to Paris before the assignation so was saved from yet another showdown with her former lover.

In June 1903 Mary was again in London ready to appear in Gounod's *Roméo et Juliette*, to be conducted by Luigi Mancinelli. She stayed at the Hotel Cecil as previously, in a room with a pleasant view over the Thames. Two days before the opening, she was found by the Belgian tenor, Ernest Van Dyck, sitting by her open window. He immediately warned her to move away, exclaiming, 'No singer can do that in London and not pay for it!' His words were prophetic, for on the morning of her performance disaster struck. She was unable to produce any high notes. She remained quiet all day, dreading the moment when she would have to put her voice to the test in public. At the vital moment she was seized by panic, and had to be virtually pushed onto the stage by the bass singer Pol Plançon. 'What a débâcle, that whole first act!', she wrote. 'Every note above A had to be imagined by the audience because there just wasn't any note.' Fortunately matters improved, and she was able to finish the opera much better than she had begun it, but the London critics were not willing to make allowances for Mary's indisposition. Although she was soon able to impress them in her performances in *Manon* and *Faust*, adverse comments from the time of her illness hurt her pride and coloured her whole view of London and the English. This misfortune also meant that she lost the opportunity to sing at a Royal Command

[16] Debussy, *Correspondance*, p. 728.

[17] 'mal vissée à votre endroit.' *Correspondance*, p. 730.

[18] *Mary Garden's Story*, p. 55.

Performance in honour of the visit of the President of the French Republic at the Royal Opera House on 7 July 1903. She preserved the beautiful silk programme for this occasion, but her name does not appear on it. Calvé sang Carmen, and Melba sang Gilda in *Rigoletto* as well as the role Mary would have performed, Juliette in *Roméo et Juliette*.[19]

Back in France Debussy still had to get the proofs for the full score of the opera ready, and in June wrote to Messager in London expressing thanks for his help in this task, once again sending his love to Mary: 'I'll be writing to Mélisande soon. Give her a kiss from both of us while she is waiting.'[20] A kiss? Perhaps she did not want one via Messager.

By September Debussy was expressing his determination to compose again, but stressing the need to get away from the style of *Pelléas*. However, as Albert Carré wrote, 'the fatal doubt fostered in him by those who laughed on 30 April 1902' had reinforced his lack of self-confidence after *Pelléas*.[21] Debussy's publisher, Jacques Durand, tried often but unsuccessfully to assuage the composer's fear that unfavourable comparisons would be made between any new theatrical work and *Pelléas*.[22] Debussy had complained to Messager the previous September that he was feeling 'like a squeezed lemon, and my poor brain has been on strike. In order to do what I want I must completely clear out the old. To begin a new work appears to me like a perilous leap, with the risk of breaking one's back.'[23] To Louis Laloy he said he never wanted to write another *Pelléas*, for 'You can't repeat a miracle.'[24]

He decided to concentrate on a work he had begun in 1889, *Le Diable dans le beffroi*, based on Edgar Allan Poe's tale *The Devil in the Belfry*. The quirky mood of this strange little story certainly contrasts with the sombre, passionate darkness of *Pelléas et Mélisande*. Debussy's comments in a letter to Messager are hardly surprising. The scenario was almost complete, but he had not decided on the 'colour of the music' he wanted to use. He refused to bow to public pressure and make compromises where the style of composition was concerned. People who wanted him to carry on composing in the same style as *Pelléas* were simply blind to reality:

> They don't realise that if that were to happen I would immediately start growing pineapples in my bedroom, for the worst thing is to 'begin all over again'.

[19] RCM, London, Mary Garden Collection, album XI.

[20] 'Voulez-vous l'embrasser pour nous deux en attendant.' Debussy, *Correspondance*, pp. 745–6.

[21] 'Le doute fatal, que les rieurs du 30 avril 1902 avaient entretenu en lui ...' Carré, *Souvenirs de théâtre*, p. 282.

[22] Jacques Durand, *Quelques souvenirs d'un éditeur de musique*, vol. 2 (Paris, 1924), p. 9.

[23] Debussy, *Correspondance*, p. 686.

[24] Laloy, *La Musique retrouvée*.

Claude Debussy

Verl. Herm. Leiser Berlin Wilm.

1 Claude Debussy, composer of *Pelléas et Mélisande*

2 The Opéra-Comique, a postcard dating from the early twentieth century

3 Portrait of Camille Mauclair by L. Lévy-Dhurmer, dated 1896

4 Georgette Leblanc in 1895, aged 26, the year she met Maeterlinck

CARMEN

5 Georgette Leblanc as Carmen 1898, as she appeared on the cover of *Le Théâtre*,
February 1899

6 Maurice Maeterlinck, Georgette Leblanc and Mathilde Deschamps out for a walk,
c. 1899

7 Mary Garden aged three. She fondly remembered standing on a table and singing to family members.

8 Mary Garden aged fourteen

9 Mary Garden and André Messager in Monte Carlo, December 1901

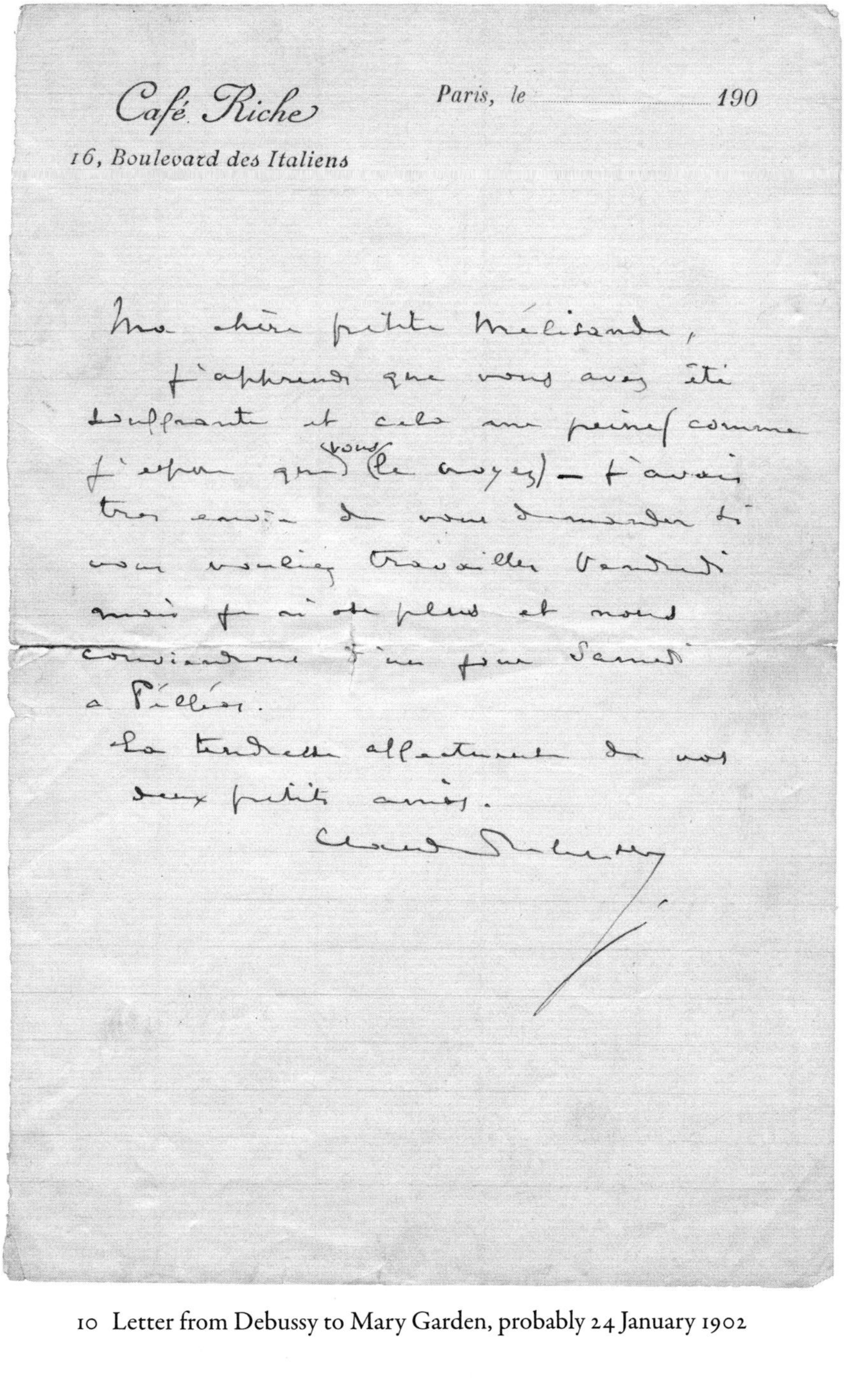

Café Riche

Paris, le 190

16, Boulevard des Italiens

Ma chère petite Mélisande,

J'apprends que vous avez été souffrante et cela me peine, comme j'espère que vous (le croyez) — J'avais très envie de vous demander si vous vouliez travailler Vendredi mais je n'ai osé plus et nous conviendrons d'un jour Samedi à Pelléas.

La tendresse affectueuse de vos deux petits amis.

Claude Debussy

10 Letter from Debussy to Mary Garden, probably 24 January 1902

11 Mary Garden as Mélisande, 1902,
as she appeared on the cover of *Le Théâtre*, June 1902

12　Mary Garden as Mélisande, 1902. Photograph signed by Mary Garden.

13 Pelléas and Mélisande by the Well of the Blind (Act II scene 1),
scenery by Jusseaume

14 Golaud surprises Pelléas and Mélisande (Act IV scene 4), scenery by Jusseaume

15 Debussy with Mary Garden and the cast of *Pelléas et Mélisande*,
undated photograph

16 Debussy in his study. On his desk is his wooden toad, Arkel.

17   Albert Carré: 'To Mary Garden, with my greatest admiration,
with my deepest affection, 14 May 1927'

18 André Messager in Monte Carlo, from the cover of *Musica*, September 1908

It is quite likely that the same people would find it scandalous for me to have abandoned the shade of Mélisande for the ironic pirouette of the Devil and it would be another excuse to accuse me once more of oddity.[25]

This project would never come to fruition. Albert Carré was certainly aware of it, for he expressed his regret that the composer did not write another work for the Opéra-Comique, although he knew he had certainly begun composing an opera based on Poe's *The Fall of the House of Usher* as well as *The Devil in the Belfry*, and had even considered a *Don Juan*, or an *Orpheus*. Debussy would never complete another full-scale opera. Catulle Mendès, so unappreciative of the combination of words and music in *Pelléas*,[26] had long been expecting Debussy to set his libretto *Rodrigue et Chimène*. This was based on the Spanish hero who was already the subject of Massenet's opera, *El Cid*, first performed in 1885. Debussy had agreed to do this as far back as April 1890, for, as Mendès had paid to have Debussy's *Fantaisie* for piano and orchestra engraved, he could hardly refuse. Hardly surprisingly, this was not a work Debussy could identify with wholeheartedly, the grandiloquent text having nothing in common with those ideals he had expressed to his teacher, Guiraud, so closely matched in the early symbolist plays of Maeterlinck. Although he told Robert Godet in 1892 that he had completed two acts, in fact there is no evidence that Debussy completed even one act. Whole pages and some of the vocal parts are missing from Acts I and III, of which only the short scores are extant. Act II appears only in a piano-vocal reduction, and also lacks some of the vocal score. Act IV has never been found, if indeed it ever existed.[27]

Whilst Debussy was searching for inspiration for a new project, rehearsals had had to resume for *Pelléas et Mélisande* for the 1903 season at the Opéra-Comique. On 16 May 1903 a significant event had occurred for Mary: that great singer who had taken her under her wing and introduced her to Albert Carré, Sibyl Sanderson, died. There are contrasting versions of Mary's attitude to Sibyl. In her autobiography Mary devotes three pages to Sibyl's death, but fails to mention two important facts. In 1902 Sibyl had repeatedly asked her for a loan, but Mary refused to grant it, in spite of Sibyl's previous assistance to her. She was later to justify this by saying she did not want to contribute to her friend's physical and mental self-destruction, or, as she is said to have put it, perhaps in more honest terms, 'Why should I loan her any

---

[25] Debussy, *Correspondance*, p. 780.

[26] See Chapter 8, p. 102.

[27] The score of Acts I to III was reconstructed by Richard Langham Smith. It was orchestrated by E. Denisov and performed by the Opéra de Lyon, May 1993. A recording of this performance can be heard on CD: Erato/Radio France 4509-98508-2 (1995).

money when all she would have done is spend it on more booze?'[28] More significant, however, was Mary's statement that she had heard stories about Sibyl's lesbianism and knew now of Massenet's alleged role in arranging for Sibyl to be seduced.[29] But Sibyl had admitted to her that she was indeed a lesbian and was no longer ashamed of it. Mary promised her not to reveal her secret, but decided that she could no longer afford to be seen with Sibyl in public.[30] The second fact is that despite their quarrel, in her will Sibyl left Mary the diamond-topped walking stick that Manon carried in the opera of that name. After her death, Mary is said to have claimed not just this, but also wigs, costumes and stage jewellery, to the dismay of Sibyl's sisters.[31] A different opinion of Mary's attitude to Sibyl was given by author William Armstrong, however, who believed she had been a loyal friend right up to the end. He pointed out that she was one of the few present at Sibyl's funeral, at which Massenet was not in attendance, 'nor did he trouble himself to send flowers. But Massenet had so many lovers that, had they died, to have provided flowers for the funeral of all would have bankrupted him.'[32]

In 1903, whilst in London, Mary had her first experience of recording onto wax cylinders with the Pathé company. The recording industry was in its infancy and she found it difficult to concentrate, complaining that the recording machine sprayed wax shavings over her.[33] The works were short, not operatic arias, but some Scottish songs. Only later recordings of these can be heard today. In 1904 it was in Paris for the Gramophone and Typewriter Company Ltd that she recorded for the first time some of Debussy's music, with the composer himself as her accompanist. The first set of songs was three *Ariettes oubliées*, settings of texts by Paul Verlaine: *Green*, *L'Ombre des arbres* and *Il pleure dans mon cœur*. Then comes the briefest of excerpts from *Pelléas et Mélisande*: 'Mes longs cheveux'.[34] However dim the tiny excerpt of Mélisande (Act III scene 1) may sound, it is apposite that the only evidence we have of her interpretation of the role should be the song of her iconic hair. We hear Debussy's rather uneven triplets precede Mary's slight scoop

[28] Hansen, *The Sybil Sanderson Story*, p. 475.

[29] See Chapter 5, p. 74.

[30] Hansen, *The Sybil Sanderson Story*, p. 422.

[31] Hansen, *The Sybil Sanderson Story*, p. 422.

[32] Armstrong, *The Romantic World of Music*.

[33] Richard D. Fletcher, 'The Mary Garden of Record', *Saturday Review*, 27 February 1954, p. 49.

[34] *Legendary Piano Recordings*, Marston 52054 (2008). Also *Claude Debussy: The Composer as Pianist*, The Caswell Collection, vol. 1, Pieran Recording Society, Pieran 0001. *L'Ombre des arbres* is also on vol. 1 of the *Opera in Chicago* series, Symposium CD 1136 (1992).

into her first note. The speed is certainly 'modéré', perhaps the reason for her splitting the first two phrases after the words 'descendent' and 'attendent'. The instruction 'librement' (freely) is observed in the stretching of 'tout le long du jour' and even more so at the end of the song, 'un dimanche à midi.' The highest notes are pure and accurate, although the sound is thin as she holds onto the last syllable of 'Raphael'. Recording techniques still had a long way to go. How Mary hated the cylinders:

> I can think of only one value that the disks made from them could have. People have a chance to hear Debussy at the piano, and the women who sing Mélisande should listen to those disks over and over again. For they would then understand the tempo to take. Otherwise those disks are worthless. Debussy didn't enjoy doing them very much. But then he never enjoyed anything really, except writing music.[35]

In the songs, the composer supports her discretely, even through a very shaky start to *L'Ombre des arbres*. Mary even seems to speak before the end of this song – perhaps she would have liked to rerecord it! To be able to appreciate Debussy's accurate observation of time values bears out what Maggie Teyte was later to insist about the necessity of treating his music like Mozart's, rigidly observing everything he wrote. Whatever Mary's disparaging opinion of the recordings, it is fascinating to be able to hear her voice, although distant, still alive after over a century thanks to modern technology. Surely we should be grateful that we have a record (in both senses of the word) of its purity and clarity and can begin to glean some intimation of her magical star quality.

Mary claims that in July 1904 she made a lightning trip with Debussy to London to see a matinée of Maeterlinck's play, *Pelléas et Mélisande*, with a woman, the great Sarah Bernhardt, as Pelléas, and Mrs Patrick Campbell as Mélisande, to be given in French at the Vaudeville Theatre.[36] Bernhardt (now aged sixty!) had originally been impressed by Mrs Campbell as Mélisande in the earlier English production, and this new collaboration was at her suggestion. She assured Mrs Campbell that her English accent would emphasise the other-worldliness of Mélisande, and indeed the production became a commercial success, the leading drama critic James Agate believing Bernhardt's Pelléas to be the best thing she ever did.[37] A question mark arises over the authenticity of this excursion,[38] simply because if Mary and Debussy did go to a matinée, this must have been on 19 July according to

[35] *Mary Garden's Story*, p. 234.

[36] *Mary Garden's Story*, pp. 76–7.

[37] Brandon, *Being Divine*, p. 343.

[38] Lesure, *Claude Debussy*, p. 262.

the dates of the performances,[39] which also happens to be the date of a letter written by Debussy to Lilly addressed from Paris. (Lilly was staying at
her parents' house in Bichain at that time, when relations between Lilly and
Debussy were strained owing to the complications arising from his relationship with Emma Bardac.) However, in Mary's defence, she does emphasise
that she and Debussy were particularly eager to see this production out of
sheer curiosity. They took the night train from Paris, lunched with a friend
and started their return journey as soon as the performance ended, arriving back in Paris about midnight. It is therefore possible that Debussy, who
quite naturally would have been preoccupied with his marital problems,
could have dated this letter 19 July if he wrote it immediately upon his return.
Mary writes that both she and Debussy were horrified at the portrayal of the
characters with whom they were so familiar. None of the cast had understood Maeterlinck's drama, and Bernhardt was 'utterly miscast.' Mary even
whispered to a restless Debussy, 'She is trying to impersonate Robin Hood.'
To the horror of both Mary and Debussy, the romantic tower scene brought
a shock: 'Debussy almost screamed when Mrs Patrick Campbell unloosed
an avalanche of jet-black hair!'[40]

Only a couple of weeks later, Debussy and Emma Bardac went to stay
in Jersey at the Grand Hotel. When he wrote to Jacques Durand at the end
of the month Debussy asked him not to reveal this address to anyone.[41] In
September, Debussy wrote to Messager from Dieppe, expressing a desire to
meet him and chat over a whisky so that he could attempt to explain why he
had not been as productive as he would have wished. The overriding emotion he felt was nostalgia for his younger self, claiming that he missed the
old Debussy who used to work so happily on *Pelléas*. 'Between ourselves', he
wrote, 'I have never found him again.'[42] One wonders under what circumstances Messager must have shown Mary Garden this letter, for she certainly
had seen it. We have read her version of Debussy's declaration of love for her,
which, if it ever happened, must have taken place early in 1904. She was to
draw the conclusion:

> I honestly don't know if Debussy ever loved anybody really. He loved his music
> – and perhaps himself. I think he was wrapped up in his genius. People say he
> married Mme Bardac for money, but I don't know. He was a very strange man.
> Perhaps he was unhappy at the end. Messager showed me a letter from him
> that might bear that out. 'Oh, how I wish I could recapture the happiness

[39] *The Times*, 6 July 1904.
[40] *Mary Garden's Story*, p. 76.
[41] Debussy, *Correspondance*, p. 859.
[42] Debussy, *Correspondance*, p. 866.

of the days of *Pelléas et Mélisande*!' he wrote. 'But it is hopeless. That joy has vanished forever.'[43]

To whom did Lilly Debussy turn on discovering her husband's infidelity, but Mary? In a frenzy of tears she told her that Debussy had simply gone for a walk one morning and never come back. A week later – it must have been shortly after 13 October 1904 – Mary received a message telling her to go to a certain hospital. The drama of the situation is grist to Mary's mill. One can imagine her voice rising with excitement as she lets the suspense build and the tragedy unfold in her telling, for on arriving at the hospital, Mary found Lilly wounded from a self-inflicted gunshot after Debussy's father had told her that his son was in Dieppe, living with Emma Bardac.[44] Other shocked visitors at Lilly's bedside included André Messager, the last person Mary wanted to see in the circumstances. He offered to see her home, and foolishly she asked him in for a cup of tea. There she felt revolted when she saw the old look of desire in his eyes and hastily showed him the door.[45] That Mary assisted Lilly throughout her ordeal is supported by a statement from Henri Busser of the Opéra-Comique, who saw Lilly at Mary's apartment on the very day she came out of hospital.[46] Now, knowing that the poor woman had no money, Mary rallied friends around and raised enough to pay for an apartment near her own in which Lilly could recuperate.

Debussy's old friends wanted no more to do with him. There they were, helping Mary to raise funds to accommodate Lilly in a small flat whilst in their eyes he was all set to live in ease with a wealthy banker's wife. Mary's handwritten notebooks contain the sentence, 'His first wife was young and poor. His second was old and rich.'[47] This despite the fact that Emma Bardac's supposed fortune, an inheritance from a rich uncle, never materialised. Debussy's divorce was financed by the sale of the score of *La Mer* and the rights to *Pelléas et Mélisande* and all future works to Durand, his publisher. This guaranteed him an annual income.[48] On 4 May 1905 Emma obtained her divorce. Debussy's divorce from Lilly was not finalised until 2 August.

Much later on, Mary's sister Helen was to tell an interviewer a shocking story, claiming that when Emma was pregnant Debussy not only went to

---

[43] *Mary Garden's Story*, p. 80.

[44] *Mary Garden's Story*, pp. 82–4.

[45] *Mary Garden's Story*, p. 84.

[46] Henri Busser, *De Pelléas aux Indes Galantes* (Paris, 1955), p. 138.

[47] Notebook in RCM, London, Mary Garden Collection.

[48] Debussy, *Correspondance*, pp. 893–5.

sleep with Lilly, but he took any money Lilly had been given by friends.[49] Truth or sour grapes? Rumours were rife, but remain only such.

At the Opéra-Comique in the season of 1904–5 Mary was much admired in two eponymous roles, Hélène by Saint-Saëns, and Chérubin, the hero of Massenet's opera. Her natural jauntiness in the *travesti* role brought comments on her appeal as a cross-dresser. Also singing in *Chérubin* was the woman who was to become Mary's rival and who was to influence future casting of the role of Mélisande, Marguerite Carré. She could not have failed to notice Mary's attractiveness in male dress. More of her later.

In October 1905 Mary visited Rome. She spent a whole year studying Italian, but apparently never really liked it. However, Vincent Sheean is convinced that the language served her well, believing it brought out tones in her voice which had hardly been heard before.[50] Whilst there she visited a friend whom she and Debussy had in common. When the young composer had been unhappily incarcerated in the city as a winner of the Prix de Rome, one of his escapes in 1885 was to the home of Count Giuseppe Primoli, whom he had met in Paris the previous year. Now, twenty years later, it was to the Count that Mary turned for advice when she received a telegram from Windsor Castle asking her to sing the following week, on 17 November, for King George of Greece. She was loath to leave the city where she was enjoying herself, but Count Primoli insisted she had no choice in the matter.[51]

On arrival at the Castle Mary found that, amongst others, Nellie Melba was to be performing. Landon Ronald accompanied both, the latter singing from *La bohème* and *Rigoletto*, and Mary singing 'Vissi d'arte' from *Tosca* and 'Depuis le jour' from *Louise*.[52] At supper after their performance, Melba left nobody in doubt as to her opinion of Mary. She suddenly announced in a loud voice: 'What a dreadful concert this would have been if I hadn't come!' Lord Farquhar hastily tried to pay Mary a compliment to cover up this remark, but Mary had not taken offence. 'I love Melba's rudeness. It amuses me', she joked magnanimously. She certainly did not bear Melba a grudge, for they travelled back to London together on the train and became firm friends.[53]

A new opera, *Aphrodite* by Camille Erlanger, took up Mary's time at the beginning of 1906. The book upon which the opera was based was

[49] Madeau Stewart notebook for BBC talk *c.* 1963, Oxfordshire Record Office, P143/04/ MS/001.

[50] Vincent Sheean, *Opera News*, 4 February 1967, p. 7.

[51] *Mary Garden's Story*, p. 91.

[52] *The Times*, 18 November 1905.

[53] *Mary Garden's Story*, p. 93.

by Debussy's great friend Pierre Louÿs,[54] and Mary was to sing the role of Chrysis. She claims it was she who had to convince Carré that the work should be performed, and chided him for being a prude, as he was anxious about the lesbian aspects of the story.[55] She, of course, relished the challenge. Carré certainly did everything he could to make her as sensuous as possible. In the scene where Chrysis was supposed to come to Demetrius almost naked, great efforts were made with lighting to give the illusion of nudity through a veil.[56] Although they had to admit defeat in this, her portrayal was declared a triumph.

Still in existence is a card from Louÿs himself, inviting Mary to lunch at 29 rue de Boulainvilliers, where she was to meet the dress designer Redfern to discuss costumes.[57] She found Louÿs a strangely intriguing creature, 'a timid, retiring, youthful looking man with a low voice and gentle manner. One could not believe that behind that wall of timidity there lay a voluptuous feline nature.'[58]

Whenever it was the turn of *Pelléas et Mélisande* to be produced at the Opéra-Comique, Debussy could not leave it alone. He felt impelled to make revisions to the score, and 1906 was no exception. This time, following his alterations, the horn parts were missing some bars.[59] Then Hector Dufranne, who was still singing Golaud, must have been at the sharp end of some criticism during a rehearsal, for in October the composer sent him a letter apologising for his 'nervosité', which had made him go 'further than he intended' in the way he had spoken to him. He and Vieuille (Arkel) were the only ones still keeping an understanding of the art he had tried to convey in *Pelléas*.[60] He must have taken for granted that Mary's performance was up to standard, for he does not remark upon it. However, advice was given to Ruhlmann (conducting eight performances in November and December 1906), to counteract the slackness of time-keeping by the singers. Debussy used the 'disorder' and his worries arising from the revival of *Pelléas* as an excuse for not writing earlier to Victor Charpentier, brother of Gustave, who wanted him to conduct an orchestra.[61] The performance of 23 December 1906 was in fact the fiftieth, and that very day Debussy wrote a letter of gratitude

54 The libretto was by Louis de Gramont.
55 *Mary Garden's Story*, p. 97.
56 *Mary Garden's Story*, p. 98.
57 RCM, London, Mary Garden Collection, album x.
58 Typescript in RCM, London, Mary Garden Collection.
59 Debussy, *Correspondance*, p. 975.
60 Debussy, *Correspondance*, p. 976.
61 Debussy, *Correspondance*, p. 977.

to Albert Carré in recognition of this.[62] He must have been pleased with Vieuille and Dufranne in the end, for he also wrote individual letters to them expressing his gratitude for their interpretations. Surely there must have been one to Mary, but we shall see eventually why this is probably no longer in existence.

On 5 October 1906 Mary signed a contract to sing at the Théâtre de la Monnaie in Brussels in which she agreed to a minimum of eight performances of *Pelléas et Mélisande* and to sing no other works in January 1907.[63] How irritated her former lover, Messager, became in his dealings with its director, Maurice Kufferath, at this time, for he had desperately wanted Mary to sing his *Madame Chrysanthème*. Now to his frustration Messager discovered she had been signed up to sing Debussy's Mélisande! Rather than employ somebody else he would rather his opera was not performed at all and demanded that rehearsals should stop. When *Madame Chrysanthème* did take place with Francès Alda in the role, it was no surprise to Messager that his opera was a flop. He argued fiercely that this was not because of the weakness of the work, nor because Alda could not sing well, but because of her inability to act and interpret the role in comparison with Mary.[64]

On 27 December, Debussy, his wife Emma and daughter Chouchou were on their way to the Hotel Metropole in Brussels. Debussy had been invited to attend rehearsals of his opera, the first time it was to be performed outside Paris. Despite a report in the paper that he was 'smiling and in good humour',[65] he did not enjoy the experience, as proved by a series of letters to Vital Hoquet and Jacques Durand.[66] The very next day he was writing, 'the rain, more Belgian than nasty, does not compensate for the boredom of rehearsals of *Pelléas*'. He was annoyed at a newspaper report that he had 'congratulated' the singers, and fed up with an orchestra which 'lacked tact and good taste.' The conductor, Sylvain Dupuis, 'more like a bull than a conductor, has a special way of deforming the simplest of rhythms ... the singers are a strange mixture.' Each of these in turn is subjected to biting criticism, except Mary Garden, for apart from her they were all new to their parts. Jean Bourbon (Golaud) had a nice voice but he declaimed like a house painter; Henri Artus (Arkel) not only lacked the build and nobility necessary for the role, he stank of wine like a furniture remover; Jeanne Bourgeois was not bad

[62] Debussy, *Correspondance*, p. 980.

[63] Her copy in RCM, London, Mary Garden Collection, album XIV.

[64] Three letters from Messager to Kufferath at Archives of La Monnaie, Brussels: 12 October 1906 (1395), 12 November 1906 (1413) and 2 December 1906 (1414).

[65] 'souriant et de bonne humeur': *L'Eventail*, 6 January 1907.

[66] Debussy, *Correspondance*, pp. 985, 986, 988.

as Geneviève, but Marguerite Das (Yniold) showed a disconcerting lack of vocal expertise. This Yniold was too young to know anything about music yet.[67] To Debussy's relief, the initial idea of having a woman to sing Pelléas had been rejected in favour of a tenor, Edmond Clément. However, when he saw Clément's markings on his score he realised he was making 'carnage' of the role, for having found the part too low, he had hardly left one phrase as originally written. Debussy therefore had to beg the director, Kufferath, to find another singer. Soon after, it was announced that Georges Petit would take over, having actually travelled to Paris to rehearse with the composer.[68] Once in Brussels, Debussy was particularly rude about the Belgians once again, his opinions no doubt having been particularly coloured by his previous encounters with Maeterlinck. 'This small nation resembles a lot of little men with a bombastic pretentiousness which is usually merely silly, but becomes dangerous when it is a question of the fate of a work of art.' He hated the sound of the bell which should have been in G but 'by some Belgian contradiction' was in C, thus sounding like a dinner bell at the castle, somehow making the death of Mélisande even sadder. 'May God preserve my friends from the artistic people of this country!', he exclaimed.[69]

Mary was ostensibly not of Debussy's opinion. Having received flowers and a telegram from impresario Gabriel Astruc, she wrote to him from her hotel, returning his good wishes, saying, 'We are rehearsing a lot. *Pelléas* is being performed next week and I think it will be a very great success for it is a very good production and is very, very well sung.' She found the directors of La Monnaie absolutely charming.[70] However, elsewhere she claimed she did not like the décor for the Brussels performance for it was too light, having been set in the Renaissance period, 'an epoch flooded with light and charm.' She pointed out that, 'Absolute latitude is permitted the stage director, as Maeterlinck has made no restrictions in the book. The Director of the Opéra at Brussels followed Mrs Campbell's example, and when I appeared in the work there I felt that I was singing a different drama.'[71]

It was Kufferath's idea to set this production in the style of early Renaissance Italy. He sketched designs which were then painted by Henry Cillard and Jean Delescluze.[72] The journal *L'Eventail* appreciated this more universal approach, stressing the importance of giving the impression that

[67] Debussy, *Correspondance*, p. 986.

[68] Denis Herlin, 'Pelléas et Mélisande à La Monnaie', in *La Monnaie symboliste*, ed. Manuel Couvreur and Roland van der Hoeven (Brussels, 2003), p. 219.

[69] Debussy, *Correspondance*, p. 988.

[70] Letter from Mary Garden to Gabriel Astruc: AML, Brussels, ML 5852/28.

[71] Van Vechten, *Interpreters and Interpretations*, p. 78.

[72] In the archives of La Monnaie.

the events were taking place outside time and history.[73] The initial sketches show, for example, an uncluttered room with graceful arches and plain furniture for the interior, and outside, a plain circular well in front of layers of trees. Yet, despite a suggestion that Maeterlinck himself may have helped Kufferath with this conception,[74] the author wrote to his friend Gérard Harry from Nice on 6 January 1907 to say that he had broken off all relations with the directors of La Monnaie. He was horrified to find that they had used old sets probably borrowed and patched up from ancient performances of *Huguenots* and *Juives*![75] Indeed, it is a fact that on the back of one sketch are scribbled the words, 'Forêt de *Grisélidis*'![76] Once again *Pelléas et Mélisande* was causing its author considerable distress.

This, in fact, was to be the last time that Mary and Debussy would work together in the opera house. Debussy remained adamant that he would give advice only from behind the scenes, and Mary claims he hardly spoke to her during rehearsals. The composer was 'silent and detached, and when he had anything to communicate to one of us on the stage, he would write it down on a slip of paper and send it up by a boy. But he never appeared on the stage and he never came over to greet me.'[77] Yet they were both staying at the same hotel, the Métropole. As Emma and Chouchou were there too, did this involve a complicated procedure for avoiding each other?

Hypocritically, having congratulated the conductor Sylvain Dupuis in florid terms after the dress rehearsal, expressing his pleasure in having worked with him, and asking him to pass on his thanks to the orchestral musicians, Debussy left on the very morning of the first performance on 9 January, so was able to avoid the curtain calls he so hated. The reviews of Mary's performance were outstanding. That in the *Guide Musical* also proved that Debussy's insistence on his interpretation of the play had paid dividends:

> We have to wonder what other musician could have brought to the stage a libretto like that of M. Maeterlinck so skilfully ... the music and the poem are so appropriate that you would think they were not only the product of the same brain but that they were both conceived simultaneously.[78]

[73] 'Il est important ... d'éviter tout rapprochement avec une époque précise et de donner l'impression d'une chose qui se passe hors du temps et de l'histoire.' *L'Eventail*, 30 September 1906.

[74] Herlin, 'Pelléas et Mélisande à La Monnaie', p. 221.

[75] Stadsarchief Gent B XLVIII.37.

[76] *Grisélidis* (Massenet), first performed at La Monnaie 18 March 1902. Scenery by Lynen and Devis. Archives of La Monnaie.

[77] *Mary Garden's Story*, p. 73.

[78] *Guide Musical*, 13 January 1907, quoted in Debussy, *Correspondance*, p. 992n.

The symbolist style of the dialogue and laboured course of events was parodied amusingly in *La Gazette* of 12 January. Two characters, 'Mélie Cendre' and 'Jenneviève', carry out an inane conversation complete with written instructions for an orchestral accompaniment. 'Dark chords' were to accompany the words 'How dark it is here!', to which the reply was 'It is always dark in this theatre.' Orchestral scales ascended and descended to the words 'It's someone coming up   Yes, it might have been someone going down.' The parody ends, 'What an interesting conversation! (the orchestra underlines the charm of the conversation)'.[79] Interestingly, this precedes by four years the famous pastiche of the opera written by Marcel Proust in 1911.[80]

Despite his kind words to the conductor, the opera's success in Brussels seems to have come as a surprise to its composer. After arriving back in his home city, Debussy wrote to Louis Laloy with a lamentable list of complaints! For two weeks he had had to re-educate the orchestra, the Flemish spirit was as easy to handle as a 100 kg weight, the woodwind were heavy and strident, whereas the brass sounded like cotton wool. The humblest rhythm was distorted and he had had a constant battle to achieve any sort of acceptable result.[81] Perhaps it was because of what he regarded as such a ponderous interpretation that he was to write to Kufferath on 11 January with the surprising opinion (expressed only on this occasion) that the five acts of *Pelléas* would have benefited from being cut to three![82]

In 1907 it was Mary's performance as Mélisande in her last season at the Opéra-Comique in Paris that Richard Strauss witnessed in person. Albert Carré ensured he sat in a first tier box with critic Jean Marnold, Romain Rolland and Maurice Ravel. Strauss whispered to Rolland throughout the performance, not taking his eyes off actors and orchestra for an instant. But he could not comprehend it. After the first act he asked Rolland: 'Is it always like this? ... Nothing more? There's nothing ... No music ... It doesn't connect ... It doesn't hold together.' He made an effort to point out what he found good in the work, but also didn't let one single Wagnerian 'imitation' pass without noticing it. His rather scornful praise was, 'It's very subtle.' 'Of course', writes Rolland, 'he was waiting for the obvious scene, and he doesn't understand that Debussy's originality was precisely that of not writing it.'

79 Roland van der Hoeven, 'De la musique des sphères aux coulisses de l'opéra', in M. Draguet, *Splendeurs de l'Idéal: Rops, Khnopff, Delville et leur temps* [exhibition catalogue] (Liège, 1997).

80 Published by Philip Kolb in *Les Cahiers Marcel Proust*; quoted in *L'Avant-Scène Opéra*, no. 9 (mars–avril 1998).

81 Debussy, *Correspondance*, p. 992.

82 Debussy, *Correspondance*, p. 990.

After the performance, discussions continued at the Taverne Pousset where Strauss rubbed his fingers together to show his appreciation of the work's subtlety, then continued, 'but it's never spontaneous; it lacks *Schwung*.'[83] The next day Rolland was invited to a dinner at which amongst others were Strauss, Mary Garden and a pretty American singer. Besides reporting Strauss's conversation, Rolland also commented on the attire of the two women, whose dresses were 'cut so low as to show their navels'![84] How typical of Mary! How she would have revelled in the sort of publicity today's stars receive as they flaunt the latest designer fashion to the flashing cameras of the paparazzi lurking outside fashionable restaurants.

Mary was a star. Her sensational entrance onto the operatic stage in *Louise* in 1900 and her creation of Mélisande in 1902, her reputation as the toast of the Paris audiences in old and new operas could not be matched in 1907. Little wonder that besides arousing the interest of the males in her vicinity this stirred jealousies and rivalry backstage at the Opéra-Comique. One woman in particular was determined to get rid of this phenomenon who was blocking her own career: Marguerite Carré, fourth wife of the director, Albert, who, as we have seen, had once asked Mary to marry him. When in 1901 Albert had auditioned a young tenor from Nantes, the unwise or naïve candidate had brought along a very pretty young girl to sing a duet with him and it was she rather than the man who was spotted. He thought 'the voice of the young girl was very pretty, her physique as well', and noted next to her name, 'Pretty voice, can do something in the theatre. To see again.'[85]

Marguerite was the daughter of the director of the theatre in Nantes, so was no stranger to the world of the stage. As Albert boasts in his memoirs, he took Marguerite twice to the registry office, for he divorced and remarried her, which gave him the dubious distinction of having had four wives and five marriages! Small wonder if other women at the Opéra-Comique, so desperate to make their mark and sing on stage, were put out at the rapid rise of this addition to their ranks, for Albert sees no irony in praising the speed at which she made her way at the Opéra-Comique. In October 1901 Marguerite made her début with a small part in *La bohème*.[86] She married Carré (for the first time) in October 1902 which clearly must have given her some influence. His support and authority must have enabled her to keep on singing despite bearing a child, born several weeks before their marriage.[87]

[83] Rolland's diary in *Richard Strauss and Romain Rolland: Correspondence, Diary and Essays*, ed. Rollo Myers (London, 1968), pp. 151–4.
[84] *Richard Strauss and Romain Rolland*, ed. Myers, p. 157.
[85] Carré, *Souvenirs de théâtre*, p. 268.
[86] Carré, *Souvenirs de théâtre*, p. 269.
[87] Carré, *Souvenirs de théâtre*, pp. 284–5.

Incidentally, when Albert Carré and Marguerite moved into a new flat in the rue Chauchat, just by the Opéra-Comique, Jusseaume, the designer of the sets for *Pelléas*, was given the task of designing frescoes for its walls. The inspirations for these were Carré's greatest operatic successes! On 14 February 1905 Marguerite sang the role of Nina in the first performance of Massenet's opera *Chérubin* in Monte Carlo, to be followed by its first performance at the Opéra-Comique on 23 May. The *travesti* title role in this opera was sung by Mary Garden to huge acclaim.

How lightly Albert Carré skips over Mary Garden's departure from the Opéra-Comique. After commenting on her sublime interpretation of Chrysis in *Aphrodite*, he merely comments that 'at the beginning of 1908 she left for America and I had the hard job of finding a replacement.'[88] It certainly was not only Mary's will that she should leave. Marguerite was making her life at the Opéra-Comique impossible. Mary wrote, 'I'm afraid the new Mme Carré wasn't a very good influence at the Comique, and besides she loathed me – why, I'm not sure, unless she knew or surmised how Carré had once felt about me.'[89] Marguerite's first line of attack was to spread the rumour that Mary was suffering from tuberculosis and would infect the other singers. She then made use of Mary's association with Sibyl Sanderson, trying to show that Sibyl had successfully introduced Mary to lesbianism. She sent Mary regular hate mail and spread scandalous stories about her, such as that she had sold her body to a man in Chicago in return for financing her studies.

It was a neat coincidence for Marguerite Carré that Mary had recently scored success in *Aphrodite*, the opera with those lesbian associations of which Carré had initially been wary. Was Mary a lesbian? Jack Winsor Hansen, who interviewed many people who knew both Sibyl and Mary whilst writing his biography of the former, quotes Quaintance Eaton as insisting that Mary was 'a closet bisexual' and says she had once made a pass at a student who later became one of America's most celebrated sopranos.[90] But Sibyl's stepdaughter Natica doubted very much that there was an affair between them. Having heard for years that her stepmother enjoyed sexual relations with women, she insisted that she never caught her in bed with any. Commenting on Marguerite Carré's smear campaign spreading the rumour that Sibyl and Mary had been lovers, she said, 'but it wasn't true. I ought to know; I lived with them.'[91]

---

[88] In fact it was October 1907. Carré, *Souvenirs de théâtre*, p. 312.

[89] *Mary Garden's Story*, p. 54.

[90] Hansen, *The Sybil Sanderson Story*, p. 475.

[91] Hansen, *The Sybil Sanderson Story*, p. 475.

Even roles outside the Opéra-Comique were now falling outside Mary's reach. What a stroke of fortune for her that the American publisher Gustave Schirmer, who had originally done his apprenticeship at the publishing house of Durand and was passionate about contemporary French music, should be determined to bring *Pelléas et Mélisande* to New York. He was adamant that Mary should perform her iconic role and insisted that not just she but all her fellow cast should be engaged.[92] It was Schirmer who persuaded Oscar Hammerstein to go to see and hear Mary singing at the Opéra-Comique, which he did first in 1906. Mary did not initially realise the importance of the great impresario and had not bothered to entertain him when he wanted an appointment, but Hammerstein did not give up that easily. This huge personality, who had made his fortune in the tobacco industry, was determined to make a resounding success of opera in America and had built his third theatre, the first Manhattan Opera House in 1893. In 1906 he opened his eighth theatre, which became the second Manhattan Opera House, and in 1908 he built his ninth, the Philadelphia Opera House.

Hammerstein was not immediately impressed with *Pelléas et Mélisande*, announcing after the first act that he had had enough and that the opera would bore the American public. Schirmer fortunately managed to persuade him to sit through the whole performance,[93] which ultimately led to Hammerstein's buying the American rights to the two operas which were most closely associated with Mary Garden: *Pelléas* and *Louise*. Now he was determined to recreate these works as closely as possible.

Mary's account of their meeting differs from the above, but is typically entertaining.[94] She claims to have returned home one day from the Opéra-Comique to find Hammerstein waiting for her in the drawing room. Without any preliminary formalities, he looked at her and said: 'Turn around, Mary, and let me see your figure.' Mary took to him at once, 'that breezy and hearty American, so unlike all the other impresarios I have ever known, with their usual questions about what other operas you've sung and how much money you want, and with whom you studied. Not Oscar! Oh, no, he wanted to know what I looked like from behind.'[95]

The impresario told her about his Manhattan Opera House, then informed her there was an opera he wanted to ask her about: 'It's called *Pelzees and Maylisander*, and it's by a man named Deboozy.' Mary laughed. 'Don't you think you'd better go and hear *Pelzees and Maylisander* yourself,

92   Durand, *Quelques souvenirs d'un éditeur de musique*, p. 129.
93   C. Engel, *The Musical Quarterly*, October 1922, pp. 615–16.
94   *Mary Garden's Story*, p. 99.
95   *Mary Garden's Story*, p. 100.

Mr. Hammerstein, and then make up your own mind?' Here Mary claims that she persuaded her sister, Agnes, to take Mr. Hammerstein to listen to the opera, and it was only at that point that he bought it. When she insisted that she would not sing *Pelléas* with anybody who was not French or at least in the French tradition, Hammerstein explained he would engage the other singers who had created *Pelléas* with Mary and have exact copies made of the scenery.

The next day they went for a car ride together. How operatic a journey (and a tale ripe for exaggeration) it turned out to be! Mary, Agnes and Oscar Hammerstein hired a car and chauffeur, and were riding along happily towards Fontainebleau[96] when suddenly a wheel fell off, throwing the three passengers into a field of poppies. 'Miraculously, nobody was hurt', continues Mary. She picked herself up and:

> walked through the poppies, which are so beautiful in the spring in France. Then I sat myself down in the middle of them, and called out: 'Mr. Hammerstein, come on over here and keep me company!' And that great and lovable impresario, immaculately dressed, with his silk hat, and that everlasting cigar in his mouth, came over and sat down beside me among the poppies on that beautiful spring day in France.
>
> 'Mary', he said, 'I've a better idea than yours. Let's sign that contract right here.'
>
> And there, propped up on a mass of lovely poppies, we signed a four-year contract [*sic*] and I'm certain that there was never another contract signed that way at any time anywhere else in the world.[97]

Mary was quick to share the news of her good fortune with her former lover. A telegram, still in existence, reads: 'Messager Directeur Opera Love Mary. Signed for three years with Hammerstein.'[98]

Two operas at La Monnaie in Brussels, *Faust* and *La Traviata* preceded Mary's departure for America. Now she was to return to the country where she had spent her childhood to demonstrate to her utmost those star qualities which had brought her such fame in Europe.

---

[96] In fact it was to Versailles.
[97] *Mary Garden's Story*, p. 102.
[98] RCM, London, Mary Garden Collection, album ix.

10 *Return of Georgette Leblanc*
(1902–7)

WHAT OF THAT OTHER Mélisande – who dreamed of being first to sing the role and was thwarted in her ambition by both opera director and composer? Georgette Leblanc and Maurice Maeterlinck had moved into the presbytery in Gruchet-Saint-Siméon in 1897 which remained their country retreat for almost ten years. Here the author completed the text of *Ariane et Barbe-Bleue*. This was first published in his third volume of collected plays in 1901, but, despite Maeterlinck's claim that he knew nothing about music, was written specifically 'to provide musicians with a theme suitable for musical development'.[1] Paul Dukas, whose *L'Apprenti sorcier* had been composed in 1897, wrote the music. Maeterlinck knew who he wanted to sing the role of Ariane. Inevitably, this role became almost as important to Georgette as that of Mélisande. However, it was to be several years before she was able to fulfil this ambition, and her life, meanwhile, was as dramatic and sensational as ever.

Lugné-Poë, who had mounted the first performance of the play *Pelléas et Mélisande*, planned to put on Maeterlinck's play *Monna Vanna* at the Théâtre Français in Paris in 1902 in the hope that this would bring him fame and financial security. Georgette claims that when writing this play the author would ask her for her views on certain scenes and she came to identify herself with 'this stubborn Vanna lady'.[2] Just as in the Mélisande fiasco, she insists Maeterlinck desired her to play Monna Vanna, and at the same time realises the irony of his pronouncement, for despite not liking music he had an acute sense of the musicality of words. How otherwise could he say, 'Your speaking voice is so beautiful, why not create Monna Vanna?'[3] She asserts that in her mind's eye she saw only her heroine, Sarah Bernhardt, in the role. Lugné-Poë definitely wanted Bernhardt rather than Georgette. However, when Bernhardt discovered that Monna Vanna did not appear until towards the end of the first act and then only to say a few words, she demanded that the script be revised to allow her immediate entry on stage. When Maeterlinck refused to do this, by default the role was allocated to Georgette.

---

[1] C. Headington, R. Westbrook and T. Barfoot, *Opera: A History* (London, 1991), p. 270.

[2] Leblanc, *Souvenirs: My Life with Maeterlinck*, p. 199.

[3] Leblanc, *Souvenirs: My Life with Maeterlinck*, p. 199.

Lugné-Poë could not stand Georgette. He was very suspicious of her influence over Maeterlinck, blaming her for his change of direction as he moved away from Symbolism. He hated the way she called Maeterlinck 'Bébé' and behaved like his wet-nurse even in public, denigrating her as 'a mediocre opera singer ... not very highly thought of amongst musicians ... Her closest friends say of her that in mime she would be incomparable.'[4] How damning. Georgette had received no formal theatrical training, had never acted professionally on stage before and was inordinately grateful for any advice he gave her. When she thanked him fulsomely for his guidance however, he suspected she was being insincere. Maeterlinck himself even accused Lugné-Poë of never having liked the play and of hating Georgette![5]

What an odd couple Georgette and Maeterlinck were. One of the reasons Maeterlinck was uncharacteristically willing to go to rehearsals of his play despite the rather seedy environment in which they took place was that opposite resided a well-known fencing master. The author went wild there with his sword, even to the extent of forcing Lugné-Poë to oppose him, pretending to be Albert Carré, so detested since depriving Georgette of the role of Mélisande! Georgette herself designed the green coat for her performance as Monna Vanna and insisted on its remaining green, making the unlikely claim that she did not know that fear of this colour was 'one of the thousand superstitions which consume actors'.[6]

So it came about that on 17 May 1902 at the Nouveau Théâtre Georgette appeared in her first stage play, another work by Maeterlinck, only a fortnight after the première of Debussy's *Pelléas et Mélisande*. Needless to say, like Mary Garden in *Aphrodite*, she revelled in the opportunity to shock, for in the second act Georgette supposedly appeared naked beneath her green coat when Monna Vanna went to Prinzivalle's tent to save the starving people of Pisa. The play achieved successful reviews and a European tour followed. In June the production arrived in London, but was banned from the Victoria Hall by the censor. Ingeniously, those who were determined to see it formed 'The London Maeterlinck Society', and organised a private showing on 19 June. The *Times* reviewer found the play ethically innocuous and considered it admirably interpreted by Georgette Leblanc, 'a beautiful woman with a resonant voice and the air of a full-blooded Madonna. If there is such a thing as voluptuous chastity, here is its

---

4 'une quelconque chanteuse ... ses plus intimes disent que dans la mime elle serait incomparable.' Aurélien-François-Marie Lugné-Poë, *Sous les étoiles* (Paris, 1933), p. 49.

5 'Il est certain que tu n'as jamais aimé la pièce ... il est plus certain encore que tu as toujours détésté Georgette.' Lugné-Poë, *Sous les étoiles*, p. 54.

6 Leblanc, *Souvenirs: My Life with Maeterlinck*, p. 202.

representative.'[7] Another admirer of her interpretation was Georges Maurevert, who even found 'Georgette of the beautiful arms' superior to 'Duse of the beautiful hands'.[8]

In view of her success, did she manage to convince Maeterlinck of her value as an actress any more than as a singer? It would appear not. She realised that in his opinion, 'the exhibitionary aspect of acting made it an inferior art. But is not art always exhibitionism? Is it more noble to reveal our thoughts in books than to divulge our personality on the stage in a fictitious form?'[9] She saw no hierarchy among the arts, believing art to be a means, not an end.

Maeterlinck accompanied his *Monna Vanna* as far as Germany and Austria, but typically returned home whilst Georgette went on to Athens. There she met King George I of Greece, who in 1901 had invited Mary Garden to his country.[10] He, with his customary generosity towards glamorous stars, wanted to present Georgette with a beautiful emerald. She, to his frustration, insisted instead on a poetic night-time visit to the Acropolis.[11] Following the success of *Monna Vanna*, Georgette's next role as Maeterlinck's *Joyzelle* in May 1903 was commemorated with her picture on the cover of the journal *Le Théâtre*.[12]

1903 is also the year of an extant recording of Georgette accompanied by Massenet, singing 'Pendant un an je fus ta femme' from his opera *Sapho*, in which she had originally performed in 1898. This was recorded by Gramophone and Typewriter Limited in Paris, and apparently was never intended for publication.[13]

What sort of a relationship was this between Maurice Maeterlinck and Georgette Leblanc? How could he treat her so dismissively? Was she clinging to some ideal that never existed outside her own mind? Here was Georgette starring in *Monna Vanna*, taking it all over Europe, appearing on the cover of a respected magazine as his Joyzelle, and what support did he give? In 1904 he addressed a letter to 'Madame Maeterlinck' at Gruchet-Saint-Siméon, informing her that his father had died in Ghent. Not long after he insisted that he did not want her stage name of Leblanc next to his.[14] Georgette was not alone when he was elsewhere, however. Whether in Gruchet or in

---

[7] *The Times*, 20 June 1902.

[8] Maurevert, *L'Art, le boulevard et la vie*, p. 294.

[9] Leblanc, *Souvenirs: My Life with Maeterlinck*, p. 206.

[10] See Chapter 6, p. 83.

[11] Leblanc, 'Histoire de ma vie'.

[12] *Le Théâtre*, July 1903.

[13] See Introduction p. 5. Note by Ward Marston in booklet accompanying *Legendary Piano Recordings*, Marston 52054–2 (2008).

[14] Benoît-Jeannin, *Georgette Leblanc*, p. 245.

Paris she had the constant companionship of Mathilde Deschamps, a girl from the Normandy countryside, who watched over her and managed the household.[15]

Mathilde was much more than a housekeeper and secretary. Mathilde ruled the roost. She contributed to the unsettled feelings Lugné-Poë experienced in Georgette's presence, for he described Mathilde as rather strange-looking, a sort of 'Irish policeman',[16] somewhat masculine in appearance. She wore a man's hat, sometimes a tie. When in Paris, Georgette frequented venues where lesbian encounters were not unusual. Nor was Maeterlinck immune to casual relationships. When he was restless and could not work, Georgette recognised the problem:

> whether the cause was blonde or brunette, whether she had black eyes or blue, there was only one way to help him out of his dilemma. 'We'll ask her to tea', I would say, to which he would add carelessly, 'And I'll take her home afterward.' The lady's home was never very far away.[17]

At Gruchet, to satisfy the author's need for regular meals, in the midst of the Normandy countryside they employed a black cook, Bamboula, gaudily attired in a red turban, gaily coloured shawls and long ear-rings.[18] There at last Georgette managed to write a book of her own. *Le Choix de la vie*[19] is a novel describing the love of a passionate, articulate woman (the similarities with Georgette are apparent) for a less sophisticated, vulnerable country girl, Rose, whose sheer beauty has captivated her. She brings her to Paris in the hope of educating her and making her more intellectually aware. She ultimately fails in this mission, and the girl eventually returns to the Normandy countryside, leaving her mentor to acknowledge her mistake in believing that she could mould her in her own image. Immediately recognisable is Georgette's own propensity to influence others, as seen in her childhood friendships, her relationship with Mathilde Deschamps, and ultimately her power over the train of Maeterlinck's thoughts on his women characters. She struggles with the realisation that some women do not want complete liberty. What matters is for a woman to have the power to choose what suits her, so that she can develop herself without restraint. The lesbian interest is evident in the account of her physical attraction to the younger girl.

---

[15] See illus. 6.

[16] 'une sorte de factotum à l'aspect bizarre … sorte de policeman irlandais'. Lugné-Poë, *Sous les étoiles*, p. 51.

[17] Leblanc, *Souvenirs: My Life with Maeterlinck*, p. 224.

[18] Described in Georgette Leblanc, *Nos chiens* (Paris, 1919); translated as *Maeterlinck's Dogs* by Alexander Teixeira de Mattos (London, 1919), pp. 53, 58.

[19] Georgette Leblanc, *Le Choix de la vie* (Paris, 1904).

The book was published in 1904, not to great acclaim at the time, but it was later noted by her admirers that it was evidence of her intellectual strength. A long appreciation eventually appeared in the *New York Times* in 1912, written by Montrose J. Moses,[20] who also wrote the introduction to an American version of Maeterlinck's *Pelléas et Mélisande*.[21] He realised it was a book into which she had unreservedly put herself. 'It is the source book for the feminism of her husband's plays', was perhaps not an opinion Maeterlinck would have seconded.

Following the successes of the plays *Pelléas* and *Monna Vanna*, in 1905 Georgette came once again to London. Here in June and July she appeared at the Criterion Theatre in a series of dramatic, literary and musical matinées three times a week presenting the poems of Maeterlinck, Baudelaire, Verlaine and others, and, in particular, poems by Judith Gautier based on translations of Chinese and Japanese songs. The music to which the poems were set was mainly composed by Gabriel Fabre. The reviewer in *The Times* was enchanted by her explanatory talk. He preferred her reading, 'the delicacy, the charm of it', to her singing, commenting, 'she is a dramatic singer – perhaps a little too dramatic – with fine notes in her voice.'[22] Not many days after this, Georgette's name appears on a list of illustrious musicians taking part in a concert in aid of the French Benevolent Society at the French Embassy in London, where the music was directed by Messager and Tosti.[23]

Georgette certainly made a lasting impression on one member of her English audience, for in 1931 Richard Jennings recalled going to see a personality 'destined to excite emotions and to inflame controversies'. He was intrigued, having heard that Mallarmé had described her as strange and entrancing, and that Sarah Bernhardt had given her encouragement. Jennings was delighted to see Georgette sitting in a high-backed, antique chair, reflected by adjacent mirrors, dramatising songs. She was 'rather small and extremely blonde', with a prominent nose, and he believed she did have a certain resemblance to Bernhardt.[24]

Back in Paris, at the end of 1905 Georgette directed a similar series of matinées at the Théâtre des Mathurins. There she also performed in Maeterlinck's *La Mort de Tintagiles*, with music by Jean Nouguès, which was given three performances. It was reported that Mary Garden was present at the third on 4 January 1906,[25] but frustratingly her opinion is not recorded.

[20] *New York Times*, 24 March 1912.

[21] See Chapter 14, p. 191.

[22] *The Times*, 17 June 1905.

[23] *The Times*, 13 July 1905.

[24] Richard Jennings, 'Elle et lui', *Life and Letters*, September 1931, p. 193.

[25] Benoît-Jeannin, *Georgette Leblanc*, p. 253.

How much more difficult could Maeterlinck make life for Georgette? In 1906 he bought a house, Les Quatre Chemins, near Grasse in the South of France, which obliged her to travel by public transport between Paris and Grasse between engagements. Even when she was with him he exercised his passion for the developing sport of motorcycling, much to her disquiet as she waited anxiously for his return from long excursions. It is hardly surprising that the same year she gave up the house at Gruchet. Georges Maurevert, when he visited Maeterlinck at Grasse, was met by him at the station and described him as looking like 'a solid English farmer from the county of Surrey'! He, in common with others, was amazed that the poet could be so at home with the mechanics of a car, and was delighted to be driven up the rose-lined drive to be greeted by Georgette, Maeterlinck's 'incomparable and glorious interpreter'. He could not refrain from describing her beauty and her extravagant dress, as together they reminisced about the old days in her salon in the avenue Victor Hugo.[26]

In 1906 a familiar old quarrel once again threatened to surface. Georgette was still desperate to fulfil her ambition of singing the role of Mélisande, this time at the Théâtre Royal de la Monnaie in Brussels. As early as 1903 Debussy had sent a letter to his publisher, Fromont, asking him to send a score of *Pelléas* to Lucy Foreau, who had written to inform him that she was going to be singing Mélisande at La Monnaie. He had already implied that he was grateful for her interest and had written to her begging her not to be put off by any rumours that the music might be difficult. This production did not materialise, but eventually on 2 September 1906 an announcement appeared in the Brussels newspaper *L'Eventail* that Georgette Leblanc and Edmond Clément were to sing the eponymous roles in the first production of the opera outside Paris.

On 15 September Georgette wrote to Kufferath, the Director of La Monnaie, desperate to know what was happening, for it had been so long since she had heard anything about *Pelléas*, and requesting details of the décor so that she could prepare her costumes. But on 8 October Debussy had to write to her to disabuse her of the impression that she was to sing her dream role. What must he have felt like? He explained that he had just been shown an article in *L'Eventail*[27] which announced the cast of *Pelléas et Mélisande* on which her name did not appear. Is he being completely truthful when he writes:

> As the details of this change are not known to me, permit me – so that there
> should be no confusion – to confirm that I have nothing to do with it and that

[26] Maurevert, *L'Art, le boulevard et la vie*, p. 70.
[27] *L'Eventail*, 7 October 1906.

I would have been happy to hear you in the role of Mélisande, having no doubt that your interpretation of the role would have been more than interesting?

Not being familiar with the workings of La Monnaie, I cannot blame any individual, but I hope you will agree that there is no point in bringing up once again the troubles that were so regrettable.[28]

Indeed, the report had enthusiastically announced Mary Garden's participation, saying, 'It is a great good fortune for our audience to be able to applaud Mlle Garden in this creation, the most rounded, perhaps, of this eminent artiste.'[29]

A couple of days later Debussy had to address another letter to Georgette, who had obviously not taken rejection lightly. He said he could only repeat what he had said in his previous letter:

The directors of La Monnaie are like all the others and did not ask my opinion once the decision was made. I thought your performance as Mélisande in Brussels was decided and settled a long time ago. Now it appears it is Mlle Garden! (according to the papers). She claims (you say) that she has not been engaged ... How do you expect me to unravel the truth amongst so many contradictory stories?[30]

He was hoping this time for Maeterlinck's full collaboration and that the author would use his influence to reach a satisfactory solution to the problem. As we have seen, Georgette and Maeterlinck did not get their way.

1906 was also the year that Dukas completed the music to *Ariane et Barbe-Bleue*. From April onwards Georgette typically threw herself into the role of Ariane. No doubt, in her mind it was inextricably and symbolically linked to the one she had previously been robbed of, for, as Maggie Teyte reminds us, before her arrival on the shores of Allemonde, Mélisande was one of the wives of Bluebeard and thus also one of the characters in *Ariane et Barbe-Bleue*. Dukas was impressed with Georgette and was determined that she should be the creator of Ariane, but once again, a fierce battle loomed with Albert Carré at the Opéra-Comique. 'As soon as he asked that I be given the role, he met with unyielding opposition', wrote Georgette.[31] The director did not want Georgette to return to the fold, and suggested other women, in particular his wife, Marguerite. This time, both the composer and Georgette held out, as did Maeterlinck. Eventually Carré had to submit. This is not, however, his own version of events. Diplomatically, he wrote that his bestowal of the role on Georgette was by

[28] Debussy, *Correspondance*, p. 973.

[29] *L'Eventail*, 7 October 1906.

[30] Debussy, *Correspondance*, pp. 973–4.

[31] Leblanc, *Souvenirs: My Life with Maeterlinck*, p. 174.

way of compensation for the 'disappointment which, in the interests of the work, I had inflicted on her with Mélisande.' He believed the role of Ariane was more suited to her build and capacity, and he was very pleased with her interpretation.[32]

The title role of Dukas' *Ariane* is intensely demanding. Although designated for a mezzo-soprano, in fact much of it is in a high register particularly in lengthy dramatic passages. Moreover, Ariane sings almost constantly through the opera, Barbe-Bleue himself only having eight lines to sing in Act I and a silent role in Act III. There are many parallels with Debussy's opera owing to the shared authorship of the text, amongst the most obvious being themes of light and dark, different levels as Ariane descends into dark dungeons to discover Bluebeard's wives, a vision of glistening sea in the distance as the women peer through a window. Here we have sparkling jewels instead of Melisande's sparkling crown and ring. When Ariane sees a woman with 'hair which seems to surround her with still flames,'[33] she asks her name. What could be a clearer link between the two operas than two direct quotations of the 'Mélisande' motif from Debussy's opera when her name is sung by Sélysette, another of Bluebeard's wives?

Rehearsals began in February 1907, but disaster almost reigned. There is no mention of it in Georgette's *Souvenirs*, but she became pregnant.[34] Not surprisingly, her travels between Paris and Grasse combined with this setback made her ill, and she suffered from loss of voice. No doubt Carré would have been glad of any excuse to deprive her of the role. Dukas supported her throughout, though, and the première was postponed. Was Maeterlinck there to help? No. He was writing about *L'Intelligence des fleurs* at his new home in the peaceful, rural surroundings of Grasse whilst here in Paris was Georgette, pregnant, no voice, about to create his heroine, Ariane. To cope with the situation, Georgette had to undergo an abortion.

Understandably, Dukas must have been anxious about the fate of his opera. Debussy was also aware of his problems, for he wrote to Dukas, acknowledging two tickets for the dress rehearsal and explained that he had not been in touch earlier for fear of upsetting him, but was sure Dukas would remain in control of events.[35] The very successful dress rehearsal earned Debussy's compliments, and the première was able to take place on 10 May 1907. Barbe-Bleue was sung by Félix Vieuille, and the conductor was François Ruhlmann. Despite the demanding nature of the role and her precarious emotional state,

---

32   Carré, *Souvenirs de théâtre*, p. 319.

33   'ses cheveux qui semblent l'entourer de flammes immobiles'.

34   Benoît-Jeannin, *Georgette Leblanc*, p. 260.

35   Debussy, *Correspondance*, p. 1006.

Georgette acquitted herself well. Gabriel Fauré wrote a review in *Le Figaro* the next day in which he praised her acting and appearance, but was less satisfied with her voice, which was sometimes too soft, so that the words did not reach the audience. Her deliberately solemn declamation also tended to hold up the musical action.[36] It is ironic that in the programme for *Ariane et Barbe-Bleue* a performance of Debussy's *Pelléas et Mélisande* is listed for the very next day. How close were Georgette Leblanc and Mary Garden at this point!

An article written by Debussy in praise of Mary Garden which was published in the journal *Musica* in January 1908 has already been quoted. It forms part of an issue of this magazine devoted largely to notable female singers of the day. It is hardly coincidence, therefore, that the same issue contains an article on Georgette Leblanc written by her friend and accompanist in his songs, Gabriel Fabre. On the previous page is a similar article about Marguerite Carré by Alexandre Georges. All three women who were vying with one another for prestigious roles at the Opéra-Comique photographed and praised in one issue! This is surely also further proof that Georgette was regarded highly enough to feature as one of the top singers of her day, despite the disparaging comments of some commentators. Marguerite Carré, judging by the pictures of her in medieval dress, was not dissimilar to Mary in build and allure, and even looks as if she has modelled her pose on Mary's. There is a large full-length photograph of Georgette on the next page. She is fuller in figure, statuesque, her eyes lifted skywards in her role as Ariane.

Fabre's account of the woman he had known now for over twelve years and who had been singing his music continuously during that time is anything but a ringing endorsement of vocal excellence, and has none of that affectionate tenderness that Debussy expressed in his appreciation of Mary Garden.[37] He begins by describing Georgette as an exceptional personality, very complex and most captivating. But it is her intellectual capacity that impresses him. He emphasises her desire to base her whole art on Intelligence, commenting, 'Without wanting to offend anyone, I will say that this is a choice that female singers do not always make – certain of them have very natural reasons for that.'[38] Is this a compliment or not? He continues, 'Her ambition to raise the level of her Intelligence every day makes Mme Georgette Leblanc a valuable collaborator for

---

[36] *Le Figaro*, 11 May 1907.

[37] Gabriel Fabre, 'Georgette Leblanc', *Musica*, January 1908, p. 8.

[38] 'Je dirai que c'est là un choix pour lequel les artistes du chant ne se décident pas toujours; – certaines même ont de trop naturelles raisons pour cela.' Fabre, 'Georgette Leblanc'.

authors.'[39] Pointing out that her book, *Le Choix de la vie*, shows a very virile mind, he then admits that this is a quality which men are not always able to appreciate in a woman. It can be attractive – or irritating. If she was ever mistaken in her conception of a role, that was above all 'because this role departed from Intelligence'. Georgette Leblanc was 'an interpreter for thinking writers and musicians'.[40] Disparagingly he notes that 'outside Paris and in Brussels she tackles traditional established roles which are assigned indifferently to any opera singer just as set menus are arranged to appeal to all appetites. Examples of these are *Carmen* and *Thaïs*. In these she provokes either enthusiasm or cries of astonishment.'[41] He mentions 'the great poet who is her husband [*sic*]' and expresses his pleasure that 'the admirable *Ariane et Barbe-Bleue* by Paul Dukas is bringing her back to the stage of the Opéra-Comique.' What a strange review this is, drawing attention to the unusual intellectual leanings of the woman above her musical ability, and to her unfeminine 'virility of mind' – both features off-putting to any male critic.

Carré was not willing to let his attitude to Georgette soften, nor would Georgette let herself be swept aside. Mélisande still lived in her heart, and now, discovering that Mary Garden was to depart for America, she had to do something about her unquenchable desire to sing the role. To this end she organised a petition for which she claims she gathered a thousand signatures:

> To Monsieur Albert Carré, director of the Opéra Comique:
> We the undersigned, patrons of your theatre, grateful for the pleasures which we owe you, beg of you to receive favourably our sincere desire, inspired by the beautiful performances of *Ariane*, to see Madame Georgette Leblanc in a revival of the role left vacant by Mademoiselle Garden in *Pelléas* – a work which is precious to us for many reasons.[42]

Georgette received no reply.

Her admirers did not desert her, however. A group of about fifty fans formed the 'Knights of Ariane'. The condition for admission to this club

39 'Son ambition de se hausser chaque jour davantage dans l'Intelligence fait de Mme Georgette Leblanc une collaboratrice précieuse pour des auteurs.' Fabre, 'Georgette Leblanc'.

40 'Parce que ce rôle s'éloigne de l'Intelligence ... une interprète pour littérateurs et musiciens pensants.' Fabre, 'Georgette Leblanc'.

41 'Elle s'attaque ... à des rôles qui ont une tradition bien établie, proposée à toutes les cantatrices indifféremment, comme les repas à prix fixe sont ordonnés pour satisfaire à tous les appétits. Au nombre de ces roles je citerai *Carmen* et *Thaïs*. Elle y provoque ou l'enthousiasme ou des *tolle* d'étonnement.' Fabre, 'Georgette Leblanc'.

42 Leblanc, *Souvenirs: My Life with Maeterlinck*, p. 181.

was that prospective members had to have attended a certain number of performances of Dukas' opera. She rewarded these faithful followers by giving a party in their honour at the amazing property she and Maeterlinck had moved into in 1907, the Abbey of Saint-Wandrille in Normandy.

11 *Pelléas et Mélisande at Saint-Wandrille*

THE ABBEY OF Saint-Wandrille was an historic building whose gothic splendour had already attracted Georgette as a child during holidays spent nearby with her parents.[1] The Benedictine monks were expelled from the abbey and departed for Belgium in 1901 as a result of anti-clerical policies of the French government which led to laws being passed to separate Church and State. In 1906, according to Maeterlinck's friend Gérard Harry, the author rescued it from vandalism by acquiring it when it was about to fall into the hands of a commercial syndicate to be converted into a chemical works.[2] Once the arrangements had been completed, Georgette's passion for these surroundings never died. It was like living on a permanent stage set, and she exploited every inch of the buildings and grounds to this end. 'I adored every stone, I knew all its echoes, each play of light, all the mysterious dwellers therein – all that little world of shadows which awakened with the night and animated in secret the lace of the capitals and the pointed arches.'[3] She would dress in medieval costume and wander round the ruins, trying to become an integral part of the buildings. To its great hall she brought her Knights of Ariane to play and listen to Dukas' score of his opera by candlelight.

Her singing career still scored notable successes. In January 1908 Georgette performed the role of Télaire in Rameau's *Castor et Pollux* in Montpellier, for which she received critical acclaim. On 16 February in Paris she sang settings of Maeterlinck by Fabre in one of the Concerts Colonne, in a programme also featuring Alfred Cortot, Jacques Thibaud and Pablo Casals. On 29 May she gave a recital in Bordeaux at the Théâtre des Arts in which she first talked then sang, including the *Poèmes de Jade*, translations from Chinese by Judith Gautier, also set by Fabre.[4]

Back at the abbey in July the couple received the great Russian theatre director Stanislavski, who wanted to mount Maeterlinck's latest play, *L'Oiseau bleu* (The Bluebird), in Moscow. Wanting to produce the play not as a simple fairy tale, but as something more serious and thus needing to discuss

---

[1] A full description and history of the abbey can be found at www.st-wandrille.com.

[2] Gérard Harry, *Maurice Maeterlinck: A Biographical Study*, trans. Alfred Allinson (London, 1910), p. 18.

[3] Leblanc, *Souvenirs: My Life with Maeterlinck*, p. 232.

[4] Programmes in AML, Brussels, Georgette Leblanc Collection, 499/118.

necessary changes, Stanislavski accepted an invitation from Maeterlinck to visit him at the abbey. The handsome chauffeur who met him at Yvetot station frightened the life out of him as he sped recklessly along the Normandy lanes. When Maeterlinck eventually revealed his true identity the pair were united in laughter. Upon their arrival at the abbey Georgette descended the great stairway to greet Stanislavski, dressed in a beautiful Norman robe. The atmosphere of the nights spent in the round tower with its mysterious noises, chiming clock, footsteps of the watchman, made an indelible impression on the Russian. Tactfully, he does not elaborate on the personal life of his host: 'So far as his private life is concerned I must lower the curtain, for it would be very immodest to describe something that was opened for me only by happy accident.'5 He had to explain in great detail the problems involved in producing *L'Oiseau bleu* and found Maeterlinck at first confused, then accepting of the demands made of him except for one thing: his desire for children rather than trained actors to appear could not be met because of child exploitation laws in Russia.6 The play received its première in Moscow on 30 September 1908, but as one might expect, Maeterlinck was not there, despite Stanislavski's desire for him to witness its success. He preferred to travel to the warmth of Grasse rather than brave the journey to Russia.

Georgette had certainly met a like-minded visionary in the Russian director, for he tells of their dreaming together of producing Maeterlinck's plays in the grounds of the abbey. They located the well of Mélisande and many other natural sets. 'Later on Mme Maeterlinck was able to bring our dreams to life when she produced *Pelléas et Mélisande*', he wrote.7 Georgette's desire to use the abbey as a stage now had highly respected support and encouragement.

When Gérard Harry visited Saint-Wandrille, he reflected upon the strangely incongruous pair, and wrote a very flattering description of Georgette in response. Having been at pains to portray the author's reticent, peasant-like simplicity, he was convinced that here was a woman of such intelligence (as usual!), that she was 'adequately gifted to reach his level, to talk to him, to understand him and interpret his creations – Mélisande, Ariane, Joyzelle, Monna Vanna – with so much genius, so much sympathy ... that *he may well end by believing them to have been modelled on her* rather than merely incarnated by her.'8 [My italics.] Surely this supports Georgette's own belief that Maeterlinck did use her ideas, her words, her behaviour, as a basis for his thoughts. 'Modelled on her'! Here is someone using a phrase

5 C. Stanislavski, *My Life in Art*, translated by J. J. Robbins (New York, 1956), p. 501.

6 Stanislavski, *My Life in Art*, p. 503.

7 Stanislavski, *My Life in Art*, p. 503.

8 Harry, *Maurice Maeterlinck*, p. 75.

which Georgette would gladly have seized upon. Harry realises this process may have been quite subconscious, but in view of later events it is difficult to believe that Maeterlinck would have appreciated his opinion that he should owe gratitude 'to the woman who, by associating her life with that of a poet or philosopher, has contributed by her grace and her share of sensibility to his happiness, his serenity, and *in consequence to the directions his work takes! Enough here to verify results!*'[9] [My italics]. As noted earlier, according to Georgette, way back in 1897 he had already admitted to 'stealing' her thoughts and ideas.[10]

An American journalist who visited the couple at the abbey in 1908 was fascinated by Georgette, noting 'her questioning eyes, her irregular, fluid features, which seem to change with every passing emotion, her tumbled mass of tawny hair, and her manner, fascinating in its exotic sort of simplicity.'[11] She realised the important part Georgette had played in the development of her husband's genius, believing she could trace her influence in the works Maeterlinck had written since what she mistakenly believed to be their 'marriage' some ten years earlier. She was left in no doubt as to Maeterlinck's opinion of opera when she tried to discover why the author had not seen *Ariane et Barbe-Bleue*, performed so recently. When told that the words of his plays gave a musical impression, his reply was that he cared a great deal for the music of words, but he hated 'that hysteria of sound they call an opera, with all its acrobatic din ... I would much rather listen to the wind caressing the grasses.' The author's appearance gave this journalist completely the opposite impression to one of romance. She noted the squareness of all aspects of his face and head, his blunt features, only his eyes having anything poetic about them. Maeterlinck had just driven from Paris with Golaud, his bull terrier, and his obvious pride in his car and down-to earth knowledge of its mechanics surprised his interviewer. 'He looked like a man who had studied the mode of his motor from below as well as above ... a transcendentalist on intimate terms with a monkey wrench', she wrote.

Maeterlinck appreciated the beauty of the surroundings, yet whilst accompanying the journalist around the grounds, in answer to her rapturous delight in the 'misty midregions of old French romance' where Pelléas and Mélisande might have loved and perished, his reply was 'No, the sea is needed.' Does this show a little remarked upon similarity of taste between Maeterlinck and Debussy, such a fervent lover of the sea, or is he simply referring to the sea being an essential part of the scenery for *Pelléas et Mélisande*?

9 Harry, *Maurice Maeterlinck*, p. 55.

10 See Chapter 3 p. 51.

11 *New York Times*, 20 September 1908.

On the other hand, once, in Grasse, Georges Maurevert had asked him if
he regretted having no view of the Mediterranean from his house there.
Maeterlinck's response was:

> I did it on purpose. I am obsessed by the sea. I fear it, I dread it. When I am
> by the sea I can think of nothing else. I do not do much work as it is; but the
> sea prevents me from doing any work whatsoever. It is better that I do not see
> it at all.[12]

On 25 January 1909 Georgette sang the roles of both Marguerite and
Helen of Troy in Arrigo Boito's opera *Méphistophélès* at the Théâtre des
Arts in her native city of Rouen. This was a charity performance in aid of
earthquake victims in Sicily and Calabria. Charles Bordes wrote a flattering
account in the journal *Musica*, describing her as the ideal interpreter of the
work, and her voice as attractive and supple.[13]

Meanwhile, Georgette's inspirational plan to use the abbey as a stage had
totally seized her imagination, and she sought a play in which 'the tragedy
would unfold under the sky among the secular scenes which the abbey provided.' Hidden by the darkness of the night, spectators would follow the
action from place to place, coming upon the actors like intruders.[14] And
the play which would fulfil this dream? Not initially one by Maeterlinck,
but Shakespeare's *Macbeth*, for which she therefore needed to find a suitable translation. This was achieved by Maeterlinck following the English text
while Georgette read aloud different French translations. He then put these
into his own words until the translated version became his own. After this
contribution, the author had unwillingly to put up with all the hustle and
bustle of the preparations for such a unique event, a horrific intrusion into
his calm routine. When he met by chance an actor and a director in the corridor shortly before the dress rehearsal, he declared to Georgette, 'I'll not
tolerate any longer this underhand invasion of the Abbey; I'll shoot the next
actor I meet.' Imaginary appendicitis, headaches, even typhoid fever were
symptoms of his anxiety at this interruption to his peace and quiet.[15]

The production, which took place on 27 August 1909, was such a success
that Georgette claims she would have liked to have made a French Bayreuth
out of Saint-Wandrille. Sixty people were welcomed by her faithful Knights
of Ariane in period costumes, those members of the audience who wished to

---

[12] 'Je l'ai fait exprès. La mer est pour moi une obsession; je la crains, je la redoute. Quand
je suis près de la mer, je ne songe plus qu'à elle. Je ne travaille déjà pas beaucoup;
la mer m'empêche tout à fait de travailler. Il vaut mieux que je ne la voie point.'
Maurevert, *L'Art, le boulevard et la vie*, p. 73.

[13] *Musica*, May 1909, p. 79.

[14] Leblanc, *Souvenirs: My Life with Maeterlinck*, p. 245.

[15] Leblanc, *Souvenirs: My Life with Maeterlinck*, p. 251.

do so changed into medieval costume, braziers were lit everywhere, and the spectators were guided around the abbey to experience the unfolding of the tragedy. Despite his grumbling and sulking, Maeterlinck soon realised the evening was not going to be a disaster. It was his translation that was being used and he was there at the end to receive praise for it.

Later that year Georgette wrote an article about the whole experience entitled *Quand j'étais Lady Macbeth*. She explained that she took her inspiration for the costumes from the Bayeux tapestry. However, of her own appearance she insisted that when she acted she had actually to transform herself completely into the woman she was representing. She used her idea of Mélisande as an example of how she approached this, saying that when she played Mélisande she managed to change her face completely. Also, letting her hair fall in long ringlets down her neck made it look straighter and her face look thinner. 'You have to turn into your image of the role. I work at this resemblance. I watch in the mirror for the moment when it appears and when I see that I have become exactly the person I must be, I feel inhabited by her sisterly soul.'[16]

Whilst Maeterlinck roller-skated round the ruins, pipe in mouth when he was not writing or fishing, Georgette wrote a children's book, inspired by his play *L'Oiseau bleu*, the first French edition of which was published by Fasquelle in 1909. Hers was not to appear in print, however, until 1913, when it was called *The Children's Bluebird*. It was translated into English by Alexander Teixeira de Mattos and illustrated delightfully by Albert Rothenstein.[17]

Meanwhile another composer had been having trouble with Maeterlinck. Henry Février had set *Monna Vanna* to music, and Messager, appointed Director of the Paris Opéra in January 1908, decided to mount this as the first new French opera to be performed there under his direction. Maeterlinck yet again argued for his rights as librettist over those of the composer, and demanded that the production be stopped. This time the musical public was rallied before legal proceedings. *Musica* in October 1908 reported Maeterlinck's veto and opened its own debate into the respective rights of composer and librettist. When the case came to court, once again the tribunal ruled in favour of the composer. Février expressed his annoyance at being estranged from a writer he much admired, writing: 'One remembers similar incidents taking place when *Pelléas* was created at the Opéra-

---

[16] 'Quand j'étais Lady Macbeth par Mme Georgette Leblanc-Maeterlinck', *Lectures pour tous*, 1909, pp. 721–8.

[17] Georgette Leblanc, *The Children's Bluebird*, trans. Alexander Teixeira de Mattos (London and New York, 1913).

Comique. The reasons and one of the people involved were the same.'[18] This time it was not Georgette who was at the root of the dispute. The author was fully capable of pushing for what he believed to be his due without her encouragement.

Pelléas et Mélisande still obsessed Georgette. She may not have been permitted to sing the role, but now had the ideal setting in which to act it, as encouraged by Stanislavski. She was determined to produce it in the same manner as *Macbeth* in the Abbey of Saint-Wandrille, bringing the characters to life in real woodland, by real water and within real ancient walls. Thus she would be presenting them as Maeterlinck had first visualised them, before having to confine their actions within the limits of a theatrical production. It was even closer to her heart than *Macbeth*, for Shakespeare's play with its witches, ghosts and walking forests could only ever remain fiction. In *Pelléas*, on the other hand, nothing was impossible in real life, for the misfortunes of the family in Allemonde are rooted in our own misfortunes, our own weaknesses and instincts.[19] She herself would, of course, represent Mélisande, and she wanted Pelléas to be acted by Sarah Bernhardt. This was six years after Bernhardt had acted as Pelléas in London at the age of sixty! On reading Georgette's description of Bernhardt's visit to Saint-Wandrille to discuss the plan, you can see why the two actresses got on so well: 'She [Bernhardt] appeared like Phèdre, leaning upon two women. Her head was wreathed in wistaria, a mauve veil encircled it and fell to her feet. A pale grey fur entirely enveloped her. She was adorable.'[20] How many years was it since the young Georgette had sewn the name of the great actress into the hem of her dress? But now the older woman was seriously ill and about to have a leg amputated, so could not possibly take on the challenge – one cannot help thinking how fortunate. What would the audience have made of an aged, limping, female Pelléas? Georgette nevertheless managed to assemble a well-respected cast around her[21] and persuade an initially resistant Maeterlinck to support the idea. Problems during preparations, mislaid parcels, spoiled rehearsals, a lawn too smoothly mown, caused Georgette so much anguish that she described herself as having become a fountain of tears, but her passion and ambition to involve all those around her, servants and labourers, on her natural stage never diminished. Maeterlinck even showed enthusiasm after the dress rehearsal, which did not prevent him

[18] Février, *André Messager*, p. 150.
[19] Georgette's thoughts on the performance at Saint-Wandrille in Leblanc, 'Histoire de ma vie', chap. 3.
[20] Leblanc, *Souvenirs: My Life with Maeterlinck*, p. 258.
[21] Pelléas: René Maupré; Golaud: Jean Durozat; Geneviève: Mlle Jeanne Even; Arkel: M. Sévérin-Mars; Yniold: Gilberte Livettini; Médecin: M. Dufay.

at the end from shooting his gun in the air so that everybody would hurry to bed![22]

On 28 August 1910 about fifty people, who had paid 200 francs per head (including a young poet, Marcel L'Herbier, later himself to play a role in Georgette's life), were guided by the Knights of Ariane around the cloisters and walls of Saint-Wandrille to see *Pelléas et Mélisande* enacted. Fauré's incidental music was played by a hidden orchestra conducted by Albert Wolff, at that time chorus master at the Opéra-Comique.[23] Since it was the play, not the opera that was being performed, all the scenes Debussy had omitted were included. No wonder Maeterlinck was to tell Georgette that he had seen his dream come to life for the first time.[24] Georgette's problems during preparations could have been as nothing when the rain poured down and thunder rumbled on the actual day. However, in her devotion, even these elements heightened the atmosphere. The clock struck seven as the play began, it was becoming dark, and stumbling down the slope from high up in the undergrowth Georgette feared she would not be noticed by her audience as large raindrops struck her face, but all turned towards her as she parted the long grass, her gold slippers getting ruined in the mud as she slipped and slid towards them. Her yellow dress with Eastern embroidery was torn, her fringed golden veil in shreds. She was crying real tears as she lay beside the water beneath a clump of fir trees. When Golaud bore her into his castle, torrents of water came belching out of the sky. But she would not wait to enter, as advised. 'Why wait, when the sky is crowning my fondest wishes! Would you have the poor little fated princess enter Allemonde castle in fine weather on a starry night?' Georgette finds it difficult to find words to express the perfection of the enchanted natural settings and deep emotions aroused by each subsequent scene. She became part of an animated and wonderful tapestry. At the end of the play, when Mélisande lay on her death bed, the spectators, who had already bent over the body of Pelléas, entered on tiptoe. The silence after the last words was palpable, and Georgette had to wait behind the drawn curtains of the great bed in order not to break the spell. Weeping, sighing, no one moved. Eventually she slipped stealthily out and shattered the dream.

In handwritten notes Georgette bemoaned the bad luck she had experienced with the difficult preparations, the weather, the grumbles she had had to put up with from Maeterlinck. Also, interestingly, she expresses her surprise that Debussy omitted one of what both she and Maeterlinck regarded

[22] Leblanc, *Souvenirs: My Life with Maeterlinck*, p. 257.

[23] Wolff was to conduct Debussy's opera many times, including three performances at Covent Garden in 1937.

[24] Leblanc, 'Histoire de ma vie'.

as the most essential scenes of the play: Act III scene 1, where Mélisande is spinning in a room in the castle, a scene which was 'full of silences in which Debussy would have had complete free reign for his genius.'[25] This scene, embellished by Fauré's music, was enacted in the chapel.

A devastating attack on the project appeared in the weekly paper *The New Age* published in September 1910.[26] It was 'grotesquely conceived ... Seldom has an actress, bent on notoriety, invented a scheme more grossly inartistic and better calculated to attract the rich open-mouthed mob.' The writer considered Georgette quite unsuitable, physically and otherwise, to play Mélisande. He was no more flattering about the author.

Others, however, were of totally the opposite opinion. The London *Times* carried a lengthy article which began with an idyllic description of the abbey and its situation. The atmosphere of theatrical Parisian excitement transferred to the worn flagstones of cloisters obviously entranced the observer. 'Select, but at the same time mixed' was how the writer described the audience, who were thankful for the awnings sheltering them from the rain. The effect as the actors and audience moved round was entrancing, the poetic illusion, a thrilling sense of mystery, and the presence that could be felt of the unseen and the unknown was 'Maeterlinckian.' The sense of reality with its 'real tower and casement as medieval as you please' was heightened by the real physical accidents of the situation: Yniold slipped as he hung on the wet ledge of the window, Pelléas was covered with mud. 'You do not have to content yourself with being told by Mélisande, as she looks over Pelléas's shoulder, that she sees Golaud, with drawn sword, lurking in the depths of the wood; you can see him for yourself.' The whole thing gave the effect of a dream and 'what is *Pelléas et Mélisande* but a dream by a dreamer of beautiful dreams?' Of histrionics there were none, and Georgette was praised for her childlike innocence, her grace, 'the mysterious fateful air of Mélisande'. And what of the author? Not until supper did anyone catch a glimpse of the Abbot of Saint-Wandrille. It seems Maeterlinck had been placidly smoking his pipe in a remote room in the abbey. Even when he did emerge, he did not discuss his plays, but preferred to talk about apples and pears.[27]

In 1910 a small volume was published by Nelson in Paris entitled *Morceaux choisis* by Maurice Maeterlinck. This contained excerpts from numerous works written between 1896 and 1909. The unusual thing about the collection is that the preface was written by none other than Mme Georgette Leblanc. Not only this, the first chapter is 'Le Silence' from *Le Trésor des*

[25] 'qui est avant tout une scène de silences et où le génie du musicien aurait eu la place complètement libre.' AML, Brussels, Georgette Leblanc Collection, 499/118.

[26] *The New Age*, 15 September 1910, p. 470.

[27] *The Times*, 31 August 1910.

humbles, which, as we have seen, was originally inspired by his discussions with Georgette. Here then, we have a book uniting their two names, in which she traced the evolution of his thoughts from the obscurity of his early plays overshadowed by the powerful shadow of death, to the gradual intrusion of bolder figures, bathed in triumphant light. She tried to explain something of the character of the author. 'We need months, years, simply to become familiar with a character. For if it is true that we judge a being by the acts he carries out, we really know him only by those he does not commit.'[28] The sense of balance in Maeterlinck's life, his calmness, stemmed from his capacity to shut himself off from his environment and to lead a routine combining his interests in nature, his physical exercise, regular meals and early bedtimes with just two hours of actual writing. Her maternal attitude is evident: 'He seems to achieve his work with no pain or effort, with the simplicity of a child who stops playing exactly at a prescribed time and begins again at the permitted time, without worrying about the page he has just begun.'[29]

Despite her eulogy, the cracks in Georgette's relationship with Maeterlinck were widening and weighing heavily upon her. In October 1910 she journeyed to Moscow with her indispensable companion Mathilde Deschamps as ever looking after both her personal and business needs. Maeterlinck did not accompany her even though it was his play *L'Oiseau bleu* which was being performed there. He had again retreated to Grasse, but as always it was torture to leave him behind. 'I had worked in haste, thinking only of my return, though Maeterlinck had approved of my going ... The fact is he never made any opposition to my activities but he was opposed to them. No sooner was I away from him than he began to manifest his resentment by a silence that poisoned my days and nights.'[30] This opposition is difficult to sympathise with, for her constant promotion of his works was steadily contributing to his widening fame and fortune. She was still giving individual recitals and talks at home and abroad about his songs and poems such as that at The Little Theatre in London on 1 December 1910 in a series called *Causeries du Jeudi*.[31]

In 1911 preparations were made for bringing *L'Oiseau bleu* to Paris. The play had at last been published there and was being promoted by the actress

[28] 'Il nous faut des mois, des années pour faire simplement le tour d'un caractère; car s'il est vrai que l'on juge un être d'après les actes qu'il fait, on le connaît d'après ceux qu'il ne fait pas.' Introduction to Maurice Maeterlinck, *Morceaux choisis* (Paris, 1910).

[29] 'Il semble accomplir son œuvre sans peine ni effort, avec la simplicité d'un enfant qui abandonne ses jeux à l'heure prescrite et les reprend aux heures permises, sans souci de la page commencée.' Introduction to Maeterlinck, *Morceaux choisis*.

[30] Leblanc, *Souvenirs: My Life with Maeterlinck*, p. 271.

[31] Programme in AML, Brussels, Georgette Leblanc Collection, 499/118.

Réjane to whom Lugné-Poë had shown the manuscript.[32] It was to receive its first performance at the Théâtre Réjane on 2 March. Georgette not only acted the key role of La Lumière (Light) but also busily supervised rehearsals and attended to costumes. Here there were no restrictions on the use of child actors. How ironic to find her notebooks, as usual covered in pencil notes, this time recording her lists and memos for the production – ironic because amongst the register of names of the many children taking part in the play is that of Renée Dahon, aged sixteen, who was to act the role of Le Rhume de Cerveau (Cold in the Head). What a headache Renée was to prove for Georgette! When Maeterlinck left Grasse to attend rehearsals in Paris his attention was drawn to this adolescent, scantily clad in a diaphanous tunic. 'Between the acts she was among the children who unceremoniously clung to Maeterlinck, climbing on his knees and looking in his pockets for the bonbons that were put there for them.'[33] Renée, referred to by Georgette simply as R in her *Souvenirs*, was from then on to form the third side of an eternal triangle. 'For eight years she was to live with us almost continually and in 1919 she married Maeterlinck.'[34] After all these years of devotion to the author, of supporting and promoting his creations, putting up with his mistresses, tolerating his sulks and silences, trying to cater for his essential daily routine, Georgette was to be ousted by a young girl. Maeterlinck knew he could always count on Georgette's constancy. Whatever their relationships with others, the stable factor in both their lives was her devotion to him. She claims it was even for the sake of allowing some levity into his life while his mother was dying that she obeyed the doctor, who said that he must have gaiety. She should distract him with something new, something that would change his habits. 'I was happy to open the door to R., who brought with her vivacity, laughter and the songs of Paris.'[35]

By now Maeterlinck had lost both parents. His reputation had spread worldwide. Perhaps for him it was time to begin anew. Perhaps he did not need Georgette's support and constant reiteration of her belief in him. He had a young, beautiful and vivacious woman to admire and who admired him. And when he did want to see his old mistress, she would surely come running. She had never refused to come to his side before.

How fortunate for Georgette that Mélisande should come to her rescue. She had the perfect opportunity to fulfil her old dream – of at last singing the role in Debussy's opera, this time not in France, but in America. Georgette

[32] Lugné-Poë, *Sous les étoiles*, p. 247.

[33] Leblanc, *Souvenirs: My Life with Maeterlinck*, p. 263, and her notebooks at AML, Brussels.

[34] Leblanc, *Souvenirs: My Life with Maeterlinck*, p. 264.

[35] Leblanc, *Souvenirs: My Life with Maeterlinck*, p. 264.

was invited by the impresario Henry Russell to act in Maeterlinck's plays *Pelléas et Mélisande* and *Monna Vanna*, but above all to sing the role of Mélisande at the Boston Opera Company where Russell had been director since its opening in 1909. She claims that she hesitated initially before accepting the role, agonising over being so far from Maeterlinck for so long. 'But what he [Russell] proposed was such an exceptional performance of *Pelléas et Mélisande* that I allowed myself to be persuaded.'[36] No doubt she was reluctant to leave Maeterlinck alone with Renée for two whole months.

Russell wanted Debussy himself to conduct the Boston performance. The two knew each other well, and the truth was that Debussy owed Russell a favour, for he had borrowed money off him in the past which he was unable to repay when the time came to do so in 1910.[37] As an impresario Russell had much influence in Paris as well as in London and Boston, so this would be another reason why it would be unwise to refuse him. There was an insurmountable problem, though. Emma, Debussy's wife, refused to let him travel there without her. 'I definitely have to renounce going to Boston', he wrote in a letter to Russell on 22 October 1911 (which he did not post until 17 November). 'I take this decision, be assured, only with regret and because of family reasons so serious that I could not carry on regardless.'[38] Not only was Emma's health not strong, but the couple had been having such difficulties with their relationship that she had even reached the point of consulting a lawyer with a view to separation. He posted this at the same time as another letter to André Caplet saying that he had lost all hope of travelling to Boston, and even if he could summon up the effort to travel alone he did not dare to do so.[39] His regret must have been sincere, for on 22 December 1911 he wrote again saying, 'You can well believe that I have not told anyone what it cost me to give up the trip to America.' Yet one can't help wondering how Debussy would have dealt with having to conduct Georgette after the historical fracas in 1902. Would he have found it in his heart to applaud her performance? How would he have coped with being present at the performance of the opera he had only ever seen in rehearsal? And what a strain he found it to conduct his own works. This too must have been a daunting prospect.

Caplet was the conductor of the Boston Symphony Orchestra, 1910–14, and a friend of Debussy who much admired his skill, so it was an acceptable solution that the task of conducting *Pelléas et Mélisande* should fall to him.

---

[36] Leblanc, *Souvenirs: My Life with Maeterlinck*, p. 264.

[37] Referred to in letter to Caplet: Debussy, *Correspondance*, p. 1549.

[38] Debussy, *Correspondance*, p. 1464.

[39] Debussy, *Correspondance*, p. 1463.

What more suitable venue for the conductor to rehearse with Georgette than the Abbey of Saint-Wandrille? In July 1911 Caplet moved into the building called the Pavillon Louis XV and emerged to enter a studio situated as far away as possible from Maeterlinck so that the author would not be disturbed by the piano and the sounds of Georgette working at her role. She had been warned that Caplet was 'the ugliest man in the world', so it is hardly surprising if he wondered why she kept staring at him when she first met him! Fortunately his charm made up for his featureless face, and his piano playing was 'as smooth as a cat's walk'. She concurred with Debussy's opinion that 'Caplet is music personified.'[40]

Georgette's recollections of collaborating with Caplet are heightened by the sensuousness of the surroundings they were working in, as well as the spell cast by the score during this marvellous month, completely devoted to music:

> Every morning when the church bell struck ten, I went out by the Gate of the Lions, crossing an avenue soft with moss, where lindens formed a green and transparent cathedral. I passed by the fifteenth century virgin that smiled at the angels and arrived at the studio where Caplet awaited me at the piano. His art and his love of perfection enchanted me and we sometimes spent hours on one small phrase in order to polish its every facet, and bring out all that was sealed in it of beauty and grace.[41]

Henry Russell also visited Saint-Wandrille to show Maeterlinck models of the sets by his revolutionary new chief designer, the Viennese Joseph Urban, with which the author was absolutely delighted, saying they were 'pure, delicious masterpieces.' Once again Maeterlinck expressed his disgust at the original Opéra-Comique production, and believed that for the first time since the Saint-Wandrille performance, the Boston production would create a living, tangible atmosphere enveloping every word and all the fatality of the drama. He loved the landscape with silhouettes of people suspended in mist and in infinity, the heavy, menacing tower which seemed to hold all the force of destiny in its shadow and weight. This production would be unique.[42]

Georgette Leblanc was about to take her Mélisande to America. Meanwhile, what had been happening at the Opéra-Comique in Paris?

---

[40] 'Caplet, c'est la musique même.' Leblanc, *La Machine à courage*, p. 173.

[41] Leblanc, *Souvenirs: My Life with Maeterlinck*, p. 267.

[42] Stadsarchief Gent BCI.

12 *Maggie Teyte: her Background (1888–1902)*

IN OCTOBER 1907 Mary Garden was on her way to America. This did not mean that *Pelléas et Mélisande* was no longer to be performed at the Opéra-Comique. Albert Carré wanted it to remain in the repertoire. But who was to sing the role of Mélisande?

One woman was now determined to do so. Marguerite Giraud had consolidated her position at the Opéra-Comique by becoming Mme Marguerite Carré. Presumably aware of her husband's earlier infatuation with Mary, she loathed her to such an extent that when Mary left for America she took over her dressing room and ordered everything to be thrown out – curtains, furnishings, everything. 'Take all that rubbish away and burn it', she ordered. 'The Scotch girl that kept this room for eight years was tubercular.'[1] Maggie Teyte had her own anecdote about the situation, although she disguised the names:

> When two leading sopranos met in the narrow passage below the stage, neither would give way to the other. One eventually said, 'Let me pass, don't you know who I am? I am Madame T..., the wife of the director.' The other replied, 'Oh, don't be silly, I was Madame T... long before you.'[2]

When Marguerite heard that Mary might return the following season to resume the role, she realised she did not have enough time to learn it herself in the summer before the 1908 season began, so another singer had to be found to fill the gap. This is where Maggie Teyte makes her appearance, only the second woman to sing the role of Mélisande at the Opéra-Comique and the second British woman to do so. By this stage in her young career, Maggie was well aware of the world she was entering, and could not fail to recognise her role in the stormy jealous relationship of the two leading ladies. On hearing the rumours that Mary Garden was to be brought back to sing Mélisande in order to keep the work in the repertoire, it did not take her long to realise why she was receiving such encouragement: 'As for me, I was just a pawn, to be used for the moment, and then thrown aside when I was no longer wanted – which would be

---

[1] *Mary Garden's Story*, p. 55.

[2] Garry O'Connor, *The Pursuit of Perfection: A Life of Maggie Teyte* (London and New York, 1979), p. 85. Anecdote told to Richard Bebb.

just as soon as Mme Carré had found time to learn the role of Mélisande herself!'[3]

Who was Maggie Teyte and how did it come about that she was ready then and there to take over the role that was so coveted?

It is necessary first to examine her ancestry, over which there has been some confusion. Maggie Tate (note the spelling) was born on 17 April 1888 in Wolverhampton in England's 'Black Country'. The Wolverhampton archives show that town's pride in its famous daughter. Search the internet and there is a picture of The Still Inn, owned by Maggie's father. From this grainy photograph, one might assume that Maggie must have been brought up as an inn-owner's daughter in the rough and ready atmosphere of pub life. What could be further from the ethereal misty pond where Mélisande dropped her crown, the mysterious grotto, the frail unearthliness of the long-haired, fragile yet psychologically complex maiden? How did the owner of a pub in Wolverhampton come to have his daughter trained to become an international opera star? In 1896, eight years after Maggie's birth, Maggie's mother, Maria, was recorded as still being the licensee of The Old Still, later to become the Saracen's Head. What role did she play in Maggie's upbringing?

Maggie's father did indeed run the pub in the picture shown on Wolverhampton's website, as well as several other public houses. This information is not passed to us by Maggie. Only by delving into historical directories and records can one trace the true family background. It is clear there is much more to find out about her than she reveals, for her autobiography, *Star on the Door*,[4] is such a strangely personal account leaving one with a feeling of familiarity with the strong character of its subject, yet frustration at the way in which she skates over and even omits important and significant moments in her life. Mary Garden wrote her autobiography in conjunction with Louis Biancolli. Maggie Teyte similarly acknowledges in an open letter at the start of her book that she was aided over six years by Cedric Wallis.

She calls her first chapter 'Background', but this title could hardly be less appropriate. The very first paragraph paints a picture far removed from public houses and city streets, and seems intended to enlighten us from the start as to the upbringing which would lead inevitably to her being ideally cast as a romantic, pre-Raphaelite beauty, leaning over a dark pond. There it is: her vivid recollection of herself as a child, a ruined castle surrounded by a moat covered by water-lilies and green weed. A forbidding tower, birds and

---

[3] Maggie Teyte, *Star on the Door* (London, 1958), p. 53.

[4] Teyte, *Star on the Door*.

bats flying in and out of its turrets. The child reaches for a lily and falls into the moat, to be rescued by her nurse. On reading further, it becomes clear that this romantic image is one of the very few carefully selected by Maggie that she wishes to pass on to us about her early childhood. How similar this approach is to the fanciful reminiscences of both Georgette Leblanc and Mary Garden. All three wanted to show in their romantic exaggerations that they felt a certainty that their rise to fame was predestined.

It seems strange that there should be so little recall of life in what Maggie describes as a family of eleven children. Not only does she seem to have got the facts of her own family background wrong, but others have unwittingly perpetuated the myths she concocted as to her family circumstances. Rather like a game of Chinese whispers, wishful thinking, vague memories, chance remarks became an elaborate family legend.

Her birth certificate confirms that she was born on 17 April 1888, christened Margaret. 'My paternal grandfather was James Tate, a Scottish Presbyterian, who became a Roman Catholic to marry my grandmother, a native of Ireland', states Maggie categorically.[5] Even in live interviews when she was in her sixties she was introduced as being Scottish on her father's side, Irish on her mother's.[6] Where is the evidence for this?

Census data and birth and marriage certificates show her origins on both sides of her family to be quite firmly rooted in Staffordshire. If Maggie had any Scottish ancestry it would relate to her paternal great-grandfather, whose birth date and place are unknown. This great-grandfather, Jacob Tate, a labourer, was a widower when in 1829 he married Rebecca Perry, a widow from Darlaston in Staffordshire. They had two sons, both born in Bilston, near Wolverhampton: Maggie's grandfather James, born 1830, and Samuel, born two years later. In 1849 James married Hannah Horn, born in 1831 in Keighley in Yorkshire. Hannah's father, Patrick, was a hawker. If Maggie had any Irish ancestry, it could relate to this great-grandfather, but in both cases, this Scottish and Irish ancestry is speculation. Both this marriage and Jacob's took place in the Collegiate Church in Wolverhampton, 'according to the Rites and Ceremonies of the Established Church', which seems an anomaly if either or both were Roman Catholic at this time. At the time of their wedding James was nineteen, Hannah eighteen. Both James and his brother Samuel were puddlers. Data for that area show that many local men were employed in the iron industry. A vivid contemporary picture of the extraordinarily demanding physical nature of the puddler's work is given in an 1862

---

[5] Teyte, *Star on the Door*, p. 13.

[6] Interview with Felix Aprahamian, BBC, 16 October 1948.

Report.[7] His task was to charge the furnace with coal and pig iron, then, having precisely judged the colour of the flame, to separate off lumps of solidified iron from the melting and boiling metal and drag these to a shingler who formed the mass of iron into a shape ready for rolling. It was a highly skilled job, needing very precise judgement and was remunerated accordingly. The operation of puddling and working the iron required 'severe and incessant labour' and the report commented on the height and muscular power required to carry it out. The birth certificate of Jacob, Maggie's father, confirms his father James's occupation as a puddler. Jacob was born on 18 November 1849, also at Bilston. There is no record of other children being born to James and Hannah.

No light can be shed on Jacob Tate's childhood, apart from the fact that he learnt the piano. Where was he at the time of the 1871 census? He would have been about twenty-two, but his name does not appear to be recorded. Maggie and her relations tell of his travels abroad for music lessons. Perhaps this occurred during this period, for in Maggie's words: 'He was a very good amateur pianist and studied at one time in Leipzig with Leschetizky.'[8] On reading biographies of musicians at the turn of the last century it is striking how often the name Leschetizky turns up in the context of ambitious young players leaving for *Vienna* to study with the famous pianist. Indeed, the great teacher, who was born in Poland in 1830, started his teaching at the Conservatory in St Petersburg, then settled in Vienna in 1878, where well over one thousand pupils from all over the world, including Paderewski, flocked to him. So why would Maggie's father have gone to Leipzig? Felix Aprahamian, introducing an interview with Maggie Teyte in 1948 was perhaps nearer the truth when he stated that 'Maggie's father was musical and had even taken *a* piano lesson from Leschetizky.'[9] [My italics.]

Maggie's mother was born Maria Doughty in 1857. Maria's ancestors can be traced back several generations in Staffordshire. In 1861 her father William was registered as a victualler and hinge-maker at the Star Inn, Horseley Heath Road, Tipton. By the 1871 census he and his wife, another Maria, née Woolley, had eight children.

The next myth is that Maggie's father Jacob was married twice and had two sons by his first marriage to a woman called Hannah. She is said to have

[7] F. D. Longe, *Report on the Ironworks of South Staffordshire* (1862). This contains an extract from the diary of a manager of a rolling mill with puddling furnaces at Bilston, the very area where James was living and working.

[8] Teyte, *Star on the Door*, p. 13.

[9] Interview with Felix Aprahamian, BBC, 16 October 1948. In a later BBC interview, *Frankly Speaking*, 31 December 1959, Maggie does refer to her father's visit to Vienna.

died bearing their third child.[10] His second wife, Maggie's mother, Maria, was supposedly twenty years younger than Jacob. All this is impossible. Jacob was twenty-five at the time of his one and only marriage to Maria, who was eighteen. The ceremony took place on 24 July 1874 at the church of St Peter and St Paul in the Parish of Aston, Warwickshire, also in the West Midlands, again Church of England, not Roman Catholic. His profession was given as wine merchant. The marriage certificate also shows that Maggie's grandfather James Tate had by now ceased to be a puddler and he too had become a wine merchant. It is not clear exactly when this change of occupation took place, but presumably it was made easier by the fact that he had been well paid as a puddler. The link between the hot labour of puddling and the quenching of thirst is not hard to imagine! William Doughty, Maria's father, who had died in 1871, had been a licensed victualler, so perhaps he was aided in this decision. The confusion about the mothers of Jacob's children must have arisen because both his wife and his mother were called Maria. This would also explain the alleged age gap of twenty years.

Despite both parents and grandparents on Maggie's father's side having been married in Church of England churches, all the children were baptised in the Roman Catholic church of St Peter and St Paul, Wolverhampton. The records of this church provide further evidence that the parents of all of them, from James the oldest, born in 1875, to Sidney the youngest, born in 1892, were Jacob and Maria. The fourth child, a daughter called Florence, was baptised and died on the day of her birth, so in fact Maria Tate bore eleven children in all. It is important to get the facts of James's birth right, for Maggie's oldest brother became an important artist in his own right, as we shall see.

By the 1881 census the family had moved further up in the world. For some reason the spelling of the surname has changed to Taite. Does it look smarter? Both Jacob, a wine and spirits merchant, and his parents are living at Spanish Vaults, Exchange Street, Wolverhampton. In the 1891 census, the surname reverts to Tate. By now there are nine children, Sidney not yet having been born. Business must have been successful, for their address is given as that house which Maggie recalls so romantically, Dunstall House, Dunstall Road. Maggie's grandmother, Hannah, died in 1886 at the age of fifty-five.

One of the arguments put forward for Jacob's being 'a little hated as well as feared by his large brood'[11] was that he was such an old father, supposedly nearly sixty when Maggie was born, older still at the birth of her younger

---

[10] O'Connor, *The Pursuit of Perfection*, p. 20.

[11] O'Connor, *The Pursuit of Perfection*, p. 26.

brothers. We know now that Maggie's father was thirty-eight, her mother thirty-one at the time of her birth. It is also quite inaccurate to say that her father Jacob spent 'forty out of his seventy years' in Wolverhampton. He did not even live to seventy, but died in his fifties. One could well imagine that Maggie's *grandfather* James, having been a puddler in his youth, was physically strong and well built, no doubt strong-minded as well, and one can imagine he might well have been a character to have been in awe of.

In 1898 when Maggie was ten years old, the family moved to London. There can be no doubt about the entrepreneurial spirit of both sides of the family, yet strangely, Maggie does not even mention the wine and spirit business in Exchange Street, Wolverhampton, which was successful enough to enable the family to move to Dunstall House, and from there to the capital to take on the Caledonian Hotel in Robert Street, Adelphi, by the Embankment. In 1901 her father Jacob is recorded as proprietor of this hotel. Only six children are now listed as living with him, the older ones having left home. In 1902, at the age of only fifty-three, Jacob died. He did not even reach his sixties, that old age he was said to have been when Maggie was born. Not only this, his father James died aged seventy in 1901 in London, only very shortly before him. He had moved as a widower to London to live at the hotel with his son's family, probably feared by the young children, until the time of his death.

Now to return to Maggie's mother and yet another puzzle. The story goes that Maggie's mother, Maria, did not want her daughter to be held back in her singing career as her sister Rose had been. Rose had a very beautiful voice, so beautiful, in fact, that the famous English tenor, Sim Reeves, according to Maggie, chose Rose to go on a world tour with him, 'an ambition never realised because of a jealous husband'.[12] This famous singer has been identified elsewhere as the baritone Charles Santley, who did indeed carry out several foreign tours.[13] It is not possible to corroborate this story. Perhaps further investigation of the census data will help. From this it becomes evident that Maria had no sister called Rose. Her mother, Maggie's maternal grandmother, also called Maria Doughty, creatively managed to lose a few years at each census! Originally stating her birth as about 1828, by the 1881 census she was registered as being born in about 1836, making her forty-five instead of her true fifty-something. This was expedient, for after the death of her husband William in 1871 she married a man fifteen years younger, Joseph Rose.

So here is the answer to the mysterious Rose. Another generation mix-up.

---

[12] Teyte, *Star on the Door*, p. 14.

[13] O'Connor, *The Pursuit of Perfection*, p. 23.

She was, in fact, Maggie's maternal grandmother. She may have had a lovely voice, but one of her two husbands, presumably her first, William, did not want her to show it off. What a shame, as she obviously must have been an attractive woman, passing as years younger than her true age. Perhaps Maggie inherited her initiative in being 'economical with the truth', not about her age, as in Maria Rose's case, but about her origins. She did, however, acknowledge that her musical talent was inherited. From her mother's side came the voice, she said; from her father's came the music.[14]

Put kindly, Maggie's memory played tricks on her regarding her true family background, and this is probably because she hated to be associated with suburbs of Wolverhampton in the Black Country and trades such as puddler, innkeeper and hinge-maker. Indeed in 1943 it is said she cancelled a tour to the town with Ivor Newton, her accompanist, saying: 'Why Wolverhampton? Didn't you know that I was *born* in Wolverhampton?'[15]

At no point does Maggie show any sign of love or appreciation of her mother, Maria. We are told that all the children learned an instrument, but, as far as we know, only one besides her, her oldest brother James, had any significant musical talent. Did she feel different from them? All the boys except the last-born son, Sidney, were sent to a Roman Catholic school, St Wilfrid's College near Oakamoor, Staffordshire.[16] Records show they each boarded there for between two and five years between 1884 and 1900. Three of Maggie's brothers also went on to be educated for a short while at Wolverhampton Grammar School: Jacob, 1890–2; Arthur and Frederick, 1891–3.

Maggie attended a Catholic school, Saint Joseph's Convent in Wolverhampton, and yet again there is no nostalgia, no sign of any affection for the place or the people. The red-brick building, built in 1860, still exists at the northern end of St John's Square. Her only reminiscences, recalled when remarking upon her superstitious nature, are of bad omens experienced in the refectory, where apparently the colour green once brought bad luck, and later a bird flying into the room foretold a death.[17] In her autobiography she makes no mention of music at this early age, but later she recalled learning about half a dozen songs at school. She found that learning the piano and learning to sing both came to her very easily. She had a natural sense of rhythm and did not regard acquiring either skill as work.[18]

[14] *Frankly Speaking*, BBC interview, 31 December 1959.

[15] O'Connor, *The Pursuit of Perfection*, p. 19. She did, however, perform there in 1942 and 1943, in spite of this statement.

[16] Later known as Cotton College.

[17] Teyte, *Star on the Door*, p. 127.

[18] *Frankly Speaking*, BBC interview, 31 December 1959.

Only one sister recurs in Maggie's life story. Maria, born in 1885, known as Marie, was crippled in a childhood accident at home in Dunstall House, and from then on she had to wear a brace on her leg. When Maggie's father took on the Caledonian Hotel in London he also bought for the sum of £5,000 the Tivoli Restaurant in the Strand. Marie Tate probably worked in this establishment, so it may have been here that she met the Italian waiter, Antonio Odoli, whom she eventually married. They had a daughter, Marguerite Nineta, born in 1907, who came to be known as Rita. Marie died when Rita was only nine months old. Odoli looked after the child with the help of a nurse until the outbreak of the First World War, when he left to fight in Italy, never to return or to be heard of again. Thus it was that Maggie eventually became Rita's guardian.[19]

It was this move in 1898 that was decisive for Maggie's future when 'we all trekked to the great city.'[20] Trekked? This must have been a brave and enterprising decision by her father and grandfather, and it is difficult to see why Maggie should regard it as anything other than exciting. It was certainly going to widen her horizons, and one can only assume that Jacob was looking forward to a more cultured environment, one that would suit his musical interests. Why Robert Street, Adelphi? Did he know that George Bernard Shaw lived in a flat just by the hotel? The great writer's name actually appears in the 1901 census immediately below that of the Tate family. Was Jacob envisaging ladies and gentlemen wining and dining, listening to music in his domain? He certainly provided the milieu, as Maggie describes it: 'a large room that was probably used for banquets', where there was a grand piano. Then she bursts the bubble, for disparagingly – and significantly – she tells us it was empty most of the time.[21] For Maggie this was an advantage, as it meant she could play and sing to herself to her heart's content, and she amused herself by the hour there. Her voice must have been admired as people coming in and out of the hotel would ask, 'Who is that singing?' But one certainly does not get the impression that she admired her father or was grateful for this access to the piano. As for the opportunity to encourage George Bernard Shaw to grace the salon, he actually sent a note to Maggie's mother, saying: 'Will you please stop that girl from making such horrible noises!'[22]

Jacob Tate recognised that Maggie had talent in spite of Shaw's remarks, and we are told that he wanted Hubert Parry to hear her sing at the Royal

[19] O'Connor, *The Pursuit of Perfection*, p. 23.
[20] Teyte, *Star on the Door*, p. 14.
[21] Teyte, *Star on the Door*, p. 14.
[22] Teyte, *Star on the Door*, p. 14.

College of Music. However, she was considered too young to study singing, and records at the College show that it was for piano that she auditioned. Her application was received and the guinea fee paid at the College on 10 October 1900 when she was aged twelve and a half. On 5 November she took the entrance examination, then attended piano and theory lessons there for just two and a half terms.[23]

There is no indication that Maggie received any further education in London. She was ten at the time of the move, but her oldest brother, James, the most musical of her siblings, was almost thirteen years older than her. After school he had left home and travelled to America, where he played the church organ, worked on a cattle train and acted. When he came back to his homeland, his considerable talent must have been recognised for he worked with the Carl Rosa Opera Company.[24] However, to the disapproval of his father, he then went on to make his career singing and dancing in musical theatre. On stage James dressed in an ostentatious manner. Besides lurid waistcoats his trade mark became his monocle. He met with considerable success in this field and in 1898, the year the family moved to London, he went on tour as the conductor of *The White Blackbird*. Here he met his wife-to-be, the leading lady known as Lottie Collins, who immortalised the raucous song *Ta-ra-ra-Boom-de-ay*, of which even Debussy had heard, for Pierre Louÿs wrote him a letter on 29 July 1894 quoting it![25] James certainly made his own contributions to the vitality of the music hall, for he composed many popular songs, improvised brilliantly at the piano, and in 1906 appeared as 'That' in the double act 'Clarice Mayne and That'. This nickname came from his stage partner's habit of banteringly pointing at him and laughing at him in his monocle. James wrote many popular songs, often performed by Clarice through the First World War, and heard in theatrical revues. What a wag James must have been, rattling out suggestive, noisy numbers, grinning wickedly beneath his monocled eye! This 'first-class composer'[26] eventually died in 1922 having been taken ill with pneumonia whilst producing a pantomime at the Theatre Royal, Hanley. Not one word about the life of this musical brother is mentioned by Maggie in her book, nor in interviews.

One of the very rare references to her family is made in a negative aside when she remembers her eldest sister, Gertrude, saying to her when she was

[23] Register at Royal College of Music, London.

[24] Andrew Lamb, 'Tate, James William (1875–1922)', *Oxford Dictionary of National Biography*, ed. H. G. C. Matthew and Brian Harrison (Oxford, 2004).

[25] It was originally written by an American, Henry J. Sayers, in 1891 then introduced to London by Lottie Collins. James Tate was Lottie Collins' third husband.

[26] W. Macqueen-Pope, *Nights of Gladness* (London, 1956), p. 171.

fifteen or sixteen: 'You are so stuck up! Why don't you talk to my friends when I bring them home to tea?'[27] Maggie's surprise at the comment may reflect her disbelief that any of the older girls would even want her to contribute to the conversation. She must have felt very isolated even within her own family. Or was her sister right to comment on her superior attitude? Was she already becoming dismissive of her relations?

The move to London proved to be a disaster for the Tate family. What a huge disappointment the whole undertaking must have been. Society, businessmen, tourists, did not flock to hear the piano being played in the salon, nor to hear Jacob's little daughter singing there. In fact, documents show first the purchase of the Caledonian Hotel by Maggie's father Jacob Tate in 1896 (two years before the move), then strangely, the mortgage of the hotel to his father James Tate in 1898. One wonders why the hotel was then assigned to Mrs Maria Tate in the same year. The answer to these questions must lie in documents dealing with a claim against Jacob and Maria by James Tate in October 1899, followed by the bankruptcy of Jacob on 9 November 1899.[28] The fact that this bankruptcy is registered so soon after leaving Wolverhampton suggests that the whole move must have been doomed from the start.

Maggie makes no affectionate references to her father in her book, and merely emphasises the parlous state of finances in which he left the hotel. Both a newspaper summary of a case heard in the Queens' Bench Division in September 1899[29] and a damning report issued at the time of his bankruptcy list several misdemeanours. Not only were Jacob's assets lower in value than the amount of his liabilities, but he had failed to keep proper accounts. Worse still, he is accused of 'rash and hazardous speculation' in mining and other shares, and has contributed to his bankruptcy by losing hundreds of pounds by betting. Not until two years later, on 7 August 1902, was Jacob discharged from his bankruptcy. Only a couple of months later he died.

Maggie wrote not a word about her grandfather James who had died so soon before, in 1901. What an awful few years this must have been for her mother Maria. We can see now that the whole stressful financial situation must have caused great grief to Maggie's parents and possibly contributed to the death of her grandfather and her father. Little wonder either that her musical education at the Royal College of Music was so brief. The fees of six guineas per term must have been hard to come by.

Knowing these facts makes the next episode in Maggie's life, one which

[27] Teyte, *Star on the Door*, p. 17.
[28] City of Westminster Archives 455/11, 455/12.
[29] *The Times*, 21 September 1899.

she does see fit to relate, far more understandable than at first sight. When Maggie was fourteen her mother called her into that large hotel room with the piano to sing for Mr George Dance, who was a song writer, theatrical producer and manager. Maggie says in her autobiography that this came about following an enquiry from Mr Dance, implying that her reputation was already beginning to spread beyond the walls of the hotel, but since he was a major figure in the field of musical theatre at precisely the time her brother James was becoming well known, one can't help wondering if her brother was the instigator of this introduction, and was trying to give her a helping hand. Dance promptly suggested that Maggie should join one of his touring companies. No doubt this would have been a most useful source of income and would have meant one less mouth to feed at home. But what was a fourteen-year-old girl to make of this? In those days no schooling was compulsory at her age, and Maggie certainly had no commitments. Here was a young child without any significant personal attachments, no close friends either here or in Wolverhampton, no marked affection for her brothers and sisters, being given the opportunity to cast off into the unknown. No wonder she felt frightened at the enormity of the implications. She was not helped by her mother, who said to her, 'You can make your own decision.' A young girl with no roots, isolated, frightened, wondering which way to go? Mélisande? Maggie's reply was worthy of her entrepreneur father. 'If you pay me what I want!'[30]

She herself, on looking back, claims to find this astonishing, but we can now see how money must have been the primary consideration in all dealings at the hotel. She interpreted her bold statement with hindsight as nothing short of the intervention of Fate with a capital F, a moment of intuition. As she herself admits, she was susceptible to superstition and believed in destiny, so to her this was the first sign that she was destined for greatness. George Dance, inevitably, was taken aback. This was not typical feminine behaviour, certainly not the sort of attitude one would expect from a fourteen-year-old, but then Maggie was in no way a conventional child with a conventional middle-class upbringing. She admits that he 'looked startled, to say the least of it' and left the hotel at once. Unsurprisingly, nothing more came of this. Judging by reminiscences from those who knew her, Maggie's outspokenness did not diminish as she grew older. Perhaps this was not just a legacy of her Midlands commercial background, but a remnant of that vital survival instinct.

Jacob by then was no longer alive, so was not there to comment on his daughter's behaviour. It would be interesting to know whether he would

---

[30] Teyte, *Star on the Door*, p. 15.

have been shocked at her outspokenness, or pleased that she had learnt the significance of finances, as he had been forced to do. Maggie does not reflect on the death of her father. Nor does she refer to her mother again in her autobiography, although Maria lived on until after her daughter was famous. She died in Wimbledon in 1913 at the age of fifty-six of pulmonary tuberculosis. Knowledge of these impoverished and stressful circumstances is a vital clue to the decisions Maggie made throughout her life. Having experienced at first hand and at an early age the distress that financial problems could bring, from now on she would eagerly take any path which would lead to security in this respect and choose a lifestyle far removed from the commercial enterprises run by her parents and grandparents. She would never have the close family support Mary Garden enjoyed, and none of the intense intellectual associations from which Georgette Leblanc benefited.

13 *Maggie Teyte's Path to Mélisande (1903-8)*

ANOTHER MALE FIGURE was to enter Maggie's life two years later, and would have a completely opposite effect on her future of any that her father could have envisaged before his death. Their meeting came about as a result of her 'always singing about the place', as she says, for in 1903 she was invited to sing at a charity concert at the Roman Catholic church of Corpus Christi, Maiden Lane (only a few hundred yards from the Royal Opera House, Covent Garden), in aid of church funds. This was one of those moments she calls Destiny. Reminiscing in her retirement, she could remember the priest announcing a number not originally on the programme, Tosti's *Goodbye*, to be sung by a very young person for whom no apologies would be needed. She recalled moving through the people standing in the aisle, but the next few minutes, those vital ones of her first public recognition, were a blank. Once back in the sacristy, there was a young man walking up and down murmuring, 'Quite extraordinary, quite extraordinary.' Only then did she become conscious of the applause. The young man, who played the accompaniment, was Walter Rubens.[1]

The number of words devoted to Walter in her book, and the sense of excitement and dedication they convey are in stark contrast to the meagre references to her father or any other member of her family. Maggie, although now fifteen, looked younger in her plain white dress. The effect was stunning. The audience was enraptured, the accompanist holding back his tears, the little soloist herself almost crying at conveying such emotion. Walter Rubens made up his mind then and there that this young girl should have a complete training as a singer.

Maggie dedicated her autobiography: 'To the memory of Walter Rubens, but for whose generosity and understanding this book could not have been written.' Indeed, Walter changed her life for ever. He was a gifted amateur musician whose brother Paul became one of the great composers of the musical comedy era. In the 1890s they had worked together writing both the librettos and the music for musicals performed by the Cambridge University Footlights Dramatic Club and elsewhere, and both continued in this vein. However, music was not the intended career of either. Paul had studied law and Walter became a stockbroker, like his father.

[1] Interview with Felix Aprahamian, BBC, 16 October 1948.

Having weighed up the potential of his young discovery and decided that she was mature enough to be trained professionally, as well as enchanting to watch and listen to, Walter spoke to his family about his plans for her future. Maggie could never have foreseen such good fortune. Not only was Walter to become her patron, but it was soon suggested that she should move in with the Rubens family. Her mother must have been relieved. Financially the situation at the hotel was disastrous and with her husband and father-in-law dead, Maria must have been leading a stressful and depressing life. There can have been little hesitation in allowing Maggie to leave behind altogether her own family of whom the details are so scant in her autobiography, and enter the wealthy society milieu of no. 8A, Kensington Palace Gardens as the protégée of Victor and Jenny Rubens, Walter's parents. Victor was a stockbroker of German origin, 'who was possibly the kindest man I have ever met.'[2] The Rubens became Maggie's surrogate family, and to them she owes all that followed in her life. Her talent was fostered and she responded intuitively, absorbing the cosmopolitan atmosphere of the wealthy society world to which the Rubens belonged, glimpsing foreign horizons vicariously as they entertained glamorous guests from abroad.

There were in fact more connections between Maggie and the Rubens than one might imagine from Maggie's account. Her brother James collaborated several times in musical theatre with Paul Rubens, for example in *High Jinks*, which had music by Paul Rubens, Howard Talbot, Jerome Kern and James W. Tate.[3] It is quite likely that the two men knew each other already before Maggie's performance at Corpus Christi church.

Walter was so bowled over by his discovery of the young, innocent singer producing such an amazing stream of pure sound that he cannot have been oblivious to her physical beauty. Maggie looked younger than her years, but at fifteen was no child. He clearly foresaw her conveying and awakening deep emotions in others through her singing, so must himself have been emotionally moved. How did he manage to avoid becoming physically attracted to her? Did he have to suppress such feelings as they were living under the same roof? Maggie never mentions any possible chink in the impeccable behaviour of her patron, nor does she ever hint at any physical attraction of her own towards him, so it must be assumed that their relationship always remained platonic. This may well have been at her insistence, for it is quite likely that Walter had indeed been in love with Maggie.[4] Comparing

[2] Teyte, *Star on the Door*, p. 16.

[3] Macqueen-Pope, *Nights of Gladness*, p. 215.

[4] O'Connor, *The Pursuit of Perfection*, p. 109.

Maggie's autobiography to Mary Garden's, one can detect immediately a contrasting attitude to the opposite sex. Maggie wants to convey the sense of a completely professional attitude to this start of her career. In similar circumstances Mary would have made much more of her closeness to any young man who had 'spotted' her, or at least managed to imply that he was unable to resist her charms! As for Walter's mother, Mrs Rubens, Maggie referred to her as 'Mama', and it is implied that she held her in more affection than her own mother.

What did Walter's idea of 'a complete training as a singer' entail? The height of achievement would be an international career in opera. He had indeed not only set his heart on a Continental musical education for Maggie, but he knew with whom he wanted her to study. First an audition would have to be arranged. A friend of the Rubens was Lady de Grey, Marchioness of Ripon, who had enormous influence at Covent Garden, both in front of and behind the scenes. She sponsored the opera to the extent, it is said, that her arrival in her seat in her box was almost the signal for the opera to begin.[5] It was she who helped to raise the £1,000 needed to send Maggie to the Paris home of Jean de Reszke, that operatic idol whom Mary Garden had first heard in Chicago.

Walter, in the role of accompanist, and his mother escorted Maggie on her first trip abroad in 1904. It was so exciting for the sixteen-year-old that all details of the expedition are blurred until the morning of the audition. On entering a big salon Maggie saw Madame de Reszke, famed for her beauty, with her husband. Amongst others present was a friend of Walter's, Olga Loewenthal, later known as Olga Lynn. Olga was awestruck by the vision of the young girl with a huge auburn pigtail, singing as though she were a fully trained artist:

> Those who were present at this audition could not refrain from shedding a tear. Her tone was round, true and noble, and of such beauty I could not believe she was real. Jean was much moved too, and from that day until the day of his death he never ceased talking of this wonderful pupil.[6]

Maggie does recall that she sang Tosti's *Goodbye* with Walter accompanying, as in that first recital at the church in Maiden Lane, and Olga completes the detail by saying she sang 'Connais-tu le pays' from *Mignon* by Ambroise Thomas and a song by Walter's brother, Paul. Jean de Reszke thanked Maggie, then said in a rather matter-of-fact way that she should make her début in two years time. His prediction proved remarkably accurate, for she took only three months longer than this. Maggie would never forget her feeling

[5] Olga Lynn, *Oggie: the Memoirs of Olga Lynn* (London, 1955), p. 43.

[6] Lynn, *Oggie*, p. 18.

of elation at being accepted so immediately by this international opera star. She called him her 'first and only master'.

'Nothing but the best would satisfy him' says Maggie of Walter's decision to send her to Jean de Reszke. This world famous opera star certainly was 'the best' for his new pupil. He nurtured her and fostered her talent, which was also recognised by her fellow pupils. Olga Lynn, who until Maggie's arrival had thought herself to be de Reszke's favourite, insists that it never crossed her mind to be jealous, 'for like everyone who heard this astonishing child, I was at her feet.'[7]

De Reszke was born in 1850 in Warsaw, his original name being Jan Mieczislaw. The de Reszke name became known throughout Europe, for both his brother Edouard and sister Josephine became famous singers. Jean's huge popularity in London dated from his performance as Radames in *Aida* at Drury Lane in 1887. One of the features of his art most commented upon was his enunciation and wonderful French pronunciation. As a teacher he encouraged 'l'amour de la parole' (love of words), and this gift he passed on to Maggie Teyte. Amherst Webber, composer, accompanist and friend of Jean, said it was 'almost impossible to recall any musical phrase one had heard him sing without also remembering the words and the peculiar charm he gave them.'[8] When Cosima Wagner heard de Reszke sing at Covent Garden in *Die Meistersinger*, 'She was in ecstasies: she kept exclaiming that she caught new beauties of melody that no German singer had ever suggested.' Queen Victoria once asked him for his autograph when he and Edouard sang in a command performance of *Lohengrin* at Windsor. She found the singing of the two brothers 'beyond praise' and adored Jean's handsome looks.[9] Unfortunately he was continually plagued by catarrh, and eventually the painful treatment of his bronchial tubes with iodine caused them to become seriously inflamed. He had to give up performance and take to teaching full time in his house at 53 rue de la Faisanderie, which is where Maggie was sent in 1904.

Maggie found that people's description of Jean de Reszke as 'le grand homme' fitted both his physique and his reputation. She was also attracted to his immense charm. Anxious and eager to absorb every word or note of advice from her new master, she now lived only for singing. 'Joy' is the word she finds to describe her attitude. 'Work! The word can have so many meanings. This work was to be my joy, my religion.'[10] Teacher and pupil were well

7 Lynn, *Oggie*, p. 19.

8 Clara Leiser, *Jean de Reszke and the Great Days of Opera* (London, 1933), foreword by Amherst Webber, p.xvi.

9 Desmond Shawe-Taylor, 'A Gallery of Great Singers', *Opera*, January 1955, p. 13.

10 Teyte, *Star on the Door*, p. 18.

suited in temperament. Unlike some of his other pupils, Maggie would do everything de Reszke told her without arguing. Both had enormous self-discipline and dedication to a task.

Jean had built a small theatre at the back of this house for performances. He taught four pupils at a time, dividing an hour up into fifteen minutes for each, but if one overran they would proceed in a different order the next day, so that the time could be made up. The lessons were not cheap by any stretch of the imagination: 200 francs or £8 per pupil for fifteen minutes (as Maggie calculated it in 1958), which was a very substantial sum of money for the times. How could Maggie possibly have been introduced into this world without her rich sponsors?

She and Olga lodged at 40 avenue Victor Hugo in a pension run by a Scottish lady, Julia Smith. One can imagine the exhilaration and sense of freedom this sixteen-year-old must have felt, away from oppressive reminders of her family and no longer under the watchful eyes of her kind sponsors. Obviously, it was a quieter city then than now. Olga describes the dignity of the Champs Élysées, the stream of elegant open carriages and fiacres bowling along towards the Bois de Boulogne, the voices of the street criers, the bleat of goats drawing little milk carts.

De Reszke supervised all lessons, starting at 10 a.m. He based his teaching on his own experience and perseverance, and insisted on a carefully graded system of certain basic exercises.[11] For ever after, Maggie was indebted to her teacher for the skill and resilience these gave her. She would also watch and listen to others in his little theatre, picking up hints not just on how to sing and act, but on how to behave. After three months she progressed to the aria 'Voi che sapete' from Mozart's *Le nozze di Figaro*. Already she recognised something special about Mozart, for she began to 'paint it with the colours which the traditions of Mozart demand, and for which Jean de Reszke was such a stickler.'[12] Indeed, she was eventually to provide a whole chapter in her autobiography 'On singing Mozart'. Her teacher believed in the virtue of trying out the most difficult things first, so that afterwards everything would seem comparatively easy. One of the arias which became a daily exercise was 'Depuis le jour' from Charpentier's *Louise*. This she sang to visitors to the school and received praise for her performances. Louise was, as we have seen, the very role which brought Mary Garden to fame.

Unfortunately, when de Reszke asked Maggie to sing to an important visitor one day, disaster struck. Heinrich Conried, Director of the Metropolitan Opera, New York, was in Paris to find French singers to

11　Reproduced in an appendix in O'Connor, *The Pursuit of Perfection*, pp. 283–91.
12　Teyte, *Star on the Door*, p. 19.

appear there in order to compete with the Manhattan Opera House, where Hammerstein was to build up his French repertoire with Mary Garden. The teacher invited Conried to hear some of his pupils in his own little theatre, and presented young Maggie singing a very long bravura aria, twenty-seven pages of 'O beau pays de la Touraine' from Meyerbeer's *Les Huguenots*. After the quiet opening passage she had a huge attack of nerves, something she had never experienced before. She stopped, and the silence seemed to go on and on. When de Reszke gently encouraged her to continue, she heard him saying to Conried, 'You understand, she has only been with me six months.' Maggie managed to finish the aria, hot with shame, then hid behind the upright piano on the stage and cried for two hours without stopping.[13]

This crushing lesson was significant, for Maggie claims that never again did she give in to self-pity about her performance. She realised she only had herself to blame if it was not good enough, and she went back to work on it. Nevertheless, if she had not had this attack of nerves, how different her career might have turned out at that crucial period in the history of opera in New York. What an opportunity she had missed to compete with her greatest rival, Mary Garden. Having taught herself this lesson in determination and endurance, she now remained totally dedicated to learning, always doing exactly as she was told. It was not all work and no play, however, for de Reszke and his wife certainly looked after the welfare of the pupils. Maggie and Olga were taken on holiday with them to Deauville, fed rich food and allowed to bathe in the sea. Perhaps this is where the seeds of Maggie's eventual love of golf were planted, for the girls used to watch their teacher on the links there.[14]

In Paris Maggie was in an ideal position to come into contact with famous and influential musicians. The school was a magnet for composers and impresarios seeking interpreters for operatic roles, and in March 1906 she was selected to sing Zerlina in *Don Giovanni* and Cherubino in *Le nozze di Figaro* in a series of concerts at a Mozart Festival organised by the composer Reynaldo Hahn.

Hahn was a man of enormous charm, a homosexual who was a lover of Marcel Proust. Georgette Leblanc had already been captivated by the man who exerted 'power enveloped in nonchalance [who] sings divinely whilst smoking cigarettes. His accompaniment is an atmosphere, he paints with vibrations.' She claimed you could not know Reynaldo Hahn until you had heard him conducting Mozart. It was a mystery to her how this could be 'so

[13]   Teyte, *Star on the Door*, p. 20.
[14]   Lynn, *Oggie*, p. 23.

precise yet so blurred ... solid yet subtle like a perfume.'[15] How greatly Maggie Teyte admired Hahn is proved by the number of references she makes to him throughout her life, describing his accompaniments and his love and interpretation of Mozart. As time went on, at intimate concerts in the great houses of Paris and London she too would see him accompanying himself in his own songs, singing in a small but melodious light baritone. Hahn must have spotted Maggie almost as soon as she arrived at de Reszke's school, for when commenting later on her performance as Mélisande in the journal *Femina*,[16] he wrote that he had realised as soon as she arrived as a timid new-comer from London that she was a born singer. This was why two years later he had invited her to sing in his Mozart Festival, where he felt that 'this little nightingale would soon grow wings'.[17] Eventually Maggie was to become an established interpreter of his songs, one whom he evidently admired, for when she once questioned him on the tempo to take his response was: '*Ma chère*, any way you sing it will always be right.'[18]

Hahn's Mozart Festival took place in the Salle Gaveau. Maggie received no fee for this, so does not rank it as her first professional appearance. Here she learnt a memorable and valuable lesson in stagecraft from the soprano Lilli Lehmann, whose niece, Hedwig Helbig, was also performing. To Maggie's astonishment, the diva was lecturing this poor young lady so volubly in German that she saw the young singer cowering with her back to the wall. Maggie had been brought up to believe in perfect silence before a concert. In fact she always claimed she never talked at all on the days that she sang. Further amazement was to follow when Maggie, who had to follow Lehmann onto the stage, saw her break out into 'a devilish grin, which stretched her mouth from ear to ear'. She realised then how broad a smile or grimace must be to be perceptible in a large theatre.[19] It had not occurred to her to act demonstratively. Now she was learning her stagecraft, not by instinct like Georgette Leblanc or Mary Garden, but by imitating experienced singers.

[15] 'Il a un pouvoir enveloppé de nonchalance, chante divinement et fume en même temps des cigarettes. Son accompagnement est une atmosphère, il peint avec des vibrations ... Là, il y a pour moi un mystère – comment être si net et si estompé ... irréductiblement solide et subtil comme un parfum.' Leblanc, *La Machine à courage*, p. 175. See illus. 20.

[16] *Femina* 15 July 1908, p. 327. Quoted in Marcel Proust, *Correspondance*, vol. 8: *1908*, ed. Philip Kolb (Paris, 1981), pp. 204–5 n. 14.

[17] 'L'on sentait qu'il pousserait bientôt des ailes à ce petit rossignol.' Proust, *Correspondance*, vol. 8, pp. 204–5.

[18] Teyte, *Star on the Door*, p. 62.

[19] Teyte, *Star on the Door*, p. 30.

Maggie retained a letter sent to her with impressions of this festival, praising this tiny sixteen-year-old who wore a short white frock, and white ribbons on her long braid. 'She was exquisite and was greeted with storms of
applause ... Tate has a wonderful future before her, and Lehmann evidently
felt that her days were over.'[20]

Her first performance outside Paris took place in Monte Carlo in February
1907. Here she was to sing Tyrcis in Offenbach's *Myriame et Daphné*, but
this was not as significant as three performances as Zerlina, with the French
baritone Maurice Renaud, the most celebrated Don Giovanni of the day.
The innocent pupil was chaperoned on her journey by 'Mama', Mrs Victor
Rubens, who had come over especially from England. First there was the
excitement of the dazzling surroundings to take in, and before returning
home Mrs Rubens wanted to go to the Casino. Permission had to be gained
for Maggie to enter as she was under age. For this she needed the assistance
of Raoul Gunsbourg, the famous Director of the Monte Carlo Opera. Once
inside, Maggie was able to take in the atmosphere of the gambling rooms,
which she found quite ugly, but she would never forget the unique sound of
real gold pieces chinking against one another.

When it came to performing in *Don Giovanni* she realised it was fortunate that as usual she had prepared thoroughly and knew her part backwards. Looking back on her professional life, she later claimed that this was
the only time she experienced stage nerves.[21] She had not been warned that
at Monte Carlo singers were accustomed to arrive in time for the performance only to disappear again immediately after it. She was to have only one
rehearsal beginning just three-quarters of an hour before the curtain rose.
The director, who was also singing Masetto in the opera, had very little time
to show her when and where to move, but 'during the performance I can
still remember the look on Maurice Renaud's face as his eyes tried to impel
me into some kind of action.'[22] This is surely a clue to the greatest difference between Maggie's style and that of both Georgette Leblanc and Mary
Garden. Georgette could always summon up histrionics and be overtly dramatic at the slightest excuse. Mary Garden's reputation as a 'singing actress'
grew with the development of her career. Maggie however, 'didn't know anything about the technique of the stage or anything. All I could do was sing ...
I went through the performance exactly as if I was doped.'[23]

It was through the larger-than-life director, Raoul Gunsbourg, that

[20] Teyte, *Star on the Door*, p. 30.
[21] *Frankly Speaking*, BBC interview, 31 December 1959.
[22] Teyte, *Star on the Door*, p. 36.
[23] *Frankly Speaking*, BBC interview, 31 December 1959.

Maggie was to have her first intimations of the power of a man in a position of authority to do more than hire and fire. She had caught his eye and ear, for he paid her the compliment of requesting that she should replace the indisposed soprano, Aino Ackté, and sing to the accompaniment of Paderewski. Maggie was struck by the sight of this great pianist pacing up and down on the stage before the concert, his hands in a muff.

There was much gossip flying around about the sayings and doings of Gunsbourg, but these must have been quite mystifying at first to the young girl who describes him as 'a short, fat, compact figure of a man, very ugly, who appeared to strut through his musical métier as though he was a reincarnation of Napoleon.'[24] She heard that Gunsbourg liked to let it be known suggestively that he entertained beautiful society ladies very late at night. However, it was not just fashionable society that received his attention. He had clearly not been immune to Maggie's young and innocent beauty. Did he know that 'Mama' had returned to England? At ten o'clock in the morning Maggie was summoned to the director's office. The conversation was trivial. Suddenly Maggie was flung back onto a sofa. Gunsbourg ran across the room to lock the door. The young girl sprang to her feet and screamed 'Ouvrez la porte! Ouvrez la porte!' She was so loud that Gunsbourg, unused to being spurned, realised others would hear, and opened the door at once. Maggie made her escape and never saw him alone again.[25]

Perhaps even more significant than this introduction to the casting couch was the presence at the Monte Carlo Opera of none other than Marguerite Carré, wife of Albert, Director of the Opéra-Comique. She must have heard (perhaps with some surprise) about Maggie's refusal to submit to Gunsbourg, for she made a point of introducing herself to the young girl. During the course of their conversation she asked if Maggie had received the traditional invitation to the banquet thrown by the Prince of Monaco in his palace at the end of each Monte Carlo Opera season. Maggie had never even heard of this event and at the time simply felt relieved to have been spared the social ordeal. In retrospect, however, she believed there might well have been a glint of malice in Marguerite's eye as her omission from the guest list was clearly a little act of revenge on the part of Gunsbourg.

Back in Paris, even if Maggie rejected the advances of men who might have furthered her career, that is not to say she did not fall in love. An early affair was kept secret until she discovered that in 1908 the Romanian composer Georges Enesco had dedicated to her the fifth of the *Sept chansons de Clément Marot*. They must have met when Enesco was playing both piano

24 Teyte, *Star on the Door*, p. 33.
25 Teyte, *Star on the Door*, p. 35.

and violin in Paris during 1907, but Maggie did not mention it until asked about the dedication about sixty years later. Her reason for not having told anyone about it, she said, was that she did not want people to think that she would go to bed with just anybody.[26] Enesco's French biographer has no further information to add to this episode, but loyally remarks that on looking at photographs of the handsome young composer at that time it is evident that he was not 'just anybody!'[27]

By now de Reszke insisted on the spelling of her surname as Teyte. Maggie had previously altered Tate to Tête to be nearer to the French pronunciation, but it was her teacher who put in the 'y'. Neither he nor she liked her being referred to as 'Mees Tat'![28] At this point she received her first contract from Albert Carré to sing at the Opéra-Comique in the role of Glycère in *Circé* by the brothers Hillemacher, which opened on 17 April 1907. Unfortunately a most embarrassing incident took place during a performance of this opera: on her feet Maggie had to wear sandals to go with the classical costume, and disastrously stubbed her toe on one of the lower steps, committing the unforgivable sin of literally falling up the rest of the flight! 'I can still hear the roar of laughter that came from the auditorium, and I can still feel the rush of hot shame to my face',[29] she wrote. *Circé* only had a very short run.

Maggie's contract was for 800 francs a month for the first year, 1,000 francs for the second, and 1,200 for the third. During that first year she sang Mallika in Delibes's *Lakmé*, prepared but never sang on stage the role of Poussette in Massenet's *Manon*, and performed the Second Boy in *The Magic Flute*. Meanwhile she practised constantly to perfect her technique. De Reszke's training was exacting and she was determined to meet the highest standards in all she did. Yet, despite her efforts, she had to bear the frustration of waiting in the wings for the realisation of her dreams. Her small roles did not lead to stardom, and Maggie did not have independent financial means to pay her way to the top as some did. The customary fee if one had to pay to make one's début with the Opéra-Comique was 10,000 francs![30] So what of that other method, used successfully by Marguerite Carré and so many other women opera singers?

One day Maggie met Albert Carré in a corridor at the Opéra-Comique.

[26] O'Connor, *The Pursuit of Perfection*, p. 71.

[27] 'Il est clair qu'Enesco n'était pas ... n'importe qui!' Alain Cophignon, *Georges Enesco* (Paris, 2006), p. 171.

[28] *Wolverhampton Chronicle*, 19 August 1949.

[29] Teyte, *Star on the Door*, p. 49.

[30] Hansen, *The Sybil Sanderson Story*, p. 73, quotes Massenet as saying he knew Sibyl Sanderson could well afford this customary fee.

He tenderly put his arm around her shoulders and asked her how everything was going. 'I withdrew myself as tactfully as I could, rather afraid of what might come next', writes Maggie:

> All seemed to be well until two or three weeks later, when I was summoned to M. Carré's office to be informed that my services would not be required after the end of the season. I was very despondent. The air of Paris is always full of love there was plenty of that to be had but I wanted roles, and it seemed there were none available. I suddenly realised how very young I was – and how very alone.[31]

Young indeed, and with no immediate family to turn to. At nineteen Maggie now faced a sudden end to her career.

This is the point at which Mélisande came to the rescue. Maggie presumably was aware that Mary Garden was about to leave for the United States, but can hardly have imagined that she would play a role in the row between her and Marguerite Carré. In September 1907, at de Reszke's suggestion, Maggie was sent to study the role of Mélisande with Debussy himself. On hearing the rumour that Mary Garden wanted to return to Paris to sing Mélisande in the 1908–9 season, Marguerite Carré urgently insisted that Albert cast Maggie in the role until she had learnt it and could take over. 'To my surprise, I was once again summoned to M. Carré's office. There was no caressing arm this time – just cold business.'[32] Carré quickly invented the excuse that he had been told gossip about her drinking and smoking too much, then generously agreed to reconsider the question of her notice.

Once rehearsals were under way, rather to her surprise, Maggie found Madame Carré very anxious that she should do well in the part, giving her a lot of useful hints. She was obviously determined that Maggie should imitate Mary Garden, for she would say 'Garden a fait ceci', or 'Garden a fait cela.' 'Even though I was young and stupid', wrote Maggie, 'I began to wonder what it was all about.' It did not take her long to realise that all of this was due to the jealousy of one prima donna for another. Maggie had seen Mary Garden in *Pelléas*. She found her an excellent actress, but criticised her French pronunciation. However, she realised that perhaps Mary cultivated this 'foreignness' on purpose to give her a special air of mystery and emphasise her uniqueness.

Maggie's descriptions of her first meeting with Debussy and her rehearsals with him in her autobiography, in BBC programmes and in journals are all very similar in emphasis and detail. She was nineteen when she was asked to present herself at Debussy's house, 80 avenue du Bois de Boulogne (now

[31] Teyte, *Star on the Door*, p. 51.
[32] Teyte, *Star on the Door*, p. 51.

called avenue Foch). She recalls it as being by the Ceinture, a railway line encircling Paris, which is why a young man remarked to her once that that was no doubt why Debussy's music was such a beastly noise! Having been shown into the *salon* Maggie's first impression was of the large collection of china cats, memorable also because of the long time she spent studying them as she waited for the composer to make his entry. When Debussy did come in, he did not look at her, but walked straight over to the little upright piano. Although he did not even glance at her, she had a good look at him. He seemed tall but thick and heavy and he slouched rather than walked. He had a black beard and a square head covered with black hair, giving him an almost Oriental look.

When Debussy did eventually turn to look at her, he was clearly taken aback by the petite figure in front of him:

> 'Vous êtes Mlle Teyte?' he asked.
> 'Oui', she replied. After another long silence he asked again, ' Vous êtes Mlle Maggie Teyte?' *(Maggie pronounced with a soft g.)*
> 'Oui.'
> Silence.
> 'Mais vous êtes Mlle Maggie Teyte de l'Opéra-Comique?'
> 'Oui.'

Debussy did not appear to believe her. She was told later that this was because he could not believe that another Scottish [*sic*] singer was to sing Mélisande. 'Quoi? Encore une écossaise?', he exclaimed. The next thing he said to her was that he would have Mélisande as *he* wanted her. Needless to say, Maggie was only too ready to agree.[33]

The composer's reaction is hardly surprising, for this must have been only shortly after dealing with the rehearsals of *Pelléas et Mélisande* in Brussels. The image of Mary Garden as his Mélisande would be very hard to match. Incidentally, Maggie was at pains to point out that the composer never touched her, not even to shake hands.

So the collaboration began. Maggie was ready to soak up all that the composer could teach her just as she had obediently and eagerly assimilated all that Jean de Reszke and Reynaldo Hahn had taught her about Mozart. Debussy found little to criticise in her work and she attributed this to her Mozartian upbringing. She often emphasised that she always approached the interpretation of Debussy as though he were a modern Mozart. 'People think I am eccentric when I say this, but like the music of Mozart, every note of Debussy must have its full value – the music must not be pulled into the

[33] Teyte, *Star on the Door*, p. 65, and interview with Alec Robertson, BBC *Music Magazine*, broadcast 27 August 1944.

shape of the poem.'[34] And again: 'You see, to sing Mozart in the true style you must be, so to speak, pedantic. You must observe exact note values. This was ingrained in me. Perhaps Debussy had not heard his music sung like this before.'[35]

'Pedantic' was the word she used to describe Debussy's teaching, and even his approach to *Pelléas et Mélisande*:

Composers are notorious for not being able to interpret their own compositions – I think this is fairly true of a great many of them – but Debussy's gifts as pianist and conductor were always sufficient to express the essence of his own music – pedantic, poetic and savage in turn, as the score of *Pelléas et Mélisande* shows to those who know and understand it.[36]

He never wasted any words. 'In fact in nine months he said hardly as many words to me.' His obsessive behaviour was striking. She had to sit and wait whilst he sat at the piano for two or three minutes getting into the mood. One day he raised his arms ready to play when he saw a little bit of white cotton on the floor. He stopped, picked it up, then rolled it up and looked everywhere for a place to put it. 'It took him quite a while to get rid of that bit of cotton', said Maggie.[37]

In another interview in 1947 she reflected, 'He was a stickler for precision. Every note had to be given its exact time-duration, even in measures that other composers might consider rhythmically rather free. Each slight stress or other marking had to be observed in order to bring out the true colours of the text.' She certainly had to work hard, studying for three hours daily for nine months, his intense concentration being matched by her desire to satisfy the demands of her exacting taskmaster.[38]

Maggie's malleable nature must have been satisfying to the composer and producer, and her attitude to her art on stage was certainly more submissive than that of Georgette or Mary. When asked in an interview in 1959 how she interpreted her roles, her reply was:

Well I suppose Debussy put me into that as well, and the man that I learnt the French [*sic*], who was the Regisseur of the Opéra-Comique ... He said – You must do this, it means that, but you know ... I did it perhaps like a parrot, let us say, perhaps a beautiful parrot, but still a parrot.

Her interviewer pressed her further. 'Were you not an actress at all?' To

---

34 Teyte, *Star on the Door*, p. 66.

35 Interview with Felix Aprahamian, BBC, 16 October 1948.

36 Teyte, *Star on the Door*, p. 66.

37 BBC *Music Magazine*, broadcast on 27 August 1944.

38 *Opera News*, 7 April 1947, p. 22.

which she replied, 'I don't think so, I don't know … but then I had a very good master again, Carré, Albert Carré of the Opéra-Comique.'[39]

She found Debussy:

> exceedingly complex and subtle … essentially a primitive, one might almost say a savage person. There was a fierce power basic in his nature. He seemed always striving for an unattainable goal and worked with such intensity that he gave the impression of being ill, breathing heavily and never at peace with himself.[40]

Maggie wondered if this breathing, which was almost whistling, could have been caused by heart trouble or nerves, but its effect was to 'key one up; one was always conscious of that powerful, nervous force at work, directing and controlling.' His singers were expected to give this same energy. His pent-up nervous force surcharged the atmosphere of a room when he entered. His appearance, his head with its distinctive bumps, his dark brown, piercing eyes contributed to the impression of immense physical power.[41] Several times she likened him to a volcano. 'A volcano that smouldered. I once saw him go white with anger, then red with the sheer effort of control. There was a core of anger and bitterness in him. Altogether my impression of him was of a man obsessed.'[42]

Maggie expressed surprise on reading biographies of Debussy that he had a circle of musicians and artists with whom he conversed, for to her his reticence was striking. He spoke very little during the nine months of her studies on *Pelléas et Mélisande* and when they were associated at concerts later on:

> Only once or twice during my studies with him do I remember this habit of silence being broken – one occasion was one morning after a rehearsal, when we were joined by André Caplet in Debussy's salon. The master suddenly let forth on the subject of Wagner and Mozart – they had spoiled a lot of paper![43]

Commenting that 'No one seemed to like him', she also remembered that 'Jean Périer, Pelléas to my Mélisande, went white with anger if you mentioned Debussy'![44]

So if he was so reticent, how did he manage to correct her? Apparently the need rarely arose. He was a man of few words, and fortunately did not find much to criticise. Maggie also recalled Debussy's wonderful eye for

[39] *Frankly Speaking*, BBC interview, 31 December 1959.
[40] *Opera News*, 7 April 1947, p. 22.
[41] *Musical America*, 13 April 1918, p. 5.
[42] BBC *Music Magazine*, broadcast on 27 August 1944.
[43] Teyte, *Star on the Door*, p. 67.
[44] BBC *Music Magazine*, broadcast on 27 August 1944.

design. 'If he were doing clothes, he would have designed some of our most beautiful modern dresses with a fine sense for the exotic.'[45]

Debussy must indeed have been impressed with Maggie – sufficiently so to ask Albert Carré specifically to allow her to sing his *mélodies* with him accompanying her at the Cercle Musical on 21 February 1908, that is almost four months before her début as Mélisande.[46] Here she sang the two sets of *Fêtes galantes* in a programme which also comprised Ricardo Viñes playing the *Images* for piano and Debussy's Quartet played by the Firman Touche Quartet. There is just one track on an LP record which has preserved Maggie Teyte's voice in 1908. In the song *Because* by Guy D'Hardelot[47] her voice already has that distinctive mellow timbre to be heard on much later recordings. It is remarkably mature, bright and confident, undimmed by the age of the recording, and instantly appealing in its clarity and expressiveness.

Talk about who was to sing Mélisande had obviously spread outside the walls of the Opéra-Comique, and no doubt others would have loved the opportunity to take over. But the composer was pleased with his new pupil. In April 1908 Debussy wrote to the singer Jane Bathori apologising for not replying sooner to a letter from her in which it sounds as if she was fishing for the part:

> I must emphasise that you exaggerate the influence I can have over M. Carré's decisions on the role of Mélisande! ... Recently I heard a young American [*sic*] girl: Miss M. Teyte; she has a charming voice and a very accurate idea of the character of Mélisande. You can be sure that she will bring to it that accent to which Mademoiselle Garden has made the audience at the Opéra-Comique so accustomed.[48]

Debussy was at the first rehearsal on Tuesday 19 May, when the conductor was Gabriel Grovlez, but François Ruhlmann took over on 23 May. Maggie was in costume for the first time on 1 June, but by 8 June Debussy was obviously exasperated at the way things were going. He wrote to Jacques Durand following six hours of rehearsals on the previous Saturday completely disillusioned: 'Believe me, it was not wonderful! – Miss M. Teyte continues to show about as much emotion as a prison door; she is a more than distant princess ... Périer mimes admirably to the music; Vieuille is the only one who is still the same as ever – i.e. very good.'[49] On 9 June Maggie wore her

45   *Musical America*, 13 April 1918, p. 5.
46   Debussy, *Correspondance*, p. 1064.
47   *L'Exquise Maggie Teyte*, EMI, RLS 716, side 8 of 4 LP set.
48   Debussy, *Correspondance*, p. 1079.
49   Debussy, *Correspondance*, p. 1093. One can't help thinking here of her own description of herself as a parrot.

iconic wig for the first time in the presence of the composer and full cast.[50] Despite his frustrations, Maggie must have satisfied the composer most of the time, for she writes that Ruhlmann got so exasperated at Debussy telling him to leave her alone that he never spoke to her again while she was at the Opéra-Comique![51] In the chapter in her book dedicated to conductors it is therefore hardly surprising that she writes, 'It is difficult for me to say very much of Monsieur Ruhlmann'![52]

Maggie herself did not dismiss the example of her predecessor. She stated, 'I am proud to say that my own interpretation was founded on hers, since Albert Carré coached us both.' How well she remembered his saying that the flowers which Mélisande carries on the castle terrace should not drip from her arms, but seem to reach up like a vine toward her shoulder.[53] As we have seen, Marguerite Carré, waiting in the wings to take over the role as soon as she had mastered it, was not slow in coming forward to tell her, 'Mary held her flowers like this.'

All were anxious that Maggie should succeed in this iconic role. Olga Lynn narrates that Mr and Mrs Rubens took both girls on a holiday to Pontresina in Switzerland in the summer before the performance, and there beside the stream amongst the trees she would help Maggie to learn her phrases, giving her the cues.[54]

After so much careful and thorough preparation, or perhaps precisely because of this, it is frustrating that Maggie did not reveal her thoughts and emotions on the first night. Typically, she claims she felt no nerves. 'I just did it', she said later.[55] Everything went so smoothly that her meticulousness led to a problem-free performance on 12 June 1908. The programme reproduced illustrations of Jusseaume's and Ronsin's stage sets, showing that the production was identical to the original one of 1902. A photograph of Maggie reveals a charmingly fresh youthful face, her thick hair piled luxuriantly on top.[56] The photograph of Jean Périer, for whom the role of Pelléas must by now have been second nature, shows him looking decidedly older, his hairline receding. He was, after all, thirty-nine years old to her twenty.[57] With Hector Dufranne as Golaud and Félix Vieuille as Arkel, she was surrounded

[50] Register at Bibliothèque de l'Opéra, Paris.

[51] Teyte, *Star on the Door*, p. 52.

[52] Teyte, *Star on the Door*, p. 107.

[53] *Opera News*, 19 November 1945.

[54] Lynn, *Oggie*, p. 21.

[55] *Frankly Speaking*, BBC interview, 31 December 1959.

[56] See illus. 21.

[57] Jean Périer, 1869–1954. Of 107 performances of *Pelléas* during Debussy's lifetime, Périer sang the role 93 times.

by a cast who knew their roles inside out. Paul Guillamat, the Doctor, had joined the Opéra-Comique in 1903 and Jeanne de Poumayrac, Yniold, in 1905. There is one anomaly between the printed programme and the Opéra-Comique register of rehearsals and performances.[58] Suzanne Brohly, who had been singing Geneviève since 1906 and who is listed as singing the role on 12 June was not the singer who performed the part. This was Mlle Berg, who had been at the Opéra-Comique since 1906. The register records categorically that Friday 12 June 1908 saw the first performance of Maggie Teyte as Mélisande and the first performance of Mlle Berg as Geneviève.

Needless to say, Maggie's English patrons were there. Paul and Walter Rubens (now with his wife), Mr and Mrs Victor Rubens, Lady Ripon – what must they have felt as they watched their protégée perform in such a masterpiece? Without them she would be nowhere. The crowning moment of her career thus far was greeted with rapturous applause and generous praise in the reviews. 'La mignonne Maggie Teyte', who had been taught by Jean de Reszke, 'the only singing teacher who knew how to teach singing', did her teacher credit. She had a sweet, pure voice, very clear diction and a graceful figure, personifying to perfection the delicate, sensitive Mélisande, wrote Adolphe Jullien (who thought Maggie was American.)[59] Pierre Lalo found the charm of the work just as powerful as when it had been heard two years previously. 'From the sound of the very first chords the subtle and deep intoxicating power of the music and poetry penetrate the depths of your soul.' Mlle Teyte had revealed a Mélisande very different from that of her predecessor, but was charming in her ingenuousness, candour, youth. She was more childlike than Mary Garden, truly the mysterious little girl found weeping by the fountain by Golaud.[60]

Debussy was pleased, for a letter to his publisher Durand written on 18 June 1908 reads:

> You will have read that Miss Maggy [*sic*] Teyte has not had to suffer too much from the memories of her illustrious predecessor? It is quite likely that the latter will at the very least accuse me of ingratitude, for no singer has the heart to understand that a work can be performed without her.

He did not change his mind about Périer, though, criticising him in the same terms as in his previous letter: 'One rather amusing detail is that people find

---

[58] Register at Bibliothèque de l'Opéra, Paris.

[59] *Feuilleton du Journal des débats*, 14 June, 1908.

[60] 'Une Mélisande fort différente de sa devancière, mais charmante aussi; charmante d'ingénuité, de candeur, de jeunesse; plus juvénile, plus puérile que n'était Mlle Garden; vraiment la petite fille mystérieuse que Golaud trouve pleurante au bord de la fontaine.' *Le Temps*, 15 June 1908.

Périer more and more admirable ... this is undoubtedly due to the fact that he is no longer singing my music at all.'[61]

Reynaldo Hahn wrote a vigorous defence of Maggie's performance as Mélisande.[62] He realised that 'taking on this role was doubly challenging because of its great difficulty and because of the memories it evoked of an ideal interpreter'.[63] He argued that Maggie's gift was something greater and even more important than simply having a beautiful voice or great determination to succeed; it was that she was a born singer: 'c'est l'instinct du chant.'

An eyewitness account of Maggie's début as Mélisande was given by that great admirer of Mary Garden, Jacques Rivière, in a letter to Henri Alain-Fournier.[64] Once again he was completely overcome by the beauty of the work and its perfect fusion of music and drama which added depth and resonance to the voices. As for Maggie Teyte, he was impressed by her intelligence. Her voice, much smaller than Garden's, was sometimes submerged, but most of the time it was fine, even excellent at times. Although Maggie later claimed the opposite, Rivière believed she was suffering from stage-fright and would therefore surely even improve with time. In some ways he found her better than Garden, in that she kept her place and did not dominate the stage as Garden had. What is striking, and must surely have been noticed by Maggie, is that at the end of the performance, cries of 'Garden, Garden!', were replaced by 'Debussy! Debussy!'[65]

As for other members of the cast, Rivière thought Périer had never sung so well. Berg, however, was a replacement for Brohly at the last minute. Here, then, we have the explanation of that discrepancy in the programme. Unfortunately, things did not go too well for Mlle Berg. She made lamentable errors in the letter scene, and as for the words, 'Aie soin d'allumer la lampe ...' ('See that the lantern is lit this evening ...') she twice came in too early!

What is even more fascinating about this account of Maggie's first night is that it contains evidence of Georgette Leblanc's presence in the audience. Jacques Rivière spotted Georgette at the exit.[66] His comment is scathing and

[61] Debussy, *Correspondance*, p. 1096.

[62] *Femina*, 15 July 1908, p. 327. Quoted in Proust, *Correspondance*, vol. 8, pp. 204–5.

[63] 'deux fois redoubtable et par sa grande difficulté et par le souvenir qu'il évoque d'une interprète idéale.' Proust, *Correspondance*, vol. 8, pp. 204–5.

[64] Rivière and Alain-Fournier, *Correspondance*, vol. 2, pp. 224–5.

[65] 'En un sens elle vaut mieux que Garden, parce qu'elle tient juste sa place, et n'usurpe pas, comme faisait Garden, malgré tout. Cela c'est fait sentir dès hier soir: aux cris de: Garden, Garden! ont succédé ceux de: Debussy! Debussy!' Rivière and Alain-Fournier, *Correspondance*, vol. 2, p. 224.

[66] Rivière and Alain-Fournier, *Correspondance*, vol. 2, p. 226.

bitter: Georgette was wearing an outrageous costume; she was plastered in make-up, old, and speaking in a sickeningly pretentious way. He termed it, 'the pitiful ugliness of an aged actress'.[67] How cruel that he whispered as he passed her: 'It's still not you singing Mélisande.'[68]

Not all the journals were so willing to allow memories of Mary Garden to be superseded. Shades of the old Maeterlinck dispute were recalled by one reviewer who found Mlle Teyte:

> a suitable Mélisande. Her gracious face and body were certainly pretty enough to stop rough old Golaud hunting in the forest, and to seduce that dreamy stripling Pelléas. But ... however graceful Mélisande was, she could only be a naive little girl, a delicate trinket, without a soul, without a heart, without real tears. Without crushing Mlle Teyte under the weight of comparison, it has to be said that her voice has a weak quality particularly in the middle register, and that the sweetness of certain sounds does not help us forget the slightness of the charm it offers.[69]

Henry Gauthier-Villars wrote that Maggie, despite the applause, was still far from being able to match Mary Garden in the role. Whilst she was intelligent and touching, with 'the fragility of an unaware doll', she had less of a foreign accent than her predecessor, 'and that artlessly sad phrase "I am not happy [je ne suis pas heureuse]", that dreadful castigating phrase, the sorrowful cry of a child about to die, which cuts you to the quick, what do you do with it, poor charming little English girl?'[70]

However, the review in *Les Annales du théâtre et de la musique* contained flattering words about Maggie:

> She does not possess that rare personality of Mlle Garden, the unforgettable creator of the role, but with a voice of delicious purity, she is the innocent and poetic Mélisande of the golden hair, the little amorous, mystical princess of legend, her whole being conveying marvellously that sensation of the unreal.[71]

Ravel went to see Maggie in the opera on 17 June. His opinion was remarkably similar to that of Gauthier-Villars, for he described her as 'an adorable doll. Physically more Mélisande than Garden was; vocally superior.

---

[67] 'la laideur pitoyable de l'actrice vieillie'.

[68] 'C'est pas encore toi qui chantes Mélisande.' Rivière and Alain-Fournier, *Correspondance*, vol. 2, p. 226.

[69] *Le Monde musical*, 15 June 1908.

[70] *Comoedia*, 13 June 1908.

[71] 'Elle ne possède sans doute pas la rare personalité de Mlle Garden, l'inoubliable créatrice du rôle, mais avec une voix de pureté délicieuse, elle est l'innocente et poétique Mélisande aux cheveux d'or, petite princesse de légende amoureuse et mystique, nous donnant merveilleusement en toute sa personne la sensation de l'irréel.' *Les Annales du théâtre et de la musique* (1909), p. 138.

But she sings it with a total lack of comprehension.' It must be noted in defence of Maggie, though, that hers was the only role that received any praise at all from this composer, who found the production a 'massacre général'![72]

In August 1908 the journal *Musica* carried a wonderful full page photograph of Maggie Tayte [*sic*] as Mélisande, her face fresh and youthful, looking even younger than her twenty years, arms appealingly outstretched, the tresses of her almost floor-length wig arranged artfully around her.[73] A couple of pages later, another photograph shows her leaning down, loose hair arranged on one side, an intense expression on her face. Her dress, medieval in style, outlines her slim body. It is embroidered with heraldic lilies climbing up from the hem and has a square neckline similar to that which Mary wore in the role. A photograph of Mary Garden as Mélisande on the same page shows a maturer face, almost glowering, hair plaited. After a glowing appraisal of Debussy's composition, the critic Georges Pioch commented that whilst Mary Garden remained unforgettable, 'Mlle Maggie Tayte [*sic*] who replaces her, looks physically more like one would imagine Mélisande than Mlle Garden. She sings with a pretty, pure voice; she acts convincingly a most mysterious little girl who is at the mercy of Fate without ever having dreamt of understanding it.'[74] He praised Albert Carré for having provided proof through 'the excellent interpretation of the very, very young Mlle Tayte [*sic*] that no artist is indispensable for any role.'

She certainly contributed to the aesthetic appeal of the work. Pioch regarded Maeterlinck's drama as ideally set to music. He had seen the first performance of the play at the Bouffes-Parisiens, but since Debussy 'completed' it, could remember little of the original production. 'In the music it finds its just fulfilment, it is completed by the music. There is no other example of a lyric drama where literature and music are so intermingled, so well blended.' Ironically the only negative criticism he made was of the 'belgicisms' in the dialogue; it was a little annoying that certain words betrayed Maeterlinck's origins and were emphasised by the music.[75] In this respect Maggie herself also noted, 'Maeterlinck was Belgian, not French' when explaining Mélisande's words 'Je ne suis pas heureuse'. 'It is wrong to translate this simply as "I am not happy"', she pointed out. 'In the Belgian idiom

[72] Debussy, *Correspondance*, p. 1096n.

[73] See illus. 23.

[74] Mlle Maggie Tayte ... a plus que Mlle Garden la vraisemblance physique de Mélisande. Elle chante d'une jolie voix pure; son jeu est fort bien celui d'une petite fille très mystérieuse qui succombe au Destin sans avoir meme rêvé de le comprendre.' *Musica*, August 1908, p. 115.

[75] *Musica*, August 1908, p. 115.

the meaning is "I am not happy *about this situation* – it is not right – I don't like this.'"[76]

When the opera returned in December 1908, Maggie had quite a following. Adolphe Jullien[77] again praised her, and commented on the considerable number of young English and American women in the audience. Still thinking she was American, he clearly believed that many had come to see her rather than the opera – but no harm in this, as she was helping to spread the reputation of this unique work. He echoed his previous admiration of her youth and charm.[78]

Maggie's magic did not fade in people's minds. Alfred Cortot wrote an appreciation of her for the sleeve notes to the LP in the HMV series Great Recordings of the Century in 1962,[79] saying, 'There is not one of the French lovers of Debussy who does not recollect the representation of *Pelléas* at the Opéra-Comique, where, succeeding Mary Garden, the excellent creator of the part, an almost childlike Mélisande brought to the interpretation of the most significant lyrical masterpiece of our time the irresistible grace of her barely unfolded springtime, the charm of her voice as pure as crystal and all the pensive melancholy of a human creature set apart by destiny.'

It was certainly predicted that Maggie would become 'a little star'. She was even described as such in an article in that very same issue of *Musica* that carried Debussy's praise of Mary Garden.[80] It is, therefore, all the more ironic that a year after Maggie's début in the opera, when *Pelléas et Mélisande* was given its first performance at Covent Garden on 21 May 1909, the role of Mélisande was sung by a French-speaking Swiss soprano, Rose Féart. Despite his pleasure at Maggie's interpretation only the season before in Paris, Rose Féart had actually been chosen by Debussy himself to sing the role, as had Edmond Warnery to sing that of Pelléas. One wonders why Féart had been selected, for Debussy made it clear in a letter to Gabriel Astruc that he did not want Maggie to think that he had abandoned her.[81]

It seems that he regretted this decision, for when in London supervising rehearsals Debussy wrote to his publisher, Durand: 'As for Mlle Féart she is unspeakably ugly, lacks poetry and I continue to miss dear Miss Teyte. Obviously she sings what is written, but there is nothing behind it. Between

[76] *Opera News*, 21 March 1970, p. 16. The same point is made in Patrick Mahony, *Maurice Maeterlinck: Mystic and Dramatist* (Washington DC, 1984), p. 74.

[77] See n. 59 above.

[78] *Feuilleton du Journal des débats*, 14 June, 1908.

[79] *Maggie Teyte: Songs by Debussy*, Great Recordings of the Century, HMV COLH134.

[80] 'Mlle Maggie Teyte ... qui pourra bien être, pour plus tard, une petite étoile.' Louis Lastret, *Musica*, January 1908, p. 12.

[81] Debussy, *Correspondance*, p. 1137.

ourselves it's a disappointment.'[82] Yet he had previously written of his new Mélisande in December 1908: 'Her voice and musicianship please me greatly.'

In London, just as at the Opéra-Comique, Debussy did not like to observe the actual performance in 1909. On 23 May he wrote to his parents (the only known letter to them), telling them of the success of the Covent Garden pre-mière, details of which had to be reported back to him, as he was not present. He had heard that not only were the performers called back a dozen times, but for another quarter of an hour they called for the composer who was in the peace of his hotel. He gathered that such a reception was extremely rare in England, 'where the public's temperature is usually somewhere below zero … So, Long live France! Long live French music! And carry on music!'[83]

The press of the day, however, was not quite as enthusiastic as one might have thought from Debussy's report. It was pointed out how difficult a work like *Pelléas* was for a Covent Garden summer audience, and there were comments on the way the interludes were spoilt by the audience's chatter.[84] Henry Wood was also frustrated by this unfortunate habit of London audi-ences, noting:

> one of the worst habits of the British public is this tendency to talk through overtures and entr'actes. This was most evident at the production of Debussy's *Pelléas and Mélisande* where some of the loveliest music is played between the acts with the curtain down. For this reason the work will never be popular over here because English audiences will not accept a stage production if they have to keep silence between the acts.[85]

The work was still being assessed and appraised in England and abroad, and audiences everywhere needed more familiarisation with this unique score.

[82] Debussy, *Correspondance*, p. 1179.
[83] Debussy, *Correspondance*, p. 1184.
[84] *Opera*, June 1958, p. 360.
[85] Henry Wood, *My Life of Music* (London, 1938), p. 54.

14 *Mary Garden in America*
(1907-11)

IN OCTOBER 1907 Mary Garden was heading for New York to perform with the Manhattan Opera Company, the first time she had returned to the States since leaving Chicago in 1896. Travelling with her on the *Kaiserin Auguste Victoria*, which left Cherbourg on 18 October, were most of the employees of the Opéra-Comique. Even the *souffleur* (prompter) and stage hands were employed by Hammerstein for the season. Mary decided to arrive in style; she thought it chic to travel with her little dog on its beautiful new leash together with thirty trunks!

First she prepared to make her début in Massenet's *Thaïs*, to be conducted by Cleofonte Campanini. Unfortunately when the day came on 25 November 1907, she was suffering from a cold and was unable to give of her best vocally. Acknowledging that she had simply 'braved the act through', she tried to explain to journalists that her art was different from everyone else's. She wanted to be judged not by singing, acting or stage appearance alone, but by all these combined into one art 'entirely different to all the rest.' The opera she emphasised as being the one that was going to demonstrate this best was *Pelléas et Mélisande*.[1] Lack of voice in *Thaïs* did not mean she did not cause a stir. Her costume – or lack of it – certainly attracted attention. Mary boasted of her boldness. 'The dress stuck to my flesh, and because it was of the palest pink it made me look as if I were naked.'[2] She sneered at critics who said she had very little on. 'I had loads on. Compared to what women wear today, that night of my début at the Manhattan Opera House I had red flannels on.'[3] Thus began Mary's love-hate relationship with the American press, one which she exploited mercilessly. In contrast with the Paris newspapers which customarily concentrated more on the qualities of a performance, she discovered that here she was able to manipulate stories and events to her own advantage, create an image of herself that had not existed in Paris and become a personality that the public was eager to know about.

How Mary loved playing to her audience at the Manhattan! She found them 'brilliant' and 'thanks to Mr. Hammerstein, they all began to understand French opera, and they came to know what a "singing actress" was

[1] *New York Herald*, 1 December 1907.
[2] *Mary Garden's Story*, p. 113.
[3] *Mary Garden's Story*, p. 110.

when I sang *Louise* on January 3 1908.'[4] A web of stories was spun about the 'idol of Parisian opera-goers'. A romantic image was portrayed of an innocent, lonely young girl who in a spirit of adventure had gone to Paris with no fixed intentions as to what she was going to do. She was credited with having avoided two pitfalls common to American students: clinging to other English-speaking students for the sake of companionship, and simply assuming a teacher to be excellent just because of his reputation, or because his studio was in Paris, where, it was claimed, many good voices were ruined. Her method was described as peculiar, for she claimed to plan nothing beforehand, simply memorising the music. Yet her spontaneity was controlled. She explained that whatever new poses she struck every night, 'where I put my feet never changes. I am always there, if it be the hundredth performance.' Her sense of style was exemplary, particularly the way she wore her French clothes.[5] The myth was spun that having taken some music-lessons before leaving her American home, Mary took so few in Paris that she could be regarded as virtually self-taught.

Mary prepared her audience for the American première of *Pelléas et Mélisande* through newspaper interviews. The settings she described as 'Scandinavian in the middle ages ... dark and sombre.' She recalled the famous row between Debussy and Maeterlinck, claiming spuriously that now she and Mme Leblanc were 'the best of friends'. 'She came to see me many times as Mélisande' is one of the very few recorded references to her relationship with Georgette.[6]

At last on 19 February 1908 the American première of Debussy's opera took place. This has been described as 'the Manhattan Opera's single greatest moment of glory'.[7] Mary found it 'something out of heaven'.[8] She certainly was in her seventh heaven, for, as promised by Hammerstein, she was singing confidently in a familiar set from the Opéra-Comique and with familiar colleagues. Jean Périer was Pelléas, Hector Dufranne was Golaud and Jeanne Gerville-Réache sang Geneviève. Arkel was not sung by Vieuille but by Vittorio Arimondi and Yniold was sung by Mme Sigrist.

The music critic Henry Finck believed that Oscar Hammerstein was running a considerable risk in engaging Miss Garden for his Manhattan Opera House, for whatever fashion hints American women still took from Paris, 'Parisian taste in music has less in common with New York taste.' Yet he acknowledged that in Debussy's *Pelléas et Mélisande* 'Mary Garden has won

[4] *Mary Garden's Story*, p. 115.

[5] *Cosmopolitan Magazine*, January 1908, pp. 295–301.

[6] *New York Times*, 10 February 1908.

[7] *American Heritage Magazine*, February 1972.

[8] *Mary Garden's Story*, p. 115.

her greatest triumph.' She loved the opera more and more, however many times she sang the role of Mélisande, and she was convinced she would never tire of it.[9] He defined the work as a music-drama rather than a traditional opera, owing to its striking lack of arias, duos, choruses, or processions. The 'mystic, shadowy remoteness and unreality' of Mary's Mélisande reminded him of paintings by Rossetti. He found her voice and her movements wonderfully consistent and her costumes thoughtfully designed. Whilst 'lithe and sinuous as a snake', Mary still managed to keep 'a singular virginal atmosphere' about her, despite her costumes closely outlining her figure. Only when Golaud abused her because her eyes feigned such great innocence, and when at last she acknowledged her love to Pelléas, was her body veiled in a heavy dress of dull colours. Her hair was stunning: 'her glorious hair meekly parted in the middle, pouring over her like a flood of sunlight!' The writer was totally captivated. It was a complete mystery to him how this exuberant, vital woman could become so monochrome in look, in voice. 'There is a forlorn groping for the tangible, a weird, uncomprehending sadness which envelops her like a mantle.'[10]

Although another critic detected Wagner's voice in Debussy's music, he found the orchestral colour so different from any other he had heard that it was as if the composer had found 'a new orchestral voice and language'. Mary's characterisation was 'truly remarkable', with a mystic quality and subtlety 'so full of half-explanation and hidden suggestion of mood and feeling as to stamp it as intellectual and emotional to a rare degree.' If she never did anything else in her artistic career, this performance would mark her as one of the great dramatic artists of her day.[11]

Books appeared explaining both the play and the opera to the American audience, that by Lawrence Gilman analysing it in detail and extolling the 'revolutionary score'. He told his readers that of all composers, living or dead, Debussy was best fitted to write music for Maeterlinck's play, in fact, 'he was ideally fitted; in listening to this music one catches oneself imagining that it and the drama issued from the same brain.'[12] On the other hand, in a preface to a translation of Maeterlinck's play,[13] Montrose J. Moses complained that those who heard the opening performance of the opera:

9 *Century Magazine,* May 1908, pp. 148–51.

10 *Century Magazine,* May 1908, pp. 148–51.

11 *The World,* 20 February 1908.

12 Lawrence Gilman, *Debussy's Pelléas et Mélisande: A Guide to the Opera* (New York, 1907).

13 Maurice Maeterlinck, *Pelléas and Mélisande,* trans. Erving Winslow (New York, 1908).

went away doubting whether they really understood the orchestration. Had
Mr. Hammerstein softened the lights on the stage to a semi-darkness or swung
a gauze curtain across the front of the scene as Mrs. Patrick Campbell did in
her production of the play; had Mary Garden, despite the fresh spirit of her
acting, been less substantial in her movements, these same folk would have
read still more into this pale tragedy of childlike love.

It gets worse, for despite appreciating the beautiful scenery and the
expressive acting, Mr. Moses found that the music 'stung and blistered and
pained the ear'. In his opinion the score was thoroughly unmelodic and the
voices were confined to the limits of Gregorian chant. He must have been
quite bored, finding that certain passages dragged and Mélisande's death
scene was unnecessarily monotone. Because Debussy did not believe in what
Mr. Moses called 'the *chanson*', presumably meaning a melodic aria, he considered that he had sacrificed some significant scenes 'that would have been
treated effectively by a musician of the *Carmen* school.' Mr. Moses had had
to struggle through the vague orchestration and dialogue. Clearly American
audiences were used to something more boisterous!

By March, when Mary crossed back over the Atlantic to resume her career
in Europe, her reputation in Manhattan was made. She had used newspapers
and magazines to promote herself. She attacked the state of opera in America
and insisted that interpretation was at the heart of the new school of opera
which she was promoting, the music of which dealt with deep human truths.
This modern music was aimed not just at the senses but also at the mind.
Musical America realised, 'It is hardly too much to say that the engagement
of Mary Garden marks the beginning of a new operatic era in America.'[14]

One can just imagine the thrill Mary must have felt when Hammerstein
suggested she should sing Strauss's *Salomé* in French at the Manhattan in
the 1909 season. Here was an opportunity heaven-sent to cause a commotion and be the centre of attention. It had already been performed at the
Metropolitan in German by Olive Fremstad, but there the Dance of the
Seven Veils had been performed by a dancer: Bianca Froelich. How could
Mary let this opportunity for self-promotion and display slip through her
hands! She told Hammerstein in no uncertain terms that she would only
sing Salomé if she could dance it herself.

On her return to Paris in 1908 she had the ideal opportunity to learn the
part. She was employed there, not by the Opéra-Comique where Maggie
Teyte was now singing Mélisande, but by the bigger Opéra Garnier, where
her former lover André Messager had been appointed director in January
1907. There she made her début in May with *Thaïs*, and was received with

---

[14] *Musical America*, 25 January 1908.

enthusiasm. Mary was described in *Musica* as a great artiste, but it was not her voice that the reviewer found special, for this was nothing exceptional. It was her extraordinarily lively interpretation of the role and the conviction with which she sang that was so striking.[15]

Now she could fill both opera houses – with men! A critic writing in the 1950s, looking back at Mary's career at the turn of the century, exclaimed 'There was a time, especially at the two Paris opera houses, which scarcely a woman could be found in the first twenty rows of the orchestra stalls; they were packed with *men* – men at an opera! – men who devoured Garden with their eyes and at the end of each act stood up to cheer wildly.' Analysing her secret, he decided that it was her 'naturalness'. Whilst most women of that era were tightly laced into completely deforming corsets, he knew (and others have confirmed) that 'Mary Garden at the turn of the century wore *none!*' This freedom of movement left her unhampered so that she could act with her body, with her heart and with her brain. He concurred with others that Mary was a 'singing actress' whose acting far outshone her voice.[16]

On 24 June 1908 the first performance in Cologne of *Pelléas et Mélisande* took place. This was not a new production, but in fact a guest performance by the whole cast, including Mary Garden and conductor Sylvain Dupuis, of the production of the Théâtre Royal de la Monnaie in Brussels, given as part of the *Festspiele zu Cöln* [*sic*]. The reception of the opera there was not as warm as in France or Belgium. Maurice Emmanuel believed this was because Germany was the country of 'forms', imbued with the spirit of J. S. Bach, even Wagner and Richard Strauss being impregnated with German classicism. The structure of *Pelléas* had nothing in common with 'those grandiose constructions which the Sonata and Germanic Symphony have erected'. Fundamental to German musicianship was a love of balance and 'regularity'. There, everything had to be related to 'codified formulae'. He quoted Joachim who, unable to explain the success of the opera, had written in 1905, 'I cannot find anything in this score but great disorder. It is not like anything that has a structure. It is as if everything has been left to chance and the composer improvises without controlling his ideas.'[17] Mary was all too well aware of the cold reaction of her German audience: 'In one of the most modern and up-to-date opera houses sat an audience who listened with deference and discordant politeness, which made us all feel we were shut in a Frigidaire', she commented.[18]

[15] *Musica*, June 1908, p. 96.
[16] *Opera News*, 5 April 1954, p. 12.
[17] Emmanuel, *Pelléas et Mélisande de Debussy*, p. 69.
[18] Typescript in RCM, London, Mary Garden Collection.

Later that summer Mary was anxious to discuss *Salomé* with Strauss himself. Having heard that problems had arisen over its production at the Paris Opéra she feared she might not be granted the role, so travelled from Switzerland, where she had been holidaying, to the composer's villa in Garmisch in Bavaria. There her fears were allayed when Strauss gave her a letter giving her permission to sing Salomé. Any reservations he might have had about her taking on both singing and dancing were rejected. As if she would have heeded such advice!

Whilst she was in Garmisch, Strauss told Mary that he was writing a new opera, *Der Rosenkavalier*, with her in mind. She was indeed to sign the contract and eventually study the role of Octavian, but the performance never came to fruition due to the outbreak of the First World War. She claimed later to be glad that she had not sung the part, for with the exception of *Le Jongleur* she did not like playing boys and objected strongly to certain situations arising in the *Rosenkavalier* plot.[19] 'Making love to women all night long would have bored me to death!', she stated bluntly.[20]

Back in Paris Mary learnt the role of Salomé in the autumn of 1908, before making her début in the role in Manhattan. She was seen practising by the correspondent of the *New York Herald*, Carl Van Vechten. He found it riveting. Van Vechten underlined the intelligence of her approach to her roles. He believed she studied thoroughly each detail of her characters, then made a careful selection of the effects she wanted to convey, occasionally rejecting her initial instinctive responses. This certainly did not eliminate feeling from her performances which still conveyed the 'deep burning flame of poetic imagination'. Like others, he wondered if Mary's insistence on singing in French had an ulterior motive: to charm her listeners. And what was Mary's greatest achievement? For him it was her Mélisande, where she had succeeded in subduing her own very definite personality and moulding it into the vague and subtle personage created by Maurice Maeterlinck.[21]

Salomé was a totally different challenge from Mélisande, but identifying with Herod's stepdaughter was every bit as consuming. Mary always felt she had all her creations already inside her. 'I never really worked over them, not in the usual sense. I just *knew* them ... I just had it *in* me, all of it. I *was* Thaïs, I *was* Mélisande, I *was* Salomé.'[22] Whilst in Paris, she learnt the Dance of the Seven Veils with a former member of the Opéra-Comique, Mlle Chasles. She wanted it to be a drama, she emphasised, not 'Folies Bergère',

[19] Typescript in RCM, London, Mary Garden Collection.

[20] *Mary Garden's Story*, p. 220.

[21] Van Vechten, *Interpreters and Interpretations*, p. 60.

[22] *Mary Garden's Story*, p. 125.

yet she delighted in the suggestive: 'Everything was glorious and nude and suggestive, but not coarse.'[23] Van Vechten was certainly seduced by Mary's costume, the 'mantle of bright orange shimmering stuff ... a close-fitting garment of netted gold', and her hypnotic, undulating dance.[24] Whatever must André Messager have been thinking as he accompanied rehearsals at the piano, watching the seductive woman he had so desired only a few years earlier?[25] Mary's obstinacy also paid dividends in another respect. She absolutely insisted that instead of 'a dreadful looking little man' who had been engaged to sing Jokanaan she should have Hector Dufranne – and she got her own way.[26]

At the same time as studying *Salomé* Mary had been learning another role, of which she was inordinately proud. She crossed the Atlantic back to New York in October and in November 1908 performed her *travesti* version of Massenet's *Le Jongleur de Notre-Dame* at the Manhattan. The part of Jean, the juggler, was first sung in 1902 by a tenor, Alphonse Maréchal, but when it was suggested to Hammerstein that 'only a woman, and a woman built like Garden, should sing it',[27] the composer remodelled the role for her. Mary loved this opportunity to demonstrate her figure. Any reservations about singing boys' roles were cast aside, for she believed she had just the body for it, claiming she had the figure of a boy. 'You see, I had no thighs, and I never had, and I don't have, any hips ... Only a woman with a body like mine could give any semblance of realism to that role.'[28] Despite critical acclaim, it is said that Massenet actually disapproved of her appropriation of the role, but in his *Souvenirs* remained tactful.[29]

In today's celebrity-obsessed society stars are schooled to deal with intensive publicity; Mary, however, knew instinctively how to keep the world at her feet. Suitors came and went, and despite constantly being at pains in her autobiography to stress that she was never interested in marriage, she positively encouraged rumours that she would be leaving opera to marry a Russian prince living in Paris. She saw an increase in her popularity as a personality, and not just as a great singer, and now the Manhattan was definitely winning the competition for survival against the Metropolitan. In order to keep up its sales the Met had to import Guilio Gatti-Casazza from La Scala, Milan, to be director and Arturo Toscanini as conductor. Hammerstein

[23] *Mary Garden's Story*, p. 124.

[24] Van Vechten, *Interpreters and Interpretations*, p. 80.

[25] Messager was planning to mount *Salomé* at the Paris Opéra the following season.

[26] *Opera News*, 5 April 1954, p. 14.

[27] Suggested by Maurice Renaud: *Mary Garden's Story*, p. 131.

[28] *Mary Garden's Story*, p. 132.

[29] *Opera*, April 1974, p. 364.

had not planned on Mary having a complete monopoly over all the leading French roles, but he learnt his lesson when she read a notice announcing that Lina Cavalieri was to sing *Thaïs*. As was seized upon by the newspapers, she wrote a letter of resignation from the company, leaving him no option but to give in.

Pelléas et Mélisande on 6 January 1909 saw Dalmorès singing Pelléas and the return of Vieuille to the role of Arkel, replacing Arimondi, who had sung it the previous season. This production, again conducted by Campanini, was taken to Philadelphia and to Boston, where it was performed on 1 and 7 April.[30] Most of the Boston audience must have had an inkling of what to expect for its members are described as being noticeably different from that of previous nights: 'It was visibly composed of those who know their Maeterlinck.' They were in for a treat, for the setting of the opera was described the next day as being 'in most delicately beautiful taste', pictures were created that could not be forgotten, and Miss Garden's triumph was 'complete'. She was totally 'in the character'. What is more, her voice was beautiful in quality – thus negating reports that she was an actress rather than a singer.[31]

On 28 January Mary's visceral Salomé, sung in French, made its mark on the audience at the Manhattan. The production was a great success, described as a credit to its conductor, Campanini, and Mary's portrayal was judged to be an astonishing achievement. The fact that she performed the dramatic and suggestive dance herself with a great variety of expression was an important contribution to the effectiveness of the whole, her seductive removal of successive layers of clothing being especially commented upon.[32] When the opera was taken to Philadelphia, however, word had spread about the supposed immorality of the work and there were protests from local churches.

1909 also brought a sudden unwelcome reminder of earlier trials and tribulations dating from before her days of fame. In March the Chicago newspapers stirred up the murky waters of Mary's private life during her student days in Paris. A journalist claimed that she had been told by Sibyl Sanderson (who had died in 1903 and could therefore no longer be asked to confirm or deny rumours) that Mary had indeed had an illegitimate child, a boy, by 'a little drummer', i.e. a salesman.

The Mayers, Mary's sponsors who had originally enabled her to study in Paris, now filed a lawsuit against her for $20,000 – the amount they had provided so many years before plus interest, angry that the stories of her immoral

---

[30] Emma Trentini replaced Sigrist as Yniold.
[31] *Boston Daily Globe*, 2 April 1909.
[32] *New York Times*, 29 January 1909.

and extravagant life-style in those early days, which had caused them so much alarm as to stop her allowance back in 1899, had never been completely dismissed. Mary's furious reaction was to deny categorically, 'with God as my witness',[33] that she had ever been the mother of a child, claiming that she would never be cowardly enough to hide it if she had had one. She did not claim to have lived the life of a saint, and argued, 'Do you not think for one instant that if I were the mother of a child – that little one would not be here – here – right here at my side?'[34] She also had to refute accusations that she had tried to commit suicide, declaring herself too much of a coward to die by her own hand. She managed to put together the money by the deadline given and was immensely relieved to pay back every dollar. But the darling of the press now quickly learned that publicity could cause mayhem in her life negatively as well as positively. Nor did Mrs Mayer like her own sudden rise to fame or the negative light it must have cast on her, for on receiving her money she suddenly turned round and asserted that Mary was innocent after all. She had investigated rumours when Mary had been her protégé, she said, and found them groundless. Now she insisted that she had never heard the 'baby' story until she saw it in the newspapers.[35]

When Sibyl Sanderson's biographer discussed the rumours with Sibyl's step-daughter, Natividad, she told him that Sibyl had asked her to keep the story of Mary's baby confidential, which she promised she did. Natividad obviously believed that Mary had had a child, for after Mary had become famous, she found herself occasionally wondering 'if that boy grew to manhood ever learning that Mary Garden was his real mother ... Catholic orphanages in France keep very private records. When they are sealed they're sealed for life.'[36] Whatever Natividad's beliefs, of course it would now be very difficult to prove or disprove them.

On her return to Paris that summer there seems to have been a hiatus in Mary's singing activity for there were reports of illness and cancelled performances. This could well have been due to stress over these tribulations, although a more mundane possibility was that she had been poisoned and almost blinded by the over-enthusiastic application of a new hair-dye,[37] a report she was later to refute. Whilst Mary appeared in *Thaïs* at the Paris Opéra, followed on 11 October by *Monna Vanna*, Maeterlinck's play set to music by Henry Février, the press was still following her amatory progress with interest. However, reports that she was soon to be married clashed with

33 *Chicago Daily Tribune*, 28 March 1909.
34 *Chicago Daily Tribune*, 28 March 1909.
35 *Chicago Daily Tribune*, 29 March 1909.
36 Hansen, *The Sybil Sanderson Story*, p. 470.
37 Untitled cutting in RCM, London, Mary Garden Collection.

the revelation that Mary was studying Roman Catholicism and intended to take the veil at the end of her opera career. In her inimitable way she manages to find a link between religion and her roles in opera, and even in this context her Mélisande becomes the touchstone. 'My greatest creations were spiritual ... even Mélisande – they touched the religious core. Most people don't think Mélisande was spiritual, but she was. And it was because of this deep spiritual side of me that I almost joined the Catholic Church.'[38] Into her scrapbooks she has stuck many newspaper cuttings announcing that she was about to embrace the Roman Catholic faith. In March she was going to 'live in retirement for a period to learn my catechism as though I were a child of fifteen.' She did not intend to leave the theatre, for she saw no incompatibility between the theatre and piety. 'Life needs confession ... that is why the Roman Catholic faith has so strongly attracted me', she proclaimed. Usefully there was a picture of herself dressed as a nun in *Thaïs* which was displayed with the heading 'Mary Garden's Conversion'.[39]

How convenient that she could blame the press for the whole plan failing to materialise. The story had spread far and wide, but when her Episcopalian mother heard of her desire to convert to Catholicism she protested, and Mary obediently agreed to abandon the idea. Rumour or reality? There is evidence that Mary was seriously attracted to Catholicism, for amongst her documents survives a full Papal Indulgence to be gained at the hour of death.[40] To obtain such a document conversion is not necessary, but it must have been some source of comfort to her. For what sins might she have been seeking indulgence? One can only speculate.

That autumn Mary seems suddenly to have tired of America, and actually moved a male reporter to tears when she told him that if it were not for Hammerstein she would not stay in the country.[41] Certainly there were problems with contracts and money on her return to New York. The world of opera was in a constant state of flux in this city as Hammerstein at the Manhattan was now losing his lead in the battle with the Metropolitan since the arrival of Toscanini and Gatti-Casazza. In Philadelphia, where Mary sang Massenet's *Sapho* and *Le Jongleur de Notre-Dame* Hammerstein was making further losses and the impresario had to make savings by cutting rehearsal time. Now a newspaper headline read 'Mary Garden *everywhere*'.[42] At the same time further competition was to appear on the scene for in December 1909 the formation of the Chicago Grand Opera Company managed by

[38] *Mary Garden's Story*, p. 134.
[39] *The Sun* [US newspaper], 20 November 1909.
[40] RCM, London, Mary Garden Collection.
[41] *Sunday American*, 5 December 1909.
[42] *Sunday American*, 5 December 1909.

Andreas Dippel was announced. Its musical director was to be Cleofonte Campanini.

In January 1910 Paris was affected by devastating floods. Concerts were organised urgently in New York to raise funds for the city. Hammerstein put Mary in charge of a benefit performance of arias from various operas, and must have been pleased to steal a march on Gatti-Casazza at the Met for Mary was able to correspond personally with the French Ambassador, 'a friend of hers'.[43]

In April the announcement was made that Hammerstein was selling the Philadelphia Opera House to the Metropolitan. Mary was making such herculean efforts in the fight to sell seats that the *New York Times* described her as 'a very busy prima donna' about to sing four times in New York and three times in Philadelphia all in one week,[44] and this was before appearing in Boston. Her Pelléas this season was first Dalmorès, then David Devries, making his début here in the role.[45] Although he was 'too obvious and too material', Mary's portrayal of Mélisande was described as 'an ethereal vision of chaste and adorable beauty.' Her power to cast off that glittering mantle of celebrity so cultivated in the press must have been astonishing, for here again she is praised for her 'repression, the gentle dignity, the patience and serene loveliness of it all.'[46] The performances were conducted by Henriquez de la Fuente.

Even so, matters went from bad to worse between Mary and Hammerstein, for he claimed he had paid her excess fees by settling in dollars rather than francs. In order to escape the threat of legal proceedings, Mary quickly packed all her costumes and possessions with the help of her sister and rushed to reach the ship bound for Europe. She claimed that Hammerstein had treated her 'worse than a chorus girl'.[47]

Back at the Paris Opéra in May, Mary's Salomé earned her high praise. However, in June 1910 she agreed with Andreas Dippel to join the recently formed Chicago Grand Opera Company for the autumn season. Her wish was his desire, according to Mary's version of their conversation, for when he asked her in which opera she would like to make her Chicago début, she answered without hesitation '*Pelléas et Mélisande*'. 'Good', he said, 'we'll make it for sometime in November', and agreed immediately that the conductor would be Campanini.[48]

[43] *New York Times*, 29 January 1910.

[44] *New York Times*, 20 March 1910.

[45] Devries also sang Pelléas at Covent Garden in 1910, with Edvina as Mélisande.

[46] *Boston Daily Globe*, 2 April 1910.

[47] Davis, *Opera in Chicago*, p. 83.

[48] *Mary Garden's Story*, p. 159.

So on 19 October 1910 Mary crossed the Atlantic yet again, voraciously pursued by the newspapers. The tale this time was of a mysterious romance between Mary and a wealthy Turk. There are various versions: he was going to cross the Atlantic to 'know his fate in December'; she had rebuffed him and refused to allow him to cross the Atlantic to visit her; he had given her a ruby ring that she had returned; she had arrived wearing his diamond ring. The press assumed it was in honour of the Turk that she wore trousers; not any old trousers but a skirt 'like a bag with two holes at the bottom', also described as 'her new bifurcated hobbled skirt'![49] She certainly whetted the appetites of her prospective audiences.

Mary was overjoyed to be reunited with Campanini. 'What a man, and what an artist! And how he loved Debussy! How delighted he was at the prospect of doing *Pelléas et Mélisande* with me again! "Mary," he said, "I could never conduct that opera for anyone but you."' She declared to reporters, 'I shall never love any role – I could not, like I do *Pelléas and Mélisande*. For Mélisande is mine. It is me.'[50]

Mary found the performance of Debussy's opera, which took place in the Chicago Auditorium on 5 November 1910, even more brilliant than it had been at the Manhattan, and was exhilarated by the response. She was proud to be the first to bring something new to that city.[51] Her new Pelléas was Edmond Warnery, who had sung the role in the first London performance at Covent Garden the previous year, and Golaud was her old colleague Hector Dufranne. Before the première, Chicagoans had been treated to an analysis of the opera by Glenn Dillard Gunn in the *Chicago Daily Tribune*,[52] extolling its uniqueness and its beauty, 'the most complete union of the arts yet accomplished', yet Gunn's review a few days after the opening acknowledges the puzzlement of the audience. He noted the arguments taking place in the intermissions between music lovers faithful to 'Teutonic creeds' and those rhapsodising on the subtlety of Debussy's musical suggestion. The performance was one of great beauty and simplicity, his only regret being that the new message was almost lost in the vastness of the Auditorium.[53] The editor of the same newspaper found this production of *Pelléas et Mélisande* the 'highest artistic achievement Chicago has ever seen', and waxed lyrical about Mary Garden. In her he saw 'a woman of the early times before women were so complex.' Her acting overwhelmed him, for in her was 'the soul of

49 Cuttings in RCM, London, Mary Garden Collection.
50 *Chicago Sunday Examiner*, 13 November 1910.
51 *Mary Garden's Story*, p. 161.
52 *Chicago Daily Tribune*, 9 October 1910.
53 *Chicago Daily Tribune*, 18 November 1910.

another'.[54] Mary herself saved cuttings of such reviews in her scrapbooks of which she must have been very proud. Her Mélisande was 'the spirit of poetry personified. Her every look, every movement has a grace, her presence diffuses an atmosphere such as we know not of, save in that realm of the Never-was, yet ever present in the fancy of man, which we call the land of romance.'[55] Both the conductor Campanini and manager Dippel expressed their delight at the 'succès immense' of his opera in separate telegrams to Debussy.[56]

Mary's reputation as an actress and her command of her roles became legendary. An incident during a performance of *Thaïs* is recounted in which she was having trouble hitting high notes. 'She came to one she knew better than to attempt, and rather than try it, she simply raised her arm, rattled her bracelets, and literally bewitched her audience into thinking they had heard it.'[57]

Salomé, performed on 25 November, was another matter. Mary was described as 'the acme of devilry', 'an unusual type of sensualist'.[58] The *Chicago Tribune* described the opera as 'the most artistic piece of indecency known to the operatic or any other stage'.[59] The Chief of Police was disgusted. 'The whole show lacked high class. Miss Garden wallowed around like a cat in a bed of catnip.'[60] When Mary refused to tone down her portrayal of lust for John the Baptist's head, the third performance was cancelled, much to her indignation. She blamed this not on the police, however, but on Mrs Harold McCormick, who had taken against the opera and complained to Mary and to the Chief of Police that her 'vibrations were all wrong'.[61]

Comparing Strauss's *Salomé* and Debussy's *Pelléas et Mélisande*, Mary wondered what Debussy would have done with *Salomé*. In her opinion, Debussy was:

> the greatest, the most original of the moderns. Strauss is a Wagnerian. Debussy is himself. He has found a new note ... of course Maeterlinck's drama is beautiful – Maeterlinck could do nothing sordid or unworthy. But it was, well, just drama after all. Debussy took it and gave it atmosphere, made it live.[62]

54 *Chicago Daily Tribune*, 8 November 1910.
55 Untitled clipping in RCM, London, Mary Garden Collection, album v.
56 Debussy, *Correspondance*, p. 1329.
57 Davis, *Opera in Chicago*, p. 87.
58 *Musical America*, 3 December 1910.
59 Davis, *Opera in Chicago*, p. 88.
60 *Chicago News*, 29 November 1910.
61 *Mary Garden's Story*, p. 210.
62 *The Inter Ocean Magazine*, 11 December 1910.

She hoped that Milwaukee, where *Salomé* was next going to be produced, would be more broad-minded and receptive, for the audience who had been robbed of their opportunity to see the scandalous performance in Chicago were transported there by two specially chartered trains.[63] There the performance went ahead successfully despite some objections.

Further roles followed: Marguerite in *Faust*, and the title role in *Natoma*. Great expectations were aroused by this opera by Victor Herbert, for it had been hoped that it would be regarded as the first great American opera. It opened in Philadelphia in February 1911 with John McCormack as the heroic American officer who rescues an Indian maiden. In the Chicago production most of the cast were French, although the work was sung in English. This led to some rather bizarre results. When Mary came to a rehearsal and heard the efforts being made, she 'just lay on the piano in hysterics!'[64] Another legend was added to Mary's history when in Baltimore she was wounded during the realistic dagger dance and had to have her arm bandaged. Heroically, she was able to remove the dressing before the end of the performance.[65] By now Mary was the singer most closely associated with the Chicago Grand Opera. She was referred to affectionately as 'our Mary' and the publicity her exploits and outbursts brought to the company certainly helped to keep the company in the public eye.

In 1911 a series of recording sessions took place for the Columbia Phonograph Company in New York in which Mary sang arias by Massenet and Verdi, but no excerpt from *Pelléas*.[66] The promotional booklet lauds Columbia's 'absolute truth to nature in vocal reproduction' as might be expected, but in particular asserts that the Garden records have 'an actual human quality that seems to transcend anything before accomplished in this particular regard'.[67]

Following this venture, Mary undertook a concert tour of several states which began at Carnegie Hall in April 1911. Her reputation preceded her. At a town in Ohio the minister preached against her and managed to get the hall locked so that the concert could not proceed, but when a famous evangelist, Billy Sunday, preached against her, endangering ticket sales in Toledo, Mary took matters into her own hands. She searched him out in his tent and charmed him with her directness and honesty, with the result that he ended their tête-à-tête by conceding that it had been a

[63] Davis, *Opera in Chicago*, p. 90.
[64] Davis, *Opera in Chicago*, p. 99.
[65] Cutting dated 10 March 1911 in RCM, London, Mary Garden Collection, album IX.
[66] Reproduced on CD: *Opera in Chicago*, vol. 1: *Edith Mason and Mary Garden*, Symposium CD 1136 (1992).
[67] A copy at National Library of Scotland, MS 12864.

pleasure meeting her. 'I guess I've been hearing lots of lies about you', he admitted.[68]

In June 1911 Mary sailed back over the Atlantic to take some singing lessons with her former teacher, Trabadelo, to spend her annual holiday in Switzerland, then to return to Paris to sing *Faust* and *Thaïs*. In view of his significance for both Debussy and Georgette Leblanc, it is worth noting that at some time between 1910 and 1914, perhaps at this stage in her visits to Paris, Mary was introduced to Gabriele d'Annunzio. Twice in her notebooks she recalls him. She was warned to be very careful, 'for if I was to fall in love with him my life would be ruined.' D'Annunzio was an extraordinarily flamboyant personality, poet, dramatist, author of the spectacular theatrical work *Le Martyre de Saint Sébastien*, for which Debussy composed music in 1911. In 1910 he had fled from Italy to Paris to escape his creditors and also to be able to continue to live a life of luxury and eccentricity. His reputation as a womaniser led to the warning issued to Mary, but on meeting him she was taken aback to see a very small man, nearly bald. He did, however, have a most beautiful speaking voice. He invited her to visit the menagerie in the Jardin d'Acclimatation in the Bois de Boulogne and enter the lions' cage with him, but she refused, noting, 'He went by himself. I'm more afraid of D'Annunzio than I would be of a den of lions. He is the sort of man who grips a woman's whole soul. What do I think of his theory of love? Why, it's warm, very warm.'[69] Fortunately Georgette Leblanc would later be able to take advantage of this warmth.

In the autumn Mary was back in the States preparing to perform *Carmen* and *Cendrillon* in Chicago. She must have been looking good after her break, for on the passenger list for the ship *George Washington* she declared her age to be thirty, just as she had done every time she had crossed the Atlantic since 1907! She was, in fact, thirty-seven. The press were ready and waiting and during an interview she modelled for reporters some of the many gowns she had brought with her. The first was made of thousands of little steel discs put together in overlapping rows like the scales of a fish. 'It is just like chain mail and it weighs twelve pounds', said Mary. 'I think it is a becoming gown for crowned heads, because it's bullet proof.' When asked what she would do if it ripped, she declared, 'Instead of a dressmaker, I'll have to find a blacksmith!' Next Mary wore a black clinging dress all of fringe, proudly confirming, 'I don't wear corsets, you know.'[70]

If Mary could ever have had a lasting relationship with a man, it was during

---

[68] *Mary Garden's Story*, p. 213.

[69] RCM, London, Mary Garden Collection.

[70] Davis, *Opera in Chicago*, p. 97.

this season in Chicago that she met the one person with whom she believed this could have been possible. In her *Story* there is a scathing paragraph in which she claims not to know how to give a picture of 'the ideal lover'. She did not believe that any man could be faithful to one woman, for a woman puts much more into romance. 'What does a man yield? Nothing in the world that I can see.' Yet only a couple of pages later begins her description of 'the longest romance of my life'.[71] At a business luncheon in a Chicago club she fell in love at first sight with a married man who had never heard an opera, knew nothing about books and had never travelled. Reminiscing, in her notebooks she has pencilled in the name Armour above a section about Chicago, but she did not reveal his name in print. J. Ogden Armour had inherited his father's Chicago meat-packing business, and by 1918 was one of America's five richest men, whose business had an annual turnover of 6.25 million dollars. In 1908 he used some of this money to build a great Italian style villa called Mellody Farms in Lake Forest, Illinois.[72] Mary enticed this magnate to her performance of *Thaïs*, following which over the years he was to pursue her to Paris, Scotland, London and France. Her sister Helen was later to talk about this relationship, referring to Armour as 'the meat-packing American'.[73] She confirmed that Mary was really in love with him, but that Armour had a wife and children he loved. Mary was his first mistress. 'He knew nothing about art – or about having a mistress', she said, but then related two anecdotes. When Mary saw Armour hand ten cents to a beggar who accosted them, she insisted he gave him instead the roll of bank notes he carried. To Armour's astonishment the beggar knelt and kissed the hem of his coat. In another version of the same story, Mary embellished it with the detail that the beggar fell to his knees in the snow. 'Get up at once!', she exclaimed. 'Never kneel to man. Only kneel to God!'[74] On another occasion, after spending a night at an hotel in Edinburgh, the couple were stopped by the police. Armour quickly asserted the lady with him was his secretary, for it was against the law for an unmarried couple to share a hotel room in Scotland.[75]

Inevitably Mary's attitude to her lover eventually changed. Not only did she tire of him,[76] but she also insisted that she would never have wanted to

---

[71] *Mary Garden's Story*, p. 194.

[72] Now Lake Forest Academy.

[73] Madeau Stewart notebook for BBC talk *c.* 1963, Oxfordshire Record Office, P143/04/MS/001.

[74] National Library of Scotland, MS 21561, pp. 274–82.

[75] Madeau Stewart notebook for BBC talk *c.* 1963, Oxfordshire Record Office, P143/04/MS/001.

[76] *Mary Garden's Story*, p. 199.

destroy his marriage. 'What intimacy we had had ceased after the third year', she wrote, but the final death knell was sounded for the relationship when Mary discovered Armour to be a secret alcoholic. In the end, not only did he lose much of his fortune in the Crash of 1921, but alcoholism eventually killed him in 1927.

In the Philadelphia-Chicago Season of 1911, it was Massenet's opera *Cendrillon* which caused a stir. At a charity performance, Mary, never one to miss a trick for publicity's sake, sold kisses to seven young men who described the experience in graphic terms: 'It lasts a long time, and believe me, it transports you into a regular paradise, and makes the world look sort of different. She doesn't make much noise about it ... she looks squarely into your eyes, and believe me, she is some kisser!'[77]

Who should be singing opposite Mary when *Cendrillon* opened in Philadelphia on 6 November 1911, but Maggie Teyte. For the first time, the two original Mélisandes were to perform together, Maggie in the role of Cinderella and Mary as Prince Charming. What had brought about this meeting of the two great British-born opera singers? How had Maggie's success in *Pelléas et Mélisande* affected her life?

[77] '50 years ago', *Opera*, February 1962, p. 125.

15 Maggie Teyte's Triumphs and Disappointments (1908–30)

MAGGIE TEYTE sang the role of Mélisande nineteen times in the two seasons 1907–8 and 1908–9, but after this Marguerite Carré obviously did not want her back at the Opéra-Comique now that she had fulfilled her function of filling the gap between Mary and herself. Maggie's progress there was to be strictly limited. However, her collaboration with Debussy continued for several years when they gave concert recitals. On 21 January 1910 she sang four of his *Ariettes oubliées*, accompanied by E. R. Schmitz, then the solo part in Debussy's *Trois chansons de Charles d'Orléans* with the choir of the Concerts Colonne, conducted by Debussy himself. He had intended to accompany her at the salon of Princesse Edmond de Polignac on 23 February 1910 if he had been well enough, but instead she had to make do with Blanche Selva.[1] The last concerts she sang with Debussy at the piano were on 25 March 1911, with Jean Périer at the Cercle Musical and on both 5 and 12 March 1912, when she sang *Le Promenoir des deux amants* and the *Fêtes galantes* at the Concerts Durand.[2] In 1913 Debussy wrote to Edgar Speyer saying he expected to be in London on 2 July. He specifically asked for Maggie Teyte to sing the *Trois ballades de François Villon* with orchestral accompaniment, rehearsed first by Henry Wood.[3] Unfortunately this concert never materialised, perhaps because of its cost, but also owing to his wife's ill health. Debussy's frustration at the cancellation is expressed in a letter to Caplet written on 2 June. How touching was a letter sent from St Petersburg in the same year, 1913, to his beloved daughter Chouchou, whom he was missing greatly. He told her that there were two bulldogs at Koussevitsky's house where he was staying, then added 'and a bird which sings almost as well as Miss Teyte.' According to Prokofiev, Debussy taught this bird a melody which it continued to sing even after he had left Russia![4]

In an article marking Debussy's death, A. R. Brugeot points out that this personal association with a performer was exceptional behaviour on the part of the composer. He rarely gave performances in which he played his own

---

[1] Debussy, *Correspondance*, p. 1249.

[2] A. R. Brugeot, 'Claude Debussy, 1862–1918', *Les Arts français*, no. 16 (1918), p. 85.

[3] Debussy, *Correspondance*, p. 1607.

[4] Debussy, *Correspondance*, p. 1722 and note.

compositions, despite being an incomparable interpreter of his own work, and two occasions Brugeot lists are those with Maggie Teyte.[5] This must be proof, indeed, of the esteem in which Debussy held her. In 1920 Vuillermoz also remarked that 'To accompany one of his interpreters or to perform one of his piano pieces in public was for him a cruel ordeal which he undertook all too rarely, with a sort of gloomy timidity.'[6]

Maggie herself, looking back on Debussy's behaviour during concerts of his music, found him both taciturn and nervous. He hated hearing someone else play his music. She recalled one evening at a concert of his works in Paris when the first violinist came off the stage in high spirits after playing Debussy's String Quartet. Debussy soon put him in place. 'You played like pigs', he said scornfully, and strode away, leaving the hapless player covered with shame and confusion. On another occasion Maggie found herself sympathising with her accompanist at the dress rehearsal of a recital of Debussy songs with the composer present. When the anxious accompanist held a note a bit too long, Maggie saw him 'actually turn red, then deathly white, every bit of colour left his face in sheer dismay'. She believed that if Debussy had been a wealthy man the world would never have heard him play, for he hated appearing in public. 'We always had a saying that we knew when Debussy needed money, for he never made any appearances except when he wished to add to his finances.'[7]

Reflecting on her career, Maggie complained that many singers seemed to think they could do what they liked with Debussy's songs, and pointed out that no composer had marked his scores with greater precision, or insisted more strongly that the interpreter should obey his instructions. She herself would always try to be pedantic when teaching the songs of a master 'who knew his own mind and allowed no liberties to be taken with his music',[8] although she admits that when she did once sing a passage slightly differently from the way in which it was indicated whilst Debussy was accompanying her, he looked up, thought for a moment then said, 'You are right, quite right; that is the way you should sing it', and passed on without further comment.[9]

Knowing Debussy's alleged reputation with women, it is hardly surprising if the question has been broached as to whether Maggie had any sort of relationship with him. No doubt she was fascinated by him. What

[5] Brugeot, 'Claude Debussy', p. 85.

[6] Émile Vuillermoz, *Claude Debussy: Conférence le 15 Avril 1920 aux Concerts historiques Pasdeloup* (Paris, 1920).

[7] *Musical America*, 13 April 1913, p. 5.

[8] Teyte, *Star on the Door*, pp. 58–9.

[9] *Musical America*, 13 April 1913, p. 5.

nineteen-year-old would not have been by this silent bear of a man whose music aroused so many sensations? But, as noted previously, she always insisted he never even shook hands with her.[10] The greatest expression of Debussy's love she ever witnessed was that which he showed for his little daughter, Chouchou. She realised that she was the centre around which his affections revolved. 'Everything else in his life was subordinated to this dominating emotion.'[11]

Just as Maggie had kept quiet about her family background in her autobiography, she gives us virtually no clues as to her private life whilst she was a young, vivacious, attractive woman learning operatic roles and building her career. What a contrast to Mary Garden, who spices up her story with endless hints and anecdotes about admirers and suitors, scandals and self-righteous denials of interest in marriage. In view of her reluctance to flaunt herself as others with such pretty features might have done, not to mention her secrecy about her background, perhaps it is hardly surprising that we know next to nothing about how she came to get married. In 1909 Maggie returned to London, relieved to 'make a graceful exit from this operatic chess game' being played by Marguerite Carré and Mary Garden at the Opéra-Comique. With her she brought the man who was to become her first husband, Eugène Plumon. Typically she remains virtually silent on the subject of her marriage. Her crucial chapter about her training, her performance as Mélisande and the rivalry of Marguerite and Mary ends in a surprisingly brief and dismissive way, with the words:

> During this year I married Eugène Plumon, a French barrister who spoke English and German, and had taken a degree in German at the University of Heidelberg. I shall always be grateful to Eugène for putting my house in order, so to speak, from the business standpoint. Up to that time business never entered my head, for I was a real bohemian – and still am. Money slipped through my fingers like quicksilver, and it was good to have someone with a level head to guide me.[12]

Where is the passion? The romance? Not a word about where or how they met, his appearance, or his background. In view of what we now know about Maggie's background and her parents' financial difficulties, perhaps it is significant that it is his financial acumen that is emphasised rather than any physical attraction. Their marriage took place at the Kensington Registry Office on 16 October 1909 with Maggie's friend Olga Loewenthal, as one of the two witnesses. To avoid any confusion about her identity, her name

---

[10] See Chapter 13, p. 178.

[11] *Musical America*, 13 April 1913, p. 5.

[12] Teyte, *Star on the Door*, p. 53.

is entered on the marriage certificate as 'Margaret Tate, usually known as Maggie Teyte', but she signed herself 'Maggie Tate'. Eugène Plumon states both his and his father's profession as 'Barrister'. He was twenty-nine at the time of the marriage; Maggie was twenty-one. By searching sources such as ships' passenger lists one can discover that Eugène was born in Armentières, near Lille, and that his family's address was in Versailles.

Mary Garden always claimed that you could not combine a career in opera with marriage, which was why she had never entered that state. Maggie was certainly not inclined to give up her singing. In an aside she is disparaging about those who do succumb to 'the temptations of Eros'. She wondered if it was due to a fundamental lack of ambition, or to some weakness of character, or failure of self-confidence. 'And why does it happen to the weaker sex? I have never known a man give up his career for such a reason.'[13] In order to avoid an unwanted pregnancy, Maggie's solution was to have an operation. Her Fallopian tubes were tied so that her career would remain uninterrupted.[14] She may well have believed that the operation was reversible.

Was it Eugène's or Maggie's wish that almost exactly three months after the Register Office marriage, on 17 December 1909, a religious ceremony should take place at the Catholic church of Notre Dame de France in London, an event which was also subsequently recorded in the register of Maggie's baptism at the church of Saint Peter and Saint Paul, Wolverhampton? Was this event of no significance to Maggie when she came to reminisce on her life? Nowhere is there any mention of it. Incidentally, there is a neat symmetry here, for this is the very church in which Lugné-Poë, the dramatist who first brought *Pelléas et Mélisande* to the stage in Paris in 1893, married another Mélisande on 23 July 1898.[15] His mother was living in London at the time, and not well enough to travel, so for the ceremony he brought over to England the actress Suzanne Desprès (whose real name was Joséphine Bonvalet), who had acted the role of Mélisande in London in 1895.[16]

Since Maggie was at the height of her career, Eugène was able to benefit from his wife's considerable income and soon gave up his career as a lawyer. He was an astute business manager and helped to promote Maggie, arranging evenings where she could sing to influential musicians and members of society, and managing her finances. It is also noteworthy that by marrying a French citizen Maggie took on French nationality. For her this may well

[13] Teyte, *Star on the Door*, p. 83.
[14] O'Connor, *The Pursuit of Perfection*, p. 104
[15] Information on both marriages kindly provided by the church of Notre Dame de France, Leicester Place, London.
[16] Lugné-Poë, *Le Sot du tremplin*, p. 19.

have been an additional attraction, for what could be further from her native roots in Wolverhampton which she was so anxious to forget.

Maggie recounts the anecdote of a trip to Germany with Eugène in 1911. Her tale shows how much older than her he must have looked, for he had even been called a baby-snatcher by some of their friends![17] He was escorting her down Unter den Linden in Berlin when a passing German officer, probably thinking the older man must be Maggie's father, made eyes at Maggie, at which her husband used his fluent German to tear a strip off him. Forty-eight hours later Eugène burst into their hotel suite telling Maggie to pack at once. They were leaving! The German officer had sent his seconds round to the lobby and unsurprisingly Eugène was in no mood for a duel. They went on to Heidelberg, and perhaps to illustrate why he was so reluctant to take on the officer, he arranged for her to watch a real duel. Maggie did not enjoy the experience, and retreated when the first blood was drawn.[18]

In the autumn of 1909 Maggie gave a series of concerts at the Aeolian Hall in London, where she became quite a celebrity. Her reputation as Mélisande also led to a role in a Queen's Hall Choral Society concert in the first performance of a now-forgotten romantic cantata by G. E. Clutsam: *The Quest of Rapunzel*. Maggie was deemed well suited to the part, even though the music was not received with enthusiasm.[19] The following year, after giving her final performance at the Opéra-Comique in Paris in *La Flûte enchantée* on 28 March, she was engaged for the autumn season of opera to be given at His Majesty's Theatre by Thomas Beecham, thus beginning a relationship described by a Beecham biographer as 'a passionate friendship which continued until the years of the First World War'.[20] If there were any 'passion' at this time it would seem to be rather precipitate in view of her quite recent marriage. Beecham was still married to his first wife Utica, and from 1912 was also in a liaison with Lady Maud Cunard. In 1910 he took over His Majesty's Theatre for a seven-week season of opéra comique, in the middle of which was a short 'Mozart Season' of nine performances. The first of these was *Il seraglio*, in which Maggie distinguished herself as Blonde, followed by a revival of *The Marriage of Figaro*, when her Cherubino was singled out for praise by the critics.

Life here was in marked contrast to life at the institution of the Opéra-Comique in Paris. She found the atmosphere 'rather *mañana*', with a frustrating lack of punctuality. 'If we were called for rehearsal at ten o'clock in

[17] Teyte, *Star on the Door*, p. 170.

[18] Teyte, *Star on the Door*, p. 171.

[19] *The Times*, 3 November 1909.

[20] Alan Jefferson, *Sir Thomas Beecham: A Centenary Tribute* (London, 1979), p. 38.

the morning, it was seldom that the Maestro would appear before half-past twelve.'[21] She told American journalists that Beecham could not bear the idea of work, study, or anything serious. Everything had to be new to interest him.[22] But she admired him for having that 'electric quality that some people call genius', and being able to transmit something of his own musical magnetism to those who worked with him, provided they knew how to work.'[23]

Maggie certainly had been trained how to work. Recitals such as that on 18 November 1910 at the Aeolian Hall won consistent praise. In this concert of modern French songs she was described as 'in her element, for no one has such wayward grace, and so much suggestion of something exquisitely remote'.[24] What could be more suggestive of the perfect Mélisande? Yet the role was a long time coming. The season continued at Covent Garden and the critics were full of praise for her performances in *Faust, The Tales of Hoffmann, Le nozze di Figaro*, and *Il seraglio*, eulogising her 'exquisite beauty', 'dainty pathos', 'the vivacity and naturalness of her acting'.

Then, at last, Mélisande. Talk about a prophet not being recognised in her own country! As previously noted, it was the Swiss soprano Rose Féart, who had sung the role the first time it was performed in England in 1909,[25] even though Debussy was happy to accompany Maggie in recitals of his music. The production of *Pelléas et Mélisande* which took place on 19 December 1910 was the same as that of Féart's the previous year, including the beautiful medieval-style costumes by Attilio Comelli.[26] This time Maggie's Pelléas was Georges Petit, Golaud was Jean Bourbon, Arkel was Murray Davey, and Geneviève was Edna Thornton. Percy Pitt conducted. By now the opera was finding greater approval in this country. 'No single touch of Debussy's is put in with any trace of hesitation', wrote the *Times* reviewer, who considered the opera 'a complete, and perfect work of art in its own way.' Maggie was 'The chief attraction of the cast' and described as 'infinitely gracious and pathetic in her girlish innocence. The tender beauty of the love-scenes owes much to her and the pathos of the scenes with Golaud was irresistible.' In contrast, Petit's acting was found lacking in spontaneity.[27] Another critic commented on the rare charm of Maggie's voice yet noted at the same time its 'peculiarly

[21] Teyte, *Star on the Door*, p. 76.

[22] *New York Times*, 13 November 1911.

[23] Teyte, *Star on the Door*, p. 81.

[24] *The Times*, 19 November 1910.

[25] See Chapter 13, p. 187.

[26] See illus. 30.

[27] *The Times*, 20 December 1910.

impersonal quality' which he regarded as precisely that required by the composer.[28]

Whatever people might think of the opera itself, the *Westminster Gazette* judged the performance excellent and Maggie 'an absolutely ideal Mélisande', finding it hardly possible to imagine a more perfect embodiment of the part. There was high praise for the beauty of her appearance, the finish and refinement of her singing, the grace and charm of her acting. It was far and away the best thing she had so far done in London.[29] The *Standard* agreed. Her looks and temperament were perfect for the part, whilst 'her clear, refined voice, and her admirable, distinct utterance invested her singing in all the great moments with distinctive interest and charm.'[30]

For Victor Gollancz, Maggie Teyte came to mean Mélisande for ever after he had heard her in December 1910. He believed she must have even surpassed Mary Garden. He loved her adorable '*mignonesse*', a quality of mingled freshness and gravity in her smooth gentle singing, 'and the child-like ingenuousness of her acting', which made him feel an affection for her such as he had felt for few other singers.[31] Sadly, though, the Beecham season at Covent Garden was not a success. Beecham himself commented that despite the general level of excellence, good press and attractive singers, the public did not give the season the support it deserved.[32]

Early in 1911 Maggie must have been hoping to acquire more engagements in Britain, for in a programme for a concert in the Edinburgh Classical Concert series on 11 February 1911 there is a substantial advertisement for her, although she was not appearing there that season.

Despite a common misconception, Maggie was certainly not singing in *Pelléas et Mélisande* at the Opéra-Comique in Paris in 1911. On 21 February of that year Marcel Proust wrote a letter to Reynaldo Hahn, telling him that that very evening he had listened to the whole of the opera on the théâtrophone.[33] He does not name the singers of the individual roles, but it is often reported that he heard Maggie Teyte as Mélisande. As we have seen, in 1911 Mélisande was sung by Marguerite Carré, and indeed the register of the Opéra-Comique for that year confirms that the latter sang the part on 18, 21, 23 and 25 February. Those who believe Proust heard Maggie Teyte as

[28] *Daily Telegraph*, 20 December 1910.

[29] Teyte, *Star on the Door*, p. 79.

[30] Teyte, *Star on the Door*, p. 80.

[31] Victor Gollancz, *Journey towards Music* (London, 1964), p. 120.

[32] Rosenthal, *Two Centuries of Opera at Covent Garden*, p. 356.

[33] Marcel Proust, letter to Reynaldo Hahn, 21 February 1911: Proust, *Correspondance*, vol. 10: *1910–1911*, ed. Philip Kolb (Paris, 1983), pp. 250–1. (Via the théâtrophone one could listen to live opera at home.)

19 Jean de Reszke

20   Reynaldo Hahn, a photograph in *Musica*, February 1910

21 Maggie Teyte, as she appeared in the programme for *Pelléas et Mélisande*, 1908

22 Maggie Teyte in 1910, the year she first sang Mélisande at Covent Garden. This photograph appeared in *Musica*, March 1910.

23   Maggie Teyte as Mélisande, 1908,
as she appeared on the cover of *Musica*, August 1908

24 Maggie Teyte as Mélisande, 1908

25 Georgette Leblanc at the Abbey of Saint-Wandrille

26 Maurice Maeterlinck on the steps of Saint-Wandrille

27 *Pelléas et Mélisande*, the play, at Saint-Wandrille, August 1910:
Pelléas (René Maupré) and Mélisande (Georgette Leblanc)

28 *Pelléas et Mélisande*, the play, at Saint-Wandrille, August 1910:
Geneviève (Jeanne Even) and Mélisande (Georgette Leblanc)

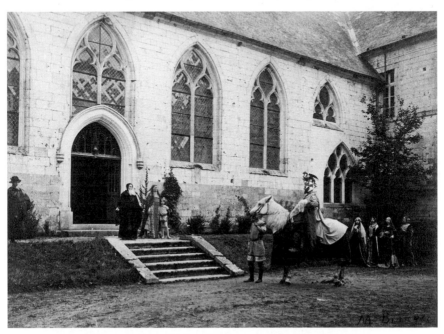

29 *Pelléas et Mélisande*, the play, at Saint-Wandrille, August 1910:
Golaud (Jean Durozat) carries Mélisande (Georgette Leblanc) to the 'castle'

30 Attilio Comelli's costume design for Mélisande, Covent Garden. Maggie Teyte wore this costume in 1910.

31 Georgette Leblanc as Mélisande in the opera, Boston 1912

32 Maggie Teyte in *Monsieur Beaucaire*, London 1919

33 Maeterlinck, his wife Renée and Henry Russell arriving in New York,
December 1919

34 Maeterlinck and his wife Renée with Mary Garden. Maeterlinck saw the opera
Pelléas et Mélisande for the first time in New York, 27 January 1920.

35 Mary Garden, Director of the Chicago Opera Association, 1921

36 Georgette Leblanc and Jaque Catelain in *L'Inhumaine*, 1924:
Georgette Leblanc as Claire Lescot in the film by Marcel L'Herbier

37, 38 Maggie Teyte as
Mélisande, New York,
25 March 1948

Mélisande are therefore mistaken. However, the work made such a haunting impression on him that, as he told Hahn a month later, he listened to
it repeatedly. He liked best the parts with no words, although he particularly loved the atmosphere created when Pelléas emerges from the vaults and
sings, 'Ah! Je respire enfin!' when the music is imbued with the freshness of
the sea and scent of roses carried by the breeze.[34]

The only specific reference to Maggie Teyte in Proust's correspondence
occurs in a letter to Hahn of the same year, when he writes that he met
Maggie on 16 August at the Golf Club ball at the Grand Hôtel in Cabourg.
Here he indicates that she sang regularly with the troupe at the Casino, but
that he had always been too ill to go to hear her.[35] An article in *Gil Blas* confirms Maggie's appearances with the Cabourg company at that time.[36]

It was not in Britain or France however, but in America that Maggie's
future was to take a more prosperous turn when she signed a contract with
Andreas Dippel, manager of the Philadelphia-Chicago Opera Company, for
the 1911–12 season. Once again she was tailing Mary Garden who had already
signed her contract with him for the previous season. Travelling as Maggie
Plumon-Teyte she sailed across the Atlantic with her husband in October
1911. Her petite figure took the American press aback: 'An opera singer
weighing around one hundred pounds made a nice change for journalists',[37]
one of them wrote. But there was to be no opportunity for the press to compare her with Mary in the role of Mélisande. Nor could she yet be compared
with Georgette Leblanc, who, ironically, was to achieve the accolade of performing as Mélisande in America long before Maggie. Improbably, Maggie
was not to perform here as Mélisande until as late as 1948.

On her arrival, Maggie did not provide the rich pickings for the press
with which Mary Garden was so accustomed to furnish them. She told them
of the rivalry at the Opéra-Comique which had led to her taking over the
role of Mélisande, of her rehearsals with Debussy, and of Thomas Beecham's
relaxed approach to rehearsals. Rather than sexual liaisons, it was her addic-
tion to sport that led to headlines. 'Tiniest prima donna an expert at all out-
door sports' was not quite in the same league as rumours of engagements
and marriage to all sorts of international figures. Besides, her husband was
there with her. When her name was associated with a scandal in the papers it

34 Marcel Proust, letter to Reynaldo Hahn, 4 March 1911: Proust, *Correspondance*,
    vol. 10, pp. 256–7.

35 Marcel Proust, letter to Reynaldo Hahn, 17 or 18 August 1911, Proust, *Correspondance*,
    vol. 10, pp. 333–4.

36 'Le théâtre possède une bonne troupe avec Miss Maggie Teyte.' *Gil Blas*, 17 August
    1911. See Proust, *Correspondance*, vol. 10, p. 336 (note).

37 Teyte, *Star on the Door*, p. 96.

was of a totally different sort, and one in which she was the righteous party. Just before she was about to make her first appearance in *Le nozze di Figaro*, a man called Nathan Arlock[38] called to see her at her hotel. He turned out to be organising a claque, a group of people who would boost or ruin the reputation of individual singers by applauding or hissing during the performance. He promised that if she made it worth his while he would ensure that she was well applauded. If not, she might well be hissed. Maggie found her husband useful at this point (one of the rare mentions of him), for he helped her to entrap Arlock by concealing newspapermen and officials of the opera company who overheard Arlock's demand for £500.[39]

On 6 November 1911 Maggie appeared in *Cendrillon* by Massenet, the only opera in which she sang with Mary Garden.[40] This was performed first in Philadelphia, then in Chicago on 27 November. Hector Dufranne, Debussy's original Golaud, was singing the role of Pandolfe. Massenet himself had predicted the greatest success for the opera as he had expressed 'the highest opinion of Miss Teyte's performance in this role', according to the American press.[41] It was Maggie's performance, not Mary Garden's, which remained in the memory of Cecil Smith when, in an article on Massenet's operas published in 1955, he commented that she lent enchantment to this work.[42] Again, it was her size that proved to be a talking point: 'There was a good deal of publicity about the size 3½ glass slippers that Cinderella was to wear, but it seemed to me that a singer only five feet tall who took size 7 would have been even more remarkable!', exclaimed Maggie. *Cendrillon* became something of a fashion during the season, the shops even selling dolls dressed up to look like the two lead singers. No wonder Maggie acquired her nicknames of 'Tiny Teyte' and 'the Pocket Prima Donna'. The remarkable versatility of this 'Irish' actress (she insisted on this version of her ancestry), turning from the pure lyricism of Mozart in an earlier recital to the broader interpretive style of Massenet, was praised as were her convincing acting skills.[43] She was compared favourably to Mary Garden in her ability to make the 'artificial style' of opera stand for sincerity.[44]

Maggie's performance as Cinderella was to lead to her one and only appearance at the New York Metropolitan under Campanini's baton on

---

38 Davis, *Opera in Chicago*, p. 111, refers to him as Nathan Arlock. *New York Times*, 15 November 1911, says Nothar Arlock.

39 Teyte, *Star on the Door*, p. 100; *New York Times*, 5 November 1911.

40 See also Chapter 14, p. 205.

41 '50 Years ago', *Opera*, November 1961, p. 721.

42 *Opera*, April 1955, p. 231.

43 *Chicago Daily Tribune*, 28 November 1911.

44 *Chicago Daily Tribune*, 1 December 1911.

20 February 1912. Her most vivid memory of this occasion was of the opening of the second act, with Mary Garden 'sitting, bored and listless on the royal throne in the centre of the stage, with her long cape hanging down the steps and her beautiful legs in their sleek tights.'[45] There is certainly no impression here of two great singers with such a similar Parisian training ever appreciating each other's company! Any conversations they may have exchanged must have been on a professional basis, for neither has admitted to anything approaching friendship.

Recitals combined American and French song, such as that on 16 November 1911 at Carnegie Hall, when her interpretation of 'Fantoches', the second song from the first set of Debussy's *Fêtes galantes*, was so successful she had to repeat it.[46] Of more lasting significance, perhaps, was the acquaintance Maggie made in Newark, New Jersey, at this time, which was to provide the precursor for her future success. She recorded several songs for Thomas Edison in his studios. His initial criticism stung her, for decades later, in 1970, she recalled it when being interviewed. Edison told her that for recording purposes her top register was no good at all! Despite her instinctive conviction that he did not know what he was talking about, she always remembered his words, reminding herself 'to be careful with the top register'.[47] Ever willing to learn, she adapted her voice well enough for Edison not only to continue recording her, but to use Maggie for an audience to compare his recordings with her singing live from behind a curtain. They were then said to be able to confirm that the recordings were indistinguishable from the live performance.

Maggie's success in America led to her singing in Chicago for three seasons, still declaring her nationality as French whenever she crossed the Atlantic, and until 1915 listing as her home contacts either her father-in-law in Versailles, or Mrs Rubens, whom she described as her 'mother', or even Mr. V. Rubens. She sang under Cleofonte Campanini several times, and gave much praised performances in Goldmark's *The Cricket on the Hearth*, as well as *La bohème*, *The Marriage of Figaro*, *The Tales of Hoffmann*, *Faust*, *Quo Vadis*, *Hänsel und Gretel*, *Madama Butterfly* and *Mignon*. In September 1912 Maggie also had the honour of featuring as soloist in the first concert given at the new Aeolian Hall in New York under the baton of Walter Damrosch.[48]

In between these seasons Maggie returned to England, but despite winning praise from the critics in recitals, particularly for her interpretations

[45] *Opera News*, 19 November 1945, p. 7.
[46] *New York Times*, 17 November 1911.
[47] In *Opera News*, 21 March 1970, Maggie remembers the year as 1911.
[48] *Time*, 11 August 1924.

of Debussy's songs,[49] she did not achieve the recognition she would have desired. Needs must, and this led to a change of repertoire – nearer to that of her brother, James. In 1912 Maggie had her first experience of music halls, appearing twice nightly in variety at London's Alhambra Theatre. She admits that what attracted her to this unusual repertoire for an opera singer was the large fee attached.[50] There she managed to fill and silence the house: 'How this can be managed in a tobacco-laden hall, ask the high gods', commented *Variety* on 1 May 1912. Even *The Times* reported the deafening applause for the song *The Minstrel Boy*, which was not to say there was any lack of it for her operatic arias. The reviewer admits that 'if we cannot see her in opera just now, it is well worth hearing her on the platform.'[51] Not all approved of her choice of repertoire, here or in more highbrow venues, however. Writing about her performance at Queen's Hall on 22 May 1913, the *Times* reviewer was disappointed. Referring presumably to American offerings such as songs by Sidney Homer, Marshall Kernochan, C. Whitney Coombs and R. Huntingdon Woodman, he complained that she was not singing 'real music', accusing her of 'deluding the taste of the public by singing bad music as though it were good music'. Charles Wakefield Cadman, whose *A Moonlight Song* started the third part, was later to play a role in her life. The critic's only outright praise was reserved for five Debussy songs which formed the central section. These she sang with depth and sympathy of expression.[52] Only four days previously, however, on 18 May 1913, Maggie had sung Puccini at the Royal Albert Hall, with Fritz Kreisler and Wilhelm Backhaus performing in the same concert, demonstrating her versatility rather than a permanent change of repertoire.

Following the bankruptcy of the Chicago Opera Company in 1914, Maggie was employed by Henry Russell's National Grand Opera Company in Boston, where she sang in *La bohème*, *Don Giovanni* and *Madama Butterfly*. Newspaper advertisements show her performances listed next to Mary Garden's – in fact Mary sang in a concert listed as 'Only time this season' on the same afternoon as Maggie's evening performance of *Butterfly*,[53] but nowhere do we have any record of conversations between the two Mélisandes. Whilst Boston was enchanted with this 'wrenlike' singer (more like a 'hummingbird' flitting from place to place was another comparison),[54]

49 E.g. *The Times*, 21 May 1912 (Aeolian Hall), 4 October 1912 (Queen's Hall).
50 Teyte, *Star on the Door*, p. 122.
51 *The Times*, 30 April 1912.
52 *The Times*, 23 May 1913.
53 *The Tech*, 19 February 1914.
54 Quaintance Eaton, *The Boston Opera Company: The Story of a Unique Musical Institution* (New York, 1965), p. 249.

she did not convey the impression being given by Mary of the grand prima donna with supreme talent, striving to find new depths in a work. With the same company she also toured to Paris, singing the role of Oscar in Verdi's *Un ballo in maschera*, and Countess Susanna in *Il segreto di Susanna* by Wolf-Ferrari.

Whilst in this city, not only did Maggie 'enchant the French capital with her voice', but she also found time to play golf on the Chantilly golf course with the American Open champion, Francis Ouimet.[55] More significantly, she was able to carry out an interview with Debussy which was printed in the May issue of the American journal *The Opera Magazine*.[56] Debussy assured her that he was going to produce no more music of the kind he had written previously, for he had reached the limit of that idiom and wanted to avoid repeating what had already been expressed. He had not deliberately invented his system, but it had been forced upon him by necessity. He disliked the plagiarisms, the 'Debussyisms' of other composers who hoped to equal his reputation, but ended up by harming him without helping themselves, and he prophesied that in ten years everyone would be singing and playing his music, by which time the general intelligence of the public would have caught up with him.

Before returning to the States, Maggie toured England with Jan Kubelík, the Czech violinist and composer, then on 10 and 24 May 1914 she sang at the Royal Albert Hall in concerts featuring Kreisler and Backhaus. Her selection of songs, which comprised compositions by such composers as Scott, Homer, Landon Ronald, Cadman and Beach besides Wolf[57] and Brahms, was again regarded as trivial by reviewers.

In 1914 *Pelléas et Mélisande* was revived at Covent Garden in June, but again, for some reason, Maggie was overlooked and must have felt sheer frustration when the role of Mélisande was performed by Louise Edvina. Instead she sang in *Don Giovanni* and a disappointing production of *Figaro*, in which she was described as the 'only' singer 'worthy of a place in the Covent Garden cast'.[58]

Since their marriage in 1909, Maggie's husband Eugène had been her business manager and had looked after her well, coping with the press, intervening with critics, entertaining to further her career, but it was this career that was paramount in their lives. Unsurprisingly, her relationship with Eugène fell to pieces as her strong personality clashed with his weaker, worldly charm, and

---

[55] Eaton, *The Boston Opera Company*, p. 262.

[56] Maggie Teyte, 'Bearding the Lion', *The Opera Magazine: devoted to the higher forms of musical art*, vol. 1 no. 5 (May 1914), pp. 10–12.

[57] Misspelt in the programme as 'Wolff'.

[58] Rosenthal, *Two Centuries of Opera at Covent Garden*, p. 387.

she began to despise his superficial delight in her music compared with the depth of knowledge and appreciation expressed by the more knowledgeable Rubens family, Reynaldo Hahn and others. In 1914 they separated. When Maggie crossed the Atlantic in November of that year she was initially listed as 'Maggie Plumon' on the passenger list, but this surname has been crossed out and 'Teyte' firmly handwritten above it.

A tour of Northwest America took place early in 1915, then in April appetites must have been whetted by an article which appeared whilst she was in Illinois entitled 'Concerning the authenticity of Miss Maggie Teyte'.[59] The author lists several spurious claims others had made on Maggie's behalf: she was said to be the inventor of a fire extinguisher adopted by the British admiralty, she was described as 'a pig-tailed prima donna astonishing Debussy' who lounged around naughtily in tight knickers and silk stockings, and was also supposedly a suffragette. The word 'naughty' was repeated as her enjoyment of wearing masculine attire was emphasised. Perhaps the reviewer was aware of a full-page illustration which had appeared in the French journal *Musica* the previous year with no fewer than five photographs of Maggie in trouser roles, entitled *Les travestis de Miss Teyte*. The text below had argued that she was one of the very few singers who looked good in masculine garb.[60] It also seems that Maggie's true origins were so mysterious that the press had had a happy time making up stories, including naming the place of her birth as Kansas City or Tipperary!

Despite her statement in her autobiography that she had to stay where she was until the end of the war,[61] Maggie did manage to return to England in the summer of 1915, for on 15 June she took a small part in a fund-raising concert, organised by the French actress Réjane, described as an 'All Women Matinée' at the Haymarket. Amongst the illustrious members of the audience were Queen Alexandra and one of Maggie's early patrons, Lady Ripon.[62] Maggie returned to the States in October, still with French nationality.

In November 1915 she was granted a divorce by a French court.[63] The news soon reached the States. 'No more husbands!', Maggie told the press.[64] 'Maggie Teyte says she is Irish again' was the headline in the *Boston Daily*

---

[59] *Chicago Daily Tribune*, 4 April 1915.

[60] *Musica*, July 1914, p. 143.

[61] Teyte, *Star on the Door*, p. 122.

[62] *The Times*, 16 June 1915.

[63] O'Connor, *The Pursuit of Perfection*, pp. 123–4.

[64] *New York Times*, 13 November 1915. This also says Eugène Plumon was attached to the British Expeditionary Forces as an interpreter. In the *Modern Language Journal* of March 1918 there is praise for a *Vade Mecum* written by Eugène Plumon to help British and French soldiers with language problems during the First World War.

Globe![65] Never would she admit her true origins. The newspapers cited the incompatibility of art with domesticity as one reason for the divorce, but there were also rumours of Plumon's extreme jealousy of his young wife. Her one ambition, claimed Maggie, was 'to go on in my career and never stop'.[66] Once back in America, Maggie wrote to her former husband telling him she wanted no more to do with him. Never again did she call herself or sign herself Madame Plumon. Not for the first time she exercised that ability to expunge from her mind all memories of her relationships with someone she did not care to remember.

Restrictions on travel as well as the danger involved made crossing the Atlantic so problematical during the war years that she was not to return to England until 1919. Andreas Dippel had arranged for Anna Pavlova, the Russian ballerina, to appear with his Opera Comique company in New York, and it was with this company that Maggie was engaged to sing in *Madama Butterfly* and *La bohème*. After each performance of either opera there would be a ballet-divertissement in which Pavlova would appear, and which always ended with the 'Dying Swan' of Saint-Saëns. Her impression of Pavlova was of a 'tragic, almost wraithlike figure' with 'that quality of romantic sadness that seems part of the Slav character'.[67] For the next two years Maggie sang operatic roles and gave concert performances, receiving accolades from the critics wherever and whenever she performed. She also sang with the Boston Opera Company as Fiora in Montemezzi's *L'amore dei tre re*, Gilda in *Rigoletto* and Desdemona in *Otello*.

At the time of her divorce Maggie was already being linked romantically to another man, the American composer Charles Wakefield Cadman, who was seven years older than her. She had sung his songs in recitals, even at the Albert Hall, as already noted, and enjoyed furthering his contributions to American music. She joined him in his recitals in California and was present at concerts given by him in conjunction with Princess Tsianina, a Native American princess who sang mezzo-soprano. Cadman suffered from poor health, however. Added to this, their feelings for each other cannot have been strong enough to withstand the separations caused by Maggie's busy schedule, for the affair did not last beyond 1916. Then in that year there was a very brief engagement. This was to a Second Lieutenant Seymour Robertson, whom she had known in her youth. Whilst in London she had noticed his name in a list of war wounded after the Battle of Ypres and must have been overcome by a rush of romantic fervour, for she tracked him down, waited

[65] *Boston Daily Globe*, 13 November 1915.
[66] *Boston Daily Globe*, 13 November 1915.
[67] Teyte, *Star on the Door*, p. 124.

while he had his arm amputated, then told him immediately: 'I want you to marry me.'[68] She must have regretted her impetuosity, for there seems to be no further reference to this relationship.

At the end of the First World War, Maggie longed to work in her homeland. When she sent a cable to her London manager, to her delight an opportunity opened up in the form of a starring role in an operetta to be performed at the Princes Theatre. Even better, it was written and was to be conducted by none other than André Messager, the original conductor of *Pelléas et Mélisande*. The work was *Monsieur Beaucaire*. Maggie accepted with alacrity. The atmosphere in the capital city was receptive after the ravages of war. As Landon Ronald wrote in the issue of *The Play Pictorial* devoted to this operetta, Londoners were craving for amusement, going from one theatre to another, ensuring that there were practically no theatrical failures there.[69]

Messager came to the dress rehearsal and also the preview given in Birmingham. He was so delighted to discover Maggie taking the leading role of Lady Mary that, believing the music not sufficiently important for her, he even wrote a new song only a day before it opened. He summoned her to his hotel at four o'clock that day to practise it, and certainly provided a suitable vehicle for her voice, for *Philomel* became a show-stopper when the operetta opened on 19 April 1919. This song was the great success of the evening and brought Maggie many new admirers.[70] Unfortunately for all concerned, the run of performances was cut short following a legal dispute over ticket sales. This must have been so frustrating and disappointing for Maggie, who was eager to make her mark again on the London musical scene. Indeed, she was one of the main signatories to a letter to *The Times* asking for reconsideration of the decision to close down at a time when it would be difficult for the performers to gain employment elsewhere.[71]

Although light opera and musical comedy were not the milieu Maggie had initially intended for herself, it is an interesting coincidence that this was the niche in which her older brother James had found success. *The Maid of the Mountains*, with music by Harold Fraser, had had its first performance in 1916. In December 1916, when the musical was tried out in Manchester before moving to London, it was felt that it needed a hit number. It was James Tate who collaborated with two lyricists to contribute four songs to the show, which actually became outstanding hits. Coincidentally, in Gänzl's

[68] *Daily Telegraph*, 18 February 1916; O'Connor, *The Pursuit of Perfection*, p. 127.

[69] *The Play Pictorial* [*Monsieur Beaucaire*], vol. 34, no. 205 (1919). See also illus. 32.

[70] *The Times*, 21 April 1919.

[71] *The Times*, 15 June 1920.

Book of the Musical Theatre[72] the entry for *The Maid of the Mountains* with its reference to the music of James Tate is followed immediately by that for *Monsieur Beaucaire* with soprano Maggie Teyte. One cannot help wondering if there was any communication between brother and sister prior to James's death in 1922. There is certainly no reference to him in her writings.

By accepting her role in *Monsieur Beaucaire* she not only found a foothold in London's theatreland, but she also met her second husband. Walter Sherwin Cottingham, known as Sherwin or Sher, was on the same ship as Maggie when she returned to England for rehearsals. His father, Walter H. Cottingham, was a multi-millionaire who owned the long-established paint manufacturers Lewis Berger & Sons. Sherwin was born and educated in Cleveland, Ohio.[73] Since 1912 Walter Cottingham had owned Woolley Hall and Grange and the surrounding estate just outside Maidenhead in Berkshire. When Maggie met him, Sherwin used to spend part of the year in Cleveland, part in England. What more romantic partner could Maggie have found? He was younger than she was, rich, tall, athletic, and a most eligible bachelor. Maggie sincerely believed her fate was being fulfilled for in New York in 1917, when she had had her horoscope read, her marriage was foretold to a tall, dark, handsome young man, and in March 1921 this prophecy was fulfilled.

It is also worthy of note that before this, on 21 May 1920, a certificate was issued granting Maggie British nationality and naturalisation.[74] All links with her first husband were now completely broken. How many people had realised that this English singer was regarded as being of French nationality during the time she was married to Plumon?

Before her second marriage Maggie lived in Knightsbridge, but she frequently visited Woolley Hall, where she was made welcome by Sherwin's father Walter. She was at that time unaware that the war had taken its toll on her future husband. Beneath that charm and vivacity he was hiding dreadful health problems. He had enlisted early and served as a naval aviator.[75] Having had to parachute out of a balloon in northern France in 1916, he had escaped with a back injury and kidney damage, but all his crew were killed. This did not stop the dashing young man from buying a flying company after the war, the Personal Flying Service, which flew out reporters and photographers to cover disasters and world events for the newspapers.[76] There was a further

---

[72] Kurt Gänzl and Andrew Lamb, *Book of the Musical Theatre* (London, 1988).

[73] *New York Times*, 12 March 1921.

[74] National Archives, Kew: HO144/1605/392194.

[75] *New York Times*, 12 March 1921.

[76] O'Connor, *The Pursuit of Perfection*, p. 140.

emotional problem. Sherwin's mother had died when he was very young. His father was always travelling and expanding his paint empire, therefore did not have much time to devote personal attention to his son, and when he remarried it was to a much younger woman, Walter being fifty-two, his wife Jacqueline twenty-six, not much older than Sherwin. For some reason, Sherwin also lied to Maggie about his age, telling her he was twenty-eight.

The marriage took place on 12 March 1921 at the Register Office, St George's, Hanover Square. At the time, Maggie was appearing at the Lyric Theatre in *The Little Dutch Girl*, an operetta by Imre Kálmán. She got married on a Saturday morning and sang in the Saturday matinée, hoping for little fuss or publicity, but was taken aback to find a throng of reporters and well-wishers when she emerged. This was not the only thing that surprised her. When Sherwin signed the register she saw for the first time his true age. He was in fact twenty-four and she would be thirty-three in a few weeks' time. Maggie resented this lie. His excuse was that he feared she would not have married him if he had told her the truth. He was probably right. Nor was she wholly honest with Sherwin. She did not reveal that she had undergone sterilisation when married to Eugène, and could not have children. There is the possibility, however, that she believed the operation could be reversed.

Now Maggie really did live a life of luxury. Her father-in-law's wedding present was Woolley Grange, the dower house a few hundred yards from Woolley Hall, where she had everything money could buy. She drove her own car and exercised her dogs. She had staff at her command, and became imperious and demanding, but at least she did allow her thirteen-year-old niece Rita to come and stay during school holidays. Rita was the sole link Maggie ever kept with her own family. She was the daughter of Maggie's sister Marie, who had died in March 1908 (the very year of Maggie's début as Mélisande) when Rita was only nine months old. Until his disappearance at the beginning of the First World War, Marie's Italian husband looked after the child with the help of her nurse, Holly, then Maggie reluctantly became her guardian. Whilst growing up, Rita had had to make do with her boarding school education, having little contact with her famous aunt. She had previously shared a flat in London with Holly in the school holidays, but at last, following the change in Maggie's circumstances, she was permitted to enjoy the lavish lifestyle at Woolley Grange.[77]

Unfortunately, after a run of six months *The Little Dutch Girl* closed on 7 June 1921 owing to a coal strike, but in 1922 the British National Opera Company was formed following the collapse of the Beecham Opera

[77] O'Connor, *The Pursuit of Perfection*, p. 144.

Company, and on 13 May Maggie scored a great personal success in a matinée performance of *Madama Butterfly* at Covent Garden.[78] She also sang at the first night of the Proms in August 1922 and made two further appearances that season. In that same year Maggie sang in the winter season at Covent Garden, performing Hänsel in *Hänsel und Gretel*, Cherubino in *Figaro*, then gave just one performance as Mimi in *La bohème*.[79] A milestone in operatic history occurred on 6 January 1923, when the matinée performance of *Hänsel und Gretel* was broadcast by the recently formed British Broadcasting Company over station 2LO, and thus became the first complete opera to be transmitted from a theatre in Europe. She also sang at some prominent social engagements and in May 1923 appeared again as Butterfly at Covent Garden. This was regarded by the critics as one of the great triumphs of the season. According to one, not only did Maggie's performance make the whole opera vital and convincing, 'It was refreshing, too, to hear a production which really sounded like that of a 15-year-old girl.'[80] There was even a special matinée performance of *Madama Butterfly* at the Chelsea Palace Theatre which was attended by the Queen. Maggie was invited to sing for the Prince of Wales after his Indian Tour after which he told her that he had carried one of her records with him through the war.[81] In the same season she sang the role of the Princess in the first performance of *The Perfect Fool* by Holst, and was described as 'an exquisite princess, one whom only a perfect fool could resist.'[82]

Despite these stage appearances, when Maggie travelled across the Atlantic to visit the Cottingham family in Cleveland, Ohio, for a fortnight in January of 1924, for the first time she described herself on the passenger list as 'Housewife'. Her professional life was becoming ever more subordinate. A recital back in England at the Aeolian Hall on 29 May 1924 did not receive glowing reviews. One critic noted that although her voice was bigger than of old, its quality was not correspondingly improved, and he criticised her for singing 'through' her tone. He complained that she now seemed to be more deliberately trying to impress, overemphasising, and singing at her audience rather than to them.[83]

There was but one British National Opera Company production of *Pelléas et Mélisande* in which Maggie appeared in the twenties. This was on 6 June 1924 at His Majesty's Theatre conducted by Eugene Goossens.

[78] Rosenthal, *Two Centuries of Opera at Covent Garden*, p. 413.

[79] *The Times*, 8 January 1923.

[80] *Opera*, January 1955, p. 23.

[81] O'Connor, *The Pursuit of Perfection*, p. 149.

[82] *The Times*, 15 May 1923.

[83] *Musical Times*, 1 July 1924, p. 646.

How different this must have been to her original interpretation of Mélisande. For a start she was now thirty-six, much more worldly-wise, no longer the tiny, innocent girl of 1908. Perhaps even more difficult to cope with was that the opera was sung in the English translation of Edwin Evans, so her part had to be completely relearnt.[84]

This was not the first time the opera had been produced in English, for in 1913 the Denhof Opera Company had included it in a season of mainly German operas in Birmingham and Manchester. Mélisande on that occasion was sung by Beryl Freeman. Walter Hyde had sung Pelléas, so was familiar with the role he was now to play in partnership with Maggie. The *Times* reviewer complained after attending that original Denhof production in the English translation by Henry Chapman, 'Debussy might cry out, like Mélisande. "Oh! ne me touchez pas," and no one could blame him, because the union between Maeterlinck's prose and his music is part of the very essence of the opera as a work of art.'[85] It was also unfortunate that Golaud (Herr von Pick) had a strong German accent and an 'inferior German tradition of declamation'! One critic regarded Denhof's fight for opera in English as 'a serious failure', exclaiming, 'No man with any sort of sense of humour could conduct *Pelléas et Mélisande* and hear it chaunted in English, as if it were a good old home-made oratorio without serious risk of a mental cataclysm, and disastrous results to everybody concerned.'[86]

The *Musical Times* considered Edwin Evans's English version a unique and risky undertaking, owing to the huge verbal importance of the vocal part. The question was posed whether it was manageable at all to translate *Pelléas*, for in English, more than any other translated opera, it became something quite different from the original, losing its childlike simplicity, thus radically altering the nature of its characters. The notes being sung had only an artificial association with their new text, creating difficulties for the singers and leading the audience then to seek interest in the music rather than the words. The quality of Maggie's singing was not commented on, but her appearance was pleasing, for she 'might have been picked by a painter as a model for Mélisande.' The 'stage pictures' by Oliver Bernard, however, were deemed harsh and lacking any dreamily romantic quality.[87] The *Times*

---

84 Andrew Clements in *Opera*, February 1991, p. 140, comments on the 'almost insurmountable problem' of producing *Pelléas* in English. 'Even the most careful translation can only render vocal lines so wedded to the rhythms and inflection of French prosody into English with enormous difficulty and unavoidable losses of expressive stress, weight and colour.'

85 *The Times*, 20 September 1913, p. 8.

86 *The New Age*, 13 November 1913.

87 *Musical Times*, 1 July 1924, p. 648.

found that not having Maeterlinck's actual words was 'the one little hitch of the evening'. Despite this, the unique qualities of Debussy's masterpiece wove their spell, although Maggie's performance did not receive unadulterated praise, for it was reported that her singing varied in quality. 'The scene with the ring was natural and vocal enough, but at other times the voice was hard and matter of fact and the action too conventional. She kept the thing moving, however.'[88] Certainly, listening to this English version can't have helped the London audience to appreciate the work. Judgements on its true merits were still being formed.

In 1924 Maggie was persuaded to perform in Mendelssohn's oratorio *Elijah* at the opening of the Norwich Festival on 30 October. Sir Henry Wood was impressed, her interpretation of the soprano part remaining one of his outstanding memories of the whole festival. She had initially been doubtful about taking on the role, regarding herself as an opera singer, but agreed to do so if Sir Henry taught her the part. As ever, she must have been the perfect pupil, for 'her rendering of the widow's part was a lesson in interpretation. I wish every oratorio singer could have heard her performance.'[89]

Sherwin, meanwhile, was becoming more and more of a liability. His illness worsened and he needed more and more medication. He drank when alone and he drank with friends. He was also prone to giving away large sums of money and was desperate for company, whether hers or that of their servants. Their relationship was unbalanced, she being the stronger, older partner. Whilst internal investigations had confirmed that Maggie would be unable to conceive a child, she at least had an interest in life which she could turn to in order to keep happy: her singing. She took to singing in the house, then singing to Sherwin's father, Walter, who in 1928 became seriously ill. He still lived in Woolley Hall, and would send for Maggie to sing to him, whether inside the house or outside in the grounds. Sherwin, however, could not stand this, particularly her high notes. He would escape, perhaps even, as Maggie suspected, to another woman.[90]

To whom could Maggie turn for company and friendship? Perhaps she would have interpreted it as fate again that brought her together with a young Jewish woman called Grace Vernon who lived in nearby Maidenhead. Grace, known as Gay, was in the opposite situation to Maggie, having been married, not to a younger, but to a much older man, Harry Vernon. She had never got over the shock of her wedding night and had a horror of sex with Harry, although they did eventually have a son. Gay was a composer

[88] *The Times*, 7 June 1924.

[89] Wood, *My Life of Music*, p. 337.

[90] O'Connor, *The Pursuit of Perfection*, p. 154.

of musical-comedy songs and proved to be an excellent accompanist for Maggie, so here was something else to draw them together. When she came to Woolley Grange in the afternoons, they could share their miseries, but more importantly, they could also make music together. Their partnership was to last many years.

With her own personal, sympathetic accompanist Maggie could now find solace in Debussy's songs, wringing the emotion out of the words and music. This constant practice and desire to sing led to successful broadcasts with the BBC. The first took place in 1927, then there were two light opera broadcasts in 1928. This was also the year that on 29 October *Pelléas and Mélisande* was broadcast for the first time on the BBC Daventry Experimental Service in a production in English with Maggie as Mélisande, Walter Hyde as Pelléas and Roy Henderson as Golaud. It received its second broadcast in 1930 on the London Regional Service with Percy Pitt conducting, one of the first studio concerts carried out in less than perfect physical conditions in 'Studio 10', a disused, rat-infested, but acoustically excellent warehouse in Commercial Road in the East End.[91]

Maggie's domestic circumstances were becoming increasingly stressful. In 1930 her father-in-law Walter Cottingham died, and she and Sherwin moved into Woolley Hall, but their relationship was stormy and even violent, for now there certainly was another woman in his life, whom he had met in 1929. Maggie's fits of anger even erupted in public. Sherwin could not take any more of this, and she could not stand his drinking and infidelity. Divorce proceedings were instigated, and on 7 May 1931 a notice appeared in *The Times* reporting the granting of a decree nisi on the grounds of Sherwin's adultery with Gladys Mary Levy.[92] Fortunately for Maggie, she was granted a generous settlement, a tax-free sum of £2,000 per year, so money worries should not trouble her in the future. She could also continue living at Woolley Grange.

Maggie was not to remain alone for long in the large house. Her friend Grace Vernon, now free of her husband, who had gone to America, moved into a flat in the stable block. Nor was Maggie willing to sit at home living off her divorce settlement. She had to resume her career and fulfil her need to sing in public.

---

[91] As described in Michael Kennedy, *Adrian Boult* (London, 1987), p. 151.
[92] An arranged co-respondent. Sherwin married Vera Owen on 11 December 1931.

16 *Georgette Leblanc's Rise and Fall (1911-19)*

EORGETTE LEBLANC at the end of November 1911 was about to
embark for America to bring *Pelléas et Mélisande* both as an opera
and as a play to the American public. In October 1911 reports had
appeared in the press that Maeterlinck would go to America to watch her,
but would travel incognito. Henry Russell had thought this up as a good
publicity wheeze, for realising Bostonians were apathetic about Debussy's
masterpiece, he had to promote the work energetically. He invented a
story that the author had wagered him a thousand dollars that he would
go to Boston and back without being recognised.[1] Russell even claimed it
was practically certain that Debussy would be at the performance of the
opera. How annoyed Maeterlinck was when an American reporter suddenly accosted him as he was alighting from the train at the Gare de Lyon
in Paris to question him about his forthcoming visit to the States. He made
his objections to being interviewed very plain, admitted he would pay a visit
to America sometime, but meanwhile, 'My wife [*sic*] does all the talking and
she is always right.'[2] The experiment of putting on both the opera and the
play of *Pelléas et Mélisande* might prove interesting to the public, but not
to him, and his well known attitude to music, 'quite unnecessary noise', was
repeated. That same evening the reporter found Georgette in her Paris studio inspecting the new costumes for the performances, which she said she
had designed herself, following Maeterlinck's conceptions. She was anxious
to show her enthusiasm not only for promoting Maeterlinck's plays, but for
studying American women, and declared that she believed that American
methods of educating young girls were far ahead of the French. She also
stated that she was no feminist. Whilst she did not condemn the activities of
the suffragettes, she found it difficult to understand how intellectual women
could worry about a vote. 'The sphere of women who confine themselves to
being just women appears to me much wider than that of those who meddle
in politics.'[3]

On 11 December 1911 Georgette arrived in New York on the *Olympic*,
having left Maeterlinck to his young mistress, Renée. She was wearing a

---

[1] *New York Times*, 8 October 1911.
[2] *New York Times*, 19 December 1911.
[3] *New York Times*, 19 December 1911.

leopard coat, a brown beaver hat trimmed with parrots' wings and a long
veil of brown chiffon. Her huge diamond, worn in Paris in her younger days,
'glittered like a headlight from her forehead'.[4] She was in the company of
Walter Straram, André Caplet's assistant, and Vanni-Marcoux, the bass who
had sung Arkel in *Pelléas et Mélisande* at Covent Garden in 1909 and was
now about to sing Golaud. The world of opera singers was a small one and
it would have been fascinating to hear what they talked about during these
lengthy crossings. Marcoux will appear in the following chapter crossing the
Atlantic with Mary Garden. What did the women say about each other? We
will never know. Mathilde was by Georgette's side, as ever, sharing her cabin
on board, ministering to her every need.

Georgette only spent one night in New York on her way to Boston, but
was caught by an interviewer for the *New York Times*. She was elusive about
Maeterlinck's whereabouts, expressed a desire to sing *Ariane et Barbe-Bleue*
in America, and was adamant that *Pelléas et Mélisande* was Maeterlinck's
greatest play. Most interestingly, however, she makes the statement that she
had seen both Mary Garden and Maggie Teyte in Debussy's opera in Paris.
Her opinion was that 'Miss Garden was ever so much better than Miss Teyte,
who seemed to be entirely lacking in atmosphere.'[5]

On their arrival in New York, Georgette and her companions went
straight away to Boston, leaving the press to search in vain for Maeterlinck,
who had stubbornly remained on the other side of the Atlantic. At long last,
ten years after being deprived of singing the role in Paris, at the age of nearly
forty-three, Georgette sang Mélisande at the Boston Opera House on 10
January 1912 in a production of *Pelléas et Mélisande* conducted by André
Caplet which she found incomparably beautiful. Pelléas was Jean Riddez,
Arkel was Edward Lankow and Maria Gay sang Geneviève. 'The perfect
Yniold'[6] was Bernice Fisher, and the Doctor was José Mardones. The experience was well worth waiting for, for she was overcome both by the production and by the music. She adored the settings and the lighting. 'It was only
on this stage that I ever saw the lighting as Maeterlinck had imagined it', she
wrote.[7]

This was the first season of designer Joseph Urban with the Boston
Opera company, whose sets Maeterlinck had already praised when Henry
Russell showed him models at Saint-Wandrille. His drawings of dense for-
ests, the medieval stone castle, the caves, all with striking contrast of light

---

[4] Eaton, *The Boston Opera Company*, p. 134.

[5] *New York Times*, 1 January 1912.

[6] Eaton, *The Boston Opera Company*, p. 121.

[7] Leblanc, *Souvenirs: My Life with Maeterlinck*, p. 268.

and dark, can be seen today in the collection of Joseph Urban Papers 1893–1998 at Columbia University.[8] However, it is clear from reviews that some felt 'the executive hand of Mme Maeterlinck' throughout the evening',[9] the atmosphere of the sets being recognised as characteristic of her home, Saint-Wandrille.

Though the lighting effects were particularly praised by some, others found them unsubtle, with 'glaring contrasts in black shadow and high-lights'.[10] An innovation for this Opera House was introduced: in order to reduce the noise of scene shifting during Debussy's musical interludes, the scenery was mounted on platforms with rubber wheels. To accommodate the amount of scenery required on the floorspace available, the area visible to the audience was confined within a narrower span than usual and surrounded by a framework of cloth graduating into darker colours. This formed a shadowy border where the subsequent set could be made ready. This more intimate setting was particularly suited to the letter scene (Act I scene 2) and Mélisande's death scene (Act V), although some found it too constricting for the castle exterior in Act I and the scene of Pelléas's murder (Act IV scene 4). After the curtain rose, each picture was gradually illuminated, and at the end the lighting faded, heightening the effect of a mystical world.[11]

First Georgette had to wait behind the curtain on the stage, kneeling by the fountain whilst the orchestra played the overture. The intensity of the sensations she experienced remained imprinted on her mind as she listened in the dark:

> Feeling very small, crouching over a zinc disk which shimmered like water from a reflected light, I could at the same time understand, analyse and enjoy the sensitive beauty of this overture as I have never been able to do in other conditions ... Hidden from all eyes, frozen in immobility, after a few moments my knees trembled so uncontrollably that I was almost forced to sit down on the edge of the zinc lake. My hands became icy, as if resting on snow. Penetrating with Debussy to the very soul of *Pelléas et Mélisande*, I forgot my own presence, I seemed to leave my body; it required the brutality of the footlights to bring me back to the role.[12]

The critics were curious to note the differences between her interpretation

---

[8] http://www.columbia.edu/cu/lweb/eresources/archives/rbml/urban/html/sub-626. html. See the section *Pelléas et Mélisande* in Metropolitan Opera 1917–1933, which were virtually the same designs.

[9] *Boston Daily Globe*, 11 January 1912.

[10] Eaton, *The Boston Opera Company*, p. 218.

[11] *Boston Daily Globe*, 11 January 1912.

[12] Leblanc, *Souvenirs: My Life with Maeterlinck*, pp. 269–70.

and Mary Garden's. Whilst Georgette preserved the naïveté and simplicity of a childlike Mélisande, it was noticed that her voice no longer had the freshness of youth and did not show a wide range of dynamics or colour. As one might expect, however, it was the expressive way in which she postured and walked across the stage that received positive praise. A review in the *New York Times* conveys an impression of Georgette's appearance.[13] All her costumes were white. Her hair – a reddish gold – streamed down her back below the waist line. Her principal gesture was one of 'supplication'. Her crying was natural, and her singing – 'what little there was of it' – was described as being that of a pure soprano of high range, but of limited power. She was clearly in 'the atmosphere'. Whether the audience could get into the atmosphere was questioned, for they lamented the absence of 'lyrics'.

Henry Russell was still suffering problems, for his publicity stunt packed the opera house as crowds tried to see the mysterious Maeterlinck. He was speechless when at the end of the opera dozens of people asked for their money back. They had thought that *Pelléas* and *Mélisande* was a double bill like *Pagliacci* and *Cavalleria rusticana*, and were feeling short changed![14] However, just as at the original performance in Paris, opinion was divided on the opera. Despite some criticisms, there were curtain calls after the various acts right up to Georgette's fourth and last performance on 22 January.

Georgette does not comment in her *Souvenirs* about her performance in the play, as opposed to the opera in Boston, showing how much more meaningful to her was the latter. Boston had already seen the play on 12 April 1902 when Mrs Patrick Campbell had acted Mélisande there with Fauré's incidental music, as in her 1898 London performance. Now on 30 January 1912 Georgette was to perform the play in French at the Boston Opera House. She had brought with her two of her cast from Saint-Wandrille: her Pelléas, René Maupré and Golaud, Jean Durozat. Yniold was played by Henry Russell's son, Sheridan. Georgette's performance was not praised as highly as that of Maupré, whose youthful and poetic interpretation took on a tragic intensity. Apparently, Georgette's Mélisande was very similar to that in the opera, slightly more obvious and accentuated. Her performance contained moments 'which invite consideration but do not have emotional appeal', was one view.[15] Fauré's music, conducted by Caplet, was found 'strangely diatonic after the exotic and fugitive character of that by Debussy.' This opportunity to compare the play and the opera served to emphasise yet again how closely

[13] *New York Times*, 11 January 1912. See also illus. 31.
[14] Henry Russell, *The Passing Show* (London 1926), p. 165.
[15] *Boston Daily Globe*, 31 January 1912.

wedded one to the other were the text of Maeterlinck and the music of Debussy.

Georgette's voice at about the time of her Boston performance as Mélisande can be heard on CDs reproducing recordings made in about 1912 by Columbia, not singing Debussy, but the arias 'Bois épais' from *Amadis de Gaule* by Lully,[16] and 'L'Amour est une vertu rare' from *Thaïs* by Massenet,[17] both to an orchestral accompaniment. The Lully is from a different era from that of Debussy, and the style, of course, differs to that in which his aria would be performed today. She takes liberties with the speed, and the interpretation is full and romantic. The intonation is true, despite some vibrato and marked downward portamenti, and the phrasing is expressive. The lower tones are particularly rich. It is a thoughtful and lyrical performance. The Massenet aria can be compared directly to a recording of the same work by Mary Garden, also made in 1912 for Columbia.[18] In her performance, Georgette demonstrates a full tone, with rich chest tones and an expressive higher register, which sounds quite unforced. Her voice is clear, the pitch is accurate and the interpretation romantic and sensitive. In comparison, Mary Garden's voice sounds brighter and more brittle, particularly in the top register. The highest notes soar above the orchestra. Here she too slides downwards with some portamenti and occasionally the intonation is slightly flat, possibly for expressive purposes. As in the aria from Massenet's *Sapho* discussed in the Introduction,[19] Georgette Leblanc's voice, whilst of a different quality, compares favourably with Mary Garden's in these two recordings.

How bitterly Georgette resented the fact that Maeterlinck made no attempt to enquire after her progress in America. Perhaps he was too preoccupied with other matters to care much about what was happening to her. He had young, adoring Renée with him and, what is more, had come to worldwide attention when it was announced on 9 November 1911 that he had won the Nobel Prize for Literature. Even the glory of the award was not enticing enough to persuade him to overcome his dislike of travel, and pretending he was in poor health he did not go to Stockholm to receive it. He would wait for public celebrations in his native country on 8 May 1912. He had also moved house again – from Grasse to Nice where the climate was

16 CD included with the book *Divas* by André Tubeuf (Paris, 2005). Original disc: Columbia MX 19763, as catalogued in the British Library Sound Archive, where a copy is held: 1LP0143717.

17 *Opera.be: The Yves Becko Collection*, King Baudouin Foundation (2006), CD 2, track 8. Original disc: Columbia A1153–19755.

18 *Opera in Chicago*, vol. 1: *Edith Mason and Mary Garden*, Symposium 1136 (1992), track 18.

19 See Introduction, p. 5.

preferable to that of Stockholm in November. There he bought a villa which
he called Les Abeilles (The Bees).

Georgette's anxiety as she envisaged him in the arms of Renée made
her want to return to France as soon as possible. First, however, she met an
extraordinary personality: Helen Keller, the gifted deaf and blind woman
about whom she wrote a book, published two years later in English as *The
Girl Who Found the Bluebird*.[20] With Maeterlinck's fame at its height, she
was also in demand as a speaker about the man she knew so intimately. Her
popularity meant that she could have stayed on in the States for after appearing in Boston she sang in New York drawing rooms for the Vanderbilts, the
Belmonts, the Duke and Duchess of Connaught and others. She believed
that if she had remained five or six weeks longer she could have brought
home a small fortune.[21] The press were certainly interested enough in her to
want to publish her views on women at home and abroad. She found little
difference between 'intelligent' women in any country, but had little time for
'frivolous' women. Young American girls were much better off than French
girls as they had so much more liberty. She approved of the idea that women
here could 'do what they want'. She liked their understanding, presumably
of sexual matters: 'it is better to understand when one is young. French girls
know nothing until after marriage, and after marriage is often too late.' A
flattering account was given of the clothes Georgette designed and made for
herself, which were soft and clinging, showing every line of her uncorseted
figure and leaving her throat uncovered. She explained about her book, *Le
Choix de la vie*, ensuring that it was realised she was not only a writer, but
acted, painted and was a sculptor. 'And she makes a wonderful cake', suggested Mathilde Deschamps – perhaps not a skill Georgette would have
emphasised![22]

She was again brought to the attention of the public as a writer in her
own right when Montrose J. Moses, the very author who had penned the
introduction to an American edition of the play *Pelléas et Mélisande* in
1908,[23] published the results of a lengthy interview about *Le Choix de la vie*.[24]
Georgette emphasised that she wanted the experiences described in the book
to be of use to other women, seeing the feminine quality in her writing as
the only quality which was truly her own, the only difference really existing
between Maeterlinck and herself. Georgette was seen as claiming for woman

---

[20] Georgette Leblanc, *The Girl who Found the Blue Bird: A Visit to Helen Keller*,
     translated by Alexander Teixeira de Mattos (New York, 1914).

[21] Leblanc, *Souvenirs: My Life with Maeterlinck*, p. 271.

[22] *New York Times*, 28 January 1912.

[23] See Chapter 14, p. 191.

[24] *New York Times*, 24 March 1912.

'a moral status on the same plane with that of men.' What must Maeterlinck have felt to read that 'more than once has Mme Maeterlinck confessed that upon *Le Choix de la vie* was most of the intent of *Ariane et Barbe-Bleue* based'? Again it was emphasised that Maeterlinck had benefited from his relationship with Georgette and that anyone reading this book would realise that 'his knowledge of women is largely the knowledge he has gained from her. The two reinforce each other; they are in perfect accord.' How ironic in view of Georgette's fully justified concerns about Maeterlinck's blossoming relationship with Renée.

So back she went across the Atlantic in time for 8 May 1912, the day of the grand ceremony to honour Maeterlinck's Nobel Prize which took place at the Théâtre Royal de la Monnaie in Brussels in the presence of King Albert and Queen Elizabeth. He was also made a 'Grand Officier de l'Ordre de Léopold'– and what role did Georgette play? Once again she acted Mélisande. What an ambassadress she had been for this play and for its author. Maeterlinck's fame had spread far and wide, way beyond his own country and in no small measure Georgette had contributed to his renown in France, Russia, London, Boston. Now he could reap the financial rewards of the Nobel Prize. What a contrast to Debussy, who, although he had been made a *Chevalier* de la Légion d'Honneur in 1903, never benefited from financial security in his own lifetime. Nor did he ever receive higher honours. His publisher and friend, Jacques Durand, was very disappointed that at a dinner to celebrate the one-hundredth performance of Debussy's opera, a government official gave a long speech declaring the artistic awareness of the Ministry of Arts, citing as proof the elevation of composers Vincent d'Indy and Charles Lecocq to the rank of *Officier* de la Légion d'Honneur. He then raised his glass and sat down again. No announcement of a similar promotion for Debussy was forthcoming. 'He had to die with just a simple ribbon!', complained Durand.[25]

That summer of 1912 was spent by Georgette and Maeterlinck at Saint-Wandrille, but by now Renée was a permanent third party in their relationship, a fact on which Georgette reflected bitterly. The *ménage à trois* had become insupportable.[26] The silence which at the beginning of their relationship had seemed so important to achieve, so symbolic in its implicit confirmation of a bond between two souls, had now been transformed into a different kind of silence: a divisive silence, isolating them one from the other. Maeterlinck had Renée, he had international fame, he enjoyed his

---

[25] Durand, *Quelques souvenirs d'un éditeur de musique*, p. 125. The *Officier* received a rosette to add to the simple red ribbon.

[26] Leblanc, *Souvenirs: My Life with Maeterlinck*, p. 283.

pleasurable life and routine of good food and company in Nice. His indiffer-
ence to Georgette meant that she was left restless and anguished.

It also meant that she sought the company of her older sister Jehanne, who
lived in a medieval château at Tancarville, not far from the Abbey of Saint-
Wandrille. Her brother Maurice, now the established author of the Arsène
Lupin books, was also there with his children. There was another young man
who took her eye – very young. This was Marcel L'Herbier, later to become a
renowned film director, who was courting Jehanne's daughter, Marcelle Prat.
The girl was sixteen; he was twenty-two years old. This young aesthete had
been at Georgette's performance of *Pelléas et Mélisande* at Saint-Wandrille
in 1910. He had already been involved in a dramatic scandal when a previous
fiancée had shot him, wounding his finger, then turned the pistol on herself,
scarring her face.[27] Although at Tancarville to court Marcelle, L'Herbier was
bowled over by Georgette and she, now forty-three, reciprocated his admiration to the extent that people started commenting on their relationship.
So that summer there was Maeterlinck visiting the abbey with the much
younger Renée, and Georgette flirting with the much younger Marcel, anxious not to let the older man have any inkling of this.

L'Herbier was to play a very significant role in her career some years later,
so it is fascinating to find not just this early link, but also to read film actor
Jaque Catelain's reminiscences of his first visit to young L'Herbier's apartment in Paris one Sunday afternoon in 1914 where he and his friends were
met by the sound of piano music: Mélisande's song from the tower in Act
III scene 1, 'Je suis née un dimanche, un dimanche à midi.' The pianist, so
captivated by Mélisande, did not hear their calls. When Catelain pushed
open a door he saw dim bluish light illuminating a fountain, ivy climbing
up trellises against the walls. Upon the exclamation of one of the company,
L'Herbier appeared and showed them into a room out of Arabian nights.
The lighting, the décor, the music, all were portents of the film career to
come.

Not long after this flirtation, however, a more significant relationship
developed between Georgette and the actor Roger Karl.[28] He was to become
a film star who lived to the grand old age of 102 (he died in 1984), and so had
plenty of time to write his own memoirs. His *Diary of a Man from Nowhere*,
written under the pseudonym Michel Balfort, contains several references to
Georgette, giving his own side of their affair.[29] Their first meeting had taken
place in 1908 in Brussels when the young man had first thrown violets to

---

[27] *Jaque Catelain présente Marcel L'Herbier* (Paris, 1950).
[28] Born Roger Trouvé.
[29] Michel Balfort, *Journal d'un homme de nulle part* (Paris, 1977).

her then gone backstage to express his admiration at a performance at La Monnaie.[30] Later, in 1913, having recognised the attractive young actor in Oscar Wilde's *Salomé* in Paris, Georgette persuaded Maeterlinck that Roger Karl should act the role of Lucius Vérus in his play *Marie-Magdeleine* which she was producing and in which she was to act the title role. She took Roger to Nice, where Maeterlinck invited Roger to participate with him in his favourite sport, boxing. The match took place with Georgette and Renée watching. Fortunately Maeterlinck did not bear a grudge at being soundly beaten. Later he was to describe Roger Karl as 'a poor actor, intelligent but with no talent'.[31] The première of *Marie-Magdeleine* took place in Nice on 18 March. There were three performances at the Théâtre de la Monnaie in Brussels on 13, 14 and 15 May, then the play was taken to Le Châtelet in Paris. Whilst Maeterlinck was becoming more and more absorbed by Renée, Georgette sought consolation in this man who 'offered me a motive for living again'.[32] By now, though, the web of relationships was becoming more and more complicated, for despite continuing to live with Renée, the author still assured Georgette, 'We will always love each other above all others and above everything.'[33]

On 4 August 1914 war was declared. On that day Georgette and Maeterlinck were at Saint-Wandrille, and to Georgette's horror, her partner's reaction was a dramatic one. He declared he was going immediately to Rouen to enlist in the Foreign Legion. She ran to her car and an hour later was at the office of the Mayor of Rouen to dissuade him from accepting Maeterlinck's services. There she was reassured that everything would be arranged. Georgette convinced herself that it was entirely her work that Maeterlinck was not accepted with alacrity as a fighting soldier and that he was persuaded instead to 'help with his pen', yet only one day after the declaration of war Maeterlinck wrote to his friend Gérard Harry that he regretted not being young enough to offer his services to the Belgian military authorities.[34] Indeed his pen was put to good use as he wrote numerous articles and delivered speeches in Italy, Spain and London during the war years.

In September they were advised to evacuate Saint-Wandrille and proceeded to make rapid preparations before the German occupation. Despite the tragedy of leaving their beloved abbey, Georgette found it amusing to watch Maeterlinck save his wine cellar. Clasping bottles to his breast, he

30 Benoît-Jeannin, *Georgette Leblanc*, p. 323.
31 Letter to Henry Russell: Stadsarchief Gent BC62.
32 Leblanc, *Souvenirs: My Life with Maeterlinck*, p. 296.
33 Leblanc, *Souvenirs: My Life with Maeterlinck*, p. 291.
34 Letter of 5 August to Gérard Harry published in *Le Soir*, 18 August 1914.

would murmur with a malicious smile: 'Here's another the Boche won't drink. See if they can find my Châteauneuf du Pape, 1902.'[35] After first taking refuge in Georgette's sister's château, in October they went via Paris back to Les Abeilles in Nice, accompanied inevitably by Renée.

When she heard that Roger Karl had been mobilised into the auxiliary army and was stationed near Angers, Georgette made the same strenuous efforts to maintain their relationship as she had done to keep in touch with Maeterlinck when he had been reluctant to travel to see her. Now, in wartime conditions, she made interminable rail journeys between Nice and Angers. Georgette realised Roger was dominated by his emotions, unable to emerge from a continual state of futile remorse and despair. The fact that she found ways of being at his side in such adverse circumstances should have reassured him, but Roger descended into deeper and deeper depression. She continued to support him when he was moved to a barracks in Paris, then worsening kidney trouble led to his being demobilised and finally discharged from the army in March 1916.

On reading Roger Karl's side of the relationship in his *Journal* one wonders if it was worth her making such an effort to keep up his morale. The very first entry, written on 29 April 1915 whilst in his barracks near Angers, contains an unflattering reference to Georgette as 'an elderly woman who has always been a flirt', bringing desperate passion to adventures of love.[36] Further entries swing between elation and bitterness, joy and despair. Roger was acutely sensitive to his surroundings and the weather. He was disgusted by the war and the destruction going on around him. He was well aware of Georgette's lesbian relationships, which caused him anguish, yet years after the end of their affair he would look back on their times together with nostalgia, recalling days such as those in a little room in a hotel in Saumur where he and Georgette took their meals. He referred affectionately to such rooms as 'rooms of intelligence, cells full of thoughts which she stirred up there'.[37] He loved her black velvet coats, her strange hats,[38] but hated having once spotted her at a production of *Oedipus* in the company of another woman, who had 'the vicious face of a lesbian'.[39]

Georgette's travels backwards and forwards to Angers from 1914 onwards must have been difficult not just logistically but financially. Her stage work was in abeyance, as Maeterlinck's plays were performed very rarely during

---

[35] Leblanc, *Souvenirs: My Life with Maeterlinck*, p. 300.

[36] Balfort, *Journal d'un homme de nulle part*, p. 24.

[37] Balfort, *Journal d'un homme de nulle part*, p. 196.

[38] Balfort, *Journal d'un homme de nulle part*, p. 34.

[39] Balfort, *Journal d'un homme de nulle part*, p. 33.

the war, although a programme shows her appearing with Maeterlinck in London on 7 July 1915 at Queen's Hall. There they both gave an evening concert and lecture in aid of the Employment of Belgian Women in Great Britain and Comfort for Belgian Soldiers at the Front.[40]

1915 also appears to have brought Georgette's first entry into the world of film. That year, the Société française des Films l'Éclair made two films with which her name is associated. *Macbeth* and *Pelléas et Mélisande*,[41] the plays she had produced at Saint-Wandrille, but, frustratingly, information on these is minimal. They were not produced commercially.

Further anxiety was caused to Georgette when in 1917 to her horror she discovered that she had been duped of her money for some years by her close companion Mathilde Deschamps, who had been at her side and looking after her financial affairs since 1898. A wealthy industrialist, Henry Deutsch de la Meurthe, had manipulated Mathilde into appropriating Georgette's money and keeping for herself the gains made on the stock exchange. Now financial disaster beckoned.[42] Not only was Georgette now bankrupt, but she had hoped to play a part in a film, *Le Torrent*, being directed by her old flame, Marcel L'Herbier, the young man she had almost enticed away from her niece, when sadly she succumbed to a lung infection and lost this opportunity. However, having been sent to the spa town of Royat in the Puy-de-Dôme for treatment, she continued corresponding with thirty-five-year-old L'Herbier, who was beginning to make his name in this world of films.

During her convalescence her tension over her relationships grew. Her relationship with Roger Karl was at an end; her constant companion Mathilde had deceived her; Maeterlinck no longer loved her. Early in 1918, when she and Maeterlinck were dining out in the company of Paris Singer (brother of Princesse Edmond de Polignac), and the dancer Isadora Duncan, Georgette suddenly found herself crying uncontrollably. Singer, worried, questioned her, but Maeterlinck interrupted. 'Never mind – it's nothing – absolutely nothing.' Georgette rose and left the room. 'Nothing, nothing ... there was nothing the matter. My great love was lost and I did not want to live.'[43] When they returned home and climbed the steep path up to Maeterlinck's villa, Georgette identified herself with another lost soul: she stumbled at every step, 'bewildered as Mélisande in the forest'. When she tried to initiate a dialogue with Maeterlinck about her troubles, his response

[40] Programme in AML, Brussels, Georgette Leblanc Collection, 499/118.

[41] 'Dictionnaire du cinéma français des années vingt', *1895*, no. 33 (2001). Online version accessed 26 June 2006: http://1895.revues.org/document96.html.

[42] Benoît-Jeannin, *Georgette Leblanc*, p. 350.

[43] Leblanc, *Souvenirs: My Life with Maeterlinck*, p. 306.

was curt. There was no point in talking. She should be able to manage her own life.[44]

Georgette returned alone to Paris, and in March moved into a flat at 95 rue Charles-Laffitte, near her sister Jehanne and her nieces Marcelle and Marie-Louise. There she earned money by giving singing lessons. She also finished a book she had been working on about the dogs she and Maeterlinck had shared, *Nos Chiens*.[45] This must have made her feel nostalgic, for it contains touching insights into the domestic life of the couple in their various residences in the past, such as references to Bamboula, their black cook, Maeterlinck's nurturing of his kitchen garden and his roller-skating round the abbey. The text was accompanied by thirty-two drawings of dogs by its author.

A further initiative was an attempt to bring *Pelléas et Mélisande* to a new audience. The play opened on 10 February 1918 at the Odéon. Fourteen performances took place with Fauré's incidental music, played by the Orchestre des Concerts Monteux. Although this was at Georgette's instigation, she did not act herself. Still she was determined to keep Maeterlinck's work in the public eye and had managed to convince a young actor, Pierre Bertin, of the originality of the play, of which his generation was virtually unaware. Bertin directed. Two friends of his, Louis Aragon and André Breton, were in the audience. *Pelléas et Mélisande* opened to a full house. However, the performance had its ridiculous moments. Mélisande's hair was too short, and Bertin as Pelléas had to pretend to cling onto it. Reminiscent of reactions at the first performance of Debussy's opera, the audience laughed at certain points, in particular when Golaud lifted Yniold onto his shoulders to spy on Pelléas and Mélisande. Aragon met Georgette afterwards in Bertin's dressing room, where he found her clearly annoyed by the portrayal of Mélisande by Mme Guereau. Aragon, Breton and Bertin all declared themselves disappointed and disillusioned. Maeterlinck's symbolism struck no chord with them.[46]

At this point Georgette suffered a bombshell. She had the opportunity to help Henry Russell to organise a tour of America for Maeterlinck on which she was to accompany him. During the war, Russell and his American wife, Donna, owned a farm near Monte Carlo to which Maeterlinck had paid frequent visits and where he had already been broached about the idea. Before their intended departure together for the States, Georgette arranged to travel to Nice on 16 December 1918, but out of the blue, three days previously,

---

[44] Leblanc, *Souvenirs: My Life with Maeterlinck*, p. 310.

[45] Leblanc, *Nos chiens*.

[46] Louis Aragon, *Projet d'histoire littéraire contemporaine* (Paris, 1994), p. 13.

she received a telegram from Renée Dahon instructing her not to come. 'Maeterlinck furious against you. He knows everything. R.' Georgette could not understand this, ignored the order and sent a telegram to Maeterlinck to confirm her arrival. The next morning she received a reply: 'Useless to come. Everything finished between us. Maeterlinck.'[47]

Georgette travelled to Nice nevertheless, and upon her arrival was informed by the cook that for several days Maeterlinck had been carrying his revolver. Her reaction to the melodramatic situation was to fall ill. Meanwhile Maeterlinck, imagining that Georgette wanted to kill Renée, sent her to a hotel out of Georgette's reach, then he too left the house.

Only two months later, on 15 February 1919, Maeterlinck married Renée Dahon, but did not tell Georgette. This lack of communication would have been most surprising news to the reporter who gave an account to the Associated Press of Maeterlinck's 'divorce' from Georgette five weeks earlier and subsequent marriage.[48] Perhaps it was Henry Russell who was trying to put the record straight and make the whole process seem respectable, for it is he who is quoted as having known of the author's attraction to Renée Dahon since her performance in *The Bluebird*.

In March Maeterlinck wrote to Georgette, not even mentioning his marriage, but baldly accusing her of having lied to him all her life. He forbade her to return to Les Abeilles in Nice, but typically, perhaps feeling unable to banish her completely from his life, he ended the note: 'As time passes we will see what we can rebuild on the ruins.'[49] Inevitably it was these final words which gave Georgette the courage to pursue the possibility that she might yet be able to see him again. She sent him a letter including the question, 'Would you like to see me sometimes?', arranged a visit to Nice where she stayed with a friend, then went up to the villa. Maeterlinck and Renée were out, but on a table she found a letter addressed to her. Upon opening it, she was amazed to read of Maeterlinck's astonishment that she had gone to stay elsewhere, for, as he said, 'Your place is here'. As for his marriage, he referred to it as an insignificant piece of paper.

How could she want to return to a man with such a fickle nature? How could she still want to rebuild any sort of relationship with him? Yet she was tempted to take him at his word. How she tossed and turned, arguing within herself for and against 'rebuilding on the ruins'. Why had she accepted the presence of that third person in the house? What had contributed to this disintegration of her character? 'Was it the effect of literature, a false

47 Leblanc, *Souvenirs: My Life with Maeterlinck*, p. 319.
48 *New York Times*, 8 March 1919.
49 Leblanc, *Souvenirs: My Life with Maeterlinck*, p. 330.

ethical standard, the misty thinking of the symbolist era?', she asked herself. 'Not only that. It was rather, a retrogression of attitude. I had become like Mélisande – a child.'[50] Once more, that enigma of a creature became the point of reference for a moment of crisis in a grown woman's life. Georgette finally made her decision, surely the only decision that could be reached, and wrote to Maeterlinck rejecting any suggestion of a reunion. They never met again.

Maeterlinck gave his side of the story to Henry Russell in a letter of 1925,[51] telling him how Georgette had persuaded him to give Roger Karl, whom he described as 'intelligent but lacking talent', a part in his play *Marie-Magdeleine*. It was not until long after this that he had received proof through letters and tales of others of her infidelity, even scandalous behaviour in Nice, and since then he had received revelations from all around about Georgette's numerous lovers.

Now, to add insult to injury, Maeterlinck sold her beloved Saint-Wandrille without informing her. She had lost not just her lover of over twenty years, but her adored abbey, her source of inspiration and fount of so much happiness.

It has to be acknowledged that Georgette had benefited professionally from her association with Maeterlinck, even though she wanted to be considered as completely independent of him. Their names were linked whether she encouraged that or not. But whatever Maeterlinck may have claimed to the contrary, he too had benefited. Others have realised that 'without her the writer's literary course would have been charted across different seas.'[52] Yet it was entirely his own decision to be taken under Georgette's wing and to allow her to spread his name far and wide by her performances and recitals. Their personalities were different, but both profited from the association. Theirs had been essentially a symbiotic relationship, each feeding off the other.

Georgette returned to Paris alone and with no money. She gave singing lessons again, but realised how problematical her career as an artist would be in future, as it would be almost impossible to separate her name from Maeterlinck's.[53] Her family tried to help. Georgette's brother-in-law and her brother Maurice managed to negotiate a monthly allowance from Maeterlinck amounting to 1,000 francs a year and the rights to *Sœur Béatrice*, which Albert Wolff set to music. However, all this came to an end when

---

[50] Leblanc, *Souvenirs: My Life with Maeterlinck*, p. 338.

[51] 26 November 1925, Stadsarchief Gent BC62.

[52] Halls, *Maurice Maeterlinck*, p. 122.

[53] Leblanc, *Souvenirs: My Life with Maeterlinck*, p. 342.

Georgette went to Belgium and gave a series of concert-lectures on the Belgian poets, Van Lerberghe, Verhaeren and, of course, Maeterlinck. Soon afterwards she received a letter from Maeterlinck saying that he considered her programme in Belgium was exploiting his name illegally and that had he known earlier, he would have stopped her allowance. That was to be the last letter she ever received from him.

At the end of 1919 Maeterlinck travelled to America with his wife Renée to give the lecture tour which Georgette had helped to plan before his marriage, and was now prevented from attending. He was to inaugurate a 'Blue Bird Campaign for Happiness': for a whole week New York department stores featured Blue Bird window displays. As he sailed towards the Statue of Liberty, aeroplanes of the Vanderbilt Squadron flew above with blue-painted wings. However, he had great difficulty preparing his speeches for he hardly spoke any English, so Henry Russell's son, Sheridan, not only gave him pronunciation lessons, but invented his own system of phonetic transcription, writing out every word in this way. Perhaps due to Maeterlinck's complete lack of any musical ear, the task proved almost impossible. 'You might as well get me to try to lift an elephant as to try to teach him English', declared Sheridan later. Tellingly, back in 1908 an American journalist visiting Saint-Wandrille had already noted that although the author read English with perfect ease, he told her that he was very diffident about his pronunciation, and would only speak English to Germans![54]

Lionised by New York society, the author found the rich and fashionable surroundings alien to his simple tastes. On 2 January 1920 he gave his first lecture (on 'The immortality of the soul') to about 3,000 people, but within a few minutes was asked to speak louder. Others said he was speaking loudly enough, but his English was incomprehensible. The chairman then ruled that the lecture should continue in French with someone translating it into English at intervals. Unfortunately Maeterlinck had only brought with him the phonetic version, so Sheridan Russell was sent to fetch the original text from his hotel.[55] The situation went from bad to worse. As it was cold, Maeterlinck suggested Russell should take his wife's fur coat for protection. At the door, Russell was stopped and questioned about the coat by a policeman![56]

Sam Goldwyn wrote a most unflattering account of Maeterlinck's American visit. Whilst other sources report the glory of the author and the success of the 'Blue Bird Campaign for Happiness', Goldwyn was obviously

54 *New York Times*, 20 September 1908.

55 Russell, *The Passing Show*, pp. 225–7.

56 Halls, *Maurice Maeterlinck*, p. 128.

not enamoured either of the author or of Renée. He expressed some sympathy for Georgette's situation, since she had been supplanted by 'the pretty little wife', and ridiculed Maeterlinck's delivery of his lecture, which many New Yorkers, who 'went to pray and stayed to laugh', still remembered.[57] Even so, this did not stop Goldwyn from recognising a possible pecuniary advantage in procuring the services of the distinguished foreigner. He arranged a meeting and as Maeterlinck entered the room was struck, as many before him, by his placid face, 'round and calm as a lake on a still August day'. Through an interpreter he explained he was anxious to procure exclusive rights to Maeterlinck's works and named a number of American writers with whom he had previously arranged contracts. The author clearly recognised none of the names, responding with a vacant smile. Only when Goldwyn offered him several thousand dollars did Maeterlinck's face brighten up. Goldwyn then organised a special train to carry Maeterlinck through America. He was pleased with the resulting publicity, but what a waste of time and effort for the film industry! One can only guess at the horror the author was experiencing at the amount of travel, life in the goldfish bowl of public appearances, lack of his beloved routine of meals and exercise. The author's first attempt at a film scenario, *The Blue Feathers*, was rejected at once. Then he tried a love story, but as Goldwyn reports, 'The type was anything but censorproof.' Maeterlinck was bewildered by this attitude. 'You asked me to write a love-story', he remonstrated, 'and then you object because my hero or my heroine is married. Yet how can you write about love when you have no triangle?'

Goldwyn was also amused to see Renée, so much younger than her husband, playing tennis on the court at the rear of Maeterlinck's Hollywood house, wearing not the customary skirt, but bloomers. There was also a report that she had asked if there might be some sort of employment for her in film, no matter how small. She would have liked some money of her own.[58]

Georgette, cast aside by the author, could certainly have done with some money. At Easter 1919 her book *Nos Chiens* had been published,[59] but was virtually ignored by the Parisian press. That same year, on 22 May 1919, the opera *Pelléas et Mélisande* had received its one hundred and eleventh performance at the Opéra-Comique with Marguerite Carré singing Mélisande. Debussy had died of rectal cancer on 25 March 1918. France offered no opportunities. Where did Georgette's future lie? Surely she must make a fresh start. Where else but back in America?

57 Samuel Goldwyn, *Behind the Screen* (New York, 1923), p. 249.
58 Goldwyn, *Behind the Screen*, p. 254.
59 See n. 45 above.

17 *Mary Garden Becomes Director (1912–31)*

*M*ARY GARDEN'S American career continued to thrive following her appearance in Massenet's *Cendrillon* in Philadelphia and Chicago at the end of 1911 with Maggie Teyte, the press picking up every little incident on and off stage. In February 1912 she sang *Carmen* at the Metropolitan Opera House, New York, under Campanini. There she also sang *Cendrillon* with Maggie Teyte on 20 February 1912 but not with as much success as in Chicago, followed by *Thaïs* and *Le Jongleur de Notre-Dame*. All three of our Mélisandes were now therefore in America at the same time. Indeed, on 30 March Mary Garden took over the role of Mélisande in the very Boston production of *Pelléas et Mélisande* that Georgette Leblanc had initiated in January 1912. Instead of Vanni-Marcoux, Golaud was sung by Hector Dufranne, but Pelléas was still sung by Jean Riddez. Here Mary made plain her dislike of the enclosed, boxed-in sets designed by Urban, complaining she could hardly turn round in them. She did not make André Caplet's job easy as she flounced in and out, but the eventual result was described as 'magical perfection'.[1] Unfortunately for Georgette, it was always Mary's Mélisande which would be linked with Debussy's princess.

Mary's next milestone was a contract with the Columbia Phonograph Company of New York. In May she recorded her old favourite, the aria from *Louise*, 'Depuis le jour', as well as excerpts from *Thaïs*,[2] *Le Jongleur de Notre-Dame*, and two Act I soprano arias from *Traviata*. The American critic Richard D. Fletcher, who had seen her performing the roles on stage, later compared her coloratura in these recordings most favourably with that of the renowned soprano Galli-Curci.[3] She also recorded five Scottish and Irish songs with orchestral accompaniment, sung with great affection and lyricism, but no Debussy.

Mary continued to sing a huge repertoire in a wide variety of opera houses and court the press. One would have thought that with her single-minded, independent attitude she would have been an enthusiastic supporter of the suffragettes. Her attitude, however, was not dissimilar to that of Georgette

---

[1] Eaton, *The Boston Opera Company*, p. 208.

[2] See Chapter 16, p. 231, where a comparison is made with Georgette Leblanc.

[3] *Saturday Review*, 27 February 1954, p. 50. Recordings from 1911 and 1912 on *Opera in Chicago*, vol. 1, Symposium 1136 (1992).

Leblanc.[4] It was not that she lacked interest, but 'Why should I want to vote? I have not time to vote … If I were a suffragist I should want to do all – lecture, write for it, live it. I can't do anything in part – I must do it all.'[5] This is an honest self-appraisal. Mary was completely devoted to her career. She had no time for marriage, nor did she have time for politics.

During her 1912 season in Paris, Mary was singing constantly both at the Opéra-Comique and at the Opéra Garnier, still drawing extremes of favourable or adverse criticism for her sensuous interpretations, particularly of *Tosca*. Perhaps this was also the season to which her sister Helen was referring when she spoke of her *Carmen* following the American tour. Because the original tenor was unwell, an unknown replacement was booked. In the last scene he should have had a dagger, but at the crucial point, the poor young man whispered to Mary, 'Je n'ai pas mon couteau!' (I haven't got my dagger!), to which she whispered back, 'Étranglez-moi!' (Strangle me!). This he proceeded to do with some enthusiasm, leaving marks on Mary's neck. The critics interpreted this departure from tradition as Mary returning from America with exciting new ideas about the production of the opera![6]

On her return to the States, Mary's name was being brought to Debussy's attention once again, for on 11 October 1912 André Caplet asked Debussy for permission to orchestrate some of the *Ariettes oubliées* for Mary to sing in America. Although he had previously refused to orchestrate his songs, Debussy agreed that Caplet might choose any of the *Ariettes*, but the choice must be his, not Mary's.[7] On 8 December this recital took place in Boston. Mary sang the two Caplet had selected, no. 1, 'C'est l'extase', and no. 5, 'Green'. She also sang *La Damoiselle élue*.[8]

Still in Boston, later that month she and Vanni-Marcoux as Scarpia caused such a scandal in their highly convincing seduction scene in *Tosca* that Henry Russell had to agree to modify their performance. Mary claimed the audience's reaction came as a great surprise to her, for she was told that, 'those very proper ladies, as if at a signal from some leader, all turned their backs to the stage.'[9] At the next performance a censor was present at the instigation of the Mayor and the Police Department. 'There is nothing in

[4] See Chapter 16, p. 227.

[5] Teddy Bean, 'Mary Garden chez elle', unidentified clipping in RCM, London, Mary Garden Collection.

[6] Madeau Stewart notebook for BBC talk *c.* 1963, Oxfordshire Record Office, P143/04/ MS/001.

[7] Debussy, *Correspondance*, p. 1549.

[8] Debussy, *Correspondance*, p. 1540 n. 4.

[9] *Mary Garden's Story*, p. 128.

the way we acted the scene that should shock anyone but a prude', was her comment.[10] Just as happens to today's film stars, this leading couple became linked in the press off stage as well as on, but when rumours of their engagement were spread, Mary, as usual, denied the story.

By now she was working constantly, her punishing schedule including performances at the Auditorium in Chicago and on tour to Los Angeles, San Francisco, Denver and Minneapolis. With her mother and forty-two trunks in tow, inevitably she was grist to the mill of the press who adored her costumes, or virtual lack of them, and her blatantly ostentatious behaviour. Crisis loomed for the Chicago-Philadelphia Opera Company when at the end of this tour, in the spring of 1913, Andreas Dippel resigned from his post as General Director to be succeeded by Cleofonte Campanini.

To compensate for the lengthy periods spent in crossing the Atlantic in those days travellers enjoyed the glamour of the company and surroundings on board the great liners. A description of life on board the *Kaiser Wilhelm II* as it returned to Europe from New York in 1913 was reprinted fifty years later. The picture is drawn of the famous singers gathered on the liner's promenade deck wearing their expensive furs. Earnings for 'operatic and phonograph' work for the season of some of those listed on board included Enrico Caruso £42,000, Geraldine Farrar £17,000, Emmy Destinn £15,000, Arturo Toscanini £8,400, Mary Garden £14,000, her fee for a single performance being stated as between £250 and £300.[11] Frieda Hempel's £2,500 was reported to be for a total of only fifteen performances. Perhaps this is why Mary, who was constantly performing, gave the impression that she did not like her fellow sopranos, sitting with her back to the stage when Frieda Hempel sang, and talking during a performance by Melba.

After a well-earned break in Scotland with her mother, father and sister, in October 1913 Mary was sailing for New York once again. Who else should be on board the *George Washington* on this occasion with Mary but Vanni-Marcoux, giving rise to yet more rumours of their romance. Perhaps this was why, once again, her age on the passenger list is declared as thirty when she was, in fact, thirty-nine! Once back in America, praise was heaped upon Mary for Dulcinée in *Don Quichotte* by Massenet in Philadelphia, *Monna Vanna* in Boston, *Le Jongleur de Notre-Dame* in Chicago. Sometimes, however, she seemed offhand in her attitude, particularly when twice she failed to perform at concerts for the Women's Music Club in Columbus, Ohio. She did not cancel the first until the audience was already seated. Then, yet again, according to the press, the marriage was about to take place between

[10] *New York Journal*, 12 December 1912.
[11] *Opera*, May 1963, p. 337.

her and Vanni-Marcoux. Who was it encouraging the rumours? In fact, following his divorce from his second wife, he did indeed get married that summer, not to Mary, but to a French dancer, Madeleine Morlay.

Following a tour of the Philadelphia-Chicago Grand Opera Company of the Far West, Mary once again had to disappoint her audience when she fell ill in Des Moines. In fact the tour was a financial disaster and dissatisfaction was expressed at Campanini's management.

On returning to the ominous atmosphere of pre-war Europe, Mary first visited her sister in Switzerland, then went to Scotland, but a few weeks after the declaration of war felt compelled to get back to Paris, despite the difficulties she knew she would encounter. On her arrival there in September 1914 she was shocked at the state of the city, trees in the Bois de Boulogne having been cut down, defensive ditches dug. All theatres and show places in Paris closed their doors until 29 November 1914, when the *Matinées Nationales* opened every Sunday until May in the amphitheatre of the Sorbonne, where Messager conducted the orchestra of the Société du Conservatoire. The first official institution given permission to reopen was the Opéra-Comique on 6 December 1914.[12]

Right from the beginning of the war Mary was determined to support the country she loved. Despite in the past having devoted so much energy to self-promotion, she seems to have found a true vocation in helping her country of adoption. For two years her singing career was virtually on hold, apart from fund-raising performances. She helped to maintain a refuge for women and children in a château at Suresnes, then became a Red Cross nurse in the Villa Trianon at Versailles, which was being used as a hospital. Amongst the photographs she kept is one of her in nurse's uniform by a soldier's hospital bed. In order to raise funds for the hospital and to see her parents, Mary braved the Atlantic crossing in December 1914 to stay in New York just for three weeks. On her return she continued her work in Paris. She was to receive two medals for her war work: the Médaille de la Reconnaissance and the Red Cross of Serbia.[13] In her *Story* Mary's wartime efforts are only given the very briefest of mentions. Here is an example of an aspect of Mary's private life that was clearly not to be trivialised.

Evidence that Mary could have escaped the rigours and emotional distress of the war years in Europe comes from Sam Goldwyn. So devoted was she to her new cause that even an opportunity to become a film star did not tempt her. Goldwyn describes how he tried to entice her into the world of silent

---

[12] J.-G. Prod'homme, 'Music and Musicians in Paris during the First Two Seasons of the War', *The Musical Quarterly*, vol. 4 (1918), p. 135.

[13] In Paris the Red Cross helped tubercular Serbians in France.

films. Admittedly, his account has her involved in a hospital in Scotland, rather than France, but the reason for her rejection of his offer remains the same: 'She refused to leave her humanitarian work.'[14]

On 27 April 1915 Mary performed in London in a much heralded concert to raise funds for the American Women's War Hospital situated at Paignton in Devon. She sang songs in Italian, English and French in a long programme at the Theatre Royal, Drury Lane, presented by many illustrious stars of opera, ballet and theatre to a large audience including the Queen and several other members of the royal family. Her dislike of London may not have been lessened by a mediocre review she received in *The Times* for her contribution to a concert of British music two days later, where it was said that her fame in America was much greater than it was likely to be here. The critic described her as being 'so certain of creating a sensation that she created nothing', and wondered what all the fuss could have been about.[15] This may have been due to Mary having to perform a song from Goring Thomas's *Nadeshda* (first produced at Covent Garden in 1885). He did have to admit that it was probably difficult for her to find anything in her repertoire which would suit the occasion!

Unhappily she had to undergo an operation for appendicitis in Paris during that summer which forced the cancellation of further charity performances. These included a single presentation of *Pelléas et Mélisande* at the Opéra-Comique in aid of war-wounded, planned for 19 June with Jean Périer and Hector Dufranne, to be conducted by Messager.[16] By 23 June Debussy was aware of Mary's appendicitis, and on 15 July, whilst staying in Pourville, he wrote to a doctor friend at the Lariboisière hospital in Paris to confirm that *Pelléas et Mélisande* had not been performed due to her illness. In a letter to his publisher, Durand, written the next day, it is clear that Debussy's obsession with his opera had hardly diminished. His mascot Chinese wooden toad, Arkel, which usually sat on his desk at home, had now been transported to Pourville, where the wonderful view of the sea, 'la mer infinie', inspired more reminders. To convey his mood, he adapted Pelléas's words (Act III scene 3) when he emerges from the vaults of the castle and breathes the fresh sea air with relief, saying that he could hear the bells ringing at midday, but if the children were not going down to the beach to bathe, as Pelléas had sung, perhaps it was because they lacked the courage.[17]

Mary was seriously ill following her operation, but on her recovery

[14] Goldwyn, *Behind the Screen*, p. 127.

[15] *The Times*, 30 April 1915.

[16] Debussy, *Correspondance*, pp. 1899, 1902.

[17] Debussy, *Correspondance*, p. 1908.

was welcomed back with open arms at the Opéra-Comique in a charity performance of *Tosca* in December. Her benevolence was further expressed when she also became 'godmother' to six African zouaves[18] on the French front, sending them regular parcels.

Meanwhile, Mary's links with Chicago did not cease. During this war-time activity she was still negotiating a contract with Campanini and crossed the Atlantic yet again in June 1916 to discuss matters. There Sam Goldwyn eventually caught up with her at the Ritz, where he was struck both by her physical appearance and her intelligence. He found she looked even taller than on stage. He was amazed when he realised the extent to which she had to transform her whole being to play *Thaïs, Mélisande, Louise, Le Jongleur*. More significantly, here was a man evidently astonished that a woman singer, a prima donna, could express coherent and convincing views on the world situation. He was greatly impressed with her eloquence, how she had grasped each industrial and economic phase of the conflict. Not only was Mary forceful in her views on current affairs, she was able to drive a hard financial bargain. When he expressed the eagerness of the Goldwyn Company for the honour of first presenting her on screen, she clearly had no doubt that she would be successful in film, her only misgiving being that he might not pay her enough. Any hesitation he may have had as to the wisdom of promising her vast sums of money was banished at the pleasure of grabbing Mary from numerous other film-producers who had been competing for her services, and the huge publicity gained for his company by the coup.[19]

Mary signed her contract in February 1917 with Goldwyn Pictures Corporation. Following a satisfactory screen test in March, Goldwyn lost no time in gaining publicity by publishing a request for the public to nominate their favourite Mary Garden role to be made in to a film. 64,000 people replied, of whom 81 per cent asked for *Thaïs*. Before crossing the Atlantic on 1 September, Mary gave a matinée performance at the Opera-Comique for American Expeditionary Forces, commemorated by a photograph of her at the piano in *Harper's Bazaar*.[20]

On her arrival in New York, her slim figure was noted, one advantage of living on war rations in Paris, said Mary, although throughout her life she maintained a slim figure through a rigorous diet. Soon after her arrival, filming began at Goldwyn's House at Fort Lee, New Jersey. Mary had had costumes brought over from France and she approved of the wonderful sets. Almost immediately, however, Goldwyn was beset with doubts, for Mary,

18 Regiments of the French Army, the first corps of which originated in Algeria in 1831.

19 Goldwyn, *Behind the Screen*, p. 129.

20 RCM, London, Mary Garden Collection, album III.

quite naturally, felt her presentation of the role of Thaïs as she was used to performing it in the opera was the one and only way of playing it. In the studio, however, it was said that she was 'acting all over the place'. He began to have grave worries regarding the outcome of his enormous investment in her. She could not bear to depart from the original with which she was so familiar, and when it came to portraying the death of *Thaïs* was furious at the mutilation of the libretto. When she saw the rushes of this scene she dashed from the projection-room down to the office, where she found the playwright Margaret Mayo. 'Did you see it?', she is reported to have shouted. 'That terrible thing? Did you see the way they made me die? Imagine a saint dying like that!', Mayo is said to have replied, 'You would have a hard time, Miss Garden, proving to anyone that you were a saint.'[21]

Mary's pride in her ability as a 'singing actress' was badly damaged when it was realised that this operatic skill was totally different from that required of a screen star. A press release claimed that the 'elaborate and dignified' film of *Thaïs* had been launched with every prospect of success and promised it would rank as one of the finest films of the year.[22] However, when it was premièred in New York in January 1918, Mary could not bring herself to watch from a box in view of the public, but retreated incognito to the gallery. It was a complete failure, both in America and abroad. In April the *New York Telegraph* complained that this purely spiritual story had turned into 'an orgy of unlovely flesh'. Words such as 'tawdry', 'crude', 'vulgar' were used to describe the result. Mary had brought to the screen 'the tedious and dismal technique of operatic acting, which is not acting at all, but slow motions made while waiting for the music to catch up with the drama'. Later, Vincent Sheean analysed the problem when he explained in his obituary of Mary, that she was probably the greatest musical actress the world had seen, and that:

> she could no more have acted without music, or made music without acting, than she could have flown to the stars. She actually could not cross a stage without music, as was proved when she tried to make a movie, and her concerts were disastrous because she had no chance to act.[23]

Meanwhile, in the same month as the première of this film, *Pelléas et Mélisande* was performed at the Auditorium in Chicago on 12 January 1918. The thirteen tableaux were those of the original American production given in February 1908 at Hammerstein's Manhattan. Emile Merle Forest was in charge of the scenery, but it was not to Mary's satisfaction. However, the

---

[21] Goldwyn, *Behind the Screen*, p. 130.

[22] *New York Times*, 31 December 1917.

[23] *Opera News*, 4 February 1967, p. 6.

reviews were positive, commenting on her contribution to the elusive beauty of this work. It was noted that this was 'her finest portrayal in a gallery of pictures that no other singing actress can rival.' The scenery was judged to be mainly 'well handled' and Mary's wig was also remembered with affection from her original Paris début as Mélisande.[24] The conductor was Marcel Charlier, her Pelléas was Alfred Maguenat, new to the role. The praise was somewhat warmer when this revival was taken to the Lexington in New York on 31 January, especially in retrospect when it was realised that this was the last American performance of the opera before Debussy's death on 25 March 1918. Admiration was expressed for Mary, who, with her calm beauty, created an atmosphere that could be almost tangibly felt by the audience. She reiterated her own opinion that it was 'the most wonderful opera in the world, a creation of genius, unlike anything that has proceeded it in music'.[25]

Mary the film star was not to be defeated. She announced that her next film was to be *The Splendid Sinner*, a story based partly on her own experiences in war-time France as a Red Cross nurse and the life of Edith Cavell. Filming began in February, but once again when the film appeared, both the story and its star were torn to pieces. 'She who is gracious, lovely and full of personality on the stage is minus every one of the qualities on the screen' and 'The picture is dressed gaudily and the story has little reason for existing save to exploit Miss Garden' were comments in the *Chicago Record*.[26] Some ridiculed the story.[27] Even Mary had nothing good to say about the film, and expressed the hope that 'nobody in God's world will ever see it again. I have heard many films called the worst ever made; I am sure those who make such judgements never saw *The Splendid Sinner*.'[28]

It is hardly surprising that silent movies were not Mary's métier. Her acting and her singing were inseparable in opera. She had surely hit the nail on the head when she realised:

> If they had been talking films, I suppose I would have been alright, because then I could have talked and brought out some sort of character ... In the silent days we didn't say anything; we just looked. That's why there was no place for a woman like me. I had to talk. Just marching around and moving my hands smothered me as an artist.[29]

Perhaps for 'talk' one should read 'sing'!

[24] *New York Times*, 1 February 1918.
[25] *New York Times*, 31 March 1918.
[26] *Chicago Record*, 24 and 25 March 1918.
[27] *New York Times*, 1 April 1918.
[28] *Mary Garden's Story*, p. 232.
[29] *Mary Garden's Story*, p. 232.

Having returned to Paris in the spring of 1918, in June she and one of her sisters (as so often, a member of her family was with her) left for the South of France. They took fifty-eight hours to travel to Monte Carlo, taking with them her jewel case, her war-disabled butler, two Turner paintings and a bust of Voltaire![30] There she rented an apartment in the Park Palace Hotel. On returning to Paris in September she cancelled all her New York engagements, including filming, and was therefore able to be in the Place de la Concorde joining in the celebrations for the signing of the Armistice in November.

When she did eventually go back to New York once again it was to sing in *Gismonda*, written and conducted by Henry Février. The work was warmly received and this was followed by further successes. *Pelléas et Mélisande* was performed at the Lexington Theatre in the same production as the previous year, which had been received with rather lukewarm praise. This time, James Huneker, usually so eloquent about Mary, restricted his comments to 'Mary Garden was Mélisande. No further praise is needful ... her Mélisande is unforgettable.'[31]

Americans were constantly being reminded of the need in Europe for used clothing and other basic necessities, and on 25 March 1919 Mary, in conjunction with the Secours Franco-Americain, gave a concert at the Metropolitan Opera House for the benefit of devastated France.[32] Back and forth over the Atlantic for another season and on her return to America in November 1919 she brought with her a fantastic gown of a thousand mirrors made out of huge rhinestones on a background of gold and silver cloth which she herself had designed. She wore this for the first time at a concert in Columbus, Ohio, causing quite a stir.[33]

December 1919 saw the death from pneumonia of Campanini, Director of the Chicago Opera. 'Nobody could touch Campanini', wrote Mary, 'nobody in the world. He was the most consummate artist in every way.'[34] His coffin was brought into the Auditorium, where the musicians and general public passed in front of it, an aptly theatrical spectacle as it was surrounded by flowers and the sets of the Transformation Scene from *Parsifal*.[35] So now a new director had to be found for the Chicago Opera Association. There were constant mutterings and tales about Mary's influence over the company, but she denied that she was going to become its artistic director and musical directorship was taken over by Gino Marinuzzi. When the company

[30] Typescript in RCM, London, Mary Garden Collection.
[31] *New York Times*, 6 February 1919.
[32] *New York Times*, 2 March 1919.
[33] Turnbull, *Mary Garden*, p. 138.
[34] *Mary Garden's Story*, p. 169.
[35] Davis, *Opera in Chicago*, p. 124.

moved to Lexington Avenue for the annual New York season a significant event took place. As we have seen in the previous chapter, the recently married Maeterlinck and Renée arrived in New York on Christmas Eve 1919 to huge acclaim. On 27 January 1920 *Pelléas et Mélisande* was performed with Mary as Mélisande, and there she had the unforeseen and unique triumph of seeing Maeterlinck and his young wife viewing the opera from a box. He had given in to curiosity, and for the first time in his life had come to see the work he had vowed never to attend.[36] His totally passive reaction was witnessed by one of Samuel Goldwyn's publicity men, who was sitting nearby. 'From the large placid face those ethereal strains which Debussy wove about his own play drew not a sign of response', was his comment.[37] Despite this, after the performance Maeterlinck told Mary 'Had I known, I should have come a long time ago. *Je suis très heureux, très heureux.*'[38] A couple of days later she received a letter from him as follows:

> I had sworn to myself never to see the lyric drama *Pelléas et Mélisande*. Yesterday I violated my vow and I am a happy man. For the first time I have entirely understood my own play, and because of you. I saw there many things which I had never perceived or which I had forgotten. Like every great artist, more than any other perhaps, you have a genius to add to a work or to vivify in it those things which I omitted or had left in a state of sleep. With all my heart's thanks for the beautiful revelation of last night's performance, in the most cordial homage of your devoted admirer, Maurice Maeterlinck.[39]

Eventually, referring to his quarrel with Debussy, Maeterlinck was to admit in writing to Henry Russell that 'Today I find that I was completely wrong in this matter and that he was a thousand times right.'[40]

During this reunion with Mary an extraordinary conversation took place in which Maeterlinck asked her if he could photograph her soul. 'That was his hobby', she noted. He showed her a large piece of paper with a flash of something that looked like the Milky Way over it. 'That is one', he said. Unsurprisingly Mary declined the request, reasoning that she wanted to keep her soul to herself![41]

In July 1920, an interview with Mary was published in which, as so often, she expressed pride in her association with Debussy, her 'greatest friend in Art!' Her memories of their rehearsals together were as fresh as ever in

---

[36] See illus. 34.
[37] Goldwyn, *Behind the Screen*, p. 256.
[38] *Mary Garden's Story*, p. 116.
[39] *Mary Garden's Story*, p. 116.
[40] 26 November 1925, Stadsarchief Gent BC62.
[41] Typescript at RCM, London, Mary Garden Collection.

her mind. She described him as 'a terribly exacting master', 'a transcendent pianist'. He would go over works with her again and again, occasionally stopping to complain, 'It's all wrong – it is all wrong.' But he was always able to pinpoint the fault and help to remedy it. When they became close friends, he would say to her, 'To think that you were born in Aberdeen, Scotland, lived in America all those years and should come to Paris to create my Mélisande!'[42]

1920 was also the year of publication of a book entitled *Bedouins* by the critic James Gibbon Huneker, who was completely besotted with Mary. He can find no adequate superlative to describe her. Using words such as 'A condor, an eagle, a peacock, a nightingale, a panther ... and a canny Scotch lassie who can force from an operatic manager wails of anguish because of her close bargaining over a contract; in a word, a Superwoman', he lauds her astounding versatility. He believed Mary's Gaelic temperament contributed to the intensity of *Pelléas et Mélisande*. He also praised her intellectual qualities, for although her chief appeal was to the imagination, she left nothing to chance. Despite her Scottish birth, Huneker was anxious to claim this paragon for America. She had remained 'invincibly Yankee'. Pages of similar hyperbole comment on her beauty, her superlative singing, the originality of her singing and acting, the 'marvellous death of Mélisande, the most touching that I can recall in either the lyric or dramatic theatre.' In a whole section devoted to this opera Huneker concludes that to him Mary Garden was Mélisande. No further praise was necessary.[43]

In 1921 Marinuzzi resigned as Musical Director of the Chicago Opera Association (the president of which was Samuel Insull) and on 14 January it was suddenly announced that the new Director of the company was to be Mary Garden. The London *Times* carried a report that Marinuzzi had resigned on the grounds that he was unable to stand any longer the 'temperamental vagaries of the stars' when Mary Garden was on stage, but did at least take the opportunity to remind its readers that she was born in Aberdeen.[44] On the very day of her appointment she sang *Monna Vanna*, and even during the interval had to give an interview in her dressing room. The prima donna was now to combine the roles of artist and impresario. She stated that she would try 'this big work' for one year and stay on if everyone was happy with the outcome. Fears were expressed that this would mean the domination of French repertoire at the expense of Italian, but Mary announced that she would give 50 per cent of operas in Italian, 35 per cent in French and

42 *The Etude*, July 1920.
43 James Huneker, *Bedouins* (New York, 1920).
44 *The Times*, 15 January 1921.

15 per cent in English. She would like to present German opera, but as she hated translations, this would have to wait until it could be sung in the original language. Any opera sung in English should be written by American or English composers. Although she was determined that she would wipe out the current $300,000 deficit, she would pay big salaries to artists who could draw large audiences. No expense was to be spared either in the number of artists she employed or in the productions. It is somewhat ironic that Mary expressed her determination that the Chicago Grand Opera Association should be an American institution, an American company welcoming young American singers. These would be 'welcomed by an American' – it must have slipped her mind that she herself was still officially British.[45]

What stamina and single-mindedness this woman showed. She had risen to the top of the tree in both the artistic and administrative world. The glass ceiling, so frequently complained about by future generations of women trying to make their way in a man's world, had not held her back. Not only was she the first woman to head an opera company, she had achieved this accolade only five months after women in America had gained the right to vote. The press had been in constant attendance, dancing after her every word and action, and she had kept herself at the height of her vocal and dramatic powers, maintained health and fitness and, although she had never married, had no lack of male, and female, interest in her. She claimed that the women were never a problem to her. 'I must say I had a difficult time with the men in the company; the women singers were charming and co-operative, but the males were just a pack of jealous boys. I've never seen such jealousy in my life.'[46] Her routine was punishing: rising at nine, devoting an hour to breathing exercises, then an hour to vocal study. Then down to the theatre for three hours for business, including rehearsals. Home about five o'clock and rest till seven. After a meal, she would return to the opera house to see how things were going, unless she herself was singing.

Mary soon learnt the perils of company management and before long experienced the jealousy and bitterness of some towards her, not to mention the attention she received from cranks, as so often happens to celebrities – not just anonymous letters arrived in the post, but once even a box of bullets including a letter saying, 'Remember that there should be twelve bullets in this box. Count them. There are only eleven. The twelfth bullet is for you.'[47] She soon felt the need to employ a personal detective who became part of her permanent staff.

[45] *New York Times*, 15 January 1921.
[46] *Mary Garden's Story*, p. 175.
[47] *Mary Garden's Story*, p. 175.

Only a few weeks later, on 22 March 1921, Mary heard that the French government was to make her a Chevalier de la Légion d'Honneur for her services to French music; she received the medal later that year in Chicago. This was after she had taken the whole Chicago Opera Association on the most expensive tour ever undertaken in America. The company was now the umbrella for four other opera companies as well, so the planning and logistics of such a tour must have been incomparable. They carried with them everything they needed for each production including scenery, lights and rigging for scene shifting.

Another first occurred when on 11 November 1921, unintentionally, Mary spoke some of the first words ever broadcast on Chicago radio from the Auditorium Theatre. She had been asked to take part in a test of the transmitter, recently installed on the top of the Commonwealth Edison Building at 72 West Adams. On the stage was a tent lit by only a single light bulb. Mary had to stand inside this and the first words heard over the airwaves were Mary saying, 'My God, but it's dark in here!' She then introduced Giorgio Polacco, who led the musicians through selections from *Madama Butterfly*. The newspapers were thrilled that no longer would it be necessary to dress up to hear grand opera, and that opera could be heard free of cost by anyone over the airwaves.[48] 'Our Mary' was presenting the Chicago Opera Company to the world.

During her year as Director there were many tempests as Mary strove to get her own way over the works to be performed and the performers. Whilst she introduced new singers, extravagantly she hired artists for more performances than they actually sang. Prokofiev himself conducted the world première of *The Love for Three Oranges* on 30 December 1921. It was performed in French at a cost of $100,000, one of the most elaborate productions ever staged by the company, yet there were only two performances.

Financial problems mounted despite Mary's initial optimism. Added to this, unfortunate clashes occurred between her opera engagements, the demands of the company and her separate concerts. In February 1922 there was a complaint from the French consul in Chicago to the Ministry of Foreign Affairs in Paris that despite her promises, French opera had not been served well. Only five French artists had been employed, one of whom was the conductor and composer Gabriel Grovlez, yet even he had not been given a work to conduct and his ballet had not been performed. The chief conductor, Polacco, was Italian. On the other hand, others grumbled that not enough had been done to make the company a truly American one. 'Miss Garden wrapped herself in the American flag ... and what has she done

[48] *Chicago Tribune*, 12 November, 17 November 1921.

256

for American artists? Nothing!' was the tenor Lucien Muratore's complaint. He then resigned, not before reporting some nasty things about her: 'To me when we sing together, she hisses "pretty boy" and when I am on stage, she talks to other members of the company about me. She calls me "pig"!' As for Polacco, the tale was spread of a row which took place on 16 January 1922 when Mary was so infuriated by his conducting of *Pelléas et Mélisande* that she pummelled him with her fists and told him to get out. He was quoted as saying that Mary 'was like a floating frog, turning first this way and then that'.[49] When it came to the last performance of the season on 21 January Polacco refused to conduct, and after harsh words Grovlez was brought in to take over. Yet artistically the season was regarded as successful, some calling it 'Chicago's big year in opera', and others admitting that Mary had managed to turn nearly every evening into a gala event.[50]

It was on 23 April 1922 that Mary succumbed and announced her retirement as Director General. During her year in the post the huge deficit of nearly a million dollars was the largest in the organisation's history. She had received no salary for this role and had put people's backs up. Prokofiev was left high and dry with another work unperformed: he had hoped she would put on *The Fiery Angel* and sing the title role herself.

To recuperate and following her customary routine, Mary spent the summer holiday of 1922 in Switzerland visiting her sister and losing weight climbing mountains. Her comings and goings to Switzerland and Monte Carlo can now be followed in the London *Times* as she was a celebrity of such note. In 1923 her European travels took her to Venice, where she was the guest of the Cole Porters, and then to the Côte d'Azur. Since 1918 she had given as her home address her apartment at the Park Palace Hotel in Monte Carlo. It was not very far from here that she found a project very dear to her heart. On the wall of the club-house of the Monte Carlo golf course she noticed a subscription opened for a war memorial in a small village called Peille. She added her name before returning to America, but on return found the necessary sum had not been raised. She promptly agreed to fund the project. The village was built steeply up the mountainside, but she insisted on the statue of a soldier being erected on the top of a hill, that a road was made up to it and that any remaining money was put towards building a public square. Construction started in 1924 and Mary was fêted as godmother of the village.[51] To this day Peille boasts a Place Mary Garden.

49 Davis, *Opera in Chicago*, p. 140.
50 Davis, *Opera in Chicago*, p. 141.
51 Typescript in RCM, London, Mary Garden Collection, and *Mary Garden's Story*, p. 134.

Further performances in Chicago, now called the Chicago Civic Opera, in 1924 and 1925 pulled in full houses and received glowing reviews, yet at the end of 1925 Samuel Insull revealed that the company had suffered a loss of $400,000. There was, however, the possibility of a new guarantee fund for the next five years and a new skyscraper opera house being built, which could be made profitable by renting out the upper floors as office space. This would mean that the Auditorium Theatre would eventually be closed.

Back in Paris in May 1926 Mary was once again acclaimed as Mélisande at the Opéra-Comique with Messager conducting. Since these two iconic initiators of the opera were appearing, this reprise was given the status of 'une grande première' by press and audience alike.[52] How could she recreate this role of a young lost princess so convincingly twenty-four years after first embodying her frailty? Here was a strong woman aged fifty-two with twenty-four years of life's experiences since that première in 1902, a prima donna, a business woman, the darling of the press, who could cast all that aside and bewitch her audience with the childlike fragility of Mélisande. On Friday 28 May there was a gala performance and in June the opera was performed four times. Singing with her were Roger Bourdin as Pelléas, Dufranne as Golaud, Vieuille was Arkel once again, Mathilde Calvet sang Geneviève, and Ernest Dupré the doctor. Mary had kept all the poetry of Maeterlinck's strange little girl-woman,[53] she was even sadder and more mysterious than before, her whole character merging with the light and shadow,[54] reported the critics.

After singing the role in October in Strasbourg Mary was back in Paris later that month for two more performances of *Pelléas* and a farewell supper in the Café de Paris. There Georges Ricou, Co-Director of the Opéra-Comique, gave a speech expressing the admiration held for Mary: 'She has been a precious example to our younger artists who worked beside her and these performances of *Pelléas et Mélisande* have forged a bond between the younger generation and their glorious predecessors.' She then received a toast from Albert Carré, to which she replied: 'Dear M. Carré, I cannot forget that I am here and I have had the career I have had thanks to you who, in days gone by, opened the gates of the Opéra-Comique to me.'[55]

Mary had her own fantastic tale to tell about this revival of the opera in Paris in 1926. Is it wishful thinking? Certainly at least one of the persons in question could well have been present. According to Mary's account, on the

52 *Le Courier musical et théâtral*, 13 June 1926, p. 331.

53 'L'étrange petite femme fille': *Le Courier musical et théâtral*, 13 June 1926, p. 331.

54 'plus pathétique, plus douloureuse, plus mystérieuse encore ... ses gestes jouent avec la lumière et l'ombre comme si toute sa personne en était impregnée.' *Le Monde musical*, 30 June 1926, p. 245.

55 *Comoedia*, 17 October 1926. Quoted in Turnbull, *Mary Garden*, p. 166.

day of the performance whilst she was still at home, a huge basket of flowers was delivered to her with the note, 'My mother, Mme Claude Debussy, is coming to the performance tonight. May I bring her up to your dressing room after the third act?' This was from Raoul Bardac, Emma Debussy's son by her first husband. Mary replied, saying it would be a privilege to meet Mme Claude Debussy. At the end of the successful performance she was in her dressing room talking to the Prime Minister, Aristide Briand, when the door opened, and in came not Emma, but Lilly, Debussy's first wife. 'We flew into each other's arms', exclaims Mary. 'Oh, Mary, you're back with *Pelléas*!', cried Lilly. What was even more startling was that Lilly declared that Claude was there with her. She claimed to have bought two tickets, and insisted, 'Claude is with me tonight, Mary, right there in the seat next to mine ... his spirit is there in the house. I feel him everywhere. Don't you?'

Hardly had Mary had time to take in this extraordinary revelation, when the door of her dressing room opened again and in came a man with an old lady on his arm, dressed in black, walking with a cane. As she came towards Mary she began to sob, overcome with emotion. This was Emma, who did not see Lilly in a corner of the room. We are not told how the conversation continued between Mary and the two Madame Debussys, but after they had departed Mary was proud to inform the Prime Minister that he had seen something that night that he would never forget, the two wives of Claude Debussy.[56]

We have proof that Mary certainly was in contact with Emma Debussy that summer, for on 15 October, the day before she left from Cherbourg to return to America, she wrote a letter of thanks to Emma having received from her a photograph of Debussy. Acknowledging her pleasure at Emma's thoughtfulness, she admitted she had no other photograph of the composer. She also said she was looking forward to *Pelléas* again the following spring.[57] Perhaps they had agreed to meet again when she sang the opera in 1927.

Back in America, the newspapers and journals were not short of copy about their favourite soprano. By now, besides her apartment in Monte Carlo, Mary owned a luxurious villa in Beaulieu on the French Riviera. On 13 September 1926 *Time* published a typically sensational anecdote describing her summer sunbathing activities in the Mediterranean. She had been lying naked on her rowing boat and fell asleep, only to be woken by splashing sounds and to see two huge sharks circling about. Needless to say, she rowed for the shore and reached it safely, despite being charged many times![58]

56 *Mary Garden's Story*, pp. 86–8.
57 Bibliothèque nationale de France, Paris, NLA-32 (81).
58 *Time*, 13 September 1926.

In October 1926 Mary made recordings for the Victor Talking Machine Company in Camden, New Jersey, her first since 1912. She had been invited to become a Red Seal artist, a marketing ploy to aid the promotion of advances which had been made in recording technique by the electric method. She was accompanied at the piano by Jean Dansereau and with an orchestra conducted by Rosario Bourdon. The aria 'Dieu de Grace' from *Résurrection* by Franco Alfano conveys the power of her voice as she clearly revels in the dramatic effects. She can be heard still enjoying 'Depuis le jour' from Charpentier's *Louise*, admittedly now transposed down a tone, that aria which had introduced the young soprano to the stage of the Opéra-Comique over twenty-six years previously. These and further recordings for Victor made between 1926 and 1929 have been transferred to CD and include just one song by Debussy, *Beau soir*, which Mary recorded in November 1929.[59] Obviously by then, at the age of fifty-five, her voice was considerably more mature than in the recordings she made with Debussy in 1904, and with better recording technology the sound is not so distant. The interpretation of this song is very romantic, with considerable use of lingering portamento and freedom with time values. In contrast, when Maggie Teyte recorded *Beau soir* in 1944, in accordance with her advice on singing Debussy, she adhered more closely to the values of the notes as written.[60] Mary Garden's pronunciation is not that of a native French speaker on certain vowels, but the enunciation is clear and she conveys richly the poetic images underlined by Debussy's setting of the words.

Back in Chicago, some unflattering references were beginning to be made to Mary's age, despite her subtracting at least seven years when declaring it on her Atlantic crossings. At the beginning of 1927 there was a somewhat comical production of *Tosca* employing a hotch-potch of languages. Mary as Tosca sang in French, except for 'Vissi d'arte', which she sang in Italian. The farce culminated in Mary demanding from Vanni-Marcoux as Scarpia, 'Combien?', and he, supposedly echoing her question, responding, 'Quanto?'[61] Language inconsistencies were also remarked upon but scarcely seemed to matter when in February 1927 she sang *Carmen* at the Eastman School of Music in Rochester, New York, conducted by Eugene Goossens. He was impressed by the intensity and vigour of her performance and believed that the fact that she sang in French, while the rest of the opera took place with the English translation, passed comparatively unnoticed.[62]

59 *Mary Garden. The Complete Victor Recordings (1926–29)*, Romophone 81008-2. Some items (not *Beau soir*) also on *Opera in Chicago*, vol. 1, Symposium CD 1136 (1992).

60 *Great Singers: Maggie Teyte: A Vocal Portrait*, Naxos Historical, 8.110757–58.

61 Davis, *Opera in Chicago*, p. 172.

62 Eugene Goossens, *Overture and Beginners* (London, 1951), p. 239.

1927 saw Mary singing in *Pelléas et Mélisande* again, this time in Geneva. The opera had first been performed there in March 1912, conducted by Antonio Bruni, with Jeanne Daffetye singing Mélisande. Debussy had expressed serious worries to his Swiss friend, Robert Godet, about this première, convinced it would not be understood, for 'Geneva is a nest of professors who only accept ideas when dressed in white ties.'[63] Now, fifteen years later, the work was an accepted part of an international exposition of music, *Pelleas and Melisande* being 'played, acted and sung as never before'.[64] The cast on this stage were Mary's familiar Opéra-Comique collaborators, Bourdin, Dufranne and Vieuille.

Immediately after this, Mary collaborated once more with Albert Carré at the Opéra-Comique in Alfano's *Résurrection*. She was delighted to be working once again with the man who had introduced her to the Opéra-Comique a quarter of a century earlier. He must have been equally pleased, for Carré dedicated a photograph of himself to her: 'À Mary Garden, avec ma plus grande admiration, avec ma plus vive affection, 14 May 1927.'[65] The première took place on 16 May. There was a dramatic opportunity to display her love of America when it was announced during a performance of *Résurrection* that Charles Lindbergh had flown across the Atlantic single-handed from New York to Le Bourget. Anyone else would have found it embarrassing to have forgotten the words of *The Star-Spangled Banner* at the crucial moment, but Mary did not mind admitting that she had had to send someone to look up the words at the library![66]

She continued singing in Chicago in 1928, and toured nineteen cities with the Company. In 1929 her work included another revival of *Pelléas*, this time in Boston. Still she was captivating her audiences and the critics – this at the age of fifty-five! Olin Downes found her voice even better and under finer control than in former years. Hearing the opera after a gap of six years, he believed that 'for the first time he had come near the secret of the piece.' He felt, 'Debussy must have listened to the heart-beat of the drama of Maeterlinck before he undertook his music', for he now realised that it was the speech of the opera which gave it its 'iron substructure and unchangeable power.' It was a complete mystery to him how Debussy had reflected so sensitively 'the most fleeting and evanescent implications of dramatic speech'.[67] In another article devoted almost entirely to Mary, he urged

[63] Debussy, *Correspondance*, p. 1471.

[64] *Time*, 23 May 1927.

[65] 'To Mary Garden, with my greatest admiration, with my deepest affection.' See illus. 17.

[66] Davis, *Opera in Chicago*, p. 175.

[67] *New York Times*, 10 February 1929.

people to make the pilgrimage to see her in Boston. When she had gone, the one and incomparable interpretation of Mélisande would have gone with her.[68] A delightful description of Mary in action at this time appeared in an article in *The Times* in 1960, when a singer who worked with the Chicago Civic Opera Company reminisced on the highlight of her short career. At the age of fifteen, she once found herself standing within three feet of Mary Garden whilst waiting to go on stage. She could not believe that Mary, who was over fifty, could transform herself in an instant into a youthful actress, running lightly onto the stage, full of grace and vitality, whilst her voice remained clear, full and mature.[69]

On 26 January 1929 the Chicago Civic Opera Company gave its final performance in the Auditorium, home of so many of Mary's triumphs and scene of her directorship. On 4 November the new Civic Opera House opened, a forty-five storey high building, financed by Samuel Insull, which Mary hated in comparison. To her it was more like a convention hall than an opera house. There was no sense of communication with the public and she could not stand the design, 'that long black hole'.[70] She was still aware that her pronouncements on life and love would be avidly seized upon by the press, and enjoyed spreading her views on the position of women in 1929. 'Women do not live for love. They work for their living.' Women were still not wholly free and may not be so for another fifty years. 'Formerly we were under the man's heel. Now just his little toe is on us. Yet how conscious we are of that little toe!'[71]

When the company went on tour that year they performed *Thaïs* in Amarillo, Texas, but Mary's appearance was not immediately appreciated. A report was published of the editor of the local *Globe News* criticising the soprano as being 'so old that she actually tottered!' Amarillo's music lovers were incensed, but she dismissed the insult exclaiming, 'Only tell him that when he's tottering I'll still be singing!'[72]

1929 was also the year she worked with Hamilton Forrest, a young American composer who came over to Paris to meet her and demonstrate his score. Through Mary, this former office boy of Samuel Insull was given the opportunity to have his opera *Camille* performed in 1930. Mary found the music hard, for 'it just screeched with modernism'.[73] Her role in this opera brought her the accolade of being pictured on the cover of *Time* magazine

[68] *New York Times*, 7 February 1929.
[69] *The Times*, 16 March 1960.
[70] *Mary Garden's Story*, p. 246.
[71] Davis, *Opera in Chicago*, p. 185.
[72] *Time*, 1 April 1929.
[73] *Mary Garden's Story*, p. 238.

in December 1930. The reviewer was reminded of Debussy's opera by the
way in which the characters seemed to talk naturally 'in the intimate, emo-
tionalised musical speech for which Mary Garden has a particular genius.'
He also emphasised the public's relief at seeing her back in the city, for
despite expectations the new opera house had not proved popular and the
affairs of the company were in a poor state. Her admirable attention to her
health and fitness was once more praised, particularly her dislike of sitting
round a table to eat. Mention was made of a project that sadly would never
materialise: she would perhaps do *Pelléas et Mélisande* for the movies. In
particular he reported the importance to Mary of wearing the correct hair
for each role, highlighted in this opera by the fact that when Mary made her
entrance, the whole house had gasped.[74] Other newspapers also commented
on her hair in *Camille*. 'The most amazing feature of the apparition was a
wig that would have shamed a Zulu medicine man', said *Musical America*.
Another observer claimed that Mary must have put up her hair with an egg
beater![75]

Pelléas et Mélisande received more performances, but the end was near
for suddenly Mary made up her mind that this was the time to finish her
operatic career in America. Her last complete performances of Debussy's
opera took place in Chicago on 22 January then in Boston on 29 January
1931. Her old colleague Vanni-Marcoux was Golaud. She had made up her
own mind that this was the time to go. 'When the final curtain came down, I
went into my dressing room, dressed myself to go home, and without saying
good-by [*sic*] to anybody I left, and I never went back. I walked out of that
vast hall without seeing a soul.'[76] When she arrived back in Paris she cabled
Samuel Insull to tell him her career in America was at an end.[77] Newspaper
reports had previously denied that she was leaving the Civic Company,[78] but
by the end of April they had to admit that she was not to return. In a farewell
eulogy, Edward Moore wrote that the opera which first came to his mind in
association with Mary was *Pelléas et Mélisande* which despite at first having
dazed its audiences was now regarded as 'the most beautiful work that ever
went upon an operatic stage'.[79] She was praised for her role in putting the
company on the map, providing constant good copy for reporters, directing the most hectic season of opera Chicagoans had known, but it had to
be admitted that it had been becoming increasingly difficult to find typical

[74] *Time*, 15 December 1930.
[75] Davis, *Opera in Chicago*, p. 190.
[76] *Mary Garden's Story*, p. 247.
[77] Davis, *Opera in Chicago*, p. 192.
[78] *Chicago Daily Tribune*, 25 January 1931.
[79] *Chicago Daily Tribune*, 26 April 1931.

Garden roles. Latterly, her appearances had been more for the glorification of her personality than for the glory of opera – so perhaps Mary had chosen the right moment to take her leave.

18 *Georgette Leblanc after Maeterlinck (1919–31)*

BOTH Maggie Teyte and Mary Garden had reached a vital turning point in their lives in 1931, when Maggie was forty-three and Mary fifty-seven. Georgette's progress after the end of her relationship with Maurice Maeterlinck in 1919 will now be followed up to that year.

Georgette at the age of fifty had lost not just a lover and companion of twenty years, but her beloved Abbey of Saint-Wandrille. She was fed up with anything to do with literature. What good had it served her? She wrote to a friend: 'Don't talk to me about writing. If you knew how literature disgusted me. Wasn't literature at the bottom of all my unhappiness.' She believed she should go to America to reconstruct her life, however mad the idea. Whatever happened, it would be interesting, 'at least for me'.[1]

However bitter she was, this had not prevented Georgette from starting to negotiate the publication of her memoirs in the United States. She was to deal with the Paris agent of the William Randolph Hearst group, a man called Vidal Hundt,[2] who had such faith in the money-spinning capacity of the story of her life and her relationship with Maeterlinck that he was proposing a contract worth $4,000 dollars to publish her story in the *Sunday American*, even though she had not yet written a word.[3] This contract would last for five years and should bring her the fame necessary to revive her own career. She had to argue with her now famous brother Maurice to try to convince him that for her life was about to begin.

'Your life has been wonderful', he argued. Having experienced great art and great love she should stay in France and simply enjoy some peace. Her life was over.

'No, Maurice', Georgette argued. 'My life is just beginning.'[4]

Life certainly was beginning anew. She had ended her close relationship with Maeterlinck. Her long term companion Mathilde Deschamps had duped her of her money. A new relationship was to be her salvation. To find its source we have to return to her earliest performances at La Monnaie in Brussels. There in 1896 she had sung the title role in Massenet's *Thaïs*, causing

---

[1] Leblanc, *Souvenirs: My Life with Maeterlinck*, p. 347.

[2] Georgette refers to him as Véral D.

[3] Leblanc, *La Machine à courage*, p. 22.

[4] Leblanc, *Souvenirs: My Life with Maeterlinck*, p. 344.

quite a stir wearing a flimsy, virtually transparent tunic, leaving her shoulders and arms bare.[5] Her interpretation of the role certainly captured the heart of a young Belgian teacher living in Brussels, Mathilde Serrure. Margaret Anderson, of whom more later, recounts that having heard Georgette sing Thaïs, Mathilde's first gesture was to buy a bunch of violets and put it on Georgette's doorstep, initiating a relationship lasting nearly fifty years.[6] She continued to express her admiration in letters to Georgette. Now, in 1919, the time had come when Mathilde could become much more than a mere correspondent.

The name 'Mathilde' had such an evil connotation for Georgette that first Mathilde Serrure must assume the name Monique – chosen because she reminded Georgette of the mother of St Augustine![7] Mathilde was then to join her in Paris. Georgette, incidentally, had deceived her as to her true age, saying she had been born in 1875, making her six years younger than she really was.[8] In fact, both were born in 1869. In September 1920 this retired schoolteacher helped Georgette to make preparations for their departure to America. Finances were still a huge problem, though. Once again she had to turn to her brother Maurice to bail her out by lending her enough money for the journey.

On 27 November 1920 she and Monique left for New York, coincidentally on the same boat, the *Olympic*, which had taken her across the Atlantic in December 1911 to sing *Pelléas* in Boston. She had no possessions of monetary value, but she took with her a goldfish in a bowl and a jar containing some earth from Saint-Wandrille.[9] To her surprise the agent, Hundt, had told Georgette to make sure she arrived in New York incognito, so she obediently hid when she saw a pack of pressmen on the quayside. Upon meeting the two women, Hundt explained he wanted Georgette to explode onto the scene with her memoirs, promising that the moment they were published in the *Sunday American*, this would lead to screen appearances, she would sing, give talks, act. This, after all, was only a few months after Maeterlinck had visited the city with Renée, and received a tumultuous welcome and been wined and dined as a literary idol. There must be mileage in her story.

Hundt found Georgette and Monique a tiny, dark flat, far from the city centre. A page from her diary scribbled in pencil reads, 'Sunday 10 a.m. In my bed – New York! Such a desire to do *nothing*, to *not exist*, that I haven't

5 See Chapter 3, p. 47.
6 Margaret Anderson, *The Fiery Fountains* (New York, 1951), p. 7.
7 Leblanc, *La Machine à courage*, p. 20.
8 Benoît-Jeannin, *Georgette Leblanc*, p. 372.
9 Leblanc, *La Machine à courage*, p. 23.

written a line since Wednesday, the day of my arrival.' She noted the names of people she had to impress, and searched around for ways of keeping her name in the public eye. Already she was considering the idea of making a *roman ciné* in which she would act herself.[10]

Georgette had hardly any knowledge of the language, yet insisted that not a single line should be published concerning Maeterlinck which she had not approved. She also demanded to meet the newspaper magnate William Randolph Hearst, a naïve request which met with derision. When she was taken to see the offices of the newspaper, she was overwhelmed by the familiarity of its employees, whom she described as 'always in shirtsleeves, both morally and physically'. She found herself surrounded by people hoping to climb onto her bandwagon, claiming they would eventually find her a part in a film or on stage, or write her a sketch for a music-hall act. Every time she received an advance from the newspaper, Hundt took a 30 per cent cut. He still insisted she did not contact the few people she did know in New York until the translation of her memoirs was completed. Once this day dawned she was indignant when informed that changes would have to be made, and again refused to allow these without her consent. Her obstinacy eventually meant the end of her financial advances and the threat that publication would never take place.

Georgette desperately wanted to terminate her contract and try to repay Hearst the money invested in her by earning it through concert performances or cinema.[11] By March money for food was so hard to come by that she even went into Central Park bearing some sketches she had done, and managed to sell one. This bought supper that night.[12] Emboldened by this little victory, she hatched a plan to take herself by bus to the Manhattan Opera House. There she knocked on the door of the box of an old acquaintance, Mrs Oscar Hammerstein, now a widow, who gave her a seat right beside her.

The opera being performed was Henry Février's *Monna Vanna*, given by the Chicago Opera Company with none other than Mary Garden in the title role. Georgette was not particularly moved by her portrayal, for Mary, wrapped in light veils, did not convey to her the character of Monna Vanna as she had interpreted her in Maeterlinck's play. She was in a rêverie at the end when she heard Mrs Hammerstein suggest that she should go backstage afterwards to congratulate Mary Garden. Despite the crowd in the dressing room, Mary spotted Georgette.

'Georgette Leblanc! How do you do?' The soprano shook hands and

[10] In AML, Brussels, Georgette Leblanc Collection, 499/118.
[11] Leblanc, *La Machine à courage*, p. 34.
[12] Leblanc, *La Machine à courage*, p. 40.

inquired as to what Georgette thought of the performance, the costumes, the interpretation. 'This isn't your first visit to New York? You must come back and see *Thaïs* next week! So pleased to have seen you again!'[13] Georgette does not tell us how she replied, for she was still feeling dazed. Her description of Mary as smiling and sympathetic, however, does not appear to be antagonistic.

Lucien Muratore, who was singing the role of Prinzivalle, also recognised her and demanded to know why he had not heard her singing in New York. At the end of the performance, Georgette took courage in her hands and courageously asked Mrs Hammerstein if she would buy the chinchilla fur she had round her neck so that she could survive a little longer. How was Georgette to have known that she too, despite being covered in diamonds and pearls, would claim to be in financial distress and unable to do anything to help?

Despite her disappointment and frustration, this visit to the opera was a vital turning point in Georgette's life, for there a young man spotted her who had admired her ever since, as a teenager, he had seen her sing Mélisande in Boston in 1912 under André Caplet. This was the pianist and composer Allen Tanner. Having heard that she was in New York, he had been looking out for her since her arrival – had even seen her in the distance on Christmas Day, when walking down Sixth Avenue singing *Pelléas* to himself![14] He took this opportunity to introduce himself, and the following day Georgette received a bouquet of lilies, a card bearing a phrase of Debussy's music, and a poetic request to visit her. On discovering her precarious situation he determined to try to help her.

To keep the wolf from the door a little longer, Georgette managed to introduce herself to a lawyer friend of Mrs Hammerstein who suggested she contacted the publishers of her book *The Children's Bluebird*, Dodd, Mead & Company. Thus it was eventually agreed her memoirs would be published in book form after their appearance in the *Sunday American* and she was paid an advance of a thousand dollars. This enabled Georgette and Monique to move into more salubrious accommodation, a small room on the twenty-first floor of the Commodore Hotel.

One day (Georgette says Sunday 13 March 1921), Allen Tanner called her down to the lobby of this hotel in order to introduce her to thirty-five-year-old Margaret Anderson, who with Jane Heap, edited *The Little Review*, the monthly journal which had first appeared in March 1914. This magazine had been founded by Margaret Anderson with the aim of publishing

13 Leblanc, *La Machine à courage*, p. 43.
14 Leblanc, *La Machine à courage*, p. 46.

anything that she regarded as true art whatever its provenance, and, as she put it, 'making no compromise with the public taste'.[15] Margaret and Jane had known even worse poverty than Georgette. Margaret had started the magazine when she had no money of her own, then managed to find a bene-factor who paid the rent for her office and printer's fees. She also persuaded advertisers to risk their money. Whilst they struggled to keep the journal in print Margaret and Jane had at one time even ended up camping out on the shores of Lake Michigan. So determined were they never to publish inferior articles and poems that one issue became celebrated for consisting entirely of blank pages, apart from a few cartoons! The list of famous contribu-tors from America and Europe grew and in 1916 Ezra Pound became their London correspondent. It was at his suggestion that they serialised *Ulysses* by James Joyce, starting in March 1918. The scandal that this 'obscene' work provoked brought a court case and a fine, but what shocked the two women most was the lack of any support for their freedom of expression from the press. In New York, Margaret and Jane became part of a lesbian subculture in Greenwich Village and campaigned for the acceptance of alternative life-styles. In March 1921, it was to these two women that Allen Tanner had the idea of introducing Georgette Leblanc.

When the moment of introduction to Margaret Anderson arrived, fifty-two-year-old Georgette emerged from a lift in the hotel foyer and was bowled over by the sight of the other woman, seventeen years her junior, 'with horizon-blue silhouette, waving a white-gloved hand and smiling beneath a toque of skunk fur'.[16] As they kissed, each left a trace of lipstick on the other's cheek. Margaret insists that their meeting was predestined. 'We knew at once that we were to join hands and advance through life together.' Neither spoke the language of the other, but this appears to have caused no barrier to their mutual understanding.[17]

Georgette and Monique moved from the noisy and uncomfortable Commodore Hotel to two tiny rooms on the fifteenth floor of the Nobleton Hotel. Meanwhile, whilst suffering from flu and lacking the strength to resist any longer, Georgette signed the final proofs of her Memoirs, thus enabling the *Sunday American* to publish them when space became available. Still she wanted to retain the right to make alterations, wary of divulging too much about Maeterlinck.

Now Georgette's particular ambition was to find a way into the world of cinema, an art form developing fast, and growing in public awareness and

[15] Anderson, *The Fiery Fountains*, p. 6.
[16] Leblanc, *La Machine à courage*, p. 62.
[17] Anderson, *The Fiery Fountains*, p. 6; Leblanc, *La Machine à courage*, p. 62.

popularity. Once she managed to get invited to an evening being hosted at the Ritz by Charlie Chaplin and acted in a game of charades with the great comedian, but this partnership developed no further. Another attempt was made when she invited Abel Gance, the French filmmaker, to her hotel room, but despite dressing up to impress him, no more came of this. In August 1921 Georgette, miserably poverty-stricken, had to appeal to Margaret for help. Her solution was to invite Georgette and Monique to move into the flat she shared with Jane Heap on 8th Street, Greenwich Village.

Monique and Margaret had helped Georgette correct the proofs of the serialisation of her memoirs in the *Sunday American*, but when the day of publication arrived, she could not suppress her horror at the newspaper's sensational treatment. She knew that scandal was the bread and butter of the press, but could not believe her eyes when she saw lurid posters showing two entwined red hearts pierced by a black arrow and her and Maeterlinck's names beneath the words 'Twenty years of Love without Marriage'.[18] The opening instalment promised 'The Intimate Details of the Most Extraordinary Romance of all History by the Woman who Fed the Fires of Poet Maeterlinck's Genius.'[19]

Whatever her shame and disgust, however, Georgette had the consolation of knowing she had found support and a love which was reciprocated. Somehow, by hook or by crook, the four women managed to gather together enough money to rent a house at Bernardsville, New Jersey. They lived on credit, and when Allen Tanner came to join them he even brought with him a Steinway piano, likewise on credit. Other artists migrated towards them including the extrovert George Antheil, avant-garde young composer and pupil of Ernest Bloch, who monopolised the Steinway. As Antheil reports, he had been invited only for a week-end but stayed for six months.[20] What an atmosphere of musical creativity flourished in the warmth of that summer! Georgette and her companions had to get used to Antheil's composing technique, which consisted of taking a theme of five or six notes, repeating it incessantly for hours, listening to the vibrations produced, then running to his room to write until morning.[21] Idyllic days were spent working separately, but in the evenings the group would meet and Georgette would sing Mélisande with Allen Tanner singing Pelléas. This role still came first to mind when she wanted to sing. Here, Allen was the perfect partner. 'His voice of bronze brought to life a Pelléas I had never heard in the theatre', she

---

[18] Leblanc, *La Machine à courage*, p. 83.

[19] Halls, *Maurice Maeterlinck*, p. 123.

[20] George Antheil, *Bad Boy of Music* (New York, 1945), p. 19.

[21] Leblanc, *La Machine à courage*, p. 90.

wrote.[22] With the arrival of cold weather their finances did not stretch to heating and the group moved down to the basement where they had found a wood stove.

Fortunately Georgette managed to persuade the property owner to keep the telephone connected and at last, towards the end of November, it rang. Allen had arranged for a rich lady on Fifth Avenue to hear Georgette sing. Her payments enabled all bills to be settled, and meant that the women could rent a small flat on the River Hudson. However, after discovering that this building was in fact a brothel, Georgette had to borrow money to rent a studio-apartment in Washington Place, Greenwich Village. To keep the wolf from the door, she managed to get some recital work and to write articles on subjects other than her life, and even get some drawings published. She also gave singing lessons. Her connections were widening, for on 10 August 1922, through Mrs Leopold Stokowski, Georgette gave a recital at Bar Harbor, Maine, accompanied by Walter Damrosch, Director of the New York Symphony Society.[23]

More hopes and plans were built up then evaporated. Left only with her belief in herself, Georgette managed to rent a hall, 47 Washington Square South, in a building due for demolition and there organised a private club to put on concerts and recitals where she sang with her devoted accompanist Margaret at the piano. Their programmes lasted for two hours, always consisting of contemporary works by such composers as Debussy, Milhaud, de Falla, Honneger, Stravinsky, Antheil, Satie, Poulenc, and Varèse. Georgette recited poems by Mallarmé, Baudelaire and Verhaeren, but the only work with words by Maeterlinck that she performed was the tower scene from Debussy's *Pelléas et Mélisande*. On 13 December 1922 she appeared at a more prestigious venue, the Town Hall, and there again had the opportunity to remind a larger public of her performance as Mélisande. 'The spare, pale figure in black, the animation of face and gesture, invited interest, even as the woman's intelligence [*always that word*!] and theatric instinct vitalized moods, vocally unrelieved by sensuous appeal, yet poetically illumined', was a critic's description.[24]

After singing and reciting for sixty-two evenings in succession the fairytale ending Georgette had been longing for came about. She was 'spotted' by a group of smartly dressed people who were representatives of Otto Kahn. At last her salvation came through this financier, art-lover and collector, benefactor and founder of the French Theatre of New York, of the

[22] Leblanc, *La Machine à courage*, p. 90.

[23] Programme in album at AML, Brussels, Georgette Leblanc Collection, 499/118.

[24] *New York Times*, 14 December 1922.

Franco-American committee, and patron of the Boston and Chicago operas as well as Covent Garden. She had originally met Kahn in April 1921 probably through Margaret Anderson, as he had already sponsored *The Little Review*. He loved France and wanted to encourage and revivify cultural links between the two countries. Acknowledging her gifts, he enabled her to benefit to the extent of founding her own company, Art Direction Georgette Leblanc Inc., based on the twenty third floor of the Fisk Building. Georgette wanted no one to suffer the indignities she had undergone on her arrival in New York, penniless and with no artistic support, and was determined that her agency would look after such artists, wherever they came from.

Meanwhile she was becoming increasingly aware of another way of achieving fame. Mary Garden had already tried to make her name in silent films. It was only a matter of time before Georgette would follow in her footsteps, but not with the famous Goldwyn Company. She managed to persuade Otto Kahn to invest in a French film to be presented in America in which she would star. With his financial backing, she sailed back across the Atlantic to France on 14 May 1923.

The film-maker Georgette contacted was Marcel L'Herbier, that young man with whom she had formed a relationship in 1912 when he was courting her niece. By now he had become a renowned and respected film director, having made his first film, *Rose-France* in 1918. In 1922 he had created his own production company, Cinégraphic. He had not forgotten his links with Georgette and Maeterlinck, for amongst early plans he announced was a short documentary entitled *Garden-Party chez Maeterlinck*.[25] At fifty-four, how could Georgette possibly star in this art form which demanded young and beautiful faces and figures? As Catelain wrote, 'Georgette, still strangely beautiful, is not exactly photogenic. This would be a hard task. But the super-woman, who had such infectious enthusiasm, managed to convince our friend.'[26]

L'Herbier wanted to produce a film entitled *La Femme de glace*, but Georgette persuaded him to adapt the scenario to be more acceptable to American taste and assisted him with this. The film became *L'Inhumaine*, in which she acted the part of an ageing singer, Claire Lescot, in love with a younger Swedish engineer, Einar Norsen, played by Jaque Catelain.[27] She invested 30,000 francs of her sponsorship money in the production and

---

[25] *Jaque Catelain présente Marcel L'Herbier*, p. 73.

[26] 'Georgette, encore d'une étrange beauté, n'est pas précisément photogénique; ce projet se présente donc comme une tâche ardue. Mais la super-femme, d'un enthousiasme si contagieux, finit par convaincre notre ami.' *Jaque Catelain présente Marcel L'Herbier*, p. 76.

[27] *Ciné-Miroir*, 1 July 1925.

planned to present the film in America as *The New Enchantment*. It was a
hugely ambitious avant-garde project, for which the artist Fernand Léger
and architect Mallet-Stevens were just two of the four set designers. The
music accompanying the silent film was by Darius Milhaud. The score does
not appear to be preserved, but as Catelain writes that 'Darius Milhaud
improvises charmingly',[28] one wonders if it was ever written down.

Despite its complexity, filming had to be finished in time for Georgette
to cross back on 10 October 1923 to New York, where she was due to open
a season of concerts. Margaret and Monique stayed at her sister's château at
Tancarville whilst she worked flat out with L'Herbier in the film studio in
Joinville-le-Pont. Catelain wrote a vivid description of the tensions aroused
while filming until the small hours each night. Further excitement was created on 4 October at a concert at the Théâtre des Champs-Elysées to which
L'Herbier took his cameras. He was able to film an extraordinary scene
when a tumultuous riot erupted spontaneously in the audience, described
by Catelain as the most extreme reaction to a performance since the *Rite
of Spring* or Satie's *Parade*![29] Here George Antheil, the 'Bad Boy of Music',
caused a commotion with his extremely dissonant music, music which had
already caused riots in Germany. When Antheil went to see the finished film,
he realised, although he was off-camera, that he himself had unwittingly
played a part in it, claiming that amongst the rioting public were such illustrious figures as James Joyce and Picasso:

> However, most curiously this riot is not a fake one. It is the *actual* riot, the
> same riot through which I played and lived that night of October 4, 1923.
> When I first viewed this movie a year later, I suddenly remembered Georgette
> Leblanc walking up to my piano while the great flood lights in the balcony
> poured on us both simultaneously. I had thought it odd then.[30]

Margaret Anderson told him she thought he would have been too nervous if
he had known that the floodlights had been previously reinforced and cameras hidden in the balcony in the *hope* that his piano sonatas would cause the
same sort of riot in Paris that they had caused in Germany.

Despite all efforts, filming was not completed in time for Georgette's
commitments in the States, and arrangements had to be made for the missing scenes to be finished when she returned to France in the spring of 1924.
She returned to New York in October 1923 on the *Aquitania* with Margaret
for company, but not with Monique Serrure, who was suffering from

[28] 'Darius Milhaud improvise avec charme.' *Jaque Catelain présente Marcel L'Herbier*,
p. 79.
[29] *Jaque Catelain présente Marcel L'Herbier*, p. 79.
[30] Antheil, *Bad Boy of Music*, p. 136.

exhaustion. During this crossing the captain organised a tombola on board for which he needed prizes. Georgette duly shut herself in her cabin and completed a sketch of Paderewski who was a fellow passenger.[31]

This return to the States could not have been more different from Georgette's last arrival there. Two events in October kept her in the news. The first was the announcement in the *Daily News* that Renée Maeterlinck, the author's wife, forbade Georgette from using Maeterlinck's name, although there was little she could do to stop the newspapers from linking her with him, and the second was Georgette's setting off on a tour of the south and west of the United States. Before this she was photographed in the foyer of the Waldorf-Astoria wearing a fur coat valued at $8,000.[32] Here she was, temporarily the darling of the newspapers, living the American dream. She wallowed in her success. She was compared in stature to her idols, Sarah Bernhardt and Eleonora Duse.[33] Later Margaret Anderson wrote nostalgically of this time, recalling concerts in cities and towns from New York to San Francisco: 'I remember critics writing that Georgette Leblanc, if asked to, could sing the multiplication table as exquisitely as Pallisy handled porcelain.'[34] So much for those who had thought Georgette would be nothing without her famous lover's name to trade on. A souvenir of this tour remains in the form of eloquent eulogies from many newspapers on a large promotional advertisement extolling 'Le plus sensationnel succès' of her performances in New York, Washington and Chicago.[35]

Yet, despite his bitterness, Georgette still felt an invisible bond to Maeterlinck. On 3 January 1924 she wrote a long emotional letter to Monique even suggesting that she should go to see him, saying she was sure that if he had been master of his own life he would not have left her. 'Send me a leaf from the garden', she begged.[36] There is, however, no evidence to suggest that any meeting between Monique and Maeterlinck ever took place.

Publicity for *The New Enchantment* (*L'Inhumaine*) progressed well at the beginning of 1924, and in a long letter of 20 February Georgette suggested a scenario for a new film to L'Herbier, with a character based on the Claire Lescot of that film and royalty based on King George I of Greece, whom she had met in 1902, and his son Constantine. In the same letter she wrote of an

---

[31] Leblanc, *La Machine à courage*, p. 180. (Her albums at AML, Brussels, are full of sketches.)

[32] Benoît-Jeannin, *Georgette Leblanc*, p. 417.

[33] *Chicago Evening American*, 17 December 1923.

[34] Anderson, *The Fiery Fountains*, p. 32.

[35] In AML, Brussels, Georgette Leblanc Collection.

[36] 'Que tu m'envoies un petit brin de feuillage du jardin.' AML, Brussels, Georgette Leblanc Collection, 499/118.

exciting plan being hatched to bring *Pelléas et Mélisande* to the public in a completely novel way. On about 20 March she would sing in a radio studio at four in the morning. The American station would broadcast the performance to Paris, to the Eiffel Tower, where it would be received at about nine in the evening. Transmitting a voice over such a long distance still presented great difficulties. She knew success depended on weather conditions and temperature, but was very excited at the prospect, and she asked L'Herbier to inform the radio magazines of the event. How thrilling would that be, to be the first to send Mélisande through the ether across the Atlantic ![37]

Frustratingly, before this could come about, at the end of February 1924 the fairy tale came to an abrupt end – as suddenly as it had begun. Georgette had to close her agency. All the money she had been receiving from her rich financier suddenly stopped. She had sunk all her profits and Kahn's money into *L'Inhumaine*. There was nothing left. The reasons for this cessation are mysterious, but it may be linked to rumours being spread about the lesbian relationship between Georgette and Margaret with which Kahn and others did not want to be associated. As Margaret wrote, the sudden end to the fairy tale was 'one of those extravaganzas that can happen only to people like us'.[38]

Georgette was ill for a while as a result of this worry, but continued to write to L'Herbier, to try to arrange recitals and to invite press attention. In March 1924 she had to resort to sensationalist means, sure to cause a stir, by touring around various cities holding a 'Love Clinic'. There were plenty of lurid headlines. 'American men can love but their technique is crude!' They should learn their techniques from the cinema, she advised, in order to gain more finesse. 'What happens when women get old? Do they miss love?', she was asked rather pointedly. She replied with a touch of asperity, 'Interesting people never get old. When passion dies, intelligence and esprit should naturally replace it.'[39]

Her last two concerts in New York took place at the Booth Theatre on 23 March[40] and 6 April 1924; they once more included the Tower Scene from *Pelléas et Mélisande* as well as songs by contemporary composers such as Stravinsky, Antheil, Satie, and Varèse and poems by Gourmont, Van Lerberghe and Verhaeren. She received warm acclaim from critics praising her interpretations. It was probably to introduce this scene from Debussy's opera that Georgette gave a talk on *Pelléas et Mélisande* in which she seems

[37] Benoît-Jeannin, *Georgette Leblanc*, p. 422.
[38] Anderson, *The Fiery Fountains*, p. 16.
[39] *New York Times*, 6 March 1924.
[40] *New York Times*, 23 March 1924.

to be trying to separate the arts of composer and writer, putting distance between the two, which runs counter to the opinion that Debussy's music and Maeterlinck's words were supremely fused in the opera. Despite the emphasis that had always been put on the fidelity with which Debussy had followed Maeterlinck's poem, Georgette found this absurd. The Mélisande of the opera was not as childlike as in Maeterlinck's conception. Whilst Debussy made an effort to follow Maeterlinck, it was impossible for an artist of his nature. They were two great individuals in two separate arts, equally consummate artists. It was not a question of supremacy of one over the other, merely that Debussy's was essentially another type of beauty. Georgette could not imagine how the beauty of Debussy's music could have a connection with the beauty of the spoken word.[41] This reminds one of her description of the two men when they originally met in her room to discuss the opera, where she emphasised the contrasts between them both physically and mentally.[42]

Before leaving New York to return to Europe, Georgette and Margaret met a personality who was to have a huge influence on the rest of their lives, George Ivanovitch Gurdjieff. Gurdjieff was the founder of the Institute for the Harmonious Development of Man at Fontainebleau near Paris, where he taught the development of a Universal Brotherhood and propounded a way of living which would help others to overcome the pressures of modern life. He was a Master, a man who did not merely teach doctrines, but was the incarnation of knowledge, who merely by his presence could help others in their search, enabling them to experience and live life as fully as possible.[43] His talks in New York were preceded by mystical dances of whirling dervishes and sacred dances he had seen in Tibetan monasteries. Gurdjieff himself had a presence about him which captivated the two women. 'In him there is a Truth', wrote Georgette.[44]

In April 1924 she and Margaret crossed back over the Atlantic and immediately Georgette returned to complete the filming of *L'Inhumaine* at Joinville-le-Pont – not without ructions. She had become aware in America of 'new methods', and she now claimed Catelain was ruining her screen career by insisting she wore too much formal make-up. This heavy mask must surely have had a dual purpose: to disguise her age and to contribute to the

---

[41] 'Georgette Leblanc talks on Debussy and Modern Music with special notes on Pelléas et Mélisande', *Musical Advance*, March 1924, in AML, Brussels, Georgette Leblanc Collection, 499/118.

[42] See Chapter 4, p. 58.

[43] See translator's note to G. Gurdjieff, *Meetings with Remarkable Men* (London, 1963).

[44] Leblanc, *La Machine à courage*, p. 195.

avant-garde sense of intensity of mood.[45] The film was at last given a private
showing in Paris on 6 May 1924 at the Colisée. It was also part of a festival
week at the Madeleine Cinéma. On both occasions it received a very mixed
reception from both general public and critics. Lively arguments, even fights
broke out. 'What anguish!' wrote Catelain. 'Never in the history of cinema
had a work provoked such a riot!'[46] People asked for their money back. It
was difficult to reconcile the age of Leblanc (fifty-five) with her romance
with the young scientist and the theme of this 'inhuman woman' who rejects
offers of marriage and associations with theatre owners and others who
promise her large audiences. Reviewers of the film in several European cities
tended either to love it or hate it, and in America it disconcerted audiences
who were unreceptive to the cinematic novelties and stark cubist settings. It
did not reach London until February 1927, when it was shown by the Film
society at the New Gallery. The *Times* reviewer had reservations but found
it original and decidedly interesting. ('Oh, that British phlegm!' exclaims
Catelain!)[47] The reviewer was particularly fascinated by the lavish inventive-
ness of the avant-garde décor. *L'Inhumaine* marked the beginning and the
end of Georgette's film career. Another crossroads had been reached.

At this point in 1924 she, Margaret, Jane and Monique followed their
desire to follow the way of life advocated by Gurdjieff and in June entered
his priory at Fontainebleau-Avon, where they were given monastic cells in
the very building where another Gurdjieff disciple, Katherine Mansfield,
had died of tuberculosis on 9 January 1923. Whilst her accommodation was
an unheated room with a hard bed, Georgette's daytime task in the com-
mune was to work in the vegetable garden. Physical labour, a frugal lunch
then readings, endless discussion and dance until bedtime were the basis
of her daily routine. The concept of simplicity leading to balance of mind
through physical work and assimilation of Gurdjieff's teachings brought her
solace and new strength.

In December 1924 Georgette accepted a recital tour of Northern Italy.
This is not a period of her life that she includes in her memoirs. Margaret,
however, who was to accompany her on the piano, does refer to it in *The
Fiery Fountains*. Monique was also there to attend to their needs. Lack of
publicity and Georgette's very contemporary programme of songs led to
hopelessly low audience figures. To add insult to injury, Georgette suffered
the theft of her mink coat, which was precious not only for financial and sen-
timental reasons, but was also a vital necessity in the cold winter. The police

[45] *Jaque Catelain présente Marcel L'Herbier*, p. 81. See illus. 36.
[46] *Jaque Catelain présente Marcel L'Herbier*, p. 82.
[47] 'Oh! ce flegme britannique!' *Jaque Catelain présente Marcel L'Herbier*, p. 82.

arrived two hours after being called and searched their trunks, on the theory that the theft was a publicity stunt.[48] It was only acknowledged to be a reality when Georgette adamantly claimed to the authorities that Mussolini and d'Annunzio would vouch for her.

We have already noted that Mary Garden was warned of d'Annunzio's reputation as a flamboyant womaniser during his period in Paris between 1910 and 1914.[49] Even before their first meeting, Georgette had heard at first hand from the great actress Eleonora Duse about her tempestuous relationship with him and the ending of their legendary love affair. Georgette herself had associated with him in salons, but although she admired his work she claims she found his exaggerated romantic airs and bombastic attitude to women irritating.[50] Now, however, it would be useful to exploit this very influential and useful connection.

Having occupied and ruled Fiume in 1919–20, d'Annunzio was now living away from the public eye in his extraordinary residence, the Vittoriale, on the shores of Lake Garda, which was being completely renovated by the architect Gian Carlo Maroni. This remains a uniquely exotic architectural and artistic realm, packed with art treasures, frozen in time. When he purchased the villa in 1921 d'Annunzio also acquired the library of about 6,000 books, a Steinway piano that once belonged to Liszt, manuscripts by Wagner, and portraits and furniture. Not long before Georgette's arrival, in April 1924 Eleonora Duse had died, and d'Annunzio, heartbroken, placed a veil over her plaster head in his study – a constant reminder of her inspiration to him.

Desperate for help, Georgette and her companions moved to a hotel on Lake Garda in January 1925, and sent the poet a letter. His immediate response was to dispatch a huge bouquet of flowers and an enormous bottle of scent. Addressing her in florid terms as 'Armide', he insisted she visit him in his 'glorious prison and voluptuous hermitage'. As evidenced by his great cabinet full of medicines, d'Annunzio was a hypochondriac and insomniac. Having just welcomed the arrival of his MAS, his Motor Torpedo Boat on which he had carried out the raid on Buccari (now Bakar, Croatia) in 1918, and gone out into the cold night to admire it, he now had to postpone Georgette's arrival due to 'illness'. Eventually he sent his chauffeur-driven limousine to fetch her.

An extraordinary series of meetings and letters followed, each eulogising the other in exaggeratedly romantic terms, some begging her not to flee

[48] Anderson, *The Fiery Fountains*, p. 33.

[49] See Chapter 14, p. 203.

[50] Georgette Leblanc, 'D'Annunzio au Vittoriale: souvenirs inédits', *Les Œuvres libres*, no. 203 (Paris, May 1938), p. 111.

from him at night, for she appears to have insisted on returning to her hotel, despite his 'daily torment and sombre melancholy'. In his house is a wardrobe containing various nightdresses in which he would dress his lover of the moment, but whether Georgette wore one or not is a moot point! The d'Annunzio connection took effect. A recital Georgette gave in Milan now achieved greater recognition. He provided further introductions for her, and she persuaded him to present her with some of his early poems written in French which she included as part of her recitals. One can only surmise what Margaret Anderson made of this association.[51]

On their return to Paris in 1925, the women once again had reason to be grateful to Maurice Leblanc, who gave them money to survive on, enabling Georgette to resume her singing and poetry recitations. In the Salle Comoedia, as ever, contemporary music featured in her programme: Honneger, Poulenc and Satie. Here she also realised another long-held ambition. At last, for the first time on French soil, she sang the Tower Scene from *Pelléas et Mélisande*. Further recitals and readings followed as Georgette and Margaret built up a following of lovers of the eclectic and eccentric. Georgette continued to widen her circle of literary contacts, socialising with artists, poets and musicians in lesbian and heterosexual circles. In June 1926 she gave a series of *concerts express* in the Théâtre du Colisée, the novel format of which was based on 'the principles of cinema' when two identical programmes were presented in succession on the same day. The contents were an extraordinary mixture of music from Bach to Irving Berlin, jazz, and her pièce de résistance, the Tower Scene from *Pelléas* in which she sang both Pelléas and Mélisande. How frustrating that there is no recording to compare her interpretation with those of Mary Garden and Maggie Teyte.

When the Swiss tenor Hugues Cuénod first met Georgette she was organising a lecture on the creation of *Pelléas et Mélisande* in which she wanted him to participate. From his description it is evident that by 1928 she had lost none of her exoticism or eccentric mannerisms. He described her as strange, tall, dressed in Eastern style of 1900. She lived with her female companion in an old-fashioned apartment with plenty of cushions, black ones decorated with sparrows, red ones with coloured patterns. 'They served me heavily scented tea; there was incense. She was very kind, but she was so unlike middle-class ladies of the time that I felt rather embarrassed.'[52]

51 Letters in AML, Brussels, Georgette Leblanc Collection, 499/118, and in Leblanc, 'D'Annunzio au Vittoriale'.

52 'Elle était très aimable, mais elle ressemblait si peu aux bourgeoises de l'époque que je me sentais un peu gêné.' Hugues Cuénod, *D'une voix légère: entretiens avec François Hudry* (Lausanne, 1996), p. 22. (He also knew Helen Garden well and had met Mary Garden at Helen's house in Vevey in 1925.)

At their meeting, Georgette told Cuénod a strange anecdote from the past, and later included it in her talk. When she and Maeterlinck first knew each other, the author was afraid Georgette's Spanish husband would search him out to wreak vengeance. When the couple were sitting on a park bench one day Georgette thought someone was spying on them from behind. Maeterlinck, having forgotten (for once) to bring his revolver with him, was so frightened he climbed the nearest tree! As Cuénod points out, there is a distinct similarity here with the fourth act of *Pelléas*! He is mistaken, however, in thinking the incident could have been an inspiration for the scene, as chronologically this is impossible.

Finding herself yet again without money, Georgette had to turn to her sister Jehanne for help. Jehanne had a penchant (and the financial means) for renting glorious old châteaux and houses, one of which was the Château de la Muette in the forest of Saint-Germain-en-Laye, to the West of Paris, and she was reluctantly persuaded to allow Georgette and her companions to live there. Georgette revelled in the romantic environment where, it was said, the Abbé Prévost had written *Manon*.[53] However, life was very spartan, for Jehanne was extremely miserly and kept a strict account of all expenditure on food and commodities, even charging six francs a time for a bath.[54] Margaret tells many anecdotes about the extraordinary lengths Jehanne went to in order to keep an eye on the supposed profligacy of the women.

It was in 1927 that an even more eccentric building with which Georgette and her companions were to be associated was spotted during a walk along a cliff above the estuary of the Seine. Appearing out of the mists they saw the lighthouse at Tancarville. They discovered that this enchanting building, so isolated and so close to nature, was uninhabited and no longer in use. It was the perfect environment for these exceptional women who found ordinary life so difficult to inhabit. Jehanne and her husband were probably only too glad to get rid of the trio to somewhere completely out of the way. They therefore agreed to finance restoration works, so summer of 1927 was spent busily making the lighthouse suitable for habitation. Now Georgette and Margaret could write undisturbed whilst Monique ministered to their every need. There, between 1928 and 1930 Georgette wrote her book *Souvenirs (1895–1918)*, later to be translated into English by Janet Flanner as *Souvenirs: My Life with Maeterlinck*. There she found the isolation she needed, 'in a dwelling as restricted as Saint-Wandrille had been vast, but its horizon was boundless – a lighthouse situated in space itself.'[55]

[53] Leblanc, *La Machine à courage*, p. 123.
[54] Anderson, *The Fiery Fountains*, p. 40.
[55] Leblanc, *Souvenirs: My Life with Maeterlinck*, p. 351.

They lived in the lighthouse in spring, summer and autumn and would have stayed on all year if they could have kept warm. Fortunately, in the winter months Georgette managed to persuade her older sister to sub-let to her the Pavillon de la Muette, a hunting lodge in the grounds of the château. Even so, this remained virtually uninhabitable as it needed huge restoration works. The three women tried to persuade the authorities at the Ministère des Beaux-Arts to restore the historic monument so that they could live with some warmth and water, but what minor improvements were made were unreliable. They had to manage without a water supply for several months; when it did materialise the pump worked only intermittently. Lighting was by candles, heating by logs. Georgette, however, always kept up appearances, and her visitors were still most likely to find her dressed in her eccentric medieval clothes, as befitted the surroundings. Whatever the deprivations, here the women 'lived as one rarely hopes to live', and retained for ever memories of the beautifully proportioned rooms, and of Allen Tanner playing Bach in the *rotonde* in the light of the stars.[56]

[56] Anderson, *The Fiery Fountains*, p. 50.

19 *Maggie Teyte's Fresh Start*
(1930-45)

*H*ow was Maggie Teyte, now single again and anxious to resurrect a career which had been sorely neglected for the latter part of the 1920s, going to imprint herself on the public consciousness? At short notice she took over the role of Butterfly at Covent Garden when in June 1930 the soprano Edith Mason fell ill. She was heard in the same role on radio, but although this brought recognition, it was not the return she wanted.

Far more meaningful to her was the work she was next engaged to sing at Covent Garden. What more could she have asked for than two performances of Pelléas et Mélisande on 17 and 23 June? Maggie was now forty-two, and here she was being asked to sing the young girl, Mélisande. The conductor she worked with knew the opera well: he had just returned to Covent Garden for the first time since 1914 from Chicago where he had been conducting Mary Garden in the same work. Maggie regarded Giorgio Polacco as the opera's ideal interpreter. She wrote:

> He had become an enthusiast for this score, and the love and devotion that he poured into the interpretation of it made the occasion one of my most outstanding memories of the opera. So beautifully did he draw out the colour from the orchestra that it seemed as though the score had become an illuminated manuscript in sound.[1]

Roger Bourdin sang Pelléas, John Brownlee was Golaud, Fernando Autori sang Arkel and Jeanne Montfort was Geneviève. Yniold was sung by Evelyn Hanson. Perhaps Maggie's own experiences of life and the tribulations she had endured, as well as her much deeper knowledge of men and relationships, gave a greater understanding and empathy to her interpretation. Yet the essence of the role is not to seem too knowing. Maggie had first been seen in the role in London when she was in her thirties, so the critics could not compare her current performance with that of the fresh young teenager who had performed it in Paris, yet some still regarded her latest performance as definitive. The *Evening News* wrote, 'Time has left her the ingenuous, forlorn little princess of Maeterlinck's and Debussy's dream.' Understanding of Debussy's opera had matured since its first performances in London, *The Times* finding that Debussy's figures had humanity, the music being gripping 'by sheer force of accumulated understatement.' Maggie Teyte, the critic

[1] Teyte, *Star on the Door*, p. 111.

remarked, was too rarely heard these days. She made Mélisande 'wistful, mysterious and tender. Her voice is of the right weight for the part, and her acting (which is important) was discreet.' Her interpretation was described as 'delicate and beautiful'.[2] Did observers realise how authentic this interpretation was? The programme for the evening gave no biographical notes.

What was her next engagement? Well might one ask. Despite this success, not for another seven years was Maggie asked back to Covent Garden. In her book *Star on the Door* she devotes a whole chapter to the 1930s and her struggle to recapture the hearts of the public. She received accolades for her appearances at the London Proms in 1932 and 1934.[3] In June 1932 a reviewer of a recital complained once again that she was not heard as often as she ought to be,[4] but one place where she was to be heard was in the Victoria Palace, where once again she tried her hand, or rather her voice, in their 'non-stop variety' season, where the programme was to be so slick that intermissions were omitted! Even in these surroundings, The Times agreed that Maggie Teyte had given pleasure by her singing.[5]

Maggie was then heard briefly in the role of Mrs Fitzherbert in Kennedy Russell's operetta *By Appointment*, which opened at the New Theatre on 11 October 1934. In the song 'White Roses' recorded for HMV with orchestra that month she sounds fresh and completely at ease in the role, the purity of her intonation and clarity of enunciation heightening the romantic sincerity with which she sings.[6] It is a shame that this show only ran for three weeks, but hardly surprising when one reads the reviews, Maggie's performance apparently being almost its only redeeming feature. A brief trip across the Atlantic in November did not result in work. An alternative way of promoting herself was via the technical progress being made in the up and coming medium of radio. Maggie tells of a useful contribution she made by aiding the improvement of the quality of broadcasting the voice. With the help of a firm called Pamphonic Ltd she actually invented a recording machine which registered the vibrations of the voice as received by the microphone and allowed the singer to see a printout so that he or she could judge when their tone was 'overloading'. The invention was called the 'Teytone' after her,[7] but has since sunk into oblivion.

Maggie's frustration at not being able to resurrect her singing career led her to cast her net further afield. She gave an account in her autobiography of

² *The Times*, 18 June 1930.

³ *The Times*, 8 August 1932, 13 August 1934.

⁴ *The Times*, 11 June 1932.

⁵ *The Times*, 11 October 1932.

⁶ *Great Singers: Maggie Teyte: A Vocal Portrait*, Naxos Historical, 8.110757–58.

⁷ Teyte, *Star on the Door*, p. 138.

a trip with the tenor Tudor Davies and pianist Yelland Richards to Australia, a country she loved, but reported honestly that whilst the trip was an artistic success, it was 'a financial fiasco, which I suppose was bound to colour one's impression of things in general'.[8] As Richard Bebb writes in his notes to the series of LPs, *L'Exquise Maggie Teyte*, 'With hindsight, we can see her flailing about, using up her abundant energies in a maze of wrong directions, almost wilfully ignoring the right path.'[9]

Maggie Teyte had not become the star she had had the potential and the desire to be before her first marriage. She could not get her career in the public eye going again. Others, from Mary Garden onwards, always seemed to be a step ahead of her in the operatic world. It was another developing technology that was to prove instrumental in keeping her singing and making her voice heard in people's homes – one that emerged just too late for Mary Garden to exploit to the full. The gramophone record would bring Maggie fame in England and the United States, and this was largely due to the admiration of a fan dating back to 1915.

When she had been in New York that year, Maggie had sung a recital in a series called 'Morning Musicales' at the Waldorf-Astoria. After the concert she had been approached by a young man in naval uniform who had introduced himself as Joe Brogan, who at that time wanted to be an opera singer. Knowing Maggie had been a pupil of Jean de Reszke, he wanted to ask her about him. Although he had not realised his ambition, he remained passionate about opera, and in the intervening years had worked in record companies, then founded his own record shop, the Gramophone Shop of New York City. This pioneering enterprise brought to the attention of the music loving public the potential of recorded music, which had been largely unrecognised. The shop soon developed a world-wide reputation. Maggie called it 'a shrine where all good classical recordings could be heard and discussed and where a good many private recordings were inspired'.[10]

Joe adored Maggie, and had the idea of trying to interest the Victor Record Company in recording an album of her Debussy repertoire. Since they did not accept this proposal he decided to come to London to see if he would fare better with HMV. There he spoke to the influential record producer Walter Legge, but he 'raised an eyebrow when my name was mentioned in connection with Debussy, and suggested the name of a well-known French artist',[11] related Maggie. Fortunately Brogan was resolute in his

[8] Teyte, *Star on the Door*, p. 141.
[9] *L'Exquise Maggie Teyte* (4 record set), EMI RLS716.
[10] Teyte, *Star on the Door*, p. 168.
[11] Teyte, *Star on the Door*, p. 168.

determination to bring Maggie's voice to a wider public, and had the temer-ity to arrange a meeting with Fred Gaisberg, Walter Legge's boss, who was more than delighted to go ahead with the recording. Describing the arrange-ment, Maggie understates her delight, and insists that her main concern was who should be her accompanist, for when she had first learnt the songs it was, of course, with Debussy himself. Gaisberg suggested Alfred Cortot, and eventually Cortot sent a telegram to confirm his acceptance.

The collaboration was recorded on 12 March 1936 on seven double-sided discs. Maggie wrote:

> I knew enough of Cortot's poetic playing of Chopin and Schumann to be sure that he would have the special kind of sensibility the music of Debussy needs – a sultry, exotic charm that one finds also in the verse of Pierre Louÿs. There seemed little need of rehearsal, for Cortot's pliable fingers found at once the inevitable nuances for the music.[12]

She remembered him achieving a special tinny quality of sound on certain phrases in Le Faune by threading a piece of thin paper through the strings inside the piano,[13] which must have been one of the earliest examples of the 'prepared piano'. It would be interesting to know what Debussy's reaction would have been to this special effect – the composer who insisted on play-ers following every nuance marked on the page. Today we can hear these recordings of the two sets of *Fêtes galantes*, the three *Chansons de Bilitis* and *Le Promenoir des deux amants* transferred to CD and appreciate the subtlety of Cortot's accompaniment (including that mysterious hollow drum-like effect in *Le Faune*), the vivid yet heartfelt sensitivity of Maggie's interpreta-tions and her immaculate, lucid enunciation.[14]

The album was a huge success, selling over one thousand copies in one year at the Gramophone Shop in New York alone. Further record contracts and recitals followed quickly, then a most successful concert of Debussy songs was given by Cortot and Teyte in London at the Wigmore Hall on 6 November 1937, to be repeated in Paris. Now the papers did appreciate the genuineness Maggie brought to the interpretation of French song. Her polish and sophistication, her declamation of the French vocal line, were praised.[15] Here was a performer making Debussy's so-called lack of melody natural and understandable.

A career on the operatic stage was not so easy to resurrect, however.

---

[12] Teyte, *Star on the Door*, p. 169.

[13] Teyte, *Star on the Door*, p. 169.

[14] *Maggie Teyte: Mélodies*, Pearl GEMM CD 9134, and *Great Singers: Maggie Teyte: A Vocal Portrait*, Naxos Historical, 8.110757–58.

[15] *The Times*, 8 November 1937.

Maggie once again found she had a champion in Sir Thomas Beecham, who was Artistic Director of Covent Garden in 1936 and 1937, and for a while he became once again more than a friend. Under his direction Maggie sang Hänsel and Butterfly, but when *Pelléas et Mélisande* was revived in the Coronation season of 1936 it was Lisa Perli (whose real name was Dora Labbette, another close 'friend' of Beecham) who sang the role of Mélisande, much to the dissatisfaction of those who had heard Maggie. Frustration was the order of the day when attempts to persuade Beecham to let her sing Strauss's Salomé were also thwarted. It would have been fascinating to be able to compare Maggie Teyte with Mary Garden in this role. Sadly, as with so many projects which should have brought Maggie well-deserved fame, the plan never came to fruition. The only evidence extant is on a recording of four excerpts made privately with George Reeves accompanying at the piano. Edward Blickstein in his sleeve notes to *Maggie Teyte in Concert* writes, 'Judging by these recordings, Teyte would have made a formidable Salomé, perhaps the closest to Strauss's ideal.' We can only hear a somewhat distant and crackly approximation to what might have been, but judging by the drama of her characterisation and the stunning clarity of her top notes there can be no doubt that this would have been a role which would have brought Maggie fervent admiration – at least for her vocal performance, if not for her dramatisation.[16]

Still casting about for a fresh start, suddenly Maggie felt nostalgia for the warm welcome she had received in America in 1912. Now aged forty-eight, she returned to New York in January 1937, and after deliberation as to how best to present herself, arranged an audition with the Columbia Broadcasting System – but under an assumed name. How miserable she felt sitting in the waiting room with her American accompanist Viola Peters, amongst a number of other unknown hopefuls. Remembering the lovely things that had been said about her by famous critics in the past, she could hardly believe that they counted for nothing in this strange new world. What came over her that she decided to sing a song by Kennedy Russell, not in her usual voice but an octave lower than the original key? She was so desperate to create an impression she thought this would catch the attention of her listeners, but the response was a mere 'Thank you.' And that was that.

Then she heard that the conductor Fritz Reiner was holding auditions for *Le nozze di Figaro* in Philadelphia. With Reiner himself at the piano she sang the recitative to Susanna's aria 'Deh! Vieni, non tardar', following which he played the introduction to the aria. Unfortunately he took this Lento instead of Andante. Realising immediately that he had no intention

[16] *Maggie Teyte in Concert*, VAI Audio 1063 (1994).

of engaging her, Maggie sang her aria as best she could, and on finishing was determined to speak first:

'Maestro', I said, 'you take it very slowly, don't you?' He turned on me furiously, and said, 'Too slowly? What do you English know about Mozart, anyhow?' 'Excuse me', I answered, 'but I learned from Continental Mozart teachers, and we have in England today one of the finest conductors of Mozart!' 'And who is that, pray?' 'Sir Thomas Beecham!' I answered.'[17]

At that she swept out of the apartment.

Still believing that the CBS must be made to remember her, she and Viola went back for a second audition so that Maggie could sing under her own name, but the result was still negative. She had left too long a gap since the years of her success. The following year Maggie followed up a suggestion that she should audition for a season of operetta to be held in California. She sang the same Kennedy Russell song, but at the right pitch, and this time met with recognition. The man listening was puzzled for a moment, wondering where he had heard that voice before. 'Ah, I know – you are Maggie Teyte!' he exclaimed. Unfortunately fate was to intervene yet again. Maggie was given a role, but a timber strike prevented the theatre from being completed, and the operetta season never took place.

Instead, back home in England, she sang the role of Eurydice in *Orphée* at Covent Garden in 1937 with Fritz Reiner conducting, as Beecham had been forced to withdraw on account of 'pressure of work'.[18] As Harold Rosenthal remarks, Reiner was 'virtually pitchforked' into conducting the opera. How ironic, in view of Maggie's recent unfortunate audition in America with this conductor. Eurydice was originally supposed to be sung by Lubin, but she returned to Paris and Maggie was brought in to replace her. Her performance was described as 'that of a fine artist'.[19] On 21 January 1938 there was another 'first' when the BBC Music Productions Unit was inaugurated with a broadcast of Massenet's *Manon*, sung in English, given at St George's Hall, Liverpool, with Maggie in the title role and Heddle Nash performing the role of Des Grieux. This proved so popular with the listening public that it was repeated in 1939. Highlights of this delightful performance can still be heard on CD.[20] The enunciation of the English translation is crystal clear and Maggie's interpretation of the young girl Manon is strong and characterful. Alan Blyth made a comparison of recordings of this opera for

[17] Teyte, *Star on the Door*, p. 112.
[18] Jefferson, *Sir Thomas Beecham*, p. 184.
[19] Rosenthal, *Two Centuries of Opera at Covent Garden*, p. 526.
[20] *Massenet Manon: Highlights from the 1939 Broadcast*, Dutton Laboratories, CDLX 7023 (1997).

the magazine *Opera* in 1974, and having heard a tape of Act I found her 'Manon to the life; frivolous, charming, romantic – her Prayer in St Sulpice is the most tenderly pleaded I know – and her re-seduction of Des Grieux irresistible.'[21]

Meanwhile what of Maggie's private life? Maggie became very self-centered, but also suffered more and more from sudden depressions. Her constant companion was Grace Vernon and she evidently received more satisfaction from this relationship than from one with the opposite sex, for she suddenly decided to break off all relationships with men.[22]

Sherwin Cottingham died on 22 January 1936 of a cerebral haemorrhage. Maggie, who, after all, was receiving an income for life from his estate since their divorce, slipped into the funeral unnoticed and sent flowers. Her base was now in London, where she took a flat in St John's Wood. Her companion and accompanist, Grace Vernon had left her flat at Woolley Grange and moved to the country. After war broke out on 3 September 1939, Maggie's London flat was requisitioned by the Air Ministry. The two women decided to live together somewhere away from the bombs where they could house their two pianos, but which was still within reach of the city. It was difficult to find accommodation at a time when empty buildings had been requisitioned and evacuees or members of the services had first priority, but eventually they were offered a butler's cottage in the grounds of an estate near Yattenden in Berkshire. Fortunately petrol was not yet rationed and they both had cars. The move was a nightmare, as everything had to be unpacked in the dark of the blackout. They had brought no food or light bulbs with them. That night, as Grace Vernon later described it, 'we were cold, we were hungry, we were near to tears ... We had never felt more homeless, cast-out and unhappy.'[23] But next morning Maggie discovered resources she had not realised she possessed. She took on all the tough physical work, even though she was the smaller of the two women, breaking up coal and carting it in from outside, chopping wood, wearing an old siren suit with a scarf over her head and motor goggles.

Country life was cut short by the introduction of petrol rationing. Maggie and Grace were forced to move back to London, where they took two flats, one above the other, in a building in St John's Wood, 73 Hamilton Terrace. The two women felt moved to do something positive to help the war effort, so Grace went into the Censorship Office. Maggie, however, was determined to undertake a more daunting task: she informed the London

[21] *Opera*, February 1974, p. 110.
[22] O'Connor, *The Pursuit of Perfection*, p. 174.
[23] Teyte, *Star on the Door*, p. 162.

County Council that she wanted to drive an army truck. As Grace wrote: 'It seems fantastic to me that they ever accepted the pocket-sized Maggie Teyte for such a job, but she got her way.'[24] She had to take a course, setting out early every morning in her dungarees, and in the evenings studying mechanics from large and formidable textbooks. Then, to her frustration, she could not be assigned work driving, for her small legs did not reach the pedals! Work as an overseer to female staff in a large garage unfortunately led to her throat being affected by the dust and fumes, so after a lot of persuasion she had to submit to finding a different way to support the war effort. She toured with ENSA, the Entertainments National Service Association, set up to provide entertainment for the troops.

Now Maggie's French repertoire became very apposite. Following the fall of France she sang an entirely French programme on 21 June 1940 at the National Gallery under Constant Lambert. Soon she was persuaded by Felix Aprahamian to continue singing French music as a gesture of defiance to the Germans and sang many times, accompanied by Gerald Moore, in a series of concerts sponsored by the French Committee of National Liberation. She could no longer be accompanied by Alfred Cortot, for in 1940 he had become persona non grata in England as he was now collaborating with the Vichy Government to the extent of becoming its special adviser on music.

Recordings of the partnership of Gerald Moore and Maggie Teyte at this time preserve evidence of perfect collaboration of singer and accompanist, their tender affection for French mélodies, and in particular the way in which Maggie makes them sound direct yet profound, always bringing a moving quality to the performances. Before their partnership, apart from hearing her in Toronto as Marguerite in *Faust*, Gerald Moore had only heard Maggie one other time and that was when she sang Mélisande at Covent Garden in 1930. He was eager to learn from her experiences of singing to Debussy's accompaniment, rightly anticipating that she would shed new light on his songs. He was amused by her description of Debussy the man: 'his impatience, his cynicism, his gloom, his gaiety, and his voracious sexual appetite'. When he ventured to ask her how she managed to resist Debussy's advances, Maggie answered demurely 'I was not his type.'[25] In 1958, looking back on her career, Gerald Moore said: 'There was never a song she sang where at some moment or other she didn't set your spine tingling. Her singing is instinct with her own warm-hearted humanity. Tears are never very far below the surface of this highly sensitive and emotional artist.'[26] Whilst he

[24] Teyte, *Star on the Door*, p. 165.

[25] Gerald Moore, *Am I too loud? The Memoirs of a Piano Accompanist* (London, 1962; Harmondsworth, 1979), p. 105.

[26] BBC broadcast, 26 November 1958.

believed there might be singers who were theoretically superior musicians to Maggie, they lacked her magic. 'None of them gave you that spine-tingling thrill which was her especial attribute.'[27]

The indefatigable Joe Brogan was still actively organising recordings of Maggie Teyte to be issued by the Gramophone Shop in New York, and in 1940 he commissioned a set in which she was accompanied not only by Gerald Moore but also by the London Symphony Orchestra conducted by Leslie Heward, conductor of the City of Birmingham Orchestra. Maggie regarded him as 'the right man for the job' of recording *Nuits d'été*, 'a sensitive musician with the give and take called for by the Berlioz songs'.[28] Recorded on the same day as two of those were Duparc's *L'Invitation au voyage* and *Phidylé*.[29] Two weeks later Gerald Moore and Maggie recorded three of Debussy's *Prose lyriques*, the songs for which the composer himself had written the words, namely 'De rêve', 'De fleurs' and 'De soir'.[30] The fourth, 'De grève', had already been recorded with Cortot in 1936, and is now often added to the others in modern compilations.

Maggie's devotion to French music was rewarded when she was awarded the gold Cross of Lorraine. This was presented to her in London in 1943. How gratifying that both British Mélisandes who had built their careers around the music of France, Mary Garden and Maggie Teyte, had now received official recognition from the French government.

Maggie's ENSA concerts continued usually with either of two great accompanists, Ivor Newton or Gerald Moore. She even agreed to sing in the town of her birth, Wolverhampton, despite her aversion to the place, and performed at the Wulfrun Hall in 1942 and 1943. In common with many other great artists in the war years, she sang at the National Gallery in London, where concerts often had to take place in the basement, and in many theatres and concert halls up and down the country. She also performed on the BBC's 'Workers' Playtime' in February 1944. Speaking on BBC radio in 1959 she looked back on some of the popular music she used to sing in the war years at the Victoria Palace which had opened as a music hall. 'They wanted a name and I went. I had a very big contract for those days. They gave me £600 for one week. And I had to sing twenty-four performances. Now there was the thing that challenged me – to do twenty-four performances in one week.' When asked who was on the bill with her, Maggie mentioned

[27] Moore, *Am I too loud?*, p. 106.

[28] Teyte, *Star on the Door*, p. 110.

[29] 31 July 1940.

[30] 14 August 1940. *Maggie Teyte: Mélodies*, Pearl GEMM CD 9134; *Maggie Teyte: 'The Pocket Prima Donna'*, Dutton CDBP 9724; *Great Singers: Maggie Teyte: A Vocal Portrait*, Naxos Historical, 8.110757–58.

jugglers and also performing dogs. 'The performing dogs and myself were the only turns that did twenty-four performances!'[31]

Cedric Wallis remembered an occasion during the war when she made a special journey from London to an inaccessible Scottish naval station, to sing for a friend who was then serving on the lower deck. 'She put up a real prima donna show in white chiffon and ermine, at great expense of time and trouble, not to mention the fee she forewent.'[32] And what a moving occasion it must have been when in March 1945 Maggie sang the closing scene from *Pelléas* in London with Pierre Bernac, accompanied by Francis Poulenc. The venue was the Fyvie Hall of the Polytechnic, Regent Street, the occasion a memorial concert for the renowned critic Edwin Evans, the translator of the English version of *Pelléas et Mélisande* that Maggie had sung with the British National Opera.[33]

To the British public Maggie now represented the essence of French song. She was proud of her heritage – her lessons with Jean de Reszke, her association with Debussy – and boasted to interviewers that even French singers were hurrying to her to learn the diction of their own language. Maggie claimed that in fact she did not really pronounce French like a Frenchwoman at all. 'French is spoken with the lips and the tip of the tongue. You can't sing that way. The French diphthongs are pointed, nasal sounds. When you sing them you have to fake them a bit, otherwise your voice could never emerge clear and free.'[34]

Yet insufficient career opportunities were opening up for her in Britain. Frustrated and ambitious what should she do? Perhaps she should grasp the nettle and travel back across the Atlantic.

[31] *Frankly Speaking*, BBC interview, 31 December 1959.

[32] *Opera*, April 1952, p. 215.

[33] *The Times*, 21 March 1945.

[34] *Opera News*, November 1945, p. 7.

20 *Georgette Leblanc Falls Ill (1931–41)*

THE FINAL CHAPTER in the life of Georgette Leblanc begins at the point in 1931 where she looked back at her own eventful life and commenced the second volume of her memoirs, *La Machine à courage*.[1] These reminiscences were to begin with her struggles in America, to eulogise her lover Margaret Anderson, and to be a testament to the teachings of the great master Gurdjieff. This was also the year in which her first volume, *Souvenirs (1895–1918)*, was published, but not before quarrels had to be overcome between her, Maeterlinck and Bernard Grasset, her publisher. In his original preface Grasset had implied that she was writing her memoirs in vengeance. Maeterlinck certainly did not want a preface hinting that he owed any of his ideas to a woman. He completely rejected any notion that the ideas which inspired *Le Trésor des humbles* and *La Sagesse et la Destinée* might have had their source in Georgette. He explained to Henry Russell that the love of a woman was not the catalyst for the ability to create, for the ability was there first. 'Believe me, the man who creates, does so at the bidding of his soul, and does not owe that soul to any woman.'[2]

He was supported in this attitude by other writers who implied that Georgette would be nowhere without his name behind her. Finally a compromise was reached. Grasset wrote a long preamble (thirty-four pages) in which he argued forcefully that Georgette had been mistaken to believe that she had ever experienced true love for Maeterlinck. In fact she had worshipped him as a creator and her feelings towards him were maternal, the child they bore together being his writings. It was almost a case of role reversal, her natural virility enabling him to nurture his feminine ability to create. As a creator, Maeterlinck had an absolute right to take material from any source, even if that source be her ideas, and in the early years of their relationship he had at least acknowledged her gifts in letters to her. Maeterlinck did owe her a debt in that through her he was able to liberate his ideas and discover himself. Grasset concluded by telling Georgette that in her book she came across as an unhappy woman, victim of a mistake which lasted too long. He begged Maeterlinck to suffer her book in silence. It would be unjust to

---

[1] Georgette Leblanc, *La Machine à courage, Souvenirs* (Paris, 1947).
[2] Russell, *The Passing Show*, p. 236.

forbid a woman who put his fecundity before her own at least to be allowed to express her frustration.

Georgette dedicated the book to her brother, Maurice, author of the Arsène Lupin detective books. Her poverty-stricken conditions contrasted severely with the luxury enjoyed by her siblings in Paris and by her former partner. The millionaire Maeterlinck now not only owned an enormous chateau at Médan in Seine-et-Oise, but also resided in the fabulous vast domaine he named Orlamonde that he had bought in Nice in 1930.[3] These ancient and mysterious castles appealed to the solitary nature of the man, where, it is said, he sat in the twilight on a throne, his coat of arms engraved above him, a sub-machine-gun in his hand watching out for thieves.[4]

Memories of the past must have been stirred when in 1932 Gabriel Astruc wrote to the author to ask him to contribute a few lines to a book in memory of Debussy. Despite having declared to Mary Garden in America in 1920 that she had given him a new understanding of Debussy's opera *Pelléas et Mélisande*, Maeterlinck sent the following reply from Orlamonde, dated 14 May 1932: 'Dear Sir, I know nothing, absolutely nothing about music. Is it not better to admit this frankly than to give you a vague reflection of the opinions of others that I am incapable of assessing?'[5]

Whilst her *Souvenirs* stirred up intense debate, Georgette continued to enjoy the companionship of a group of intellectual American women who visited Tancarville, including Kathryn Hulme, author of *The Nun's Story*.[6] She was never to leave Margaret Anderson and Monique Serrure, but there was a complicated web of relationships between a number of American lesbians in her circle which, besides Margaret and Kathryn, included Jane Heap, Solita Solana and Janet Flanner (translator of *Souvenirs*). In 1933, the year Hitler came to power in Germany, Georgette and six American women friends[7] found the means to take two cars and tour Bavaria and Austria. As they witnessed unpleasant scenes of violence in Bavaria they could not remain unaware of the potential dangers of the situation in Germany.

In the spring of 1933 the renovated Pavillon de la Muette became too expensive for the trio of women to continue paying the rent. The following year the

---

[3] Maeterlinck used this name first in 'Les Sept Filles d'Orlamonde', the seventh of his *Quinze chansons* (1896–1900), then in 'Les Cinq Filles d'Orlamonde' in *Ariane et Barbe-Bleue* (begun in 1899).

[4] Roger Bodart, 'Actualité de Maeterlinck', *Europe*, July–August 1962, p. 52.

[5] 'Je n'entends rien, mais absolument rien à la musique. Ne vaut-il pas mieux vous l'avouer franchement que vous donner le vague reflet d'opinions étrangères que je suis incapable de controller?' Vuillermoz, *Claude Debussy* (1957), p. 97.

[6] Kathryn Hulme, *The Nun's Story* (Boston, 1956), later made into a film.

[7] Margaret Anderson, Jane Heap, Florence Reynolds, Janet Flanner, Solita Solano and Noel Murphy.

time came when they also had to abandon the lighthouse at Tancarville, for finding the means to survive there had become too time-consuming, leaving too little time for writing. Where could they go to where they would feel at home and near friends? The obvious answer was back to Paris, where they moved into rooms in the rue Jacob.

The New Year did not commence well. Georgette contracted pneumonia. In hospital she needed oxygen which had to be paid for. Her millionaire brother-in-law Fernand Prat was at the door of her room when the doctor emerged to tell him that she was playing her last card, yet there was a chance for her. Despite his wealth, Fernand took the doctor aside and murmured a request that he make his bill as low as possible. The doctor looked at him. 'Cher monsieur', he said, 'there *is* no bill for Georgette Leblanc.'[8] Although she survived this, kidney problems followed and it was necessary for her to travel at her family's expense with Monique (who only had her teacher's pension) to the spa at Vernet-les-Bains in the Pyrenees. Margaret managed to afford to join them later in the year. They loved the little house they rented there and spent 'the beautiful sad autumn days'[9] writing. Margaret emphasises Georgette's selfless attitude to her living conditions, an echo of the way in which she ceded space to Maeterlinck when living with him.[10]

By the spring of 1935 Georgette had recuperated enough to return to Paris, where she, Margaret and Monique rejoined Janet Flanner and Solita Solano. A friend in Grasse, hearing of Georgette's poverty, wrote to the editor of the newspaper *L'Eclaireur de Nice et du Sud-Est*, Georges Maurevert, who had known Georgette since her youthful days in Paris at the outset of her career.[11] A collection of money for her resulted in only a minuscule amount, so Maurevert appealed to Maeterlinck himself. The reply was negative. The author did not want even to talk about Georgette, as he would not be able to find anything pleasant to say about her.[12]

For the sake of her health Georgette returned to Vernet-les-Bains during the cold winter of 1935. While in the south she gave lectures in Toulouse and Castres, where on both occasions she was introduced as the 'ex-collaborator of Maeterlinck'.

On her return to Paris in May 1936, where she, Margaret and Monique rented a flat at 17 rue Casimir-Périer, the women made contact once again with the master, Gurdjieff. Georgette devoted herself entirely to following

[8] Anderson, *The Fiery Fountains*, p. 51.

[9] Anderson, *The Fiery Fountains*, p. 99.

[10] Anderson, *The Fiery Fountains*, p. 58.

[11] Maurevert, *L'Art, le boulevard et la vie*. See Chapter 2, p. 34.

[12] Benoît-Jeannin, *Georgette Leblanc*, p. 511.

his method in the hope that she would not only be cured of her illness, but that she would achieve some sort of mental equilibrium. She was one of that group of women, predominantly American, following the teachings of Gurdjieff, who became known collectively as 'The Rope'. They included Margaret Anderson, Kathryn Hulme, Solita Solano and Louise Davidson. The master treated them differently and kept them separate from his other disciples, giving them intensive instruction in his method. The results of Georgette's spiritual search exceeded her wildest hopes. She found the will to live, renewed energy and despite the preparations for war proceeding all around her, she found an inner peace.

In the autumn of 1938 Georgette travelled to London and, as Margaret Anderson relates, actually made a series of recordings of songs by Hahn, Duparc, Ravel and Debussy including some extracts from *Pelléas et Mélisande* in which she sang both eponymous voices.[13] Intriguing though this is, apparently she was dissatisfied with the results and, as she fell ill before she could make further recordings, the project was abandoned. This must have been a sensible judgement, for surely her voice at nearly seventy could only have been a shadow of that of the passionate, vigorous woman who sang these works in her youth.

A revival of Maeterlinck's play *Pelléas et Mélisande* took place in Paris at the Théâtre de l'Odéon in January 1939, not with Georgette in the role of Mélisande, but Maeterlinck's wife Renée, now aged forty-six. A long review of this production in the *New York Times* determinedly clings to the point of view that without Debussy's music, even with Fauré's incidental music, '*Pelléas* is – and remains – only half *Pelléas*.' Numerous precise examples are cited of points at which the words sounded flat and insignificant without Debussy's 'poignant and searching harmonies'. Paradoxically, in this critic's opinion, the characters (apart from Mélisande herself, portrayed by Renée), appeared more artificial in the play than in the opera. It was evidently far more difficult to create atmosphere in Maeterlinck's *Pelléas* than in Debussy's opera, where the music conveyed the deepest implications of the text.[14] Pierre Brisson in *Le Figaro*, who had been looking forward to seeing the play again, was horrified by the appalling scenery and the best he could say of Renée was that she was true to herself and died 'according to all the rules'.[15] Public reaction was not encouraging and there was talk of shelving the play after less than half a dozen performances.

[13] Anderson, *The Fiery Fountains*, p. 220. No further information is given about these recordings.

[14] *New York Times*, 2 April 1939.

[15] 'La plupart des décors sont affreux ... Mme Renée Maeterlinck ... reste très fidèle à elle-même ... Elle meurt selon toutes les règles.' *Le Figaro*, 5 February 1939.

The declaration of war in September 1939 coincided with more personal tribulations for Georgette. In that very month she had to undergo the
urgent removal of a breast tumour. Whilst many of their American friends
returned to the States, Georgette and her constant companions, Margaret
and Monique, managed to make their way to the lighthouse, but on arriving
at Tancarville found Georgette's sister Jehanne in mourning for her husband
Fernand. Despite the privations of war, the women managed to survive in the
cold, very basic conditions, once again sharing their time between the lighthouse and the Pavillon de la Muette near Paris, but Margaret and Monique
knew full well that now it was only a matter of time before Georgette would
succumb to her cancer. They decided to make their way to America.

To put this plan into action, Georgette contacted her niece, Marcelle Prat.
In common with many civilians anxious to escape the threat of a German
advance, Marcelle had gone south to Hendaye with Roland, her son by
Bertrand de Jouvenel.[16] In November, ahead of the main exodus from north
to south, Georgette, Monique and Margaret had a relatively smooth journey to the Atlantic coast, where Marcelle had found them a house. The plan
was to cross the bridge from Hendaye to Irun, then pass through Spain to
Portugal in order to take a ship to America. Georgette was convinced that in
New York she would find a remedy for her cancer and once again be able to
accept radio, concert and lecture engagements. In the peace of Hendaye, by
its beautiful beach, fortified by the lessons she had learnt from Gurdjieff, she
was able to continue work on *La Machine à courage*. On 20 November a piece
of good fortune arrived in the form of a large cheque from America in payment for a de-luxe edition of her book *The Children's Bluebird*. The women
then had a change of plan, for knowing that Georgette would need constant
medical attention, friends found them a flat at Le Cannet near Cannes. They
arrived there on 10 February 1940. At first life was blissfully peaceful on the
shore of the Mediterranean and Georgette believed herself cured. But dreadful international events of May 1940 coincided with Margaret and Monique
being informed by the doctor that Georgette had only six months to live.

Fearing an Italian invasion in the south the women once again resurrected
their plans to escape to the States. Maeterlinck had already abandoned his
villa in Nice and gone to Portugal, where he had been welcomed by the Prime
Minister, Dr Salazar, then continued on to America. The women filled their
car with petrol and journeyed west until they reached Bordeaux early in June.
Georgette and Margaret were granted visas to travel on the *SS Washington*,
but Monique was refused one. She was a Belgian citizen; her country was

---

[16] Her husband: stepson and lover of Colette, also partner of journalist Martha Gellhorn,
third wife of Ernest Hemingway.

now occupied by the Germans. Ever faithful to each other, the trio refused to be separated and travelled together to Bayonne, but still were frustrated in their effort to get a visa for Monique. The German occupation now covered the whole Atlantic coast. Bordeaux was bombed and they feared the same fate for Bayonne. They were still there when the Germans marched in. Not until August were they able to get exit visas to leave the town. They set off to travel to Marseille and took refuge near Georgette's sister, Jehanne, who now lived in a château at Saint-Pardoux-la-Croisille, Corrèze, with her daughter Marcelle and grandson Roland. A peaceful month was spent in an inn until September 1940, when they travelled back to Le Cannet. Despite severely worsening health, Georgette was able to finish *La Machine à courage* in a tiny house on a hillside, the Chalet Rose, all they could afford to rent there, and contact was made with Jean Cocteau, who was eventually to write the preface to the book.

Throughout 1941 her health worsened. Margaret describes how Georgette would sing songs softly to herself before sleeping, including scenes from *Pelléas*. How fervently her companions longed for a miracle. How painfully difficult it was for them to conceal their grief. There was a slight remission towards September when Georgette was able to summon the strength to go to a concert at the Casino in Cannes to which Reynaldo Hahn, who was conducting, had invited her. It took her three hours to dress and arrange her hair with one hand. When she arrived, Reynaldo gave her red roses.[17] How typically chivalrous of the man who had so inspired not just her but Maggie Teyte.

In October Georgette had to go to hospital, but knowing her end was near insisted after a week on returning to the house to be with her companions. She still received inspiration from her teachings from Gurdjieff, and just three days before her death received a note of encouragement from the great master. Georgette died on 26 October 1941.[18] She was buried in the Cimetière Notre Dame des Anges at Le Cannet. Margaret Anderson's final words describing Georgette's death echo those of Arkel at the death of Mélisande, calling her 'ce petit âme mysterieux et silencieux'. She had lost her lover of twenty years whom she described as 'the perfect human being'.[19] On 26 October 1945 a memorial service was held in Paris at the Dominican church on the rue du Faubourg Saint-Honoré at which Reynaldo Hahn

[17] Anderson, *The Fiery Fountains*, p. 228.

[18] Patrick Mahony claims to have been in the same room as Maeterlinck when he read of Georgette's death in the *New York Times*. Maeterlinck shouted to Renée, 'La viper [*sic*] est morte!' However, he dates this as February 1941, so it may be unreliable. Mahony, *Maurice Maeterlinck*, p. 63.

[19] Anderson, *The Fiery Fountains*, p. 179.

was present.[20] Jean Cocteau, in his eulogy to Georgette in *La Machine à courage*, published in 1947, exclaims that this magnificent title is the only way of describing such an astonishing woman, who continually possessed the energy to struggle against hostility and arise phoenix-like from the ashes. Cocteau himself was later to have a close connection with the opera *Pelléas et Mélisande*, for in 1962 it was his sets that aroused great controversy, first in Metz and Marseilles, then in 1963 at the Opéra-Comique. Anything further from Jusseaume and Ronsin's original conception could hardly have been imagined at that time, and was considered by some to be shocking and damaging.[21]

In Le Cannet Monique Serrure continued to care for Georgette's grave. Eventually Margaret Anderson found a new partner, Dorothy Caruso, the widow of the great tenor, and led her too to study with Gurdjieff. Maeterlinck spent the war years in America with Renée. In 1941 a report appeared in *Time* magazine of the couple's attendance at a performance of the opera *Pelléas et Mélisande* given by the Philadelphia Opera Company with John Toms and Frances Greer singing the title roles. The journalist, who was under the misapprehension that Maeterlinck had never before sat through a complete performance of the opera, reported that he had refused to promise to applaud, 'but he did'.[22] When he returned to France in 1947, the beautiful villa, Orlamonde, was in a terrible dilapidated state since being occupied by Italian, German, then French troops, but he was able to move in after staying with friends while it was made habitable. There he remained faithful to his sub-machine gun, keeping it under his bed in case of prowlers, firing off warning rounds when innocent intruders penetrated the grounds.[23] On 6 May 1949 he died.

Georgette, Margaret and Monique remained inseparable even in death. Monique died in June 1961, aged ninety-two, Margaret in October 1973, aged eighty-seven. They were both buried in Le Cannet next to Georgette, beneath the same tombstone.

[20] Benoît-Jeannin, *Georgette Leblanc*, p. 538.
[21] *Opera*, July 1963, p. 468.
[22] *Time*, 10 February 1941.
[23] Halls, *Maurice Maeterlinck*, p. 163.

21 *Mary Garden's Retirement (1931–67)*

*J*UST BECAUSE she had left the Chicago Civic Opera Company, it did not mean that Mary Garden would not continue singing. She was a great hoarder of photographs and cuttings. Many scrapbooks and albums survive with pictures of her in her operatic roles, but also of an extraordinarily varied collection of personalities. Many of these she met and sang to, and was obviously interested enough to cut out and keep souvenirs of them years afterwards. Little wonder then that we find John D. Rockefeller, to whom she sang at Daytona Beach in February 1931, and a rather dark photograph of a large luncheon party given 'in honour of Mary Garden and Gutzon Borglum at the 2000 Foot Level of the Homestead Mine at Lead in South Dakota'.[1] Borglum was the designer of the huge Mount Rushmore National Memorial. In 1931, when Mary gave a concert at Rapid City to raise funds for its completion, she was told that a new road leading over Iron Mountain to the Memorial was to be named 'The Mary Garden Way'.[2] Despite her glee at this accolade, and mention of it in the newspapers, it appears that since then the road has not been referred to as such, so the idea probably never survived beyond the banquet![3] A more musical memento of this year is the photograph Koussevitsky dedicated to Mary, 'L'inoubliable *Damoiselle élue*', after conducting a much-praised performance of Debussy's work in Boston.[4]

With her penchant for self-promotion, it is hardly surprising that her name was sought after to endorse fine products. As long ago as 1909, 'as a friendly gesture', she had allowed an agent for the Paris perfume manufacturer Rigaud to use it for one of their wares. The firm had then taken advantage by using her name to promote virtually all its products. In 1931, when she realised she was not free to lend her name to other firms, she brought a lawsuit against Rigaud, claiming damages and compensation. The matter was not settled until 1933, when she won an injunction restraining the firm from selling cosmetics labelled 'Mary Garden perfume'.[5] To this day one can

[1] RCM, London, Mary Garden Collection, album XI.
[2] *New York Times*, 20 October 1931.
[3] Reply to personal enquiries.
[4] RCM, London, Mary Garden Collection, album XIII.
[5] RCM, London, Mary Garden Collection, album XI.

obtain advertisements and packaging from collectors for products bearing her name and image.

Advertising must surely have been a natural extension of Mary's personality. She must have loved the exposure it brought her and the grandeur it lent her as she graciously permitted her name to endorse the liners on which she crossed the Atlantic and her favourite car, the Pierce Arrow. Chocolates were named after her, and in 1925 there was even 'Mary Garden The World's Most Democratic Woman' promoting the Mary Garden Summer Chautauqua and Winter Forum. And it was not just products and events which bore her name. It already adorned the square in Peille in France where she had financed the war memorial.

Back in Europe in 1932 Mary's association with the role of Mélisande was brought into sharp focus. On 17 June there was a Debussy festival in Paris, at which she represented the United States. A monument to Claude Debussy was dedicated by President Lebrun on the boulevard Lannes near the Bois de Boulogne. That evening she sang the last act of *Pelléas et Mélisande* at the Théâtre des Champs-Elysées, with Hector Dufranne, Félix Vieuille and Roger Bourdin, conducted by Inghelbrecht.

When Mary returned to America the Great Depression was taking its toll. At the beginning of 1933 she took the uncharacteristic step of singing in vaudeville in Washington. If she was experiencing difficulty finding big operatic roles at this time, no wonder Maggie Teyte was also singing in 'non-stop variety' in London in the same year! Later in 1933 Mary decided to return to Paris in the expectation of singing *Pelléas*. How shocked she was to discover that the Opéra-Comique had changed the design in 1930, and nothing was the same as it had been. She definitely did not want to sing on the new sets by Valdo-Barbey. These aimed to concentrate the mind on the words and music by being simpler, stronger, not so decorative. It was, however, at the Opéra-Comique the following year, 29 May 1934, that Mary announced her retirement at the final performance of the season of Alfano's *Résurrection*. She was sixty years old.

When she returned to the States, Mary proceeded to give lecture recitals and concerts, using her association with Debussy as the main focal point. She soon discovered that people were fascinated by her tales of their collaboration and of his life, and responded typically with anecdotes and comments spiced with scandal and enticing hints about her own love life. In a typical concert, Jean Dansereau played some Debussy piano music then Mary sang to his accompaniment. 'Her singing, as ever, was curiously uneven and husky, a weird combination of song and emotionalized speech', wrote a reporter, yet he regarded each of her Debussy songs as a perfect blend of text and music.[6]

Mary was then employed to give master classes at the Chicago Musical College for six weeks. The course was called 'Opera – Stage Deportment – Dramatic Song', and from the hundreds of applicants, she selected fifty-one. She must have been a very imposing personality, for her pupils were too 'religiously awed' to laugh at their teacher's quips. A typical class is described where 'restlessly, ceaselessly between the stage and the aisles moved a rusty-blonde woman in white sports dress, white low-heeled shoes ... prowling round, never sitting down.'[7] Others are less polite about her methods of tuition. Jack Winsor Hansen claims 'within six weeks [she] almost tore the Chicago Musical College apart brick by brick.' Hansen was informed by its President that complaints rained down upon him when Mary habitually arrived up to half an hour late for classes and ended them early, but worst of all, repeatedly hailed her pupils with insults.[8] However, Michael Turnbull, in an appendix to his biography of Mary Garden, reproduces extracts from the notebooks of a participant in this course.[9] The instructions she passed on demonstrate the acutely observed body movements and gestures Mary wanted to convey to her pupils and show how thoughtfully they were co-ordinated with particular words. Such careful premeditation of facial expression and eye movement, the precise indications of tonal value and emphasis, the expressiveness with which she describes the emotions her pupils are to arouse, demonstrate the thrill she herself must have experienced when on stage.

In April 1936 Mary was engaged as a consultant to Metro-Goldwyn-Mayer on their musical picture productions. She was thrilled with the notion of training young and beautiful singers to appear in operas adapted for the screen. Firmly believing glamour would return to opera in the guise of film, she toured Europe to find suitable candidates to be given screen tests. One of her successful protégées was the American soprano Grace Moore, who made her name in both opera and films in a sadly short life.[10] Another young hopeful was not so lucky. She arrived without a hat, with coils of golden hair twisted round her head. When Mary asked her what role she would like to sing, out came all the hairpins, down fell the hair and she answered

[6] *Time*, 17 December 1934.

[7] *Time*, 8 July 1935.

[8] Jack Winsor Hansen, 'Mary Garden: Queen of Chutzpah', *Massenet Society Newsletter*, January 1992.

[9] Turnbull, *Mary Garden*, pp. 214–25.

[10] 1901–47. Killed in a plane crash in Copenhagen. There are many photographs of her in Mary's albums at RCM.

'Mélisande'. Mary admits her breath was taken away for a moment, but soon 'I was forced to realise that she needed more than her hair to be able to understand the genius of Claude Debussy.'[11] When she tried to find suitable candidates in Scotland she was reported as saying that 'the girls with personality hadn't voices and those with the voices were short of personality.'[12] Glamorous photographs attest to the good-looking male and female candidates she did pick out.

According to Mary's original memoirs she was in Scotland with her family when the outbreak of the Second World War was announced. This must have been doubly sad, for her father died in Scotland at the age of eighty-eight on 19 November 1939. She and her mother then returned to Paris, but in May 1940 plans had to be made to escape quickly. They managed to take one of the last flights out of Le Bourget back to Scotland. Her faithful maid, Françoise Donnadieu, took it upon herself to hide the books, furniture and pictures that Mary had to leave behind. The war years were spent in Aberdeen, where she made the acquaintance of Noël Coward, amongst others, who ensured she was given celebrity status when she watched him at the theatre there.[13]

It was difficult to reclaim her career after the war (she was, after all, now in her seventies), but help was at hand. In 1946 Mary was back in America, where she was hired to teach French repertoire to six scholarship students, including Beverly Sills. In her autobiography the latter wrote a telling description of her lessons. Despite her white hair, she was struck by Mary's trim figure and extraordinarily beautiful legs which she saw plenty of, for Mary used to stand on a chair whilst teaching her, being much smaller than her pupil. 'Audiences have *always* looked up to me – that's why.' Appearance was very important. Mary was particularly aware of Beverly Sills' feet, telling her to stop taking vitamins, so they would get no bigger. 'Ladies simply do not wear size nine shoes', she declared. Miss Sills' comment that Mary was 'the meanest woman I'd ever met' tallies with those descriptions of her in classes at the Chicago Musical College. Significantly, Mary concentrated primarily on her acting, only hinting at how she should sing certain phrases.[14]

Mary's mother died on 18 December 1948 at the age of ninety-one. Mary herself by then was seventy-four yet still fit and energetic enough the following September to travel yet again to New York to carry out a lecture tour for the American National Arts Foundation, an organisation trying to

[11] Typescript in RCM, London, Mary Garden Collection.
[12] *People's Journal*, 14 August 1937.
[13] Turnbull, *Mary Garden*, p. 191.
[14] *Opera*, March 1988, pp. 270–1.

bring about a revival of the arts. On the ship she had her first encounter with a television camera when she was asked to walk and talk as a man filmed. When she saw the result she found it 'indescribable! The most awful thing I have ever seen. I looked like nothing living.' However, she was soon to discover the advantages of the medium when she watched opera from the Metropolitan on a large television set without having to leave home.[15]

She was also given the task of auditioning talented young Americans who would be eligible for operatic fellowships to study in Europe.[16] Mary was exhilarated to find that she had not been forgotten. Once again column inches were devoted to her arrival. Her pronouncements on the decline of opera, her love of America and her philosophy of choosing between a career or marriage, supported by her claim that she had always been determined never to fall in love, were still as eagerly reported as ever. She campaigned energetically for an opera house in each great American city, and was even received by President Truman. Her final lecture on 26 December in New York Town Hall ended with the Tower Scene from *Pelléas et Mélisande* sung with the baritone Martial Singher – although her singing was described rather as speaking a few brief lines whilst she showed her acting skill.[17] It was at this performance that Maggie Teyte witnessed her 'rambling concoction of supposition, scandal and promiscuous adventure'. What a mixture of emotions the younger singer must have felt, knowing the glory and notoriety Garden had received in America throughout her career. Now she simply found her ridiculous.[18] Not all were so dismissive, for this was the year in which Monmouth College, the oldest Scots college in the USA honoured Mary by making her a Doctor of Music.[19] She was never to receive such an accolade in her native country.

On 7 May 1950 Mary was reunited with Gustave Charpentier at the Opéra-Comique in Paris during celebrations of the composer's ninetieth birthday and the fiftieth anniversary of *Louise*. This opera was performed with many celebrated singers in the audience. The conductor was André Cluytens and the scenery was specially designed for the occasion by Maurice Utrillo. What nostalgic memories and emotions must have been aroused as Mary watched frail Charpentier appear on stage at the final curtain, taking a bow at the end of the work which had launched her onto the opera stage in 1900.[20]

[15] *The Press and Journal*, 13 January 1950, in RCM, London, Mary Garden Collection.

[16] *The Times*, 28 December 1949.

[17] *New York Times*, 27 December 1949.

[18] O'Connor, *The Pursuit of Perfection*, p. 198.

[19] *People's Journal*, 7 October 1950.

[20] *Opera*, June 1950, p. 35; *The Times*, 1 March 1950.

After a brief spell at home in Aberdeen, Mary was back in America in October 1950 as chairman of the Opera committee of the National Arts Foundation Fellowship. After an illness, her sister Agnes died in 1951 in Aberdeen. On her return to the city, Mary wrote to a friend, 'Sometimes it seems I can't stay here, I miss Aggie so! It's awful!'[21] In August of that year she summoned up the energy yet again to leave for the States for another lecture tour. Meanwhile her book, *Mary Garden's Story* which had been ghost-written by Louis Biancolli, was published in America in 1951, then in England in 1952. In both countries it was regarded as an inaccurate and exaggerated account of her life and loves which trivialised its subject matter, although her large audiences on her lecture tours queued up enthusiastically to have their copies signed.[22] When Maggie Teyte was given the book to review, she wrote, 'I cannot reconcile the wonderful illusions she gave us before the scenery with what, Miss Garden would have us believe, happened behind it.'[23]

When the fiftieth anniversary of the première of *Pelléas et Mélisande* took place at the Opéra-Comique in April 1952, Mary was certainly not forgotten. Two souvenirs of this occasion survive: the first a copy of the programme dedicated to her as follows: 'Chère Madame, Les interprètes de *Pelléas*, ceux d'hier et ceux d'aujourd'hui regrettent votre absence et vous disent toute leur fidélité.'[24] It was signed by Louis Beydts, the Director of the Opéra-Comique, and fourteen others, including Jean Périer and Félix Vieuille who had sung with her in the original performance (Vieuille's son Jean was now singing the role of the Doctor), Jacques Jansen, Janine Micheau and Henri Etcheverry. The current Mélisande, Irène Joachim, whom Mary had earlier helped in her preparation for the role, also added her signature.[25] The second souvenir was a photograph taken of Mary and Louis Beydts in front of a portrait of Debussy, which appeared in the press.[26] An even more personal recollection of her presence in the city at this time came from Hélène de Tinan, Emma Bardac's daughter by her first marriage. She remembered a concert being given in the Debussy's house in the Square du Bois de Boulogne.

[21] Letter from Mary Garden to D. C. Parker, 18 August 1951: National Library of Scotland, MS 21555, fol. 209.

[22] Letter from Helen Garden to D. C. Parker, 9 November 1951: National Library of Scotland, MS 21555, fol. 213.

[23] *Sunday Times*, 12 March 1952.

[24] 'The interpreters of Pelléas, those of yesterday and today, miss you and assure you of their loyalty.'

[25] RCM, London, Mary Garden Collection, album XIII.

[26] Untitled clipping and photograph at Bibliothèque de l'Opéra, Paris: Mary Garden Portraits, Res. 2156.

There she was delighted to meet Mary again, who was still charming, elegant and wearing sapphire jewellery which matched the colour of her eyes. Mary came to see her again privately the next day, a gesture which Mme de Tinan found very touching.[27] This visit must have been fresh in Mary's mind when she gave a lecture at the Edinburgh Festival on 22 August 1952. There she held her audience spellbound, standing alone on the stage for over an hour, with just an occasional slight movement of her hands, as she spoke of her career.[28]

In 1954 at the age of nearly eighty she was still crossing the Atlantic and appeared on CBS television on the *Ed Sullivan Show* talking to young opera singers. An article published in the *Saturday Review* exclaims that Mary 'still packs a terrific wallop', and was still able to command the press as she always did. One wonders why, given her age, the author is so surprised that she was now beginning to be remembered and valued more as a personality than for 'the most electrifying singing-actress ever to perform on the American operatic stage'.[29] The reporter went on to evaluate her legacy on record, believing that her attitude to this repertoire was too modest. Another American, Ernest de Weerth, published an article in 1955 in which he eulogised Mary as 'one of the most fascinating women of this century ... she need only to walk onto a stage or into a room to seize one's attention.' He mentioned in particular 'her back which was perhaps her most famous attribute'![30]

Plans were made in 1958 for a film and television series about Mary's life. On 24 August she actually travelled to Paris to sign an agreement with the National Arts Foundation of New York.[31] Vincent Sheean remembers with affection a visit to the Metropolitan Opera during this, her last visit to the United States. She had clearly retained her charisma. He arrived on a Wednesday night at her hotel to find her in the vestibule wearing deep mourning clothes. When he asked her with concern who had died, she explained it was Good Friday. He tried to explain that by the calendar it was a Wednesday, but Mary rose majestically saying, '*Parsifal* is always Good Friday.'[32] Sadly, a year later she had to decline all invitations and engagements in America for she had a domestic accident in Aberdeen in which she was overcome by gas fumes.

[27] 'Causerie sur Claude Debussy faite par Hélène de Tinan à la Discothèque de Londres en décembre 1972'. Unpublished document, Centre de Documentation Claude Debussy, Paris, RESE – 08.07(1).

[28] D. C. Parker, Notes: National Library of Scotland, MS 21561, fol. 274–282.

[29] *Saturday Review*, 27 February 1954, p. 47.

[30] *Opera News*, 5 April 1954, p. 12.

[31] *The Times*, 25 August 1958.

[32] *Opera News*, 4 February 1967, p. 7.

1962 was the year of Debussy's centenary and to mark the occasion on 21 May *Pelléas et Mélisande* opened the season at Glyndebourne. In recognition of Mary's role in the first performance, the eighty-seven-year-old was interviewed for BBC radio by Madeau Stewart who travelled to Aberdeen to meet her on 31 August 1961.[33] Even at this advanced age Mary knew how to court publicity. Having chatted for a while to Mary's two sisters, Amy and Helen, Madeau Stewart noted that 'Mary Garden did not, after an interval, "come" into the room: she *made an entrance*.' She found her still beautiful, commenting in particular on her very long, white, slim hands. Her voice was low. She expressed herself in few words, almost defiantly. She was more striking in appearance than photographs suggested, partly because of her colouring, her white skin and vivid blue eyes, and partly because of her gestures. She was very forthright and uncompromising in her comments about people, and was able to evoke an impression in one trenchant phrase. She called Richard Strauss 'a cross old thing'. Debussy, however, she found very difficult to describe. He was, she said, very 'in'; he never talked much. But Mary's frustration during the interview grew until she cried out to her interviewer, 'My dear, what I could tell you, but I can't remember.'

Whatever faculties Mary may have been losing, she was still aware of the opposite sex. Madeau Stewart felt it was best that a woman should interview her for 'even at 88 men were still attractive beings to be shared if possible.'[34] Nor had the old lady lost her love for publicity, and was still able to take advantage of the situation to show her belief in herself as a uniquely creative opera singer. She spoke of her care over her figure, and perhaps now because of her age was not so insistent that Debussy had ever been in love with her. Needless to say, when asked what was the thing that stood out as the most important in her whole career, Mary answered:

> *Pelléas* – most difficult. Debussy's the most difficult because you have to sing him as he writes – not as you want to. Everything that he wrote, every word of Mélisande or the other characters, has the right music tone. And they mustn't sing *their* way. They must sing his way. Because everything that she does, or her husband did, or Pelléas – it was perfectly human, and you had to make it that way.

Debussy, she said, had commented to her that no one sang his music as she did, for 'you sing talking.' She was proud of her friendship with the composer and declared that if they ever discussed his work, he was always right. He would sing his music when he came to her home, and told her, 'Now, Mary, that's the colour of the voice I want.' Mary emphasised that he was

33 Madeau Stewart interview notes, Oxfordshire Record Office, P143/4/MS/5.
34 Madeau Stewart interview notes, Oxfordshire Record Office, P143/4/MS/5.

always insistent on putting the voice into the colour of the people being sung. He explained that when you sing Carmen, 'You have to be very impertinent, very rude.' That was entirely different from Mélisande, when, 'You have to be very careful and very sad.' Mary exclaimed, 'Oh, it's a lovely opera!'

At this point in the interview, to her astonishment and horror Madeau Stewart was told by Mary that she had burnt all her correspondence with Debussy. She had kept nothing, not even his photograph, because she had it all in her mind and simply could not see the point of keeping 'just a lot of paper' in her drawers.[35] How this attitude contradicts the evidence of her own and her family's love of hoarding mementos in scrapbooks and albums.

In June 1962 Mary was admitted to hospital in June, having broken both arms in a fall. The next five years were sad times of deterioration, both mental and physical, as she lived in the past and became very difficult to care for. Madeau Stewart maintained her contact with Mary's sister Helen, and visited her again in November 1963 while she was in Scotland, sorting out Mary's affairs, many of which Helen wished to sell. Helen, now seventy-six, lived in France, at the Villa Antoinette, Peille, that village for which Mary had provided funds for the war memorial. She emphasised Mary's love of her family and her generosity. Some of Helen's reflections were bitter, even about Debussy. 'Debussy had ugly hands', she remembered. 'The nails were bent over the ends so that when he played the piano they clattered on the keys.'[36]

Mary died at a Scottish country hospital, the House of Daviot near Inverurie, on 3 January 1967. About fifty people attended her funeral at Aberdeen Crematorium. There were four wreaths from old friends and a tribute from an unknown admirer – two chrysanthemums bound simply together.[37] Her grave is in St Nicholas Church Graveyard in Aberdeen.

And what of all those letters that Debussy had written to his 'chère petite Mélisande'? Had they really been burnt before 1962, as Mary claimed in her interview with Madeau Stewart? Mary's sister Helen had been unable to attend the funeral owing to a fall, but eventually travelled to Pitmurchie House, home of her sister Amy. The Aberdeen manager of the BBC drove to see her there and as he was motoring up the drive saw smoke from a bonfire. The explanation he received from Helen was: 'These are a lot of letters of Mary's from Debussy. Nobody will be interested in them now. I've just burnt

35 *Prima Donna: Mary Garden*, BBC Scotland broadcast, 28 December 1961. See also *The first Mélisande* (transcript of this interview) *Opera*, May 1962, pp. 305–8.
36 Madeau Stewart notebook for BBC talk *c.* 1963, Oxfordshire Archives, P143/04/MS/001.
37 Untitled cutting in folder compiled by Dr Oliver Davies in RCM, London, Mary Garden Collection.

the lot.'[38] This would imply that Mary had not destroyed them earlier. It is a fact that, as far as is known, only one letter exists from Debussy to Mary Garden.[39] It is that dated 24 January 1902, addressed to 'Ma chère petite Mélisande.' Debussy was a prolific letter writer with a unique style. What a mine of information and insight into both the relationship between him and Mary Garden and quite probably his ideas on the interpretation of the role of Mélisande have disappeared for ever.

[38] Told to Michael T. R. B. Turnbull by Geoff Collie, Mary Garden's solicitor: Turnbull, *Mary Garden*, p. 200.

[39] Debussy, *Correspondance*, p. 637. See Chapter 6 and illus. 10.

22 *Maggie Teyte after the War*
(1945–76)

A T THE END of the Second World War, once again it was not England but America that fêted Maggie Teyte's talent and gave her due recognition. In February 1945 she received a telegram from an old friend: 'Have contract of thirteen weeks for you with Columbia Broadcasting System can you come please reply immediately love Joe Brogan.'[1] One can just imagine the thrill of this bolt out of the blue. Her recordings had sold so well on the far side of the Atlantic that she was a sought after and marketable interpreter of French song basically owing to Brogan, who had achieved his aim both of promoting her and being able to be reunited with the woman he so admired.

Getting across the Atlantic was still a huge problem. Maggie needed a permit from the wartime Ministry of Transport to be able to purchase a ticket, so there was an inevitable delay. In March another telegram arrived from Brogan, telling her to accept no more engagements and that there was a possibility of her singing eighteenth-century French songs. Yet another stated, 'Rodzinski and New York Philharmonic want you for complete recording of Pelleas for God's sake don't fail me love Joe Brogan.'[2] On her birthday, 17 April, he informed her that there was a feud as to who she should appear with first. The telegram read: 'believe it will be Telephone Hour July 23'. It was Maggie herself who almost ruined the whole plan, for she had no idea that there were two broadcasting companies in America, and that the original CBS contract was not the same as the *Telephone Hour*, which was an NBC programme. After meeting the London representative of NBC and thus discovering her confusion, she was advised eventually to see Ed Murrow, the respected American war-time broadcaster. It was he who managed to get her a berth on the *SS Eros*, a banana boat departing from Glasgow on 2 July 1945, on which she sailed as Margaret Cottingham. He also informed her that CBS were no longer interested in her. Fortunately, this was now of no consequence, as Joe Brogan sent her a cable telling her that her *Telephone Hour* broadcast for NBC would go out on 23 July.

Maggie's difficulties were still not over. Not only did all this rushing around and excitement cause the fifty-seven-year-old considerable stress, but she also had to visit the dentist before her departure, who gave her an

---

[1] Teyte, *Star on the Door*, p. 176.
[2] Teyte, *Star on the Door*, p. 177.

injection. One or both of these factors affected her jaw, and at the crucial time she found herself unable to sing. On her arrival in New York on 11 July 1945 she saw a dentist, and was informed she would not be able to sing for three months! What must Joe Brogan have felt like when he told the sponsors of *Telephone Hour* that Maggie was not going to be able to participate? They insisted that she received a second opinion. To everyone's relief this was more positive, but to be on the safe side her first broadcast was postponed to 20 August.[3]

Time magazine took the opportunity to remind its readers of 'the tiny English soprano' who in 1911 had 'trilled like a bird and danced on legs as dainty as the Philadelphia opera house had ever seen', and explained that most of her new waiting fans were unaware that she had ever been in the United States before.[4] Maggie herself quotes a long account of her first post-war broadcast in America written by Wallace Magill, who had sponsored the arrangements. He pointed out that the younger generation did not know Maggie had ever been to America before, and those who did remember her had thought that she was dead and was now being impersonated by her daughter![5] Edward Blickstein commented on her radiant and vivacious appearance, and reported that the radio station was besieged with requests for tickets.[6] She herself could not help being pleasantly surprised that 'the singer who had been of no interest to anyone at fifty was received with open arms when she finally returned after the war at the age of nearly sixty.'[7]

Maggie sang on twelve *Telephone Hour* programmes between 1945 and 1949 and in 1947 on one *Standard Hour* programme. She was paid well enough to stay in a suite of rooms at the Waldorf-Astoria. *Opera News* exclaimed about the remarkable vivacity, wit and gaiety of this 'small, blonde, youngish-looking woman' who produced recordings of such 'crystalline beauty'.[8]

Now it was as if Maggie were taking a leaf out of Mary Garden's book, for she revelled in the long awaited fame and publicity. On 31 October and 28 December 1945 she gave two concerts in New York Town Hall. How triumphant she must have felt to see and hear the capacity audience at the end of the first, cheering and calling for more. Her programme included Geneviève's letter scene from *Pelléas* and Debussy's *Le Tombeau des Naïdes*. Whilst these were described by Olin Downes as being 'a part of her', he had

---

[3] Teyte, *Star on the Door*, p. 182.

[4] *Time*, 23 July 1945.

[5] Teyte, *Star on the Door*, p. 183.

[6] Sleeve note to LP *Magge Teyte at Town Hall, January 15, 1948*, Desmar GHP 4003.

[7] BBC interview with Madeau Stewart, 7 March 1968.

[8] *Opera News*, 19 November 1945, p. 6.

not forgotten Maggie's Mélisande in the opera house which he had regarded as an interpretation of unforgettable distinction and vocal quality. In this recital, however, he found she departed widely from precedents she herself had established. He was astonished to record her 'tendency to obviousness and exaggeration'. She overacted, both histrionically and vocally, making the evening, in his view, something less than a triumph.[9]

There followed a Washington recital with President Truman in the audience and a trip to Toronto to open Canada's ninth War Loan drive.[10] A report of her recital early in 1946 back at the Town Hall in Manhattan highlights Maggie's popularity, but also her blunt attitude to her work. When she had opened her mouth to sing a top A flat in Henri Duparc's *Phidylé*, not a sound came out. Even so, the audience applauded. Maggie, however, obviously felt she had not given good value, for she snapped to her accompanist, 'To hell with them', and sang the last ten bars again, this time perfectly. She received a huge ovation, reminiscent of the old days over thirty years previously.[11]

Another recital took place at New York Town Hall on 23 October 1946 which Olin Downes found finer than her first appearance there. Included in the programme were two sets of Debussy's songs, the *Trois chansons de France* and *Trois poèmes de Stéphane Mallarmé*. Now Maggie was singing with confidence, for he saw her exerting true authority with less distracting extraneous effects. Her mastery of French diction and capacity for colouring her tone contributed to the impressive performance. The clarity of this diction was even such that he wondered if 'less clean-cut and definitely inflected phrases' would have been more consonant with Debussy's intentions.[12] Maggie claimed that after this series of fourteen concerts, she would return to England to rest, to cut some more records and to lose ten pounds she had put on, which she blamed on rich American food. 'Most people say I'm better than the records. On records they don't see me being lively, gay and expressive', she said.[13]

In 1947 an American tour with Pierre Monteux conducting the San Francisco Symphony Orchestra at last included the work which had given her such inspiration at the beginning of her career: she sang seven scenes of *Pelléas* in a concert version – the first time Maggie had sung Mélisande in America. Theodore Uppman was her Pelléas, the first time he came to national notice. Maggie, now aged fifty-nine, was still feeling able to portray

[9] *New York Times*, 1 November 1945.
[10] O'Connor, *The Pursuit of Perfection*, p. 195.
[11] *Time*, 4 March 1946, p. 75.
[12] *New York Times*, 24 October 1946.
[13] *Time*, 4 March 1946, p. 75.

the young princess. How sad that even with Joe Brogan behind her she never managed to record this whole opera, despite his initial hopes.

Today we are able to hear transferred to CD some of the works she broadcast live on radio in the *Standard Hour* from the Marines Memorial Theatre in San Francisco during this tour on 23 February 1947 and further songs recorded by EMI for the Gramophone Shop in October of that year and issued by subscription.[14] They include works by Ravel and Hahn, and also two excerpts from *Pelléas et Mélisande* with Gerald Moore accompanying. The first is Geneviève's letter scene (Act I scene 2), the second the meeting of Pelléas and Mélisande by the well (Act IV scene 4). This is a somewhat disturbing interpretation, as Maggie has to personify both characters, at times almost in the same breath, with piano rather than orchestra to provide further atmosphere. The words are crystal clear, but emphasised so dramatically to convey their message that the excerpts sound almost like arias. Mélisande's quiet responses join onto Pelléas's passionate outpourings sometimes in one breath. It is somewhat unsettling to hear her admission of love entering on a lower note than his, only the singer's clear diction making the change of character evident.

On 15 January 1948 Maggie's recital at the Town Hall in New York was recorded. There, besides some individual songs, she sang the whole of Benjamin Britten's *Les Illuminations*, four excerpts from *Salomé* by Strauss, and five excerpts from *Pelléas*.[15] In the latter she can be heard singing the letter scene, Act I scene 2; the scene outside the cave Act II scene 3, omitting the interior of the cave; Act IV scene 3, in which Yniold questions the shepherd; and Act IV scene 4, when Mélisande and Pelléas admit their love for each other. John Ranck provided the piano accompaniment to this extraordinary selection, for on this occasion Maggie sang not only Mélisande, but *all* the other roles except that of Golaud – from Yniold to Arkel – even the shepherd! In fact, the amount she sang as Mélisande was restricted to her quiet responses to Pelléas's passionate outpourings in Act IV scene 2. It must have been a puzzling selection to those members of her audience who did not know the opera. No doubt her characterisation on stage was sufficient to separate the roles, but whilst the ardent determination to communicate the music is impressive, it is the beauty of the music that is being conveyed as dramatic song with piano accompaniment rather than the tragedy of the opera. The performance provides confirmation of Debussy's opinion that a concert performance of excerpts would be unsatisfying. Surely he could not

---

[14] Now on CD: *Maggie Teyte: French Songs & Arias*, Naxos Historical, ADD 8.110147.

[15] On LP: *Magge Teyte at Town Hall, January 15, 1948*, Desmar GHP 4003. On CD: *Maggie Teyte in Concert*, VAI Audio VAIA 1063 (1994).

have imagined one soloist singing all the male and female parts – except perhaps himself when trying to persuade others to accept the embryonic work.

Perhaps this was intended as a 'trailer' for the opera to come, for only a couple of months later the most extraordinary comeback of all took place. How incredible that on Thursday evening, 25 March 1948, Maggie made her New York début in the complete opera, *Pelléas et Mélisande* at the New York City Center of Music and Drama with the New York City Opera Company, just a few days before her sixtieth birthday![16] One must ask oneself, how does this comply with the original vision of Debussy and Albert Carré when they were trying to select the ideal Mélisande for the first performance: that she should be 'someone young – above all, young'? Maggie enjoyed telling the press of her original rehearsals with the composer, once again perpetuating the myth that she had taken to the part like a duck to water because she was 'Scottish', as Mary Garden was before her.[17] The conductor was Jean Morel. Pelléas was to be sung by Theodore Uppman again, but for the first two performances he had to be replaced by Fernand Martel as he did not feel fully prepared.[18] The whole production was a new one, with costumes by H. A. Condell and sets designed by Komisarjevsky. These involved platforms at different levels approached by stairs, daunting for the ageing Maggie in the dim light. The *New York Times* reviewer must have sympathised with her plight, for he found the scenery 'magnificently bad'! It was claustrophobic and much too dark. He praised Maggie's fundamental virtues of musicianship and style, reserving only faint criticism for 'infelicitous details of action and now and again of costuming.' It seems almost unbelievable that a sixty-year-old woman could have created the illusion of a young girl sufficiently to convince the audience of her veracity. Did she really look nubile enough to entrance her twenty-eight-year-old Pelléas? Not everyone thought so. 'The New York City Center's 1948 production, with Maggie Teyte looking middle-aged, did no good for the cause of French opera' is one lasting judgement.[19] Despite this, the opera was sold out on the first night and played to a full house for four performances. It was then taken on tour. When the production returned to New York on 6 December a different Pelléas was singing to Maggie's Mélisande: Robert Rounseville.

In an article published after this revival, an American interviewer praised Maggie's tonal quality and the impact of her voice projection, and considered her March performance 'of historic value'. Her interpretation of Mélisande

---

[16] See illus. 37 and 38.

[17] *New York Times*, 21 March 1948.

[18] *New York Times*, 26 March 1948 reports he was indisposed.

[19] W. Brockway and H. Weinstock, *The World of Opera* (London, 1963), p. 573.

with its vocal perfection, beauty of characterisation, and its complete, elusive charm was lauded. Maggie took the opportunity to look back once again to her lessons with Debussy, describing the composer as 'rather odd' and stressing his silent, introspective nature. Paying homage to the two other great influences on her musical life, Reynaldo Hahn and Jean de Reszke, she revealed that even now at sixty she still went through de Reszke's exercises every morning of her life. She gave detailed advice on how to sing French song, how to master the French accent and strike a balance between music, declamation, colour and rhythm, but claimed that the most difficult thing was to teach people how to *feel*. Her interviewer seems to have inspired a more emotional response from Maggie than usual, for she expounded upon her notion of living intensely, being alert to the beauties of nature, above all avoiding being nonchalant. 'Live fully your own life, and that of others, through sympathy and compassion', she advised.[20]

Outwardly, life was amazing. Maggie kept her name in the public eye through magazine and newspaper columns, and she was entertained, wined and dined by Joe Brogan and his friends. Letters to Grace Vernon dated 1948, however, show her continual worry about money. She was even at one point considering returning home, as she now had no work in prospect. She was surviving on her savings.[21] This led to her giving singing lessons. During the summer Grace crossed the Atlantic to join Maggie in New York in the venture they called 'The Teyte-Vernon School of Singing.' No longer could Maggie afford the Waldorf-Astoria, so in March 1949 she moved to a studio in a high-rise building at no. 404 East 55th Street, which she nicknamed Mélisande's Tower. In June 1949 she was grateful for the income from another *Telephone Hour* broadcast, and in August was both producer and singer in a concert production of Gounod's *Faust*, with English dialogue by the poet Stephen Spender, whom privately she described as 'a handsome brute'![22]

Meanwhile Maggie had been crossing back and forth over the Atlantic to undertake recitals, such as that in April 1946 at the Wigmore Hall, and on 1 September 1948 in Edinburgh with Gerald Moore. Her records with Gerald Moore at the piano were being imported to America by the Gramophone Shop and advertised in the same programmes as those for her *Pelléas et Mélisande* as 'Made in England by His Master's Voice for the Gramophone Shop, Inc.' In a BBC broadcast in 1958 Gerald Moore looked back with affection on his collaboration with Maggie. He felt privileged to play Debussy

[20] *The Etude*, October 1948, pp. 593, 628.
[21] Copies of letters to Grace Vernon in Royal Opera House Collections, JC 7/06/05.
[22] Ibid.

songs with an artist who had studied them with the composer. He emphasised the spine-tingling thrill of her singing, and her instinctive, sensitive
interpretations. 'I shall never be able to sing this song', she declared to him
when they were rehearsing one day. 'It upsets me too much.' Maggie was
proof, he said, that English artists were anything but phlegmatic, as some
claimed.[23]

However, it was not just Maggie's beautiful voice, but her sharp wit and
incisive tongue that were becoming proverbial. Gerald Moore describes her
unpredictability with wry affection. Once, when time was very short, they
booked a Wigmore Hall rehearsal room for two hours to follow on from
a lesson Maggie was giving. Not only did Maggie tell Gerald on his arrival
that she had left the music at home, she then made him accompany her pupil
and had the temerity to criticise him for playing a lot of wrong notes. On
another occasion at the Wigmore Hall he was rehearsing for a recital with
a lady singer when he suddenly heard a voice boom from the gallery at the
far end of the hall: 'In what language are you singing?' It was Maggie, whom
he had thought was still in America. Cedric Wallis recalled a Wigmore Hall
recital when Maggie forgot her words in the middle of a song, and had to
stop. Looking severely at the audience, she said, 'I *insist* on learning the
words of that song!' The audience fortunately was amused and applauded
her aplomb.[24]

In 1949 the Opéra-Comique company came from Paris to Covent
Garden to perform *Pelléas et Mélisande* on 20 June. The conductor was
Roger Désormière. The role of Mélisande was sung by Irène Joachim, who
had been coached in the role by Mary Garden. There is no evidence that
Maggie heard this. Her bitterness at the lack of recognition she received for
public performances and the laggard progress of her career in England was
leading to cutting comments to interviewers in America which then made
their way back to the British newspapers. Her reception as a recording star
across the Atlantic resulted in a report in the *Wolverhampton Chronicle* on 19
August, 1949 that she was about to become a naturalised American citizen.
'What has caused her to take this step so late in life?', asked the reporter. He
then quoted words she had said in New York: 'The whole business of music
in England has gone to pieces because they don't appreciate it any more. I
don't intend to go back unless they ask me. Musical appreciation and culture
is far greater in America today. I remember when it used to be the other way
round.' The journalist recognises the bitterness in her tone, commenting:
'We now know what she really thinks of us and our music. But what a pity if

[23] BBC broadcast, 26 November 1958.
[24] *Opera*, April 1952, p. 215.

we lose her – even to our friends across the Atlantic.' Although she had not sung in Wolverhampton for six years the reporter still believed the town had reason to be proud of Maggie and expressed the hope that someone would invite her to come and sing there again before long, clearly not realising that Maggie herself did not feel any pride in her origins. Once again the myth of Maggie's Scottish and Irish ancestry is repeated. The article ends with more of Maggie's acerbic words as she criticised the conservatism of modern musicians who 'cannot, or will not, see further than any work which they happen to know by heart. They lack the flexibility of taste or brain to get themselves out of the rut into which they have fallen ... Of the new they are ignorant and distrustful.' She believed musicians lacked sufficient intelligence to overcome prejudices.[25]

Maggie's hard exterior belied the worries about her lack of work in America, however. Back in New York she complained to Grace Vernon in September that she had to economise 'like the very devil' as business was so bad. No wonder she felt frustrated and angry at the sight of Mary Garden still being fêted on her lecture tour in December 1949.[26] By January 1950 she was asking Grace whether there was a good concert agent in London, fearing she would have to return for good.[27]

In a BBC interview with Alec Robertson in 1950[28] Maggie's views on modern music were becoming more trenchant. She disliked its lack of melodic line, found it too fast. She did not, however, waste time grumbling, for the following year she embarked on a brand new mission, a challenge for a singer in her sixties: to try to 'unlock the obscure treasures in the music of Arnold Schoenberg'.[29] The stimulus for this was the preparation she had been doing for hearing *Pierrot Lunaire* in London when she had found that her 'whole musical background had revolted at this rebellious new idiom'.[30] Bravely, in 1951 she travelled to Vienna, where she stayed in the Pension Schneider where other famous musicians also lodged. She wrote to Grace, however, complaining that her money was not going very far. She also took some German lessons at the Berlitz School, but in spite of these efforts she found her 'search' was unsuccessful, her only consolation being that many other famous musicians were in agreement with her over the incomprehensible nature of Schönberg's music. Whilst in Vienna she took the opportunity

[25] *Wolverhampton Chronicle*, 19 August 1949.
[26] See Chapter 21, p. 302.
[27] Letters to Grace Vernon, Royal Opera House Collections, JC 7/06/05.
[28] *Personal View*, BBC, 18 September 1950.
[29] Teyte, *Star on the Door*, p. 172.
[30] Teyte, *Star on the Door*, p. 172.

of visiting another composer, Joseph Marx, with whom she sang some of his songs.[31]

Back home again, Maggie's last appearance in an opera took place on 9 September 1951. This 'delightful experience', as she described it, resulted from meeting Bernard Miles, the actor, who had converted an outbuilding in his garden in St John's Wood into the little Mermaid Theatre. There he produced Purcell's *Dido and Aeneas* with Kirsten Flagstad as Dido and Maggie as Belinda. It was conducted by Geraint Evans. The opera was rehearsed and performed in such intimate conditions and the company was so sympathetic that it was clearly very rewarding for Maggie, both artistically and socially. The performance received due praise, although William Mann, writing in *Opera* was not very complimentary about Maggie, whom he found ideal in appearance and manner, but, 'the voice we love in so much music made heavy weather of Belinda's; her singing was too rich and, surprisingly, too inflexible.'[32] A recording of a broadcast in October demonstrates the strength and conviction of her interpretation.[33]

At the end of that season Maggie considered a new departure, planning ahead for the time when she would no longer be able to sing. To her interviewer's surprise, she had already announced in a broadcast that she would give up singing and turn her attention to Greek drama.[34] She got as far as declaiming to Tyrone Guthrie at an audition in the Old Vic Theatre, and whilst, unsurprisingly, he had no part to offer her in London (and perhaps correctly forecasting her response!), he did eventually write to her to ask if she would consider studying at the Bristol Old Vic. Needless to say, this suggestion was never followed up.

Maggie also still managed to keep up her radio work despite somewhat autocratic behaviour when it came to rehearsals and arriving late for recordings, but her expensive lifestyle was by now proving unsupportable. She had been crossing the Atlantic in luxury befitting the status of prima donna and keeping up the payments on two flats, one in New York and one in London. The money she received from the Cottingham estate was not covering her needs. She decided to return home permanently, and in 1952 bought the lease on a property in London, 42 Hamilton Terrace in St John's Wood.

Now another significant change took place in Maggie's life. Grace, her faithful companion, who had ministered to her needs for many years whether at home or abroad and carried out Maggie's imperious commands

[31] Teyte, *Star on the Door*, p. 175.
[32] *Opera*, September 1951, p. 657.
[33] CD: *Purcell: Dido and Aeneas*, Walhall WLCD 0186
[34] *Personal View*, BBC, 18 September 1950.

without question and who had taught with her in the Teyte-Vernon School of Singing in the States and in London at the Dinely Studios, now accepted a proposal of marriage. She too was now in her sixties and perhaps was thankful for this means of escape from a retirement of obeying orders from the stronger-willed woman. Her new husband was a well-known violinist, Alfred Cave. In the 1930s Cave had been leader of the City of Birmingham Orchestra, then the BBC Midland Orchestra. From 1946 to 1952 he was a member of the Aeolian Quartet. Whatever the case, this was the end of Maggie's relationship with Grace, for feeling betrayed, she refused ever to see her again.[35] That tough ability to pull down the shutters and cast off those she had been close to, was just as powerful now as it had been at the very beginning of her career when she had left her family to live with the Rubens and when she had ended her marriage with Eugène Plumon. Grace Vernon died in 1974, her husband Alfred having died in 1966.

In 1954 Maggie performed her last recitals in America, with George Reeves accompanying. At home she still sang recitals with Gerald Moore at the piano, but was becoming increasingly outspoken and unpredictable. Although they were close neighbours, Moore reported that they never met except by appointment. If they did happen to run into one another, they avoided looking at one another. Gallantly he insisted Maggie was a perfect neighbour, 'as vivacious, intriguing, lovable, and thank God, unpredictable as ever'.[36]

At the Festival Hall on 17 April 1955, on her sixty-seventh birthday, Maggie's last official concert took place. In this final public performance what more fitting work could she perform than the one that had brought her to fame: excerpts from *Pelléas et Mélisande*? Neville Wallace wrote of this concert: 'Her voice had retained its individual beauty of timbre; the charm and the interpretive skill were still there. One felt that Jean de Reszke, who in 1907 had inscribed a photograph with the words "à ma chère élève, l'exquise Maggie Teyte", would have been proud of his pupil.'[37]

Accolades followed: at last, in 1957 Maggie was made a Chevalier de la Légion d'Honneur, for her contribution to French music, thus matching Mary Garden. The following year she was recognised by her own country when she became a Dame of the British Empire – an accolade Mary Garden never received.

35 O'Connor, *The Pursuit of Perfection*, p. 218.
36 Moore, *Am I too loud?*, p. 107.
37 Notes to LP *Maggie Teyte: Songs by Debussy*, Great Recordings of the Century, HMV COLH 134

In 1959 Maggie was the subject of the BBC programme *Frankly Speaking*.[38]
The questions were probing and personal, to the extent of asking her whether
her love of music had made it difficult for her to love in a human sense. 'Yes',
she admitted. There had been a moment in her life when she had had to
decide between love and companionship or music and solitude. She chose
the latter. 'The other could never have made up for what I would have lost in
music', she replied. She did not reveal to whom she was referring. Even more
personal was the question, 'Are you afraid of death?' 'No. Not at all. In fact
I prepare every day of my life now for death', was the unexpected response.
She claimed she did this by remaining very occupied. Although she did not
go to church she regarded herself as religious, for 'when you are brought up
in the Catholic faith, you can never forget it.' So here is one of those very
rare references to her early upbringing. Further questions led to Maggie's
admission that she was 'a bit rough, perhaps. And I'm a very plain-spoken
person', that she was impatient and could not abide 'lack of intelligence in
other people. Lack of common sense in other people.' Defiantly she claimed
not to be lonely and not to miss the crowds and the applause.

A letter dated 12 May 1965 to Douglas Charles Parker, a Scottish writer
on music, contains some rather strange references to *Pelléas et Mélisande*.
Maggie says she had, of course, been to the production of the opera which had
taken place at the St Pancras Arts Festival that year. Her memory must have
been slipping, for referring to the 'original' version of the opera, she seems
to think it was first sung at La Monnaie in Brussels and that Debussy might
have added the music for the interludes after this for the Opéra-Comique.
Not only this, despite having herself sung the scene with Yniold and the
sheep on record, here she claims: 'I disagree with present day producers who
have brought back the *silly stupid* scene of Yniold.' (She underlines these
words.) She then expresses disgust for a certain producer (unnamed) who
is doing his best in London and Glyndebourne to 'bring out the Symbolism
of Maeterlinck – Symbolism – my foot! Excusez-moi – they just make it
difficult to enjoy the blood and thunder of Maeterlinck's drama.'[39]

Until 1966 Maggie continued to teach in her Teyte School (no longer
called the Teyte-Vernon School since Grace Vernon had left). She enjoyed
this, feeling that passing something on 'becomes the children that I never
had, really'.[40] But with her strength and health failing, as she grew older
she became more and more irascible and suffered a long deterioration, sadly
difficult, both for herself and for others. She moved to a new flat and was

[38] *Frankly Speaking*, BBC interview, 31 December 1959.
[39] National Library of Scotland, MS 21156, fol. 116–117. D. C. Parker also corresponded
    with Mary Garden. See Chapter 21, notes 21, 22 and 28.
[40] *Frankly Speaking*, BBC interview, 31 December 1959.

certainly not forgotten by the public, for the BBC broadcast a commemorative programme on her eightieth birthday and she even gave a talk the following year. In 1968 her name became synonymous with the best aspiring young singers when she established the Dame Maggie Teyte Prize, which is still awarded today and for which particular emphasis is placed on the interpretation of French song.

In 1970 a substantial article about 'Dame Maggie' was published in the American *Opera News*. The interviewer approached this 'grande dame' with some trepidation. However she was welcomed graciously and enjoyed the experience, feeling the attraction of Maggie's personality and finding it easy to understand why the singer would always be identified with Mélisande. The lofty position of Maggie's flat was likened to Mélisande's tower as she spoke with intensity about *Pelléas*. Despite her lively powers of conversation, Maggie was clearly feeling her age, for reminiscing on her 'one and only meeting' with Thomas Edison in 1911,[41] she hoped the BBC would broadcast the tapes she was trying to compile of her memories 'and pay me for them; it's so bloody expensive to die in luxury nowadays!' Her main concern, however, was that the interviewer should emphasise the Mélisande connection. She had obviously forgotten nothing of the opera and could still virtually reproduce it by heart. She stressed the need to give as much weight to Maeterlinck's libretto as to the music, describing the opera as 'a beautiful monologue.' (Perhaps this explains her own interpretation in New York, later transferred to record, when she sang all parts as one continuous item.) Vocal strength had to be divided equally between music and word, which demanded a great technique. 'Debussy has as much *bel canto* as Puccini, but you must have the technique to do it right.'[42]

Sadly, following several falls, in 1974 Maggie had to go into a nursing home. She was consequently moved to other homes and, as so often happens at this stage, finances disappeared into their coffers to the extent that just before her death it was going to be necessary to seek financial support to pay the bills. Indeed, money was needed not only for this purpose but to enable the continuation of the Maggie Teyte Prize fund and very shortly before her death an appeal was published for contributions from the opera-loving public.[43] Just after this had gone to press, however, having become both deaf and blind, Maggie died in Pitt Street Nursing Home on 27 May 1976. On 1 June 1976 Low Mass was said for Maggie at the Carmelite Church, Kensington,[44]

---

[41] See Chapter 15, n. 47.
[42] *Opera News*, 21 March 1970, p. 15.
[43] *Opera*, May 1976, p. 456.
[44] *The Times*, 2 June 1976.

and on 12 October a Requiem Mass took place at St James's, Spanish Place.[45]

Maggie's obituary in the *Musical Times*[46] described her voice as 'pure, steady, of no great volume, but faultlessly projected. Intelligence and musicianship infused tone and words with high expressiveness.' *The Times* described her as 'a person of great courage, considerable humour and a sensible philosophy of life.' Her singing combined innocence and sophistication, purity and warmth, particularly the top of her range being of singular beauty.[47] Above all it was her identification with French music which was at the root of Maggie Teyte's fame, and in particular her association with Debussy and the role of Mélisande.

45 *The Times*, 13 October 1976.
46 *Musical Times*, July 1976, p. 596.
47 *The Times*, 28 May 1976.

23 Silence

THE DEATH OF Mélisande was the overwhelming culmination of the opera, the moment which had moved Mary Garden to tears when she first heard Debussy gruffly singing along to the 'very strange and unbearable' music. 'The human soul is a very silent thing ... But the sadness, Golaud, the sadness of everything one sees',[1] sings Arkel. Silence and sadness.

Silence is the last thing one would associate with an opera singer. The turbulence of the lives of Georgette Leblanc, Mary Garden and Maggie Teyte, their efforts to retain some control over their destinies in the cauldron of artistic and political affairs in the early twentieth century seem far removed from the love affair in Allemonde. Yet *Pelléas et Mélisande* is the one work all three singers kept coming back to. At key moments in their lives Mélisande became a symbol of their own searching, their own feeling of being swept along by powers beyond themselves. Perhaps they each wanted to be as innately attractive as the foreign princess. The brilliance of Maeterlinck's play lies in the fact that it seems so simple yet is so universal. The fresh, youthful love of Pelléas and Mélisande contains the essence of pure feeling distilled into a few words. Beauty and innocence are punished for a crime not committed because of the all too human passion of Mélisande's husband. Nothing must detract from the intensity of the emotions which lead inevitably to the deaths of the two lovers. Debussy assimilated the souls of these 'children' to such an extent that he lived with them, dreamed of them, spoke to them, and finally expressed them in perfect musical terms, leading even Maeterlinck finally to understand his own characters.

All three women had huge personalities. Of that there can be no doubt. Mary Garden pencilled in over her original typescript a reminder to emphasise that 'personality cannot be acquired – one must be born with it for it's a magical quality which cannot be explained.'[2] Surely each was born with a surfeit. Their memoirs are idiosyncratic and fanciful, but then, as was said about Mary, 'one feels, as with all the great prima donnas that life and art

---

[1] 'L'âme humaine est très silencieuse ... Mais la tristesse, Golaud, la tristesse de tout ce que l'on voit.' Act V.

[2] Notebook in RCM, London, Mary Garden Collection.

are inextricably bound up together. Art is selective, and so, therefore, is the memory of life itself.'[3]

It is extraordinary, comparing Georgette Leblanc with Mary Garden and Maggie Teyte, that she got so far in the world of opera without any conventional training. Her personality could be overpowering and extravagant. She lived life with an intensity which was too great for some people to take. Everything she did, she did with passion. She spent her life seeking for a meaning to it, yet at the same time endeavoured to give others room to fulfil their own dreams. Her intellectual capacities, her intelligence, that word so often used when people tried to describe her, certainly put off many. Her lesbianism and unconventional lifestyle caused her to be marginalised in some circles. Yet the humanity conveyed in her writing, the genuine enthusiasms, her searching, and her efforts to survive in the artistic world with few material means at her disposal draw one to her. She was not 'a poor little creature' like Mélisande by any stretch of the imagination, but one can understand why she would be desperate to enter the soul of this mysterious person to experience another facet of life and art. Her frustration at not being allowed to sing the role in the original performance was channelled into the creation of her own version of the play in the grounds of Saint-Wandrille, but even this was not enough. She finally achieved her ambition in Boston in 1912, the one and only time she was to sing the complete opera, but to her an intensely emotional experience, especially as she had been so closely associated with the work since its inception. After this, she only performed excerpts from the opera, and no doubt these were sung with great passion. They would have fitted well into her programmes of contemporary song and verse.

Debussy himself had wondered how he could persuade people to accept his Mélisande, 'so difficult to bring into the world' and realised with relief that Mary Garden would fulfil the task to perfection. 'Voilà ma Mélisande', he said and begged her never to change her accent. It was useful to remain the strange girl from afar, lost in the forest. As Vincent Sheean wrote, the magic of Mary Garden's Mélisande came partly 'from her accent in French, which although, wonderfully clear and comprehensible, was never that of a Frenchwoman. The little wanderer from afar should not, of course, pronounce her words in any accent which has the associations of every day'.[4] It was quite often said that Mary Garden did not have a great voice, yet she

[3] Alastair Selway in *Prima Donna: Mary Garden*, BBC Scotland broadcast, 28 December 1961. Also Madeau Stewart files, Oxfordshire Record Office, P143/04/ MS/007.

[4] *Opera*, October 1984, p. 1079.

managed to turn it into an instrument which conveyed a huge variety of moods and subtleties of expression.[5]

Whilst Debussy identified her with the lost princess, it is again difficult to imagine anyone less lost and embodying great innocence than Mary. Yet she had the huge capacity to enter the heart of a role. Mary Garden was a singing actress. She always claimed that she simply *became* the person she was singing. Her critics agreed. 'For each new creation Garden managed to undergo complete psychological transformation, bending her voice, like the actress's other instrument, her body, to the requirements of the new creature', wrote Richard Fletcher.[6] Yet of all her roles she always claimed that the most important one she ever created was Mélisande, not only for its poignancy, but also because 'it was the most difficult, because you have to sing him [Debussy] as he writes, not as you want to.'[7] She said she had nothing to learn from the death of Mélisande:

> Death was somehow embedded in the pattern of my living self, and in the last scene I surrendered completely to it. But what a beautiful death was Mélisande's ... Never in the world would I take a curtain call after the death of Mélisande. I never did, because, you must understand this, *I really died.*[8]

Having sung Mélisande sixty times at the Opéra-Comique between 1902 and 1907, Mary was to sing the role approximately eighty times more in her life. No wonder she became identified with it in the minds of so many admirers.

Describing her life, one sees a woman bathing in self-glorification who adored publicity and knew how to manipulate journalists and businessmen. Yet this very manipulation in itself was a facet of her great intelligence and concealed much of her private life. The many red herrings thrown out to journalists were snapped up eagerly, leaving her to enjoy private moments with her family, with whom she was always close. Her sister Helen, who like many others realised her book was but a façade, emphasised that she always wanted to have one of them with her.[9] How the storm of publicity contrasts with her unselfish acts during war years and her desperate desire to do something worth while for the country of her adoption, including her sponsorship of the war memorial in the little French town of Peille. Yet

---

[5] E.g. Russell, *The Passing Show*, p. 168.

[6] Fletcher, 'The Mary Garden of Record', p. 49.

[7] Madeau Stewart notebook for BBC talk *c.* 1963, Oxfordshire Record Office, P143/04/MS/001.

[8] *Mary Garden's Story*, p. 65.

[9] Madeau Stewart notebook for BBC talk *c.* 1963, Oxfordshire Record Office, P143/04/MS/001.

Mary would not have changed her life. 'It was a beautiful career I had. It was quite different from a lot of people – quite different. My art was my life. My art – oh, it was lovely. And especially *Pelléas*', she said in one of her last interviews.[10]

Maggie Teyte had to work hard not only to establish herself but to maintain esteem in the world of singing. She certainly fought to rise above her background and must be admired for her steely determination. What would her puddler grandfather have made of having an opera-singing Dame of the British Empire for a granddaughter? Listening to her imperious voice introducing her own songs or in radio interviews she certainly sounded like a *grande dame*. It was unfortunate that because other established prima donnas preceded her, also perhaps because she was years younger and less assertive than they were, she did not get the opportunities to create such a vast range of characters as Mary. Who knows how far she would have progressed in the world of opera in France or America if she had not been supplanted by the machinations of rival prima donnas? Having sung the role of Mélisande nineteen times at the Opéra-Comique between 1907 and 1909, she was only given the opportunity to sing it in a complete staged performance three more times in England, in 1910, 1924 and 1930. She was to return to it in New York in 1948, where she sang it twice, this production being repeated in Chicago later the same year. This did nothing to enhance her reputation as an interpreter of the role, for by now Maggie was sixty years old.

Finding it so hard to establish herself in England when young, then even harder after the War, Maggie developed a defensive shell which led to a sharp tongue. John Ranck, her friend and accompanist, called her a 'steel butterfly'. She had extraordinary bad luck, in that when she did have major roles in operetta in London, for various reasons their runs were cut short. The few songs on record which are a memento of these productions prove her voice to be entirely suited to the romantic lyricism required to bring out the characters she was portraying. Yet, like Georgette and Mary, Maggie refused to give up at any setback. Her childhood taught her resilience, and her perseverance led to her name and her voice living on in treasured recordings which continue to be reproduced on CD. She brought character and a distinctive timbre to her interpretations of French song, a repertoire which clearly suited not just her voice but her personality. Perhaps the more intimate surroundings of the recital room and recording studio were better suited to the projection of her personality than the larger opera platform. One does not get the impression from reviews that Maggie was a singing actress as Mary Garden was. Yet it is ironic that we have far more evidence of Maggie Teyte's singing voice

---

[10] *Prima Donna: Mary Garden*, BBC Scotland broadcast, 28 December 1961.

than of Mary Garden's simply because the recording industry was at a more advanced stage of development.

It would be fascinating to discover how Debussy and Maeterlinck would react to contemporary productions of the opera. Maeterlinck provides no precise stage directions to restrict the setting so the director has latitude as to the era in which to place it. However, the author and composer might be somewhat taken aback by contemporary productions which can be so visually distracting that their impact diverts concentration away from the music and words, that combination so consummately realised by Debussy. Even as long ago as 1928, a similar opinion was expressed by Louis Laloy, who would have been quite happy to dust down the original sets. 'It's too often forgotten by the modern reformers of stageing that you go to the theatre to hear the work rather than to contemplate the scenery, especially when it's *Pelléas*.'[11] Lugné-Poë remarked that Maeterlinck's hair grew visibly when he was stressed about the performance of his plays. He would probably have been tearing it out today! At least the interpretation of Debussy's music has not gone as far as Mary once feared: 'I wouldn't be surprised that in fifty years from now, if all his musical rules are not prized and considered, little Mélisande's timid cry "Ne me touchez pas" will be thundered out like hojotoho in Wagner's Valkyrie', she commented wryly.[12]

Nevertheless, it is nowadays as if directors are afraid of allowing Mélisande to be a creature of dreams. Subtlety should be at a premium, but rarely is. In many contemporary productions the characters are portrayed as full-blooded, emotional people, whose psychology is worn on their sleeves. The singer Pauline Viardot wrote in 1908 that whenever she thought of Mary Garden in her Mélisande costume in the original setting of *Pelléas et Mélisande* she was reminded of a figure in a deliciously illuminated manuscript from a Missal.[13] In contrast, contemporary productions present strong vibrant Mélisandes. Some are dressed in bright red; each is energetic, manipulative, anything but the frail figure weeping at the well whose death approaches with a fatalistic inevitability. Mélisande today chops her hair off before the action begins. She very deliberately drops her crown into the water and is seen to think about tossing her ring down into the well. Despite her pregnancy she can be a trapeze artist, writhe around on a piano, balance on

[11] 'ce fait, trop souvent oublié par les réformateurs modernes de la scène, qu'on vient au théâtre pour y entendre la pièce plutôt que pour contempler les décors, surtout quand il s'agit de Pelléas.' Laloy, *La musique retrouvée*.

[12] Notebook in RCM, London, Mary Garden Collection.

[13] 'C'est Mlle Garden, que je ne retrouve jamais dans des décors de Pelléas et Mélisande, que comme une figure de missel parmi des pages délicieusement enluminées d'un précieux manuscrit.' *Musica*, January 1908, p. 2.

thin boards over water. She is so energetic that she does not lie down to die until the very last moments. There is almost a fear of creating silence. That 'silence extraordinaire ... on entendrait dormir l'eau'[14] cannot be imagined if real water on stage is making so much noise it can be heard above the music, or if the characters are having to jump from plank to plank to avoid getting wet. Some productions go to the other extreme: no water, no hair, minimal props.

However, problems with productions of the opera are nothing new. On 5 May 1963 a performance took place at the Opéra-Comique in Paris with sets designed by Jean Cocteau. The critic André Tubeuf described the production as 'vile and nauseating – thanks to Mr. Cocteau'. He went on to remark that 'the freedom with which Cocteau was permitted to lay this damaging touch on *Pelléas*, and at the Comique itself, is all the more shocking in the light of an interesting recent legal-aesthetic affair.'[15] He was referring to the action Durand, Debussy's publisher, had taken to forbid the Lyons Opera to continue performing a version staged by Louis Erlo. Durand's representative decided his 'renovations' were harmful to the interests of the composer. When the courts decreed that the publisher did not have the right to forbid performances, Durand got round the decision by refusing to rent out scores! The finest performance Tubeuf had ever seen was one put together hastily in December 1962, the centenary of Debussy's birth, when the Opéra-Comique suddenly realised that nearly all opera houses in Europe were producing *Pelléas* except themselves, its original home. They used the original 1902 Jusseaume–Ronsin sets, and in his opinion, 'The beauty and *rightness* of the original designs were a revelation.'[16]

'C'était un petit être si tranquille, si timide et si silencieux.'[17] Our three Mélisandes are now silent. No recordings of Georgette Leblanc singing Debussy survive. She was fortunate in being able to display her love of Mélisande in performances of Maeterlinck's play, having initially been deprived of her ambition to sing in the opera. She, Mary Garden and Maggie Teyte were the first singers to 'catch the fever', a phrase which Jacques Jansen, who first sang the role of Pelléas in 1941, later used to describe the way in which the score of the opera overwhelmed him and became the centre of his life.[18] Whilst we can hear tiny excerpts with Debussy at the piano accompanying

---

[14] 'Extraordinary silence ... One can hear the water sleeping.' (Act II scene 1).

[15] *Opera*, July 1963, pp. 467–8.

[16] *Opera*, July 1963, pp. 467–8.

[17] 'She was such a quiet little creature, so shy and so silent.' Act V.

[18] Jacques Jansen, *My Pelléas*, in booklet accompanying CD set, *Debussy: Pelléas et Mélisande*, conducted by Roger Désormière, EMI CHS 7 61038 (recorded 1941).

Mary Garden, and Maggie Teyte singing scenes as a monologue, neither of them recorded the complete opera, so the full mystery of the spell they wove with their voices remains unheard today. *Pelléas et Mélisande* may illustrate the futility of trying to find any answers to the struggle of life and the role of fate, but these three Mélisandes, spellbound by the role, certainly did their utmost to lead full and significant lives and bring pleasure to their audiences through the extraordinary strength of their personalities and their talent. The drama and pathos of their lives is a testament to the struggle they fought to remain strong and independent in the competitive world of opera and theatre. Their pride in their association with Mélisande never diminished and is fully justified.

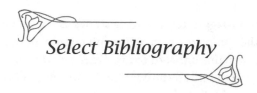

Select Bibliography

❦   About Debussy

The literature on Debussy is extensive. The following is necessarily a select list of works for reference:

Dietschy, Marcel, *La Passion de Claude Debussy* (Neuchâtel, 1962); translated by William Ashbrook and Margaret G. Cobb as *A Portrait of Claude Debussy* (Oxford, 1990)

Langham Smith, Richard (ed.), *Debussy Studies* (Cambridge, 1997)

—— and Caroline Potter (eds.), *French Music since Berlioz* (Aldershot, 2006)

Lesure, François, *Claude Debussy: Biographie critique* (Paris, 1994)

Lockspeiser, Edward, *Debussy: His Life and Mind*, 2 vols. (London, 1962)

Nichols, Roger, *The Life of Debussy* (Cambridge, 1998)

—— *Debussy Remembered* (London, 1992)

Peter, René, *Claude Debussy* (Paris, 1944)

Trezise, Simon (ed.), *The Cambridge Companion to Debussy* (Cambridge, 2003)

❦   Debussy on Pelléas et Mélisande

Claude Debussy, *Correspondance (1872–1918)*, collected and annotated by François Lesure, Denis Herlin and Georges Liébert (Paris, 2005) [An invaluable resource containing in one volume more than 3,000 letters, over 2,500 by Debussy himself.]

Debussy on Music, collected by François Lesure, translated and edited by Richard Langham Smith (London and New York, 1977)

❦   About Pelléas et Mélisande, the opera

L'Avant-Scène Opéra, no. 9 (mars–avril 1977) and *L'Avant-Scène Opéra*, no. 9 (mars–avril 1998) [Both contain a full text with 'Commentaire Musical' by Henry Barraud and informative articles. The latter also includes: 'Miroirs pour Pelléas et Mélisande' by Pierre Boulez.]

Caillet, Aude (ed.), '*Pelléas et Mélisande*: étude de Charles Koechlin', *Cahiers Debussy*, nos. 27–8 (2003–4)

Couvreur, Manuel, and Roland van der Hoeven (eds.), *La Monnaie symboliste* (Brussels, 2003) [This includes a chapter by Denis Herlin, '*Pelléas et Mélisande* à la Monnaie', pp. 209–31.]

Emmanuel, Maurice, *Pelléas et Mélisande de Debussy: étude et analyse* (Paris, 1926)

English National Opera, *Pelléas et Mélisande,* Opera Guide no. 9 (London, 1982).
This gives a parallel rendering of the text of the opera in English translated by Hugh
Macdonald and of Maeterlinck's play in French. Debussy's alterations to the text
are also indicated.

Gilman, Laurence, *Debussy's Pelléas et Mélisande: A Guide to the Opera* (New York,
1907)

Grayson, David, *The Genesis of Debussy's 'Pelléas et Mélisande'* (Ann Arbor, 1986)

Grayson, David, 'The Libretto of Debussy's *Pelléas et Mélisande*', *Music & Letters*,
vol. 66 (1985), pp. 34–50

Lecler, Eric, *L'Opéra symboliste* (Paris, 2006)

Messager, André, 'Les premières représentations de Pelléas', *La Revue Musicale*, vol. 7
(May 1926), pp. 206–10

Nichols, Roger, and Richard Langham Smith, *Claude Debussy: Pelléas et Mélisande*,
Cambridge Opera Handbooks (Cambridge, 1989)

❧   About Maurice Maeterlinck

For a comprehensive bibliography of works by Maeterlinck and concerning him see:

Rykner, Arnaud, *Maurice Maeterlinck: bibliographie des écrivains français* (Paris, 1998)
See also:

Compère, Gaston, *Maurice Maeterlinck* (Besançon, 1992)

Crawford, Virginia, *Studies in Foreign Literature* (Boston, 1899)

Samuel Goldwyn, *Behind the Screen* (New York, 1923) [This contains a chapter
entitled 'Some authors who have travelled to Holywood.']

Halls, W. D., *Maurice Maeterlinck: A Study of his Life and Thought* (Oxford, 1960)

Harry, Gérard, *Maurice Maeterlinck: A Biographical Study*, translated by Alfred
Allinson (London, 1910)

❧   About Pelléas et Mélisande, the play

Pélléas et Mélisande (Brussels, 1892) [The original edition. Note the spelling 'Pélléas'.]

Pelléas et Mélisande, with preface by Henri Ronse and discussion by Christian Lutaud
(Brussels, 1983)

Pelleas and Melisanda and The Sightless: Two Plays by Maurice Maeterlinck, translated
by Laurence Alma Tadema (London, 1895)

Pelléas et Mélisande, translated by Erving Winslow, with an introduction by Montrose
J. Moses (New York, 1908)

English National Opera, *Pelléas et Mélisande,* Opera Guide no. 9 (London, 1982)

Martin-Lau, Philippe, *Centenaires de Pelléas, de Maeterlinck à Debussy* (Orléans, 2001)
[This includes contemporary reviews of the first performance of the play by Léon
Bernard-Derosne, Jules Lemaitre, Francisque Sarcey, Adolphe Retté, Jacques des
Gachons and Alfred Vallette; also a chapter, 'Pelléas lyrique?', by Bertrand Degott.]

❦   *Other works by Maeterlinck*

Three collections of essays by Maeterlinck mentioned in the text are:

Le Trésor des humbles [The Treasure of the Humble] (Paris, 1896)
La Sagesse et la destinée [Wisdom and Destiny] (Paris, 1898)
Le Temple enseveli [The Buried Temple] (Paris, 1902)

❦   *About Georgette Leblanc*

Benoît-Jeannin, Maxime, *Georgette Leblanc (1869–1941)* (Brussels, 1998)

Also:

Anderson, Margaret, *The Fiery Fountains* (New York, 1951)
Mauclair, Camille, *Le Soleil des morts* (Paris, 1898)

❦   *Writings by Georgette Leblanc*

The Archives & Musée de la Littérature in Brussels hold a collection of correspondence, documents and press cuttings relating to Georgette Leblanc. (See the online catalogue, *Plume*). Amongst these is Leblanc's unpublished manuscript, 'Histoire de ma Vie', MLT 00536.

Published works:

Souvenirs (1895–1918) (Paris, 1931); English version: *Souvenirs: My Life with Maeterlinck*, translated by Janet Flanner (New York, 1932)
La Machine à courage: Souvenirs (Paris, 1947)
Le Choix de la vie (Paris, 1904); English version: *The Choice of Life*, translated by Alexander Teixeira de Mattos (New York, 1914; reissued Charleston, 2007)
Introduction to Maurice Maeterlinck, *Morceaux choisis* (London, 1910)
'Mes conversations avec Eleonora Duse', *Les Œuvres libres*, no. 66 (1926)
The Children's Blue Bird, translated by Alexander Teixeira de Mattos with illustrations by Albert Rothenstein (London and New York, 1913)
The Girl who Found the Blue Bird: A Visit to Helen Keller, translated by Alexander Teixeira de Mattos (New York, 1914)
Nos chiens (Paris, 1919); translated as *Maeterlinck's Dogs* by Alexander Teixeira de Mattos (London, 1919)
'D'Annunzio au Vittoriale: souvenirs inédits', *Les Œuvres libres*, no. 203 (May 1938)

❧ *About Mary Garden*

Turnbull, Michael T. R. B., *Mary Garden* (Portland, OR, and Aldershot, UK, 1997)

Also:

Goldwyn, Samuel, *Behind the Screen* (New York, 1923)

Hansen, Jack Winsor, *The Sibyl Sanderson Story: Requiem for a Diva* (Pompton Plains, NJ, and Cambridge, UK, 2005)

Huneker, James, *Bedouins* (New York, 1920)

Rutherford, Susan, *The Prima Donna and Opera, 1815–1930* (Cambridge, 2006)

Stewart, Madeau, 'The First Mélisande', *Opera*, May 1962, pp. 305–8 [Transcript of BBC radio interview with Mary Garden, followed by an excerpt from Debussy's article on Mary Garden translated from *Musica*, 1908]

Van Vechten, Carl, *Interpreters and Interpretations* (New York, 1917)

❧ *Writings by Mary Garden*

Mary Garden Collection, Centre for Performance History, Royal College of Music, London. This collection contains Mary Garden's unpublished typescript of the original version of her autobiography and several early notebooks. It also contains volumes of albums of photographs and cuttings collected throughout her life.

Published works:

L'Envers du décor: souvenirs d'une grande cantatrice (Paris, 1952)

'The "Know How" in the Art of Singing', *The Etude*, July 1920, pp. 439–40

with Louis J. Biancolli, *Mary Garden's Story* (New York, 1951; London, 1952)

❧ *About Maggie Teyte*

O'Connor, Garry, *The Pursuit of Perfection: A Life of Maggie Teyte* (London and New York, 1979)

Also:

Anon. 'An Hour with Maggie Teyte', *Opera News*, 19 November 1945

Spaeth, Sigmund, 'Maggie Teyte's Training', *Opera News*, 7 April 1947

Stanley, May, 'Debussy the Man, as Maggie Teyte Knew him', *Musical America*, 13 April 1918

Wallis, Cedric, 'People xv: Maggie Teyte', *Opera*, April 1952, pp. 215–20

Writings by Maggie Teyte

Star on the Door (London, 1958)

'Bearding the Lion', *The Opera Magazine*, vol. 1 no. 5 (May 1914), pp.10–12 [Interview with Debussy]

'Mastering the "French Style", A Conference with Maggie Teyte', *The Etude*, October 1948

Other Works

Carré, Albert, *Souvenirs de théâtre* (Paris, 1950)

Davis, Ronald, *Opera in Chicago: A Social and Cultural History, 1850–1965* (New York, 1966)

Eaton, Quaintance, *The Boston Opera Company: The Story of a Unique Musical Institution,* (New York, 1965)

Lugné-Poë, Aurélien-François-Marie, *La Parade*, 1: *Le Sot du tremplin* (Paris, 1930); 2: *Acrobaties* (Paris, 1931); 3: *Sous les étoiles* (Paris, 1933)

Robichez, Jacques, *Le Symbolisme au théâtre: Lugné-Poë et les débuts de l'œuvre* (Paris, 1957)

Rosenthal, Harold, *Two Centuries of Opera at Covent Garden* (London, 1958)

Russell, Henry, *The Passing Show* (London, 1926)

Wolff, Stéphane, *Un demi-siècle d'Opéra-Comique* (Paris, 1953)

Index

(GARDEN, MARY, *continued*)

Philadelphia-Chicago Grand Opera
Company, *see* Chicago Opera
Company

press and publicity, 65, 76, 128, 189–90, 192,
195–6, 197–8, 200, 203, 205, 245, 254,
258, 302, 304, 323

product endorsement, 298–9

radio and television broadcasts, 255, 304,
305–6

recitals, *see under* Garden, Mary: Concerts
and recitals

recordings, 5, 118–19, 202, 231, 243, 259, 327

retirement, 262, 299

reviews and opinions, 80, 81, 101, 103–4,
106–11, 112, 114, 115, 122, 123, 126, 138,
177, 190–3, 199, 200–1, 243, 247, 249–
50, 253, 257, 259, 260–1, 299–300, 301,
304

Roman Catholicism, 198

Rome, 122

singing lessons, 69, 71–3, 75, 190, 203

sponsorship, 67, 69, 71–2, 75–6, 196–7

teaching, 300–2, 314

travesti roles, 122, 129, 194, 195

vaudeville, 299

vocal quality, 5, 79, 81, 104, 106, 114, 118–19,
122, 191, 193, 196, 259–61, 299, 322–3

war service, 246–8

women, views on, 243–4, 254, 261

🎜 MARY GARDEN AND ...

Annunzio, Gabriele d', 43, 203, 277

Armour, J. Ogden, 204–5

Bernhardt, Sarah, 31, 78

Carré, Albert, 56, 57, 61, 77, 78–80, 84–7,
108, 117, 128–9, 257, 260

Debussy, Claude, 5, 66, 83, 86–9, 94, 96,
105–8, 112–16, 118–21, 124, 126, 140,
183, 201, 244, 247, 252–3, 258, 259, 299,
302, 303–4, 305–7, 322

Debussy, Emma, 258

Debussy, Lilly, 83, 88–9, 121, 258

George I, King of Greece, 83

Goldwyn, Samuel, 246–7, 248

Hammerstein, Oscar, 130–1, 172, 198–9

Leblanc, Georgette, 78, 109, 136, 140, 190,
230, 231, 243, 266–7

Maeterlinck, Maurice, 64, 88, 201, 252, 292

Messager, André, 80, 82–6, 111, 112–13,
115–16, 120–1, 124, 131, 195

(GARDEN, MARY, *continued*)

(Mary Garden and ..., *continued*)

Sanderson, Sibyl, 73–5, 76–7, 78–9, 81, 82,
117–18

Teyte, Maggie, 177, 182, 183–6, 205, 213–15,
216–17, 243, 283

🎜 PERFORMANCES

Aphrodite, 122–3, 129, 133

Ariettes oubliées, 244

Beau soir, 259

Camille, 261–2

Carmen, 65, 203, 243, 244, 259

Cendrillon, 203, 205, 214–15, 243

Chérubin, 122, 129

Damoiselle élue, La, 244, 298

Don Quichotte, 245

Faust, 115, 131, 202, 203

Fille de Tabarin, La, 85

Gismonda, 251

Hélène, 122

Jongleur de Notre-Dame, Le, 194, 195, 198,
243, 245, 248

Louise, 78–81, 84, 85, 90, 92, 94, 122, 128,
130, 171, 190, 243, 248, 259, 302

Madame Chrysanthème, 85, 124

Manon, 85, 92, 112, 115, 118

Marseillaise, La, 81

Monna Vanna, 197, 245, 253, 266

Nadeshda, 247

Natoma, 202

Pelléas et Mélisande

announcement of appointment, 61

introduction to role, 86

preparations for first performance, 86–9,
92, 94–5, 97–8

Boston, 196, 260–1, 262

Brussels, 124–7

Chicago, 199–201, 249–50, 262

Cologne, 193

Geneva, 260

New York, Lexington, 250–2

New York, Manhattan, 130, 189–92, 196,
199

Paris, 100–11, 247, 257–8, 299

Philadelphia, 196

Strasbourg, 257

see also Mélisande: sung by Garden,
Mary